Helseth argues that the Old [...] Hodge, Warfield, and Mache [...] today) but had a nuanced epistemology including subjective and emotional factors. I think he and they are right, and that Helseth is also right in deriving this epistemology from Scripture and the Reformed theological tradition. His argument is cogent, and it clears away the debris of unjust criticism so that we can again be delighted in the insights of Old Princeton Calvinism. As it turns out, the Old Princetonians are an attractive alternative to the confusions of modern liberalism and postfoundationalism.

—**John M. Frame**, J. D. Trimble Chair of Systematic Theology and Philosophy, Reformed Theological Seminary, Orlando

Challenging the prevailing academic views can be a lonely place. Paul Kjoss Helseth seems not only comfortable with the challenge, but adequate to the task. Armed with primary sources from major Old Princeton scholars, Helseth critically examines the prevailing notions of academic "orthodoxy" concerning the religious epistemology of Machen, Hodge, and Warfield and finds them wanting. Helseth . . . then develops the insights of Princeton theology and its challenge of nineteenth-century theological liberalism to challenge contemporary trends prevalent in postconservative theology. While not everyone may share his assessment of this particular trend, Helseth is conscientious enough in his critique that all disagreement must be equally thoughtful. While standing outside of the academic mainstream can be a lonely place, I suspect that soon this "voice calling in the wilderness" will be received as a clarion call joined by many.

—**Todd Bates**, Associate Professor of Philosophy, California Baptist University, Riverside, CA

At last—a book that gets the Princeton theology right! Helseth's "unorthodox proposal" challenges the commonly held view that Alexander, Hodge, and Warfield compromised their Reformed theology by a commitment to Scottish Common Sense philosophy that rationalized their theology and apologetics and stressed head over heart in Christian living. Helseth's treatment is scholarly, patient, and careful. He has read the Princetonians widely and with great care to rescue their "holistic epistemology" from the charge that they were "the purveyors of an essentially humanistic philosophy rather than the champions of Reformed orthodoxy." This book not only corrects an injustice to the Princetonians but also argues persuasively that "contemporary evangelicals would be much better off if they did theology more like the theologians at Old Princeton Seminary."

—**David B. Calhoun**, Professor Emeritus of Church History,
Covenant Theological Seminary, St. Louis

Paul Helseth is to be commended for challenging a common but wrong-headed interpretation of the theologians of Old Princeton Theological Seminary and attempting to set the record straight. His familiarity with the primary sources, his more accurate reading of Alexander, Hodge, Warfield, and Machen, and his superior scholarship enable him to dismantle the prevailing view and to demonstrate that these theologians were not the blind captives of Common Sense Realism that the "orthodox" view has portrayed them to be. Rather, Helseth shows from their own words that these Princetonians were faithful to a genuinely Reformed epistemology. In the process, he shows as well that the misguided prevailing view has been used in the service of a growing departure from a truly evangelical theology and the movement toward a neoliberalism that is as dangerous as the old liberalism. This book offers a much-needed corrective to both current historical scholarship and current theological directions. I recommend it highly on both counts.

—**Terry A. Chrisope**, Professor of History and Bible,
Missouri Baptist University, St. Louis

The question of how we should interpret Old Princeton epistemology and theological methodology is a watershed issue in the current battles between conservative and postconservative evangelicals. Paul Helseth convincingly shows that, rather than accommodating wholeheartedly to Enlightenment rationalism and Scottish Common Sense philosophy, the Princetonians articulated their epistemology well within their Reformed tradition. The Old Princeton theologians believed that the soul is a unity of mind, will, and emotions; thus, apprehension of truth is not only a cognitive activity, but a moral one as well. This "unorthodox" interpretation of the Old Princeton theology flies in the face of the current consensus on Old Princeton and has serious implications for the legitimacy of many postconservative evangelical commitments. Helseth has done his readers a great service with his careful research and insightful analysis of one of the most hotly contested issues in evangelicalism today.

—**George Coon**, Associate Professor of Theology and
Church History, Calvary Baptist Seminary, Lansdale, PA

From time to time a book comes along that reverses a widely shared paradigm. This wonderful study is such a volume. It presents a much-needed corrective to the "orthodox" interpretation of the Old Princeton theology, which is that Common Sense Realism and rationalism so shaped the approach of Archibald Alexander, Charles Hodge, B. B. Warfield, and their peers that they often sounded more like Enlightenment thinkers than Calvinists. In his characteristically careful and thorough manner, without denying some appropriation of the prevailing philosophy by these giants, Helseth shows that they were theologians of the heart, in essential continuity with the Reformation approach. In the bargain we are given a sane look into the relation of Kuyper and Warfield, Machen and Van Til, and much more. The book is especially timely in that postconservative evangelicals often claim that Old Princeton elevated ideas at the expense of piety. Helseth puts that view to rest, in a powerful plea for right doctrine alongside fervent piety. This is essential reading for all who care about that balance.

—**William Edgar**, Professor of Apologetics,
Westminster Theological Seminary, Philadelphia

Helseth has engaged in a compelling and thorough reexamination of the theologically rooted epistemology of the Old Princetonians, and then used the results to offer a winsome and penetrating critique of the so-called postconservative evangelical movement. He demonstrates convincingly that the giants of Old Princeton were not—contra much scholarly consensus—simply beholden to modern and Enlightenment thinking. Rather, the Old Princetonians were true Augustinians and stand in the line of the best of Reformed thinking, including their thinking on the nature of knowledge, whether of God or of the created order. Like Augustine, Hugh of St. Victor, Calvin, and Pascal, the Old Princetonians repeatedly argue that knowledge in the truest sense is always related to—and dependent on—the state of one's heart. Helseth shows that "right reason" is rooted in being rightly related to the risen Jesus. Helseth also demonstrates that at the end of the day, it may not be the postconservatives who offer the most compelling way for evangelicals, young or old, to resist and counter the acids of modernity. He demonstrates, paradoxically, that one of the most promising roads to be traveled in attempting to faithfully and properly follow Christ in our modern and so-called postmodern world might actually take one right through New Jersey.

—**Bradley G. Green**, Associate Professor of Christian Studies, Union University, Jackson, TN

I have followed Paul Helseth's development of this research for almost fifteen years. His abilities and analysis remain, even if we quibble over a few matters, among the most impressive in this field. In *Right Reason*, he attempts, and I believe largely succeeds, to rehabilitate an important aspect of Reformed epistemology in America. Rather than repeating the often-incorrect caricatures of some of the strongest Princeton leaders, Helseth has cut through the mist in order to clearly present their thinking on key epistemological matters. He does for these Princetonians what Richard Muller has done for Calvin's successors. We need this corrective, and I am deeply thankful for Dr. Helseth's research and fine work in this needed volume.

—**David Hall**, Senior Pastor, Midway Presbyterian Church, Powder Springs, GA

Not very long ago, evangelical Protestants in the United States regarded the theology of Old Princeton Seminary as a source of wisdom and inspiration because of its scholarly rigor and theological depth. Today's evangelicals often view Old Princeton in a very different and antagonistic light, as wooden, rationalistic theologians who have little to teach those living in postmodern times. Paul Helseth believes this is an unwelcome development and defends the Princeton theologians, Archibald Alexander, Charles Hodge, Benjamin Warfield, and J. Gresham Machen, as thoughtful students of Scripture and defenders of orthodox Christianity whom evangelicals need to read and heed. This is a timely defense of Old Princeton and thoughtful challenge to the confusion that bedevils contemporary evangelical theology.

—**D. G. Hart**, Adjunct Professor of Church History,
Westminster Seminary California, Escondido, CA

Paul Helseth's book is a notable example of intellectual reclamation and recovery. By careful research the author shines a critical new light on the oft-repeated claim that Princeton theology was deeply in debt to Enlightenment rationalism, and especially to the Common Sense philosophy of Thomas Reid. Helseth claims that its roots lie not in the Enlightenment, but in the Augustinian anthropology of the Puritans and of Reformed orthodoxy. Thorough and persuasive, Helseth sensitively and knowledgeably discusses the issues of faith and reason, particularly in relation to apologetics, and then assesses the strength of the critique of postconservative orthodoxy against the Princeton theology.

—**Paul Helm**, Teaching Fellow, Theology and Philosophy,
Regent College, Vancouver, BC

"Right Reason" and the Princeton Mind: An Unorthodox Proposal is a major accomplishment on many fronts. Historically Paul Helseth advances the four-decade reassessment of Old Princeton theology. Philosophically he demonstrates that Princeton advocates Alexander, Hodge, Warfield, and Machen, by rejecting speculation and emphasizing the moral aspects of "right reason," are more fully allied with the Reformers and Augustine than with their Enlightenment predecessors. Apologetically Helseth contends that evidentialism and presuppositionalism may have more in common than previously acknowledged.

And his trenchant analysis of postconservative rejection of Princeton contributes substantially to contemporary evangelicalism. *Right Reason* is well worth reading to follow Helseth's intriguing themes, skillfully woven together.

—**Andrew Hoffecker**, Professor of Church History Emeritus, Reformed Theological Seminary, Jackson, MS

Unlike so many who never take the necessary time and effort to grapple with the Old Princeton theologians and instead rely on hand-me-down opinions, Paul Helseth has coupled a close reading of Old Princetonians with great sensitivity to their concerns and the context in which they wrote. Helseth demonstrates over and over again that much of what has been written about Old Princeton stands in need of major revision. Anyone wanting a reliable analysis of the Old Princetonians should be directed to Paul Helseth's work.

—**Gary L. W. Johnson**, Senior Pastor, Church of the Redeemer, Mesa, AZ

In spite of the daunting title, *"Right Reason" and the Princeton Mind: An Unorthodox Proposal*, this book is a not-to be-missed discussion of the spirited modern debate within evangelicalism with regard to the nature of truth and the place of doctrine. Helseth elegantly and convincingly argues for the biblical and Reformed nature of nine-teenth- and early-twentieth-century theological orthodoxy and shows how contemporary postconservative evangelicalism, in misrepresenting as rationalism the great achievement of our Princeton fathers, inadvertently exposes itself as a contemporary version of the very liberalism that Hodge, Warfield, and Machen brilliantly unmasked in their day.

—**Peter Jones**, Director, truthXchange; Scholar-in-Residence and Adjunct Professor, Westminster Seminary California, Escondido, CA

Helseth urges postconservative and conservative evangelicals alike . . . to heed Old Princeton's critique of theological liberalism. He corrects widespread misconceptions about the Princetonians' thought and applies that thought to an incalculably important controversy of today.

This thoroughly researched and insightfully argued work merits the attention of all thinking evangelicals.

—**Dennis W. Jowers**, Associate Professor of Theology & Apologetics, Faith Evangelical College & Seminary, Tacoma, WA

Right Reason is both a stinging and stunning defense that the Princetonians shared in the theological and epistemological assumptions of the Reformers rather than accommodating their theology to the Enlightenment rationalism of Scottish Common Sense Realism of their day. The book comprehensively demonstrates that the Princetonians were not Enlightenment rationalists, an allegation so often leveled by postconservatives. Consequently, Helseth demonstrates that the current debate between conservatives and postconservatives over the role and purpose of doctrine is actually a debate about the very nature of Scripture. Helseth has given the church an incredible gift. *Right Reason* is an outstanding achievement marked by thoroughness and fair scholarship, all in a readable, accessible presentation.

—**David Mappes**, Associate Professor of Systematic Theology, Baptist Bible Seminary, Clarks Summit, PA

There are those in contemporary evangelicalism who see Old Princeton and what it represents as a relic of a bygone era. Days gone and, thankfully in their view, forgotten. I am mystified. More importantly, Professor Helseth is mystified, and in this book he shows rather deftly how the Princetonians are woefully misunderstood and misinterpreted and too readily and easily cast aside. Helseth further shows how—once the Princetonians are understood rightly, once this critical concept of "right reason" is understood correctly—the Princetonians are a healthy and worthy model for theologians today. Ignore what people claim that the Princetonians said, and read this book to find out what they really said.

Next to the writings of the Princetonians themselves—the grand works of Hodge, Warfield, and company—this is the best and the most important book on Old Princeton ever written.

—**Stephen J. Nichols**, Research Professor of Christianity and Culture, Lancaster Bible College, Lancaster, PA

This book needed to be written in order to reinvigorate the evangelical view of the inspiration of Scripture as held by Archibald Alexander, Charles Hodge, B. B. Warfield, and J. Gresham Machen. Written in that way, it now needs to be read and recognized by those who claim to know and share this as the "Princeton view." When this presentation is known, it will not be possible to dismiss the Princeton view as simply an outworking of Scottish Common Sense philosophy. It will be acknowledged as drawn from the Scriptures and intended as the biblical view of inspiration.

Buy this book!

—**Roger Nicole**, Professor of Theology Emeritus,
Reformed Theological Seminary, Orlando

Paul Helseth's detailed and careful arguments against the received view of Old Princeton's epistemology are convincing and possess the conceptual precision to break the stale impasse in evangelical hermeneutics and epistemology and to open up refreshing lines of research.

—**Walter J. Schultz**, Professor of Philosophy,
Northwestern College, St. Paul

Grounded in painstaking and thorough engagement with the writings of Archibald Alexander, Charles Hodge, and B. B. Warfield, as well as today's debates about them, Paul Helseth's *"Right Reason" and the Princeton Mind* issues an important challenge to the dominant way of reading the Old Princetonians—a reading that has deeply influenced many interpretations of contemporary evangelicalism. Emotions can run deep in debates about these interpretations, and these emotions occasionally surface when Helseth responds to charged statements by some postconservatives. Nevertheless, it is to be hoped that scholars on all sides of these questions will give careful and sober attention to Helseth's contention that the Princetonians—far from being in hock to Enlightenment rationalism—held a view of "right reason" deeply indebted to classic lines of Augustinian and Reformed thought. Helseth's argument in *"Right Reason" and the Princeton Mind* deserves a careful reading by all who are concerned about the important questions regarding the Princetonians and their place in understanding the past, present, and future of the evangelical church.

—**Bradley N. Seeman**, Assistant Professor of Philosophy, Taylor University, Upland, IN

Old Princeton theology and epistemology is often caricatured as modernistic rationalism, with no room for the crucial elements of subjective experience. But in this careful study, Paul Helseth persuasively argues that the Princetonians saw the reception of truth as involving the "whole soul," apprehended by the regenerate with "right" (or saving) reason and uniting both head and heart. Helseth not only overturns a historical misunderstanding, but also undermines a common narrative used to explain the development of North American evangelicalism. In addition, his work provides a practical and theological corrective for the life of the church and the academy today. I hope it will be widely read and appropriated.

—**Justin Taylor**, Managing Editor, *ESV Study Bible*

I confess I have trouble containing my enthusiasm over the publication of *Right Reason*, but why should I try? In these pages, Paul Helseth has done a fantastic job of defending the theology and theologians of Old Princeton, and has done so in a way that demonstrates their continuing relevance in these days of postorthodoxy.

—**Douglas Wilson**, Pastor of Christ Church and Senior Fellow, New Saint Andrews College, Moscow, ID

This book is overdue. The apologetic task as understood by the Old Princetonians is too often mischaracterized and too seldom investigated with thoroughness and care. Helseth has read the primary sources more thoroughly and more carefully than most and has provided a needed corrective. His *Right Reason* deserves a wide hearing and will serve well toward a more accurate understanding of the Princetonians' robust doctrine of man and sin and corresponding apologetic outlook. Heartily recommended.

—**Fred G. Zaspel**, Pastor, Reformed Baptist Church, Franconia, PA

"Right Reason"
and the
Princeton Mind

"Right Reason"
and the
Princeton Mind

AN UNORTHODOX PROPOSAL

P AUL K JOSS H ELSETH

P&R
P U B L I S H I N G
P.O. BOX 817 • PHILLIPSBURG • NEW JERSEY 08865-0817

Printed in the United States of America

Library of Congress Cataloging-in-Publication Data

Helseth, Paul Kjoss, 1962-
 "Right reason" and the Princeton mind : an unorthodox proposal / Paul Kjoss Helseth.
  p. cm.
 Includes bibliographical references (p.   ) and index.
 ISBN 978-1-59638-143-8
 1. Faith and reason--Christianity. 2. Knowledge, Theory of (Religion) 3. Reformed epistemology. 4. Princeton Theological Seminary. I. Title.
 BT50.H55 2010
 231'.042--dc22

                              2010024760

This book is dedicated
in the hope of the resurrection
to
Hovald Kjoss Helseth
September 17, 1934–January 3, 2007
and
Torger Kjoss Helseth
June 5, 2008

It is because we cannot be robbed of God's providence that we know, amid whatever encircling gloom, that all things shall work together for good to those that love him. It is because we cannot be robbed of God's providence that we know that nothing can separate us from the love of Christ—not tribulation, nor anguish, nor persecution, nor famine, nor nakedness, nor peril, nor sword. . . . Were not God's providence over all, could trouble come without his sending, were Christians the possible prey of this or the other fiendish enemy, when perchance God was musing, or gone aside, or on a journey, or sleeping, what certainty of hope could be ours? "Does God send trouble?" Surely, surely. He and he only. To the sinner in punishment, to his children in chastisement. To suggest that it does not always come from his hands is to take away all our comfort.[1]

1. B. B. Warfield, "God's Providence Over All," in *Selected Shorter Writings of Benjamin B. Warfield*, 2 vols., ed. John E. Meeter (Phillipsburg, NJ: P&R Publishing, 2001), 1:110.

Contents

Foreword:
JOHN D. WOODBRIDGE

───⊗───

Voltaire (1694–1778), the famous French *philosophe*, sparkled as a brilliant and witty conversationalist in the *salons* of Parisian women of letters and at the *Café Procope* in Paris. During the so-called "Enlightenment," Voltaire often starred at center stage in European culture. Not only did he write popular plays (*Irene*, 1778) and pen provocative essays and fascinating stories (*Candide*, 1759), but he battled against social injustice and intolerance (the Calas Affair, 1762–65). As a prolific wordsmith, he bequeathed to later generations an astonishing legacy of fifteen million words.

Voltaire often used his remarkable literary gifts to criticize contemporary Christians, especially those he deemed "superstitious," hypocritical, or power hungry. After all, it was they who peopled the "Age of Superstition," the other age besides the "Age of Lights" (*Siècle des lumières*) in which Voltaire said he lived. He worried that defenders of the Christian faith remained so powerful in the eighteenth century that they might thwart the advance of the "Age of Lights" that he and other *philosophes* were promoting with missionary zeal. The article *Philosophe* in Diderot's *Encyclopédie* drew a sharp distinction between *philosophes* and Christians: "Reason is to the *philosophe* what grace is to the Christian. Grace determines the Christian to act; reason determines the *philosophe*." In 1769, Diderot complained to David Hume about Christianity's residual influence among their contemporaries: "Ah, my dear philosopher! Let us weep and wail over the lot of philosophy. We preach wisdom to the deaf, and we are still far indeed from the age of reason." By the 1770s, Voltaire bemoaned the fact that the "philosophic" movement devoted to the propagation of *la philosophie* was in noticeable retreat.

As a worldly wise gadfly, Voltaire spread his criticisms around— beyond the ranks of European Christians. For example, on occasion he launched sharp barbs at historians. One barb was especially painful. Probably with a mischievous twinkle in his eye, he wrote: "History is a bag of tricks we play on the dead." In this brief dictum, Voltaire reduced the study of history to malicious tomfoolery.

Most historians, even radical postmodernists, bristle if aware of Voltaire's charge. They shudder at the characterization that they are purposeful "tricksters" who manipulate their subjects from the past for personal advantage or to enjoy a playful whim. After all, do not many historians carefully eschew misrepresentations of the "facts"? Do they not try to eliminate or minimize the influence of personal biases from overpowering and distorting the way they relate historical narratives? Do they not assume their "accounts" or "discourses" contain at least a modicum of "truth"? Even the most radical postmodernist historians—those who have abandoned the quest to practice "objective history" and compare the doing of history to the writing of propaganda—believe their own analyses are somehow "reliable." Ironically, a number of postmodernists who dispute the very existence of "truth" have become publicly vexed and angry when the "truthfulness" of their own pronouncements is challenged or questioned.

As for Voltaire's claim that "History is a bag of tricks," this rebuke does not fully represent his final judgment on the discipline of history. After all, he was a serious historian himself. He devoted five years to researching and writing *The Age of Louis XIV* (1751)—a landmark historical piece. He apparently believed he had represented the royal actors in his story in a reliable manner.

Despite the postmodern onslaught of the last four decades, many historians still pursue and practice a chastened form of "objective history." They admittedly invoke less precise standards for what constitutes "objectivity" in historical writing than the precise measurements natural scientists employ to describe their "objective," repeatable experiments. Sometimes historians cite as a heuristic stopgap measure their commitment to peer review as a means to protect them from slipping into radical personal subjectivity in historical writing. Historical articles and books generally undergo a robust review process before they are deemed worthy contributions to the scholarly world. Expert reviewers for university presses and scholarly journals are charged to offer ostensibly fair-minded assessments of the quality of manuscripts submitted for publication. Then, after publication, works are further reviewed in scholarly journals. Reviewers often point out weaknesses and strengths of the publication and sometimes note suspect ideological proclivities of the author—biases that might compromise or jade the "truthfulness" of the book's central contentions.

Should well-respected reviewers concur that a particular study is genuinely superlative, their approval might propel the book toward becoming a "standard," authoritative source on the topic it addresses. Other historians who read the positive reviews may conclude that so persuasive and conclusive is the book's coverage and central argument that the need no longer exists to do further research in the field. Did not distinguished reviewers of the volume, the quality control gatekeepers for the historians' guild, put seals of approval on the newly minted "standard" interpretation?

With the passage of time, a consensus in favor of the "standard" interpretation may grow even stronger among historians. Additional studies may appear that seem to confirm its basic premises. The new "standard" interpretation takes on the allure of a historical "orthodoxy"; that is, a received interpretation that knowledgeable scholars in the field should adopt regarding the topic under consideration. The "orthodoxy" can become so ingrained in the collective consciousness of the historical community that few historians ever contemplate doubting its validity.

In this context, any enterprising scholar who should dare to offer an alternative, "unorthodox proposal," to the effect that the "orthodox" interpretation may need serious revision, undertakes a daunting challenge. To gain a respectable hearing, he or she must offer compelling evidence and arguments in support of the claim. Longstanding "orthodoxies" of historical interpretation are not easily dislodged.

This brings us to the present study by Professor Paul Kjoss Helseth, an accomplished theologian, philosopher, and historian. In his "Unorthodox Proposal," Professor Helseth, writing in the respected tradition of a gatekeeper reviewer, challenges the validity of one of the most influential "orthodox" interpretations related to the history of American evangelicalism and fundamentalism. Helseth has an especially keen mind and a gracious spirit. He does not believe the historians who created this "orthodox" or consensus interpretation did so with malicious intentions à la Voltaire. Moreover, Helseth recognizes that some of the arguments sustaining the "orthodox" interpretation possess merit. At the same time, his close textual reading of pertinent primary sources leads him to conclude that in aggregate, the "orthodox" interpretation should be reconsidered and his "unorthodox" proposal should replace it. No postmodern historian or partisan of Voltaire's silly sally against historians, Helseth assumes that his mustering of substantial documentary evidence should still count for something in convincing readers they ought to give his "unorthodox proposal" a fair hearing.

What is the "orthodox" historical interpretation Professor Helseth calls on scholars to reconsider, if not jettison? He contests the "orthodox" proposal that the Presbyterian professors at Old Princeton Seminary (1812–1929) betrayed traditional Reformed theology by their alleged claim that human reason was in certain significant ways unaffected by the fall. The proposal suggests the Princetonians were prompted to accept this anti-Augustinian teaching owing to the supposed influence of Common Sense Realism and Baconianism in shaping their theology.

The origins of this "orthodox" historiography date back to at least the 1950s. In a seminal article, "The Scottish Philosophy and

American Theology,"[1] Professor Sydney Ahlstrom of Yale University laid out the interpretation in a cogent manner. Thereafter numerous distinguished historians adopted it, added to it, and converted it into an "orthodox" historical interpretation.

For self-identified Reformed Christians, the implications of the interpretation are no less than staggering. This is particularly the case for Reformed Christians who have appreciated and appropriated elements of the theological reflections of the Old Princetonians. The thesis suggests that if Reformed Christians embrace aspects of the Old Princetonians' theology, they thereby become doctrinal innovators, philosophically "modernists"—and betrayers of critically important doctrines of the Reformed faith. Believing that these are in fact the entailments of espousing the theology of the Old Princetonians, a number of commentators have criticized the "Old Princetonians' theology" in very severe terms. Little doubt exists that the theological reputation of the Old Princetonians has suffered gravely in consequence.

The late George H. Williams, professor of church history at Harvard Divinity School, was once asked what trait he thought should characterize a historian. His answer was quite surprising. He replied that among other traits, a historian should be generous. This generosity would exhibit itself when a historian defends the reputation of people in the past who can no longer defend themselves. Perhaps Williams's own academic career during which he called for a more sympathetic understanding of Anabaptists provides a superb example of what a historian's generosity may look like in action.

In one sense, Professor Helseth's study is also a work of generosity. In it, he calls on readers to reassess the validity of the "orthodox" interpretation regarding the Old Princetonians by giving his own "unorthodox" proposal a fair hearing. Should readers do this, they may discover a very persuasive new read of what the Old Princetonians actually believed regarding reason's powers and the way theology should be constructed. Readers may become convinced that the Old Princetonians did not betray their Reformed tradition

---

1. *Church History* 24 (1955): 257–72.

but amplified it. In this study, Professor Helseth makes a formidable argument that such really is the case. Perhaps in decades ahead, his "unorthodox" proposal regarding the Old Princetonians may become the new "orthodox" proposal. Should this occur, it would signal a major historiographical revolution in American religious studies devoted to the history of evangelicalism and fundamentalism. It would constitute no small historical corrective, one that is needed. It would also represent a generous accomplishment in exonerating the reputations of the theologians at Old Princeton Seminary from unfortunate and misleading accusations.

Preface

A Tendentious Analysis?

A number of years ago I had the privilege of interacting with a prominent evangelical historian about the role of "right reason" in the Princeton Theology. In one e-mail exchange, this historian—a giant in the field with a well-earned reputation for competence and scholarly integrity—encouraged me to remember that there is a difference between real historical analysis and tendentious historical analysis. Whereas real historical analysis attempts to interpret a "historical situation" dispassionately, tendentious analysis often supplants real analysis, often in a duplicitous attempt to garner historical support for a particular proposal "for how theology should look [now]." In short, this scholar—a leading architect of the standard interpretation of the Princeton Theology who was skeptical of the thesis I was then and am now defending—was gently admonishing me "to differentiate historical assessment from theological construction" as I pursued a line of inquiry that is, at least as far as the standard interpretation of Old Princeton is concerned, nothing if not "unorthodox."

While I appreciated this historian's counsel and am willing to acknowledge that I think contemporary evangelicals would be much better off if they did theology more like the theologians at Old Princeton Seminary, I have yet to be convinced that the substance of the proposal that follows is grounded in a tendentious—and therefore suspect—analysis of Old Princeton. In fact, I remain convinced that the forthcoming analysis is a needed corrective to a historiographical consensus that is itself grounded in a tendentious reading of the Princeton theologians, a reading that more and more scholars are recognizing is far too eager to view the Princetonians against the backdrop of Scottish Common Sense Realism and far too reluctant to consider the paradigm-shifting implications of Old Princeton's holistic epistemology. Since this reluctance and the historical analysis that follows from it continue to have a profound impact on how much of contemporary evangelical theology in fact "looks [now]," at least some now suggest that the architects of the historiographical consensus—along with their theological allies—should ask themselves whether and to what extent their concern for tendentious analysis cuts both ways. Indeed, in light of the fact that the consensus of critical opinion is now being used, as Part Two of the forthcoming discussion attempts to make clear, to justify constructions of theology that some insist are barely Christian let alone faithfully evangelical, many are now asking—I think legitimately—whether it is time to revisit what has come to be regarded as the "orthodox" assessment of Old Princeton. Are the more progressive proposals that are currently being offered "for how [evangelical] theology should look [now]" really justified, these scholars are asking, by an interpretation of the Old Princetonians that is looking increasingly tenuous? Lest that question sound much more combative than I (and others) intend for it to sound, let me make it clear that to the extent that the study that follows has been compromised—despite my best efforts to the contrary—by historical eisegesis, then it is my prayer that the substance of the analysis will, to that extent, be rejected.

About the Dedication

This book is dedicated to my father, Hovald Kjoss Helseth, who died of cancer on January 3, 2007, and to my first son, Torger Kjoss Helseth, who was stillborn on June 5, 2008. The last few years have been difficult for my immediate and extended family for a number of significant reasons. We have been refined by the bitter providence of

God and learned a number of good but difficult lessons along the way. Two of the most painful trials have been the death of my dad, a man for whom I had and still have profound respect and affection, and the death of Torger, the son I will come to know in the new heavens and the new earth. The Warfield quote at the bottom of the dedication page is an indication of the depth of the influence that the theologians at Old Princeton Seminary have had on my worldview. I have come to love not just the Old Princetonians, but more importantly the God of the Old Princetonians, who is, as far as I can tell, the God of the Bible, the God whose hope-giving promises are yes and amen in Jesus.

Acknowledgments

I have been encouraged, assisted, and challenged throughout this project by a number of important individuals. I am grateful to my wife Marla for her unfailing love, support, and faithfulness. She is a wonderful friend and companion to me and a wonderful mother to our children Margrethe Pearl and Benjamin Paul, both of whom are good gifts from the Lord who have made our lives unspeakably fulfilling and sweet.

My mother Betty and my siblings Peter, Anne, and Sara along with their families continue to support and encourage me in ways that are significant.

My friends Ardel Caneday, Ian Hewitson, Douglas Huffman, Joshua Moon, and Walter Schultz are kindred spirits who have done more than they can imagine to sharpen my thinking on all things theological.

Michael Gurney, David P. Smith, and Jeffrey Waddington have kindly given of their time to read and critically assess the penultimate draft of this manuscript. Their suggestions have served to make for a better, although by no means flawless, argument; whatever shortcomings remain are, of course, entirely my own.

I am also grateful to Nathan Strom for his fine work on the bibliography, and to Marvin Padgett and John Hughes at P&R Publishing for embracing this project with such enthusiasm.

Finally, I am thankful to John D. Woodbridge, research professor of church history and the history of Christian thought at Trinity Evangelical Divinity School, for doing me the honor of writing the foreword to this volume. A number of years ago, Dr. Woodbridge—who is a giant in the field of church history—encouraged me to publish a book on the Old Princetonians that challenges the "orthodox" assessment of the Princeton Theology. This volume is, among other things, my response to his encouragement.

Introduction: An Unorthodox Proposal

The Question

J. Gresham Machen is widely regarded as having been the leading spokesperson for Princeton Theological Seminary's Reformed orthodoxy during the fundamentalist-modernist controversy of the early twentieth century. At a time when many within the denominational power structures of North America were calling for denominational unity on the basis of the accommodation of doctrine to the theological and philosophical presuppositions of modern biblical and historical scholarship, Machen, holding fast to the theological and philosophical presuppositions of the Princeton Theology (a major nineteenth- and early twentieth-century North American school of Reformed thought), was uncompromising in his condemnation of this growing trend. Denominational unity on the basis of doctrinal accommodationism cannot be tolerated, he argued, because doctrines are not merely the changing symbolic expressions of an ineffable subjective experience. Rather, they are the objective foundation upon which the Christian life is based, for they both participate in and provide a truthful witness to the historical facts that ground and shape the Christian religion.[1]

1. Machen insists that doctrines set forth the meaning of the facts upon which the Christian way of life is based. According to Machen, "The primitive Church was concerned not merely with what Jesus had said, but also, and primarily, with what Jesus had done. The world was

Given Machen's commitment to the objective rather than the merely subjective nature of religious truth, the question arises as to what was the driving force behind his repudiation of theological liberalism. Was his repudiation of liberal accommodationism informed by a theological commitment to the epistemological assumptions of the Reformed tradition? Or was it informed by a philosophical commitment to a kind of Enlightenment rationalism that came to reign in modern America, as many believe? Since the publication of Sydney Ahlstrom's seminal analysis of the influence of Scottish Common Sense Realism on the development of North American theology, the historiographical consensus has clearly been that Machen was a practitioner of the "Old Princeton" approach to apologetics, and as such indebted to epistemological assumptions that are diametrically opposed to those of the Reformed tradition.[2] The problem with the Princeton Theology, so the argument goes, is that while it made a show of orthodoxy, in fact it was built on an accommodation of theology to the epistemological assumptions of an essentially humanistic philosophy.[3] Those who concur with this analysis conclude that Machen's views are more or less suspect because

---

to be redeemed through the proclamation of an event. And with the event went the meaning of the event; and the setting forth of the event with the meaning of the event was doctrine. These two elements are always combined in the Christian message. The narration of the facts is history; the narration of the facts with the meaning of the facts is doctrine. These two elements are always combined in the Christian message." J. Gresham Machen, *Christianity and Liberalism* (Grand Rapids: Eerdmans, 1990; 1923), 29. Note that I am using the word "objective" in this study not in the sense of Enlightenment foundationalism, i.e., to suggest that neutral, comprehensive, mathematically indubitable knowledge is possible for finite human beings, but in the much less ambitious sense that affirms that at least some true knowledge of real states of affairs in the "world as it is" is possible for finite human beings, the influence of culture notwithstanding.

2. Cf. Sydney Ahlstrom, "The Scottish Philosophy and American Theology," *CH* 24 (1955): 257–72.

3. Critics contend that this accommodation is evident in a number of places, including the understanding of language that informs Old Princeton's understanding of doctrine. A helpful discussion of this point can be found in John Stewart's incisive analysis of Charles Hodge. According to Stewart, Hodge endorsed "a language structure rooted in Scottish realism. That linguistic commitment enabled Hodge to construct a coherent description of the actual cultural realities of the everyday, common sense world: reliable human testimonies in law, business, and politics; a confidence in the historicity of past events and precedents, including creedal traditions; a vehicle for human community and communication; and an accessible language for reasonable scientific and religious discourse." John W. Stewart, *Mediating the Center: Charles Hodge on American Science, Language, Literature, and Politics* (Princeton: Princeton Theological Seminary, 1995), 58.

he stood in a tradition that they suppose is "utterly rationalistic,"[4] for they are convinced that the "source"[5] of Old Princeton's commitment to the objective nature of religious truth is found in the (perhaps unwitting) endorsement of assumptions that are bound inextricably to the mind-set of "the modern scientific revolution."[6]

An Unorthodox Proposal

While this conclusion appears at first glance to be justified because it seems to offer a plausible explanation for Machen's rather uncompromising defense of what he regarded as the objective foundations of the Christian religion, the question remains as to whether or not it in fact is justified. Were Machen and his predecessors at Old Princeton Seminary really the purveyors of an essentially humanistic philosophy rather than the champions of Reformed orthodoxy? Was the driving force behind their theological labors, in other words, an understanding of religious epistemology that supplants the epistemological assumptions of the Reformed tradition with those of an "alien philosophy"?[7]

The study that follows is grounded in the conviction that the reigning (or "orthodox") interpretation of the Princeton Theology cannot stand because it ignores the moral rather than the merely rational nature of the Princetonians' thought. When Old Princeton's religious epistemology is interpreted within a context that regards the "faculties" or "powers" of the soul as the functional manifestations of a unitary whole rather

4. William Livingstone, "The Princeton Apologetic as Exemplified by the Work of Benjamin B. Warfield and J. Gresham Machen: A Study in American Theology 1880–1930" (PhD diss., Yale University, 1948), 342. See also Ernest Sandeen, "The Princeton Theology: One Source of Biblical Literalism in American Protestantism," *CH* 31 (1962): 307–21.

5. George Marsden, "Understanding J. Gresham Machen," *PSB* 11, 1 (1990): 57. See also George Marsden, "J. Gresham Machen, History, and Truth," *WTJ* 42 (1979): 157–75.

6. George Marsden, "The Collapse of American Evangelical Academia," in *Faith and Rationality: Reason and Belief in God*, ed. Alvin Plantinga, Nicholas Wolterstorff (Notre Dame, IN: University of Notre Dame Press, 1983), 241.

7. This is the general theme of John Vander Stelt's *Philosophy and Scripture: A Study of Old Princeton and Westminster Theology* (Marlton, NJ: Mack Publishing, 1978). According to Andrew Hoffecker, Vander Stelt's treatment is "the most comprehensive, and critical, study of Scottish influence at Princeton." Andrew Hoffecker, "Benjamin B. Warfield," in *The Princeton Theology*, Reformed Theology in America, no. 1, ed. David Wells (Grand Rapids: Baker, 1989), 81.

than as essentially autonomous substances that have the ability to act independently of one another,[8] it becomes clear that the Princetonians were not Enlightenment rationalists whose confidence in the mind led them to ignore the import of the subjective and the centrality of experience in religious epistemology. Rather, they were more or less consistently Reformed scholars who insisted that these kinds of factors play a critical role in every attempt to lay hold of what God has revealed, because laying hold of what God has revealed is something that is done by whole persons, not by autonomous faculties or powers.[9] Indeed, they insisted that "right" assessments of revealed truth are grounded in more than merely rational analyses of objective evidence, for they recognized that the operation of the intellect involves the "whole soul"—mind, will, and emotions—rather than the rational faculty alone.[10]

8. On the "faculty psychology" see, for example, Lefferts Loetscher, *Facing the Enlightenment and Pietism: Archibald Alexander and the Founding of Princeton Theological Seminary* (Westport, CT: Greenwood, 1983), 168; Norman Fiering, "Will and Intellect in the New England Mind," *WMQ* 29 (1972): 515–58. According to Bruce Kuklick, many North American theologians embraced the "faculty psychology" so they could respond to Edwards's work on the freedom of the will. "The Scots and their disciples in the United States," he argues, "shifted discussion [on the freedom of the will] from the Edwardsean functionalist view of the mind to a three-substance view." This "faculty psychology" held that "the mind had three functions, not two, and they were more clearly separated into ontological faculties. The understanding was not so much an activity as a substance that *did* the cognizing. So also the will, which was divided into a substance capable of *affection*, which might include sensation and emotion; and the will *proper*, which was the capacity for choice, or a substance that often clearly had what was known as a power to the contrary. Thus, in human behavior the reason (or understanding or cognition) set out goals; the affections provided the motives; but the will made action possible." Bruce Kuklick, "The Place of Charles Hodge in the History of Ideas in America," in *Charles Hodge Revisited: A Critical Appraisal of His Life and Work*, ed. John W. Stewart, James H. Moorhead (Grand Rapids: Eerdmans, 2002), 72.; see also Kuklick, *A History of Philosophy in America: 1720–2000* (New York: Oxford University Press, 2001), 52.

Throughout this study, I am not absurdly denying that the Princetonians often referred to the various "faculties" or "powers" of the soul. What I am suggesting is that they did not regard these "faculties" or "powers" as ontological substances that have the ability to act independently of one another, but as particular functions of a unitary thinking-feeling-willing whole. For example, as we will see in Chapter Four, Machen argues that "what we call the will is just the whole man willing, as what we call the intellect is the whole man thinking, and what we call the feelings is the whole man feeling." J. Gresham Machen, "Sinners Saved by Grace," in *The Christian View of Man* (Edinburgh: The Banner of Truth Trust, 1965; 1937), 236.

9. For a discussion of the impact of the demise of this emphasis on the wholeness of the person on the study of psychology at Princeton College and elsewhere, see Bryan M. Maier, *The Separation of Psychology and Theology at Princeton, 1868–1903: The Intellectual Achievement of James McCosh and James Mark Baldwin* (Lewiston, NY: The Edwin Mellen Press, 2005).

10. In his analysis of Charles Hodge's ongoing "quest for the harmony of science and religion," John Stewart argues that "purpose, benevolence, and rationality were the deep assumptions of

In response to those who suggest that Old Princeton's understanding of the theological enterprise was grounded in the accommodation of assumptions that find their genesis in a rather naïve form of Enlightenment rationalism, the following chapters argue that whatever Enlightenment assumptions the Princetonians did embrace altered the form more than the substance of their theology, and that despite what the consensus of critical opinion would have us believe, the religious epistemology of the Princeton theologians was principally informed by anthropological and epistemological assumptions that are consistently Reformed.[11] As such, the following chapters call for

---

Hodge's approach to scientific agenda." In an intriguing footnote in this analysis, Stewart notes: "I suspect that larger doctrinal commitments of the Augustinian-Calvinist tradition surface in these three characteristics. Doctrines of creation and redemption are equally rooted in God's sovereignty in the Reformed tradition and, I suspect, Hodge's doxological science merely extended those Reformed convictions to encompass teleology, benevolence, and rationality." Stewart, *Mediating the Center*, 25–26. In my estimation, Stewart's suspicions are correct and—assuming Hodge's approach to science is representative of his colleagues at Old Princeton—point to the reason why the reigning interpretation of the Princeton Theology must be significantly qualified if not abandoned.

11. Please note the important qualifications in this sentence. I am not suggesting that the Scottish philosophy had no impact whatsoever on the substance of Old Princeton's Reformed commitments or that Scottish Common Sense Realism was totally irrelevant to the Princetonians' religious epistemology. Thus I am not denying that in a certain sense, what John Stewart says about Charles Hodge is true of the Princetonians in general, namely, that their theology was "conditioned and nuanced by political and cultural realities peculiarly American." Stewart, *Mediating the Center*, 112. Rather, what I am suggesting is that we ought not to overestimate the impact of the Scottish philosophy on Old Princeton, for this impact, I would argue, was largely held in check by the Princetonians' classically Reformed commitments despite the fact that they were—as all of us are—children of their time to one degree or another. For an example of how the epistemological assumptions of Scottish Realism had a negative impact on the theology of Charles Hodge, see how his appeal to "the consciousness of men" leads him to be surprisingly critical of the doctrine of concursus in *Systematic Theology*, 3 vols. (Grand Rapids: Eerdmans, 1989; 1871–73), 1:603–5.

See also Mark Noll's contention that "Hodge's ad hoc use of common sense moral intuition as a building block of his theology" is seen "most clearly" in his revision of the Federal Theology's understanding of the relationship between the sin of Adam and the guilt of his posterity. Mark A. Noll, "Charles Hodge as an Expositor of the Spiritual Life," in *Charles Hodge Revisited*, 202, 205. According to Hodge, the guilt and/or righteousness of a covenant head is reckoned to the members of a covenant neither because there is a "mysterious identity" between the two parties of the covenant, nor because the covenant relationship is the basis for a transfer of moral "turpitude" or "excellence" from one party to the other, but because there is a forensic relationship between the covenant head and those who are "in" him. Charles Hodge, *Commentary on the Epistle to the Romans* (Grand Rapids: Eerdmans, 1980; 1886), 178. The Federal Theologians typically "*added* their conception of a covenant solidarity with Adam to the Augustinian conception of natural solidarity as it had been sanctioned by Calvin and his immediate followers."

a fresh (or "unorthodox") interpretation of the Princeton Theology and its relevance to the historiography of North American Christianity by building on the insightful analyses of scholars such as Andrew Hoffecker and David Calhoun. Whereas Hoffecker has successfully challenged the notion that the Princetonians were indifferent to the subjective and experiential components of the Christian religion,[12] and Calhoun has demonstrated conclusively that the Princetonians "never allowed Scottish Common Sense Philosophy to stand by itself or to determine their theological outlook,"[13] the following chapters

George Hutchinson, *The Problem of Original Sin in American Presbyterian Theology* (Nutley, NJ: Presbyterian and Reformed, 1972), 102; for discussion that is relevant to Noll's critique of Hodge, see pages 5–9, 28–35, 109. Hodge separates liability to blame (*reatus culpae*) from liability to punishment (*reatus poenae*) by subordinating the natural relationship to the federal relationship, and by rejecting outright the notion of "a kind of Platonic unity of human nature acting in Adam." Noll, "Charles Hodge as an Expositor of the Spiritual Life," 202. As a consequence, he insists that those who are "in" Adam are not finally condemned for the imputed guilt of Adam's first sin alone, for the guilt that is imputed is penal, not moral. It does not entail, in other words, "criminality or moral ill-desert, or demerit, much less moral pollution, but the judicial obligation to satisfy justice." Hodge, *Systematic Theology*, 2:194; cf. Hodge, "Review of an Article in the June Number of *The Christian Spectator*, entitled 'Inquiries Respecting the Doctrine of Imputation,'" *BRPR* 2 (October 1830): 433.

According to Hodge, the justification for conceiving of the relationship between the sin of Adam and the guilt of his posterity in this fashion becomes immediately clear when we consider the person of Christ. We can continue to maintain that Jesus was sinless, Hodge argues, only by supposing "that the federal, and not the natural union is the essential ground of the imputation; that the sense in which Adam's sin is ours is a legal and not a moral sense and that the sense in which we sinned in him is that in which we act as a representative and not a literal sense." Hodge, "The First and Second Adam," *BRPR* 32 (April 1869): 367. For Hodge, then, Jesus was sinless not because the corruption of sin was not transmitted to him by means of natural generation, but because Adam did not represent him in the original covenant of works; Adam was not his covenant head. Note that Noll accounts for Hodge's separation of liability to blame from liability to punishment—and the "ingenious distinction between imputed sin (which only grace could overcome) and actual sinning (which condemned people to hell)" that is entailed in it—by pointing to a nominalist tendency in Hodge's thought, a tendency that Noll believes is grounded in common sense rather than in Scripture or in faithfulness to the classically Reformed understanding of the unity of the race in Adam. Noll, "Charles Hodge as an Expositor of the Spiritual Life," 204, 202.

12. Scholars who recognize that the Princetonians were not rationalists are indebted in one way or another to Andrew Hoffecker for his seminal work on the place of the subjective in the Princeton Theology. While Hoffecker believes that Scottish Common Sense Realism played an important role in the Princeton Theology, nevertheless he establishes that "Not only is this subjective element present [in the Princetonians' thought], but the omission of it renders . . . interpretations of [their] thought as a whole radically incomplete." Andrew Hoffecker, *Piety and the Princeton Theologians: Archibald Alexander, Charles Hodge, and Benjamin Warfield* (Phillipsburg, NJ: Presbyterian and Reformed; and Grand Rapids: Baker, 1981), 157, 159–60, 157).

13. David B. Calhoun, *Princeton Seminary*, vol. 2, *The Majestic Testimony, 1869–1929* (Edinburgh: The Banner of Truth Trust, 1996), 414.

call the prevailing historiographical consensus into question by establishing that Old Princeton's religious epistemology focused much more on the heart than it did on the head. Indeed, they establish that the Princetonians—while certainly "distinctively American" in a contextual sense[14]—nevertheless were neither scholastic rationalists nor Enlightenment humanists, but more or less consistently Reformed theologians who stood in the epistemological mainstream of the Reformed tradition while self-consciously opposing what they regarded as the "great intellectual drift"[15] of the nineteenth and early twentieth centuries.[16]

An Entrenched Bias

As such, the forthcoming chapters suggest a promising perspective for interpreting the Princeton Theology, one that helps to explain, among other things, why Charles Hodge would conclude his famous discussion of the inductive theological method by insisting that, "The question is not first and mainly, What is true to the understanding, but what is true to the renewed heart?"[17] They also challenge the tendentious nature of historical analysis that reflexively overestimates the influence of Scottish Common Sense Realism on the theologians at Old Princeton Seminary. Representative of such analysis is E. Brooks Holifield's recent survey of the history of theology in America. In this otherwise remarkable contribution to the study of American intellectual history, Holifield argues that Charles Hodge's critique of Nathaniel William Taylor and Charles Finney

---

14. Stewart, *Mediating the Center*, 13; cf. 112–13.

15. Stewart, "Introducing Charles Hodge to Postmoderns," in *Charles Hodge Revisited*, 22.

16. At no point in this study do I want to suggest that the Princetonians were always perfectly consistent in putting their Reformed commitments into practice. I want to suggest that they were "more or less" consistently Reformed in their actual doing of theology. For those who might conclude that I am conceding too much by granting this point, what I am simply saying is that the Princetonians, while essentially Reformed in practice, nevertheless were not perfectly Reformed in practice. At this point I would ask any reader who might imagine that he is perfectly consistent in his own doing of theology to cast the first stone.

17. Hodge, *Systematic Theology*, 1:16. This is one of the passages Calhoun cites to establish that Hodge "gave great importance to the inward teaching of the Holy Spirit, not as a substitute for external revelation but as a guide in determining what the Bible teaches." Calhoun, *Princeton Seminary*, 2:405.

signified an alternative reading of Scottish mental philosophy. Hodge made a portion of his case against Finney, for instance, by arguing that direct acts of volition lacked the power to govern emotions and affections. The argument against New Haven depended not only on biblical exegesis but also on an appeal to "consciousness," through which the Princetonians tried to ground a distinction between acts and dispositions, and between liberty and ability. When Hodge found "moral propensities, dispositions, or tendencies, prior to all acts of choice," or when he contended that the will was always determined by "the preceding state of mind," he was offering a particular reading of the Scottish philosophy. The philosophical views suffused the theological judgments.[18]

While Holifield does not deny that Hodge's critique was also informed by "a reassertion of an older Calvinist piety," nevertheless he gives pride of place to "philosophical difference[s]"[19] for explaining Hodge's repudiation of the New Haven Theology. Indeed, he privileges philosophical explanations for understanding the theological judgments of the Princeton theologians on matters relating to the nature of free agency, and thereby reinforces the prevailing assumption that Scottish Realism's conquest of Old Princeton was complete. But why, one wonders, does Holifield assume—particularly in this context—that philosophical factors have more explanatory power than theological factors do? Why does he insist, in other words, that "philosophical views suffused the theological judgments" when—given the clear presence of theological judgments that can only be described as standard Reformed fare—he just as easily could have argued that "theological judgments suffused his philosophical analysis"?[20] I would suggest that the answer is found in a bias

18. E. Brooks Holifield, *Theology in America: Christian Thought from the Age of the Puritans to the Civil War* (New Haven, CT: Yale University Press, 2005), 383–84. See also Holifield, "Hodge, the Seminary, and the American Theological Context," in *Charles Hodge Revisited*, 103–28.

19. Holifield, *Theology in America*, 384.

20. This question is particularly relevant when one considers just how different the philosophical views of the Scottish philosophy and the theological views of Reformed theology often are despite their apparent similarities. For example, although Scottish philosophers and Reformed believers both recognize that dispositions are related to the beliefs that humans hold, they think about dispositions in significantly different fashions. Whereas Reformed believers think about dispositions in moral terms and thus relate them to the inclination of the human

that is entrenched in the historiography of the Princeton Theology, a bias that I hope to challenge in the analysis that follows.[21]

---

heart, Scottish philosophers regard them as: (1) innate capacities with which human beings are endowed by their Creator and thus possess by nature, and (2) capacities that human beings acquire throughout life "by way of conditioning." Thus, while Reformed believers are quite sensitive to how sin and grace shape the beliefs that we hold, such considerations do not play a major role in the Scottish philosophy. According to Nicholas Wolterstorff, "[Thomas] Reid nowhere recognizes the ways in which sin inserts itself in the workings of our belief-dispositions. He bases his epistemology on those dispositions with which we have been endowed by our Creator. He hardly recognizes how those dispositions are now intermingled with all sorts of dispositions that we have by virtue of our fallenness. In this respect, Calvin and Kuyper were more insightful." Nicholas Wolterstorff, "Thomas Reid on Rationality," in *Rationality in the Calvinian Tradition*, ed. Hendrik Hart, Johan Van Der Hoven, Nicholas Wolterstorff (Lanham, MD: University Press of America, 1983), 66.

21. I realize that I am slicing things rather thin in this paragraph, particularly since there is a sense in which Hodge would agree with Holifield's basic point. After all, Hodge argues that "every theology is, in one sense, a form of philosophy. To understand any theological system we must understand the philosophy that underlies it and gives it peculiar form." Charles Hodge, "What Is Christianity?" *BRPR* 32 (1860): 121. Hodge's mentor, Archibald Alexander, had a similar assessment of the role of philosophy. See Hodge, "Memoir of Dr. Alexander," *BRPR* 27 (1855): 141. What I am challenging in this paragraph is not that the Scottish philosophy played at least an ancillary role in Hodge's defense of a classically Reformed understanding of human freedom, but that this philosophy should be afforded a privileged status when explaining the substance—and not merely the form—of the theological judgment that is rendered. It seems to me that those who insist there is such a thing as objective, transcultural truth can acknowledge on the one hand that philosophical systems influence how individuals do and think about theology, and reject on the other hand that those systems adequately account for the substance of their theology. Certainly it is possible to be influenced by a philosophy without being wholly at its mercy, and thus there is no compelling reason to conclude that particular theological judgments can be explained only in terms of particular philosophical systems, especially when the theological judgments in question—such as those referred to by Holifield in the quotation above—are not necessarily bound to the categories of one philosophical system or another. A case in point serves to illustrate my concern, and it has to do with whether or not one must be a commonsense foundationalist in order to subscribe to a "Calvinistic natural theology." In his consideration of this question, Paul Helm examines the work of two Reformed theologians who subscribe to natural theology, and then draws the following conclusion: "So here is evidence that there is only a contingent relationship between common-sense philosophy and the views of Calvinists on the place of reason in the development of natural theology. Not only is it logically possible to be a Calvinist and believe that there is a natural theology—and yet not be a Scottish common-sense philosopher—but many actually *have been* such." Paul Helm, "Thomas Reid, Common Sense and Calvinism," in *Rationality in the Calvinian Tradition*, 85.

In light of the fact that it is possible to endorse the view of human freedom that Hodge endorses in the block quotation above without being a Scottish realist, might it be the case that he was offering not "a particular reading of the Scottish philosophy" in his response to the New Haven theologians, but a theological judgment that is both essentially "Reformed" and capable of being defended in terms of common sense? If it is true that there is only a contingent relationship between Scottish Common Sense Realism and Hodge's understanding of the relationship between moral character and moral activity, then why privilege that which is contingent in one's explanation of the theological issue at the heart of the exchange?

The Argument

Terry Chrisope has argued that the primary question that confronts modern interpreters of the Princeton Theology has to do with the role of the subjective in that theology. "The real question regarding the Princetonians," he writes, "is not whether this element was present in their thought, but how it fit in with their other philosophical commitments."[22] If the argument of this investigation is to be established, the following chapters need to demonstrate that not only did subjective concerns occupy a place of central importance in the Princeton Theology, but more importantly these concerns are the key to understanding the epistemological assumptions of the Princeton Theology in general and the Princeton apologetic in particular.

I attempt to substantiate both of these claims in Part One of this study by examining the epistemological assumptions of four of the primary representatives of the Princeton Theology.[23] I begin this examination in Chapter One by outlining the epistemological context within which Old Princeton's compatibility with the Reformed tradition is found. After summarizing the formative commitments of the "evidential Christianity" that captivated the American theological mind in the eighteenth and nineteenth centuries, I consider the work of Archibald Alexander and Charles Hodge and suggest that Old Princeton's religious epistemology is compatible with the assumptions of the Reformed tradition because its emphasis on "right reason" is moral rather than merely rational. I suggest it is grounded, in other words, not in the accommodation of one form of Enlightenment rationalism or another, but in the endorsement of the classical Reformed distinction between a merely speculative and a spiritual understanding of what God has revealed.

That the "intellectualism" of Old Princeton in fact is moral rather than merely rational, and that classically Reformed assumptions do indeed take precedence in the religious epistemology of the Princeton

22. Terry Chrisope, "The Bible and Historical Scholarship in the Early Life and Thought of J. Gresham Machen, 1881–1915" (PhD diss., Kansas State University, 1988), 99.

23. I acknowledge that the scope of my study is rather limited. It is limited, however, to the analysis of those giants who in my estimation are the best representatives of the Old Princeton tradition as a whole.

theologians, is the focus of Chapters Two and Three. In these chapters I examine the work of B. B. Warfield and show how the Princeton apologetic and the understanding of Christian scholarship that follows from it are grounded in epistemological assumptions that are consistently Reformed. While critics would have us believe that Warfield was a rationalist because he argued that the primary mission of the believing apologist "is no less than to *reason* the world into acceptance of the 'truth,'"[24] these chapters establish that such a conclusion cannot be justified because Warfield retains an important role for subjective factors in his evidentialist apologetic. Whereas Warfield certainly affirms that a saving apprehension of what God has revealed entails the rational appropriation of objective evidence, he nonetheless recognizes that the quality of this apprehension is determined neither by the scholarly prowess of the perceiving mind, nor by the objective sufficiency of the evidence that is presented to one's consciousness, but by the moral or ethical state of the knowing soul. In short, these chapters establish that the Princeton apologetic is grounded not in one form of Enlightenment rationalism or another, but in the acknowledgment that fallen sinners are absolutely dependent on the sovereign grace of God not only for salvation, but also for the "right" apprehension of revealed truth by which salvation is obtained and the kingdom of God is advanced.

In the concluding chapter of Part One I finally consider J. Gresham Machen's critique of theological liberalism and ask whether it is ultimately grounded in theological or philosophical concerns. I suggest that the answer is found in Machen's solution to the problem of the relationship between Christianity and culture. Through an examination of what Machen calls the "task of consecration," I establish that the theological concerns that are manifest in Old Princeton's understanding of "right reason" are sustained in Machen's understanding of "true science." I argue that since the scientific enterprise for Machen is an inherently moral enterprise involving the "whole soul," it follows that he repudiates theological liberalism because he is convinced that it is "un-Christian," and that it is "un-Christian" precisely because it is "unscientific." In short, Chapter Four establishes that Machen

---

24. B. B. Warfield, "Christianity the Truth," in *Selected Shorter Writings of Benjamin B. Warfield*, 2 vols., ed. John E. Meeter (Phillipsburg, NJ: P&R Publishing, 2001), 2:213.

repudiates theological liberalism because he is critical of theology that is grounded in a kind of humanism that is without the moral ability to take account of all the facts that impinge on the integrity of the gospel message. As such, it serves as the transition to the discussion in Part Two, which suggests, among other things, that the conservative critique of postconservative evangelicalism is grounded in the same kinds of concerns that led Machen to repudiate theological liberalism.

In Part Two, I discuss the relevance of my proposal to the contemporary debate between conservative and postconservative evangelicals over the precise nature of the theological enterprise. In Chapters Five and Six I argue that the postconservative critique of conservative evangelicalism—which imagines that the rationalistic bent of some conservatives represents a faithful appropriation of the Princeton Theology—cannot be sustained because the Princetonians conceived of "right reason" in an Augustinian and not in a scholastic or an Enlightenment sense. I argue that the Princetonians sought to discern the difference between truth and error not by appealing to the magisterial conclusions of the rational faculty alone, but by hearing the message of the text with "right reason," which for them was a biblically informed kind of theological aesthetic that presupposes the work of the Spirit on the "whole soul" of the believing theologian. What I suggest in these chapters, then, is that when all is said and done, the postconservative critique of conservative evangelicalism fails for the same reason that the standard critique of Old Princeton fails; it misconstrues the nature of Old Princeton's understanding of "right reason" and then repudiates the conservative approach to theology on the basis of that misconstrual.

In the conclusion of this study I explore the relevance of my proposal to the assumptions at the heart of the ongoing debate within the evangelical camp over the role and function of doctrine. What I suggest is that despite what a growing consensus would have us believe, conservative and postconservative evangelicals are at odds not because conservatives have accommodated habits of mind that were born in the Enlightenment and embraced by those at the fountainhead of the conservative mainstream. Rather, evangelicals are at odds because conservatives are committed to the convictions of their theological forefathers and thus refuse to conceive of moral and religious truth in what they regard as a theologically liberal sense. Indeed, they are committed to a view of moral and religious truth that stands in self-conscious opposition to those cultural forces that reduce moral and religious truth claims to little more than expressions of the subjective preferences of those who hold them, and thus their views on such matters are nothing if not out of step with the spirit of the age. As such, the discussion in the concluding chapter challenges the assumptions at the heart of postconservative evangelicalism's critique of the "received evangelical tradition"[25] by considering those assumptions in light of Old Princeton's insistence that the regenerate alone can reason "rightly." It concludes that the postconservative critique is dubious at best because the best thinkers in the conservative mainstream—like the best thinkers at Old Princeton Seminary—are convinced that objective doctrinal knowledge is possible not because finite human beings have the ability to lay hold of what God has revealed in an unbiased, comprehensive, and mathematically indubitable fashion. Such knowledge is possible, rather, because those who have been given eyes to see and ears to hear lay hold of this revelation in a fashion that is biased by the work of the Spirit and the formative assumptions of the biblical worldview.[26]

A Consistently Reformed Perspective

In short, the study that follows examines Old Princeton's understanding of "right reason" and concludes that the Princeton theologians

25. Roger E. Olson, "Postconservative Evangelicalism: An Update after a Decade," http://www.thedivineconspiracy.org/Z5209W.pdf.

26. While the Princeton theologians acknowledged that the Christian religion is "founded on faith," they insisted that the faith on which it is founded "does not destroy or demand the destruction of reason, but elevates or perfects it." This is why they were convinced that believers can know, "in some degree, the great truths of religion as they are in themselves." Note, however, that although the Princetonians insisted that believers could have objective knowledge of doctrinal truths, they never presumed that believers could know these truths in "all their relations," or that they could know them precisely as God knows them. Charles Hodge alludes to the palpable tension between objective doctrinal knowledge—knowing doctrinal truths "as they are in themselves"—and mystery—truly knowing these truths, but only "in some degree"—in the following quotation: "A Christian introduced by the Spirit into the glorious temple of truth, may well be blinded by excess of light, but he can still clasp in his arms the great pillars of the faith." Charles Hodge, "Reid's Collected Writings," *BRPR* 32, 3 (1860): 509–10.

have been significantly misunderstood. According to the consensus of critical opinion, the theologians at Old Princeton Seminary were something less than authentically Reformed because they accommodated epistemological assumptions that were born in the Age of Reason. This study establishes that such an assessment must be revised if not abandoned because the Princetonians in fact conceived of reason in a fashion consistent with the assumptions of the Reformed tradition even if they were not always perfectly consistent in how they put this conception into practice. Indeed, they conceived of reason in a fashion that is moral rather than merely rational, and thus they recognized that the ability to reason "rightly" involves the "whole soul" and has to do with objective as well as subjective factors. As such, the following chapters call the justification for the postconservative project into question by challenging what has come to be an article of faith in the historiography of North American Christianity. They establish that the Princetonians simply were not rationalists by pointing to the anthropological and epistemological context within which Old Princeton's "blend of reasoning and piety, evidentialism and fideism, defense and proclamation"[27] is properly understood, and thus they offer a consistently Reformed—even if unconventional—perspective from which to assess the ongoing debate between conservative and postconservative evangelicals over the precise nature of the theological enterprise.

27. Mark A. Noll, ed., *The Princeton Theologians, 1812–1921* (Grand Rapids: Baker, 1983), 72.

Abbreviations

BRPR	*The Biblical Repertory and Princeton Review*
BRTR	*The Biblical Repertory and Theological Review*
CC	*The Christian Century*
CH	*Church History*
CR	*Critical Reviews*
CSR	*Christian Scholar's Review*
JETS	*Journal of the Evangelical Theological Society*
JHI	*Journal of the History of Ideas*
JPH	*Journal of Presbyterian History*
ModRef	*Modern Reformation*
Guardian	*The Presbyterian Guardian*
PJ	*The Presbyterian Journal*
PR	*Presbyterian Review*
PSB	*Princeton Seminary Bulletin*
PTR	*The Princeton Theological Review*
RTJ	*Reformed Theological Journal*
RTR	*Reformed Theological Review*
TrinJ	*Trinity Journal*
USR	*Union Seminary Review*
WSC	Westminster Shorter Catechism
WesTJ	*Wesleyan Theological Journal*
WMQ	*The William and Mary Quarterly*
WTJ	*Westminster Theological Journal*

PART 1

"RIGHT REASON" AT OLD PRINCETON SEMINARY

If men are unaffected with the truth known it must be because they do not know it aright. . . . Did any man ever see an object to be lovely and not feel an emotion corresponding with that quality? And what unconverted man ever beheld in Christ, as represented in Scripture, the beauty and glory of God? Hence that doctrine is not true which confines depravity or holiness to the will, and which considers the understanding as a natural and the will as a moral faculty. The soul is not depraved or holy by departments; the disease affects it, as a soul; and of course all faculties employed in moral exercises must partake of their moral qualities.[1]

1. Archibald Alexander, *Thoughts on Religious Experience* (Edinburgh: The Banner of Truth Trust, 1989; 1844), 63.

1

1

The Moral Context

Radical Rationalists?

Princeton Theological Seminary was founded in 1812 in order to defend biblical Christianity against the perceived crisis of "modern infidelity."[1] Its founders took their stand between the extremes of deism on the one hand and "mysticism" (or "enthusiasm") on the other, and resolved "to fit clergymen to meet the cultural crisis, to roll back what they perceived as tides of irreligion sweeping the country, and to provide a learned defense of Christianity generally and the Bible specifically."[2] Throughout the nineteenth and into the twentieth centuries theologians from Princeton Seminary proved to be the most articulate defenders of Reformed orthodoxy in America. Their theological efforts have come under intense critical scrutiny, however, because critics are convinced these efforts were compromised by Old Princeton's accommodation of the Scottish Realism that engulfed the churches and seminaries of antebellum America. The Princeton theologians were not immune to

1. Mark A. Noll, "The Founding of Princeton Seminary," *WTJ* 42 (Fall 1979): 85.
2. Mark A. Noll, "The Princeton Theology," in *The Princeton Theology*, Reformed Theology in America, no. 1, ed. David Wells (Grand Rapids: Baker, 1989), 24.

the philosophical developments of the eighteenth and nineteenth centuries, these critics insist. On the contrary, their emphasis on "science," "facts," and the primacy of the intellect in faith is clear evidence that they accommodated these developments despite their pretensions of orthodoxy.[3] Critics conclude, therefore, that the theologians at Old Princeton Seminary were not the champions of Reformed orthodoxy that they claimed to be. Rather, they were the purveyors of a theology that had been bastardized by what Gordon Jackson calls "the Enlightenment's one-sided emphasis on reason."[4]

3. John Stewart argues that it is "simply ill-informed" to maintain that the Princeton Theology "was a mere repristination of seventeenth-century Reformed orthodoxy." According to Stewart, Charles Hodge and his colleagues at Old Princeton Seminary were committed to mediating Reformed orthodoxy to a distinctively American context. One of the essential components of this "Americanized nineteenth-century Reformed theology," he contends, is an understanding of science that is informed by what he calls the "Princeton paradigm." The Princeton paradigm, he insists, "mixed . . . three interactive elements: 1) an epistemological grounding in the Scottish common sense realism of Thomas Reid; 2) a commitment to a 'doxological science' that assumed no insurmountable demarcation between science and religion; and 3) a growing notion that theology itself was understood and pursued as a science." John W. Stewart, *Mediating the Center: Charles Hodge on American Science, Language, Literature, and Politics* (Princeton: Princeton Theological Seminary, 1995), 13, 21–22, 112–13.

4. Gordon E. Jackson, "Archibald Alexander's *Thoughts on Religious Experience*, a Critical Revisiting," *JPH* 51, 2 (1973): 143. The Dutch and Neoorthodox branches of the Reformed camp generally agree with this critique of Old Princeton, as do the postconservative evangelicals with whom I am familiar. Contemporary interpreters who endorse this critique are indebted in one way or another to Sydney Ahlstrom, "The Scottish Philosophy and American Theology," *CH* 24 (1955): 257–72. See, for example, Ernest Sandeen, "The Princeton Theology: One Source of Biblical Literalism in American Protestantism," *CH* 31 (1962): 307–21; Mark A. Noll, "The Irony of the Enlightenment for Presbyterians in the Early Republic," in *Reckoning with the Past: Historical Essays on American Evangelicalism from the Institute for the Study of American Evangelicals*, ed. D. G. Hart (Grand Rapids: Baker, 1995) 131–53; Noll, "The Contested Legacy of Jonathan Edwards in Antebellum Calvinism," in *Reckoning with the Past*, 200–17; John Vander Stelt, *Philosophy and Scripture: A Study of Old Princeton and Westminster Theology* (Marlton, NJ: Mack Publishing Co., 1978); George Marsden, "The Collapse of American Evangelical Academia," in *Faith and Rationality: Reason and Belief in God*, ed. Alvin Plantinga, Nicholas Wolterstorff (Notre Dame, IN: University of Notre Dame Press, 1983), 219–64; and Steven B. Sherman, *Revitalizing Theological Epistemology: Holistic Evangelical Approaches to the Knowledge of God*, Princeton Theological Monograph Series 83 (Eugene, OR: Pickwick Publications, 2008). Older studies that are critical of the religious epistemology of Old Princeton include Ralph Danhof, *Charles Hodge as Dogmatician* (Goes, Netherlands: Oosterbaan and le Cointre, 1929); John O. Nelson, "The Rise of the Princeton Theology: A Generic History of American Presbyterianism Until 1850" (PhD diss., Yale University, 1935); William Livingstone, "The Princeton Apologetic as Exemplified by the Work of Benjamin B. Warfield and J. Gresham Machen: A Study of American Theology, 1880–1930" (PhD diss., Yale University, 1948).

What, then, are we to make of this conclusion? Were the Princeton theologians "nineteenth-century positivists who did not reject theology"?[5] In other words, did they bend their theology into conformity with philosophical assumptions that are diametrically opposed to those of the Reformed tradition, and did they thereby compromise the integrity of their Reformed commitments? Most interpreters regard Old Princeton's religious epistemology as evidence that such a conclusion is justified. The Princetonians' emphasis on "science," "facts," and the primacy of the intellect in faith is incompatible with the assumptions of the Reformed tradition, they reason, for such emphases manifest profound indifference to the subjective and experiential components of a consistently Reformed religious epistemology. But is this assessment accurate? Are Old Princeton's epistemological commitments in fact evidence that the Princeton theologians responded to the perceived infidelity of the age by embracing "a radical rationalism"?[6]

In this chapter, I argue that such a conclusion cannot be justified because it ignores the moral rather than the merely rational nature of the Princetonians' thought. When Old Princeton's religious epistemology is interpreted within a context that acknowledges the soul is a single unit that acts in all of its functions—its thinking, feeling, and willing—as a single substance, it becomes clear that the Princeton theologians were not Enlightenment rationalists whose confidence in the mind led them to ignore the import of the subjective and the centrality of experience in religious epistemology. Rather, they were Reformed scholars who insisted that subjective and experiential factors are of critical importance in every attempt to lay hold of what God has revealed. Indeed, they recognized that the operation of the intellect involves the "whole soul"—mind, will, and emotions—rather than the rational faculty alone, and as a consequence they insisted the ability to reason "rightly," i.e., the ability to see revealed truth more or less for

5. Marsden, "Scotland and Philadelphia: Common Sense Philosophy from Jefferson to Westminster," *RTJ* 29 (1979): 11.

6. Jackson, "Archibald Alexander's *Thoughts on Religious Experience*," 144. The word "rationalism" is used in this chapter to refer to a confidence in the mind that springs from not taking the noetic effects of sin as seriously as one should, an oversight that is supposed to have its origin in the accommodation of the assumptions of Enlightenment philosophy.

what it objectively is, namely glorious—presupposes the regenerating activity of the Holy Spirit on the "whole soul" of a moral agent.[7]

How, then, should we approach the religious epistemology of the Princeton theologians? While the consensus of critical opinion would have us believe that the theologians at Old Princeton Seminary were less than authentically Reformed because they accommodated the formative commitments of the "evidential Christianity"[8] that came to dominate the American theological landscape in the eighteenth and nineteenth centuries, this chapter suggests that the Princetonians, on the contrary, stood in the epistemological mainstream of the Reformed camp. After a brief survey of the epistemological commitments that informed the "evidential Christianity" of antebellum America, and following a cursory analysis of the challenge these commitments posed for those who claimed to be standing in the Reformed tradition, I establish the plausibility of this claim by considering the place of the new birth in the religious epistemologies of Archibald Alexander, the theologian who is rightly regarded as "the father of the Princeton Theology,"[9] and Charles Hodge, the foremost expositor of the Princeton Theology throughout most of the nineteenth century. What I establish, in short, is that Old Princeton's religious epistemology is compatible with the assumptions of the Reformed tradition because it is grounded not in the Enlightenment's overblown confidence in the epistemic competence of the rational faculty, but in the classical Reformed distinction between

7. What I am saying about "right reason" in this chapter will be explored in greater depth in Part Two of this study. For now, though, note that what I say in this chapter is similar to what Robert Hoopes says about reason in Augustine's thought. Cf. Robert Hoopes, *Right Reason in the English Renaissance* (Cambridge, MA: Harvard University Press, 1962), 64, 72, 111. Jack Rogers and Donald McKim summarize Hoopes's discussion of Augustine as follows: "For Augustine, only the righteous could rise to an understanding of truth. Right reason was reason that acknowledged the authority of God and which functioned for moral, not speculative ends." Jack Rogers and Donald McKim, *The Authority and Interpretation of the Bible* (San Francisco: Harper & Row, 1979), 202. On Hoopes's treatment of "right reason," cf. Jack Rogers, *Scripture in the Westminster Confession* (Grand Rapids: Eerdmans, 1967), 82–85. Ironically, it is Old Princeton's imagined departure from Augustine's understanding of "right reason" that gets its theologians in trouble with the likes of Rogers and McKim.

8. E. Brooks Holifield, *Theology in America: Christian Thought from the Age of the Puritans to the Civil War* (New Haven, CT: Yale University Press, 2003), 5, 173–96.

9. Donald McKim, "Archibald Alexander and the Doctrine of Scripture," *JPH* 54, 3 (1976): 356.

a merely speculative and a spiritual understanding of what God has revealed, a distinction that clearly has more to do with moral factors than it does with rational factors alone.

The "Evidential Christianity" of Antebellum America

Formative Commitments

E. Brooks Holifield has argued that "The most notable feature of American religious thought in the early nineteenth century was its rationality."[10] Theologians from differing denominational backgrounds were all trying to demonstrate that rationality supported orthodoxy, he suggests, because they were all convinced "that revealed theology . . . had the sanction of the 'understanding.'"[11]

But where did this conviction come from? According to historians such as Holifield, the nineteenth-century "quest" to establish the "reasonableness"[12] of the Christian religion was informed by two commitments, both of which played decisive roles in the rise of "evidential Christianity" in the eighteenth and nineteenth centuries. The first has to do with a cluster of ideas that is closely associated with what A. C. McGiffert refers to as "supernatural rationalism."[13] "Like contemporary deists, supernatural rationalists were confident that careful observation of history and nature can lead to reliable knowledge of God's existence and attributes. Like pietists (and unlike deists), however, supernatural rationalists also believed that this natural knowledge of God is inadequate."[14] They believed, in other words, that although natural revelation communicates reliable knowledge of God, only the revelation that is given in Scripture—which "is above or beyond reason's ordinary range of discernment"[15]—can meet the

10. E. Brooks Holifield, *The Gentlemen Theologians: American Theology in the Southern Culture, 1795–1860* (Durham, NC: Duke University Press, 1978), 3.

11. Ibid., 71.

12. Holifield, *Theology in America*, 4.

13. A. C. McGiffert, *Protestant Thought before Kant* (New York, 1912), 189, quoted in Conrad Wright, *The Liberal Christians* (Boston: Beacon Press, 1970), 5.

14. Grant Wacker, *Augustus H. Strong and the Dilemma of Historical Consciousness* (Macon, GA: Mercer University Press, 1985), 24–25.

15. Ibid., 25.

supernatural need of the sinful soul. While supernatural rationalists were more or less confident about human rational ability and thus more or less convinced of the extent to which human beings need special revelation in order to know God rightly, nevertheless they all shared the same governing assumption: that revealed truth could be known with certainty because God had endowed human beings with the ability to apprehend this truth whether it was disclosed in nature, history, or Scripture.

If the "quest for theological rationality"[16] was informed on the one hand by a more or less orthodox commitment to the epistemological reliability of both general and special revelation, it was informed on the other by a more or less progressive commitment to the Scottish Common Sense Realism of Thomas Reid, the philosophical system that came to reign as "the *lingua franca* of philosophical discourse [in] early nineteenth-century Protestant America."[17] According to Henry May, Scottish Realism was the primary means by which the Didactic Enlightenment came to exercise a formative influence on the American mind in the eighteenth and nineteenth centuries. While the Didactic Enlightenment was clearly an outworking of the humanistic tendencies of the Age of Enlightenment, it was also, May argues, in part a counter-Enlightenment because it espoused "a variety of thought which was opposed both to skepticism and revolution, but tried to save from what it saw as the debacle of the Enlightenment the intelligible universe, clear and certain moral judgments, and progress."[18]

What, though, did the Didactic Enlightenment in general and Scottish Common Sense Realism in particular have to offer to religious conservatives who were disturbed by many of the more radical trajectories of the Age of Enlightenment? According to George Marsden, many believers in the eighteenth and nineteenth centuries were attracted to Scottish Realism because it affirmed the existence "of both reality and morality," and thus supplied the philosophical justification for "both a popular intellectual defense of the faith and

---

16. Holifield, *Theology in America*, 5.

17. John W. Stewart, "The Tethered Theology: Biblical Criticism, Common Sense Philosophy, and the Princeton Theologians, 1812–1860" (PhD diss., University of Michigan, 1990), 244.

18. Henry May, *The Enlightenment in America* (New York: Oxford University Press, 1976), xvi.

a clear rationale for moral reform."[19] Indeed, these believers found the Scottish philosophy to be compelling precisely because it offered a realistic conception of the universe that grounded a coherent response to the philosophical underpinnings of what they regarded as the rising infidelity of the age. In the first place, it challenged a perceived defect in Locke's concept of "idea." Whereas Locke and his followers insisted that the immediate object of every movement of the mind is an idea, the Scottish philosophers insisted that perception is a dynamic activity in which the mind establishes contact with "the real empirical lineaments of the thing itself."[20] In short, the Scottish philosophers looked with scorn on Locke's "theory of ideas" because they were convinced it left the mind without access to objective reality and thereby denied the possibility of objective knowledge. "If the only possible objects of thought are possible objects of sense or introspective experience," the Scottish philosophers reasoned, "and if the objects of sense experience are ideas (counting 'impressions' as 'ideas'), then the world becomes at once exclusively my world, its history part of my biography, and I become what is introspectively discoverable in me."[21]

If Scottish Realism was compelling in the first place because it challenged Locke's imprisonment of the mind "within its own sensations," it was so in the second because it affirmed that true knowledge of objective reality is possible because of how our minds are constructed.[22] Unlike the more skeptical philosophers in the Age of Enlightenment, Scottish Realists were convinced that the "organic complex" of perception is trustworthy because the "direct intuitions" or "first principles" that inform our cognitive activity afford us direct and reliable access to the world in which we live. Since the "first principles" of common sense are "prerational" and act as "the forms that organize thought and make experience meaningful,"[23] the Common Sense philosophers insisted

---

19. George Marsden, *The Evangelical Mind and the New School Presbyterian Experience* (New Haven, CT: Yale University Press, 1970), 48, 233.

20. Theodore Dwight Bozeman, *Protestants in an Age of Science: The Baconian Ideal and Antebellum American Religious Thought* (Chapel Hill, NC: University of North Carolina Press, 1977), 9.

21. S. A. Grave, *The Scottish Philosophy of Common Sense* (Oxford: Clarendon Press, 1960), 50–51.

22. Holifield, *The Gentlemen Theologians*, 115, 63.

23. Wacker, *Augustus H. Strong and the Dilemma of Historical Consciousness*, 27.

that the denial of these principles as well as of the self-evident truths manifest by them is "absurd."[24] It is nonsensical, they argued, to deny the self-evident truths manifest by "the common sense of mankind," for whether the truths disclosed are moral or whether they relate to objects in the world outside our minds, their truth is simply "forced upon us by 'the constitution of our nature.' "[25] To be sure, the Scottish philosophers did not insist that the beliefs of Common Sense are held on the basis of reasoning. Rather, these beliefs "are basic beliefs, beliefs not established by arguments, but caused immediately by 'common sense,' or the belief-producing faculties that underlie all reasoning."[26]

Finally, Scottish Realism was found to be compelling because it commended the "Baconian Philosophy"[27] as the means to achieving rational certainty in an age of increasing skepticism. According to Holifield, Christian evidentialists in the eighteenth and nineteenth centuries learned three lessons from Francis Bacon via the Scottish philosophers that accentuated the epistemological significance of facts and induction:

> The first was that progress came through the observation of particular facts as a prelude to generalization. Whether the facts were construed as descriptions of natural phenomena, delineations of mental states, or readings of discrete biblical passages, the careful thinker assembled them diligently before reaching a conclusion about general laws or higher truths. The second was that theology should avoid the metaphysical, or speculative, or theoretical. Theologians were to draw inferences from the facts of consciousness and biblical revelation and to go no further. . . . The third was that the theologian, like the naturalist, should become an expert in taxonomy, the discipline of classifying the facts and ordering the classifications.[28]

In short, Scottish Realism was compelling to many believers because it directed their attention not to the consideration of one abstract

24. Grave, *The Scottish Philosophy of Common Sense*, 114.
25. Ibid., 108.
26. Marsden, "The Collapse of American Evangelical Academia," 226.
27. Bozeman, *Protestants in an Age of Science*, 3.
28. Holifield, *Theology in America*, 174–75.

philosophical concept or another, but to the analysis of the facts received by our senses. It is not through speculation but through the inductive analysis of objective data, the Scottish philosophers reasoned, that errors are avoided, knowledge of the truth is acquired, and epistemic certainty is realized.

Theological Implications

As E. Brooks Holifield and Theodore Dwight Bozeman have correctly noted, the theological implications of "supernatural rationalism" and Scottish Realism were clear. By encouraging believers to affirm the reality of objective truth and the reliability of knowledge, these commitments not only "supported a natural theology in which scientific investigation of the created order disclosed the existence and nature of the Creator,"[29] but they also encouraged scientific investigation to be regarded as a "doxological" enterprise that "dealt in the hard currency of substantial, reliable, verifiable fact."[30] As such, "evidential Christianity" offered a solution to the problem of the relationship between Christianity and culture that allowed religious conservatives to stand in the intellectual mainstream of the day without accommodating speculative hypotheses that would overtly compromise their theological commitments. Not only could they embrace modern learning for their defense of the faith, but they could do so with confidence because it seemed to substantiate everything they already believed in.

The Problem with "Evidential Christianity"

According to the consensus of critical opinion, the impact of Christian evidentialism is perhaps nowhere more clearly manifest than in the peculiar approach to apologetics that was embraced by many Protestant apologists in the nineteenth century. Not only did many Protestants adapt the inductive method of Bacon "directly to the uses of biblical exegesis,"[31] but they also insisted that "intuition or common

29. Holifield, *The Gentlemen Theologians*, 121.
30. Bozeman, *Protestants in an Age of Science*, 141. For a helpful summary of Old Princeton's understanding of the doxological nature of science, cf. Stewart, *Mediating the Center*, 25–26.
31. Bozeman, *Protestants in an Age of Science*, 131.

sense provided certain unquestionable starting points from which good arguments could rise to rebut skepticism, defend the existence of God, and support the truthfulness of Scripture."[32] While the widespread endorsement of this approach is thought to be clear evidence that the Enlightenment's conquest of antebellum America was complete, historians have long suspected that this conquest was perhaps nowhere as comprehensive as it was among the Reformed scholars at Princeton Theological Seminary. Indeed, ever since Sydney Ahlstrom's seminal analysis of the relationship between the Scottish philosophy and North American theology was published in 1955, "it has become a commonplace to hold," as Mark Noll has insightfully noted, "that Old Princeton was heavily, even uniquely, indebted to this philosophy."[33]

But is there not "something ironic," critics ask, "about the fact that among the Americans to wed themselves most permanently to Common Sense were the staunch defenders of confessional Calvinism at Princeton Theological Seminary"?[34] Those who endorse Ahlstrom's analysis generally conclude that there is, because they are convinced the epistemological assumptions of Scottish Realism are opposed to those of the Reformed tradition in a number of significant ways.[35] Whereas

32. Mark A. Noll, ed., *The Princeton Theology, 1812–1921* (Grand Rapids: Baker, 1983), 34–35. An evidentialist apologetic is positive or constructive rather than defensive, for it seeks to *constrain* belief by establishing the trustworthiness of the facts with which systematic theology is concerned. Note that many evidentialists—including the Princetonians—distinguish between "historical" or "speculative" faith, and "spiritual" or "saving" faith. At least for the Princetonians, attempting to constrain belief meant attempting to constrain speculative rather than saving faith; they not only recognized that the Holy Spirit alone could constrain saving faith, but they were also aware that there could be no saving faith without first having speculative faith. On the difference between a merely speculative and a spiritual understanding of the gospel, see the forthcoming discussion. On the distinction between an apology, which is defensive, and apologetics, which is positive and constructive, cf. B. B. Warfield, "Apologetics," *Studies in Theology*, vol. 9, *The Works of Benjamin Breckinridge Warfield* (Grand Rapids: Baker, 1991, 1932), 3–4.

33. Noll, "The Princeton Theology," 21. Elsewhere, Noll notes that "many of the supposed distinctives of the Princeton Theology were simply the common intellectual affirmations of the day." Noll, *The Princeton Theology, 1812–1921,* 62.

34. Marsden, "Scotland and Philadelphia," 9.

35. Other scholars, of course, are not convinced that Ahlstrom's analysis is entirely accurate. See, for example, Kim Riddlebarger, "The Lion of Princeton: Benjamin Breckinridge Warfield on Apologetics, Theological Method and Polemics" (PhD diss., Fuller Theological Seminary, 1997); Paul Helm, "Thomas Reid, Common Sense, and Calvinism," in *Rationality in the Calvinian Tradition*, ed. Hendrik Hart, Johan Van Der Hoeven, Nicholas Wolterstorff (Lanham, MD: University Press of America, 1983), 71–89.

Reformed scholars typically insist the mind has been so blinded by the fall that a saving apprehension of what God has revealed necessitates that the eyes of the mind be opened by the regenerating activity of the Spirit of God, those who accommodated "the optimism of the Scottish Renaissance" often gave the impression that the mind was essentially undisturbed by sin's influence, and that saving faith could be practically induced through the clear presentation of objective evidences.[36]

Because critics are appropriately critical of such thinking, they insist that Christian evidentialism must be repudiated because it is grounded in an almost "Pelagian confidence"[37] in the epistemic competence of the unregenerated mind. Not only does it imagine there is no difference intellectually between the believer and the unbeliever, but more importantly it ignores the important role that subjective and experiential factors play in religious epistemology.[38]

36. Ahlstrom, "The Scottish Philosophy and American Theology," 266. Ahlstrom argues that "the humanistic orientation of the Hutcheson-Reid tradition" is the necessary consequence of the loss of "the fervent theocentricity of Calvin." Ibid., 268. Cf. Marsden, "Scotland and Philadelphia," 10.

37. Rogers and McKim, *The Authority and Interpretation of the Bible*, 290.

38. According to critics such as Ernest Sandeen, Old Princeton's preoccupation with "the external not the internal, the objective not the subjective" is nowhere more clearly manifested than in the Princetonians' doctrine of the inspiration and authority of the Bible. Sandeen, "The Princeton Theology," 310. Sandeen and others argue that in response to the theological and philosophical developments of the modern era, the Princetonians embraced an understanding of biblical authority that was nothing if not rationalistic. Not only did they come to regard the created order as "a precise, 'factual,' unalterable objective order open to unbiased cognition" (Bozeman, *Protestants in an Age of Science*, 171), but they also insisted "that reason established the criteria for recognizing and validating the Biblical revelation itself." Holifield, *The Gentlemen Theologians*, 85; see also Martin Marty, *The Irony of It All, 1893–1919*, vol. 1, Modern American Religion (Chicago: University of Chicago Press, 1986), 14, 208. Indeed, they transferred the locus of biblical authority from "that conviction of mind and heart which may be termed the *testimonium Spiritus Sancti*" to those evidences they presumed could be rationally verified. Livingstone, "The Princeton Apologetic," 184. For these critics, then, Old Princeton's understanding of biblical authority is suspect because the Princetonians shifted the locus of religious authority from the internal to the external evidences for the authority of Scripture. They insisted the Scriptures are authoritative not "because in them God speaks to the believer in such a way as to convince him that it is God who is speaking," but because the apologist can gather rationally compelling evidences that establish that the Scriptures are inspired and as such are the word of God." Ibid., 346.

Those who concur with this assessment of Old Princeton generally conclude that the Princetonians were not the champions of Reformed orthodoxy that they claimed to be. Rather, they were "participants in a portentous transition in the interpretation and application of the Bible." Holifield, *The Gentlemen Theologians*, 96. According to these critics, the Princeton theologians "substituted a doctrine of inspiration for the witness of the Spirit" (Ernest Sandeen,

For example, critics such as George Marsden are convinced that evidential Christianity is problematic because it fails to acknowledge how much "basic first beliefs and commitments can pervade the rest of one's intellectual activity,"· thus precluding the "possibilities for objectivity."[39] It is simply not true, he argues, that, "By clearly definable scientific, rational, and objective procedures, one can simply eliminate subjective or culturally conditioned aspects of knowing,"[40] for the "first principles" that inform the activity of the mind are themselves conditioned by a host of factors, including spiritual factors. Interpreters who are convinced that there is a difference between the epistemic abilities of the regenerate and the unregenerate therefore insist that a sound approach to apologetics must take into account not only the objective components of the Christian religion, but the subjective and "superrational" components as well. Many thus advocate a presuppositional approach to apologetics because they believe such an approach is more compatible with the assumptions of the Reformed tradition than is the kind

---

The Roots of Fundamentalism: British and American Millenarianism, 1800–1930 [Chicago: University of Chicago Press, 1970], 119), human rational capacities for the "material principle" of "Old Calvinism," namely the "cataclysmic apprehension of divine potestas" in Scripture, and thereby fell prey to a narrowly defined biblicism that sought to establish the authority of Scripture on rational grounds rather than on a "direct apprehension of God [in the Scriptures]." These critics conclude that although the Princeton Theology "built its fully furnished house upon the formal principle, Scripture," nevertheless the Princetonians undermined the true basis of Scripture's claim to religious authority by elevating the external over the internal evidences. Nelson, "The Rise of the Princeton Theology," 7, 365. For these critics, then, it is in this subversion of Scripture's true locus of authority that the perilous nature of Old Princeton's "rationalistic departure from the Reformed faith becomes apparent." Livingstone, "The Princeton Apologetic," 346. For compelling responses to this line of argumentation, see Randall H. Balmer, "The Princetonians and Scripture: A Reconsideration," WTJ 44 (1982): 352–65; John D. Woodbridge, "Biblical Authority: Towards an Evaluation of the Rogers and McKim Proposal," TrinJ n.s. 1 Fall (1980): 208; John D. Woodbridge, Biblical Authority: A Critique of the Rogers/McKim Proposal (Grand Rapids: Zondervan, 1982); John D. Woodbridge and Randall H. Balmer, "The Princetonians and Biblical Authority: An Assessment of the Ernest Sandeen Proposal," in Scripture and Truth, ed. John D. Woodbridge, D. A. Carson (Grand Rapids: Zondervan, 1983).

39. Marsden, "The Collapse of American Evangelical Academia," 256–57. Note the sense in which Marsden uses the word "objective" here. While he uses it to refer to an unbiased or neutral view of reality, for the Princetonians it refers to the reality that is outside our minds and independent of our preferences and desires. Yes, the Princetonians affirm that we can have knowledge of objective reality, but as I hope to make clear, they do not necessarily affirm that we know this reality objectively.

40. George Marsden, "J. Gresham Machen, History, and Truth," WTJ 42 (1979–80): 169.

14

of evidentialism that is typically associated with the theologians at Old Princeton Seminary.[41]

The Moral Context

The Enduring Question

Despite the fact that the Princeton theologians have come under heavy criticism for their assimilation of the Scottish philosophy, it is altogether clear, as Terry Chrisope has incisively argued, that "they never became [the] mere tools of this philosophy."[42] That Scottish Common Sense Realism had a marked impact on the theological method of the Princeton theologians is unquestioned, even by their most uncompromising defenders.[43] That fact, however, cannot justify the misrep-

41. The dispute between evidentialists and presuppositionalists centers largely on the following question: Do regenerated and unregenerated human beings know "essentially alike"? Whereas evidentialists argue that they do and that the chains of apologetical reasoning should therefore begin with an appeal to the mind rather than to special revelation and faith, presuppositionalists argue that they do not, because there is "an antithesis between Christian thought, the first principles of which recognize God's sovereignty over all creation, and *non*-Christian thought which [is] predicated on human autonomy." George Marsden, *Fundamentalism and American Culture: The Shaping of Twentieth Century Evangelicalism, 1870–1925* (New York: Oxford University Press, 1980), 115; see also Marsden, "The Collapse of American Evangelical Academia," 253. Because they are convinced that believers see the world much differently than unbelievers do, presuppositionalists insist that Christians should not do apologetics by piling up evidences in the vain attempt to constrain belief. Rather, they should do apologetics by arguing at the level of presuppositions and worldviews. They must convince the unregenerate that their worldview is absurd, and that human experience will ultimately make sense only with a Christian worldview. See, for example, Cornelius Van Til, *Christian Apologetics*, 2nd edition, ed. William Edgar (Phillipsburg, NJ: P&R Publishing, 2003). As I hope to make clear, a good case can be made that these two camps often talk past one another on a number of important epistemological matters. It might be the case that a proper understanding of "right reason" would reveal more common ground between evidentialists and presuppositionalists on epistemological matters than most commentators have acknowledged.

42. Terry Chrisope, "The Bible and Historical Scholarship in the Early Life and Thought of J. Gresham Machen, 1881–1915" (PhD diss., Kansas State University, 1988), 98. While Chrisope does not deny that Scottish Realism played an important role at Old Princeton, nevertheless he insists that the Princetonians "may not have been so captive to Scottish common sense realism as some historians have contended." Ibid., 283–84.

43. For example, John Gerstner, "The Contributions of Hodge, Warfield, and Machen to the Doctrine of Inspiration," in *Challenges to Inerrancy*, eds. Gordon Lewis, Bruce Demarest (Chicago: Moody Press, 1984), 352. On how Old Princeton embraced induction yet rejected the "philosophy of science consistent with the secular scientific culture of its time," see Donald Fuller and Richard Gardiner, "Reformed Theology at Princeton and Amsterdam in the Late Nineteenth Century: A Reappraisal," *Presbyterion* 21, 2 (1995): 89–117.

resentations of their views that have been put forward by a host of modern interpreters. This is the contention of Andrew Hoffecker in his groundbreaking study of the role of piety in the Princeton Theology. In response to historians who insist that subjective and experiential factors play little or no role in Old Princeton's otherwise intellectualistic treatment of the faith, Hoffecker demonstrates that not only do these factors have a significant impact on their thought, but more importantly that the Princeton Theology will never be understood correctly if these factors are ignored.[44]

So how are these factors related to Old Princeton's religious epistemology? Are they largely irrelevant to the Princetonians' understanding of knowledge, as the consensus of critical opinion would have us believe? Or, do they play an important role, and if so, what is that role? Beginning with a brief examination of the classical Reformed distinction between a merely speculative and a spiritual understanding of what God has revealed, and concluding with a cursory analysis of the place of the new birth in the religious epistemologies of Archibald Alexander and Charles Hodge, the remainder of this chapter outlines the context within which the answer to this question is found. It suggests that subjective and experiential factors play a critical role in Old Princeton's religious epistemology because Old Princeton's "intellectualism" is moral, not merely rational. It has to do, in other words, with the "whole soul"— mind, will, and emotions—rather than the rational faculty alone, and for this reason it is simply wrong to conclude that the orthodoxy of Old Princeton was subverted by the Enlightenment's Pelagian confidence in the epistemic competence of the human mind.

Merely Speculative versus Spiritual Knowledge

Whereas historians such as Ernest Sandeen virtually dismiss Old Princeton on the presumption that subjective and experiential factors play little or no role in the religious epistemology of the Princeton Theology, a growing number of scholars recognize that these factors do play a de-

---

44. Andrew Hoffecker, *Piety and the Princeton Theologians: Archibald Alexander, Charles Hodge, and Benjamin Warfield* (Phillipsburg, NJ: Presbyterian and Reformed; and Grand Rapids: Baker, 1981).

cisive role despite the Princetonians' relentless emphasis on the primacy of the intellect in faith.[45] Those who concur with this assessment do so because they recognize that the intellectualism of Old Princeton must be interpreted in the same manner as the intellectualism of Calvin. According to Edward Dowey, there is an emphasis on the primacy of the intellect in faith in Calvin's thought because Calvin recognizes there can be no saving faith—and therefore no salvation—"without *knowledge*."[46] But does Calvin believe that all human beings—by virtue of being rational agents—have the natural ability to know what God has revealed in a true and therefore saving sense? Does Calvin believe, in other words, that there is no more to a saving apprehension of what God has revealed than "a simple, natural perception of what God sets clearly before the mind of man"?[47] While a comprehensive discussion of Calvin's doctrine of the knowledge of God is beyond the scope of this chapter, it is clear that he does not, because he recognizes that knowledge is a function of the "whole soul" rather than of the rational faculty alone.[48] In short, Calvin recognizes that apart from the work of the Spirit in the new birth the unregenerate remain blind to the saving significance of what they can rationally perceive, not because of "an intrinsic obscurity" in what God has revealed, but because the "subjective imperfection" of the sinful soul leaves them without the moral ability to see what God has revealed for what it objectively is, namely glorious.[49] Heinrich Heppe summarizes the nature of the case: "The unconverted can at best appropriate only a theoretical and pure external knowledge of truths of faith. As an animal can quite see the body of a man but not his spirit because it has not one itself, even the unspiritual man may see and understand the letter but not the Spirit of the Scripture."[50]

45. Cf. Sandeen, "The Princeton Theology," 310; also Sandeen, *The Roots of Fundamentalism*, 119. See also R. C. Sproul, John Gerstner, Arthur Lindsley, *Classical Apologetics: A Rational Defense of the Christian Faith and a Critique of Presuppositional Apologetics* (Grand Rapids: Zondervan, 1984); Jonathan A. Gerstner, "Reason as Starting Point: The Rationality of Classical Apologetics," *ModRef* 7, 1 (January/February 1998): 17–20.

46. Edward Dowey, *The Knowledge of God in Calvin's Theology* (New York: Columbia University Press, 1952), 172.

47. Ibid., 173.

48. Ibid., 3.

49. Ibid., 32.

50. Heinrich Heppe, *Reformed Dogmatics*, ed. Ernst Bizer, trans. G. T. Thomson, foreword Karl Barth (London: George Allen and Unwin, 1950), 33.

What, then, does the work of the Spirit in the new birth entail, and how does it foster the capacity for discerning the saving significance of what the unregenerate can only rationally perceive? The regenerating work of the Spirit, i.e., Christian experience, properly understood, accomplishes this end not by operating exclusively on the rational faculty of the sinful soul—as if the rational faculty had the ability to act independently of the unitary whole of which it is a functional manifestation—but by changing the moral disposition of the sinful heart and thereby enabling the regenerated sinner to see what unregenerated sinners cannot see, namely, "the beauty and 'sweetness' of revealed truth."[51] It is the gift of what Jonathan Edwards calls a new heart or "principle of nature"[52] that enables the elect to see revealed truth more or less for what it objectively is, classically Reformed scholars insist, for it is the new heart that enlightens the mind to the spiritual beauty and "sweetness" of the truth that comes to it "through the door of the understanding."[53]

Given the epistemological significance of the Spirit's regenerating activity, it follows that a spiritual or saving apprehension of what God has revealed is in classical Reformed thought not the result of a merely speculative analysis of assorted truth claims, nor is it the consequence of "a hasty, ill-considered capitulation of the mind or abandonment of reason."[54] Rather, it is the result of the mind being enabled to reason "rightly" through the regenerating activity of the Spirit of God. Through the regenerating activity of the Holy Spirit, the mind—which without the Spirit is enslaved to the blinding disposition of a sinful

51. Sproul, *Classical Apologetics*, 299.

52. Jonathan Edwards, "A Divine and Supernatural Light," in *The Works of Jonathan Edwards*, 2 vols. (Edinburgh: The Banner of Truth Trust, 1992; 1834), 2:12ff.

53. Edwards, "Christian Knowledge," in *The Works of Jonathan Edwards*, 2:158. Many Reformed scholars are convinced that in classical Reformed thought, the noetic influence of sin is not "direct through a totally depraved mind, but . . . *indirect* through the totally depraved heart." Sproul, *Classical Apologetics*, 243. In my estimation, the language of directness and indirectness is problematic because it presupposes that the mind and the will are essentially distinct or independent faculties of the soul. While it is one thing to insist that the rational power of the soul was not destroyed by the fall, it is an entirely different thing to suggest that "Something is wrong with the heart—not the mind—which needs the nonrational, super-rational revelation of divine majesty." Sproul, *Classical Apologetics*, 242. If the mind is nothing but the "whole soul" thinking, then it seems such a comment is problematic because it betrays a denial of the essential unity of the soul.

54. Dowey, *The Knowledge of God in Calvin's Theology*, 111.

18

heart—"receives new keenness and a new taste for things it formerly did not relish."[55] It is this taste for the divine, then, that enables the regenerate to see revealed truth more or less for what it objectively is, for it is this taste for the divine than enables regenerated sinners to see what God has revealed in its true light, or as that which is declaring the glory of God in some sense. In light of the fact that the testimony of the Spirit is not merely rational but has to do with what Edwards calls the "sense of the heart,"[56] we must conclude that the knowledge of God that is communicated to the regenerated soul via the combined action of Word and Spirit is in classical Reformed thought "not something purely theoretical, but a practical experience, engaging the whole human personality, soliciting all the energies of the conscience and heart, putting in motion all the spiritual faculties."[57] As such, neither speculative knowledge nor spiritual knowledge is

> intended in the doctrine [of Christian knowledge] exclusively of the other: but it is intended that we should seek the former *in order* to the latter. The latter, or the spiritual and practical, is of the greatest importance; for a speculative without a spiritual knowledge, is to no purpose, but to make our condemnation the greater. Yet a speculative knowledge is also of infinite importance in this respect, that without it we can have no spiritual or practical knowledge.[58]

55. Ibid., 183.

56. Edwards, "A Divine and Supernatural Light," 2:17–18.

57. Dowey, *The Knowledge of God in Calvin's Theology*, 25–26. The distinction between a merely speculative and a spiritual understanding of what God has revealed is grounded in the conviction that the soul is a whole unit that is comprised of two rather than three "faculties" or "powers": the understanding, which takes precedence in all rational activity, and the will, which is broadly defined to include not just the power of self-determination but the feelings and emotions as well. While the will is a power of the mind, it is not a self-determining power, but one that is determined by the motives or sensibilities of the mind. For an excellent analysis of the understanding of free agency that is associated with this anthropology, see Paul Ramsey's introductory essay to Edwards, *The Freedom of the Will* (New Haven, CT: Yale University Press, 1957), especially pages 38–40. For an excellent discussion of how the faculties or powers of understanding and will are related to each other, and for a particularly relevant discussion of "Augustinian voluntarism," see Norman Fiering, "Will and Intellect in the New England Mind," *WMQ* 29 (1972): 515–58.

58. Edwards, "Christian Knowledge," 158. This statement gives some indication as to why some would argue that Edwards was an evidentialist rather than a presuppositionalist. See, for example, Sproul, *Classical Apologetics*, 185, 297–98. Like Edwards, more conservative evidentialists insist that "It is impossible that any one should see the truth or excellency of any doctrine

The Princeton Theology and Old School Calvinism

It is my contention in this chapter that the Princeton Theology in general and the Princeton apologetic in particular must be interpreted within the epistemological context articulated in the foregoing discussion. That this is the likely context within which Old Princeton's emphasis on science, facts, and the primacy of the intellect in faith is best understood will be clear after we consider the place of the new birth in the religious epistemologies of Alexander and Hodge. Before we move on to this consideration, however, I must emphasize that the interpretation I am commending is warranted because the Princetonians stood squarely in the tradition of Old School Calvinism, particularly in their understanding of the essential nature and operation of the soul. This is clearly revealed in their repudiation of the attempt to free evangelistic outreach from the strictures of the doctrine of inability throughout the early decades of the nineteenth century.[59] Whereas New England theologians such as Nathaniel William Taylor fell prey to the Enlightenment humanism practically manifest in the rising tide of evangelical revivalism because they severed the connection between moral character and moral activity and thereby destroyed the distinction between natural and moral ability,[60] the Princetonians were essentially unscathed by this assault

of the gospel, who knows not what the doctrine is. A man cannot see the wonderful excellency and love of Christ in doing such and such things for sinners, unless his understanding be first informed how these things were done." More conservative evidentialists concur with Edwards that the fallen sinner "cannot have a taste of the sweetness and excellency of divine truth, unless he first have a notion that there is such a thing." Edwards, "Christian Knowledge," 158. Because of this, and because they recognize with Edwards that the Spirit moves beyond though not against reason, more conservative evidentialists conclude that the primary function of the apologist has to do with satisfying "the fundamental needs of the human spirit. If it is incumbent upon the believer to be able to give a reason for the faith that is in him, it is impossible for him to be a believer without a reason for the faith that is in him; and it is the task of the apologist to bring this reason clearly out in his consciousness, and make its validity plain." Warfield, "Apologetics," *Studies in Theology*, 4. For a compelling counterargument to the notion that Edwards was an evidentialist, see K. Scott Oliphint, "Jonathan Edwards, Reformed Apologist," *WTJ* 57, 1 (Spring 1995): 165–86.

59. On this attempt, see, for example, Perry Miller, *The Life of the Mind in America from the Revolution to the Civil War* (New York: Harcourt, Brace and World, 1965), 9, 34; Bozeman, *Protestants in an Age of Science*, 33.

60. For an excellent analysis of the difference between revival and revivalism, see Iain H. Murray, *Revival and Revivalism: The Making and Marring of American Evangelicalism, 1750–1858* (Edinburgh: The Banner of Truth Trust, 1994). On the decline and fall of Calvinism in the American

because they recognized that the soul is a single unit that always acts as a single substance. Indeed, like classically Reformed thinkers before them, they acknowledged that the soul is a whole unit rather than a collection of more or less autonomous faculties or powers, and they also insisted that the acts of the soul are always determined by the moral character or inclination of the acting agent.[61]

This is historically significant for two reasons. In the first place, it suggests that the Princetonians' appropriation of Scottish Realism was qualified and conditioned by their Reformed commitments. We have already acknowledged that defenders of Old Princeton must concede that the Scottish philosophy had a marked impact on the theological method of the Princeton theologians. Defenders of Old Princeton need not concede, however, that this impact was so profound that it altered much more than the framework of the Princetonians' theology.[62] Indeed, as

---

church, see Glenn Hewitt, *Regeneration and Morality: A Study of Charles Finney, Charles Hodge, John Nevin, and Horace Bushnell*, vol. 7, Chicago Studies in the History of American Religion, eds. Jerald Brauer, Martin Marty (New York: Carlson, 1991), 14; James Turner, *Without God Without Creed: The Origins of Unbelief in America* (Baltimore: Johns Hopkins University Press, 1985); William McLoughlin, "Introduction," in *The American Evangelicals, 1800–1900*, ed. William McLoughlin (New York: Harper Torchbooks, 1968), 1–27.

61. On the philosophical psychology that this understanding of free agency entails, see note 57 above. Historians such as Bruce Kuklick would have us believe that a primary explanation for why the Princetonians were not "satisfied" with the theology of Jonathan Edwards is found in their repudiation of his understanding of the mind or soul. According to Kuklick, "The mind for Edwards was not so much an entity as a function, and there were two reciprocally related functions—cognition and volition. Following the Scots, Hodge [and his heirs] found comfort in a different conception of mind that divided mental substance into a series of separate powers. For those opposing Edwards (and Hume) the mind had three functions, not two, and they were more clearly separated into entities—thus the phrase 'faculty psychology.' " Bruce Kuklick, *A History of Philosophy in America: 1720–2000* (New York: Oxford University Press, 2001), 52.

While the Princetonians did refer often to the various faculties or powers of the soul, nevertheless they did not regard these powers as distinct or separate entities, for they recognized that the soul is a single unit that always acts as a single substance. As such, they would likely have agreed with the following definition of "true psychology" even though it appears to affirm—although it does not necessarily require that we affirm—the existence of three rather than two faculties or powers, for it attests to the existence of separate faculties while simultaneously maintaining the essential unity of the soul. "True psychology maintains the unity of the soul. . . . It thus makes of the soul no mere mosaic, after the old 'faculty psychology' conceptions, composed of so many separatist and distinctive parts. This unity of the soul, as monistic, is fundamental in modern psychology, and has led to a true sense of the interdependence of the faculties—will, thought, and emotion." James Lindsay, "Psychology of the Soul," *PTR* 6, 3 (1908): 438.

62. Mark A. Noll, "Jonathan Edwards and Nineteenth-Century Theology," in *Jonathan Edwards and the American Experience*, eds. Nathan O. Hatch, Harry S. Stout (New York: Oxford University Press, 1988), 268.

scholars such as Mark Noll and David Wells have carefully argued, the Scottish philosophy moved New England theologians such as Nathaniel William Taylor much farther from Reformed orthodoxy than it did Old Princeton, because Taylor and his associates endorsed "the estimate made of human nature by Scottish Common Sense Realism."[63] The New England theologians endorsed, in other words, the latent humanism of the Common Sense tradition, and as a consequence they passed on to their descendants a version of Calvinism that was, as Joseph Haroutunian has incisively argued, "not Calvinism. It was the faith of the fathers ruined by their children."[64] To suggest that the

63. David Wells, "Charles Hodge," in *The Princeton Theology*, ed. David Wells, 43. In an important essay, Noll argues that the extent to which Edwards's theological commitments were subverted by the participants in the nineteenth-century struggle for his mantle was largely dependent on the strain of the Scottish philosophy that the participants themselves embraced. Whereas Princeton "showed greatest fondness" for the "methodological aspects" of Scottish Realism, Andover and Yale embraced its anthropological commitments and thus "moved further from Edwards's theology than . . . Princeton." "Jonathan Edwards and Nineteenth-Century Theology," 268. According to Noll, this way of subverting Edwards's legacy is particularly evident in the theology of Nathaniel William Taylor. "More than other heirs of Edwards," Noll argues, "Taylor also accepted the Scottish philosophy of Common Sense which . . . made much of innate human freedom and the power of individuals to shape their own destinies." Mark A. Noll, "New Haven Theology," in *Evangelical Dictionary of Theology*, ed. Walter Elwell (Grand Rapids: Baker, 1984), 763; see also Noll, "The Contested Legacy of Jonathan Edwards in Antebellum Calvinism," 200–217. Douglas Sweeney and Allen Guelzo concur with Noll's assessment, arguing that Taylor and his colleagues "repackaged Edwardsean ideas for antebellum America. Focusing mainly on the doctrines of sin and spiritual regeneration, they formed a kinder, gentler evangelical Calvinism. . . . Denying that humans are born guilty of the sin of Adam and Eve and affirming that people play a role in their own regeneration, they seemed to some Edwardsean siblings to have sold the farm to save the family business." Douglas A. Sweeney and Allen C. Guelzo, "Theology in New Haven," in *The New England Theology: From Jonathan Edwards to Edwards Amasa Park*, ed. Douglas A. Sweeney, Allen C. Guelzo (Grand Rapids: Baker, 2006), 188. Note that Wells regards Taylor as "the stepping stone to the next generation's Liberalism" because of the prominent role that he played in the decline and fall of Calvinism as the dominant force in the North American church. Wells, "Charles Hodge," 58.

64. Joseph Haroutunian, *Piety versus Moralism: The Passing of the New England Theology* (New York: Holt, 1932), 281. Haroutunian posits that Calvinism fell from preeminence in the North American church because the Common Sense or Enlightenment humanism practically manifest in the rising tide of evangelical revivalism subverted the theocentric piety of many in the Reformed camp shortly after the death of Jonathan Edwards. Revisionist scholarship has challenged this argument in two ways. First, revisionist scholars have discovered a diversity of theological opinion within the New England camp itself. As William Breitenbach notes, "This discovery of diversity makes older assumptions about the inevitable organic evolution of a universally accepted Covenant theology into Arminian moralism seem too simplistic." Second, revisionist scholars have recognized that piety and moralism are not necessarily incompatible

Princetonians embraced the Scottish philosophy to the same degree that their more progressive brethren in New England did is to seriously misrepresent the Princeton Theology. It is to ignore, moreover, what the Princetonians themselves regarded as the historiographical key to understanding the theological tensions between Princeton and New England throughout most of the nineteenth century. According to Hodge, whereas Princeton was theocentric in that it had for its object "the vindication of the Divine supremacy and sovereignty in the salvation of men," New England was increasingly anthropocentric.[65] It came to have for its "characteristic aim," in other words, "the assertion of the rights of human nature. It is specially solicitous that nothing should be held to be true, which cannot be philosophically reconciled with the liberty and ability of man."[66]

If Old Princeton's emphasis on the unitary operation of the soul is significant in the first place because it establishes that the Princetonians repudiated the anthropocentrism that was an essential component of the Enlightenment, it is significant in the second because it neutralizes the assumption that is often at the heart of commentary that is critical of the religious epistemology of Old

in Reformed thought. According to Breitenbach, historians now recognize "that Reformed theology, even in its pristine formulations, did not set piety against moralism." William Breitenbach, "Piety *and* Moralism: Edwards and the New Divinity," in Nathan O. Hatch, Harry S. Stout, eds., *Jonathan Edwards and the American Experience* (New York: Oxford University Press, 1989), 178–79. For other examples of revisionist scholarship, see William Breitenbach, "The Consistent Calvinism of the New Divinity Movement," *WMQ* 41 (April 1984): 241–64; Joseph Conforti, *Samuel Hopkins and the New Divinity Movement* (Grand Rapids: Christian University Press, 1981); Allen Guelzo, "Jonathan Edwards and the New Divinity, 1758–1858," in *Pressing Toward the Mark: Essays Commemorating Fifty Years of the Orthodox Presbyterian Church*, eds. Charles Dennison, Richard Gamble (Philadelphia: The Committee for the Historian of the Orthodox Presbyterian Church, 1986), 147–67. In response to this revisionist scholarship I would suggest that although Haroutunian's critique may suffer from a lack of nuance, nevertheless it is compelling because it accurately describes—albeit in general terms—the impact that the optimism of the Scottish philosophy had on evangelical theology in general and Reformed theology in particular in the nineteenth century.

65. Charles Hodge, "Remarks on the Princeton Review," *BRPR* 23 (1851): 309. I say "increasingly" simply to acknowledge that the early advocates of the New Divinity did not "sell Edwards and New England down the Connecticut River" like their New Haven descendants did. Guelzo, "Jonathan Edwards and the New Divinity," 148.

66. Hodge, "Remarks on the Princeton Review," 309. On the difference between the starting points of Princeton and New England, and on the implications of these starting points for the historiography of the nineteenth century, see Wells, "Charles Hodge," 44ff.

Princeton. Commentary that is critical of the intellectualism of Old Princeton—be it the contention that the Princeton theologians had "unbounded confidence" in the epistemic competence of the rational faculty or the related assertion that they were indifferent to the subjective and experiential components of a consistently Reformed religious epistemology[67]—is often grounded in the at least implicit assumption that the Princetonians fell prey to the ideas of Enlightenment humanism because they endorsed a "faculty psychology."[68] The Princeton theologians sacrificed anthropological and epistemological integrity to the assumptions of an essentially humanistic philosophy, it is commonly assumed, because they failed to recognize that "our intellect, will and emotions are inseparably connected with our whole personality," and as such cannot operate independently one from the other.[69] While critical analyses grounded in this assumption would be valid if the Princetonians in fact denied the unitary operation of the soul, that they are not valid is clear from their repudiation of the revisionist tendencies of those driven by their zeal for revival to embrace what Old School Calvinists regarded as the abuses of revival*ism*,[70] and from their insistence that the ability to reason "rightly" presupposes the regenerating activity of the Holy Spirit on the "whole soul" of a moral agent. As the remainder of this chapter attempts to make clear through a brief examination of the religious epistemologies of Alexander and Hodge,

67. Rogers and McKim, *The Authority and Interpretation of the Bible*, 245.

68. On the "faculty psychology," see note 61 above, note 8 in the Introduction to this volume, and the forthcoming discussion of Charles Hodge.

69. William Masselink, "Professor J. Gresham Machen: His Life and Defense of the Bible" (ThD diss., Free University of Amsterdam, 1938), 153–55; see also Rogers and McKim, *The Authority and Interpretation of the Bible*, 290.

70. On the doctrinal revisionism that was occasioned by the rise of evangelical revival*ism*, see note 60 above. See also Marsden, *The Evangelical Mind and the New School Presbyterian Experience*; Earl Pope, *New England Calvinism and the Disruption of the Presbyterian Church* (New York: Garland, 1987); H. Shelton Smith, *Changing Conceptions of Original Sin: A Study in American Theology Since 1750* (New York: Charles Scribner's Sons, 1955); Maurice Armstrong, Lefferts Loetscher, Charles Anderson, *The Presbyterian Experience: Sources of American Presbyterian History* (Philadelphia: Westminster, 1956). Marsden notes that the doctrinal revisionism that came to be associated with the rise of evangelical revivalism "was not a liberalism that involved intentional concessions to secularism (as in later modernism). Rather, it was an outgrowth of pietist zeal for revivalism." George Marsden, "Reformed and American," in *The Princeton Theology*, ed. David Wells, 5.

Old Princeton's emphasis on "right reason" is neither the supreme manifestation of a loss of "Reformation bearings,"[71] nor evidence of what Lefferts Loetscher refers to as Old Princeton's "startling confidence in the competence of human reasoning powers."[72] It is evidence, rather, of Old Princeton's conscientious attempt to retain a place for both the objective and the subjective components of a consistently Reformed religious epistemology in an age increasingly characterized by religious subjectivism.

The Religious Epistemology of Archibald Alexander

The Right Use of Reason in Religion

In the first chapter of his *Evidences of the Authenticity, Inspiration, and Canonical Authority of the Holy Scriptures*, Archibald Alexander makes the rather startling claim: "Without reason there can be no religion."[73] The rational faculty "was certainly given to man to be a guide in religion, as well as in other things," he argues, for without it, man "can form no conception of a truth of any kind."[74] Indeed, since reason is the "constituent power of the soul"[75] that apprehends and judges truth, man "possesses no other means by which he can form a judgment on any subject, or assent to any truth; and it would be no more absurd to talk of seeing without eyes, than of knowing any thing without reason."[76] Given the intimate nature of the relationship of truth, reason, and the claims of the Christian religion, Alexander concludes that it would be "a great mistake to suppose that religion forbids or discourages the right use of reason. So far from this, she enjoins it as a duty of high moral obligation, and reproves those who neglect to judge for themselves what is right."[77]

71. Ahlstrom, "The Scottish Philosophy and American Theology," 268.

72. Lefferts Loetscher, *The Broadening Church: A Study of Theological Issues in the Presbyterian Church Since 1869* (Philadelphia: University of Pennsylvania Press, 1957), 70.

73. Archibald Alexander, *Evidences of the Authenticity, Inspiration, and Canonical Authority of the Holy Scriptures* (Philadelphia: Presbyterian Board of Publication, 1836), 9.

74. Ibid., 9–10.

75. Alexander, *A Brief Compendium of Bible Truth* (Grand Rapids: Reformed Heritage Books, 2005; 1846), 136.

76. Alexander, *Evidences*, 9.

77. Ibid., 9.

What, though, does "the right use of reason" entail? What does it mean, in other words, to exercise the rational power of the soul in a "right" or "proper" fashion? Alexander suggests the answer:

> There is no just cause for apprehending that we shall be misled by the proper exercise of reason on any subject which may be proposed for our consideration. The only danger is of making an improper use of this faculty, which is one of the most common faults to which our nature is liable. Most men profess that they are guided by reason in forming their opinions; but if this were really the case, the world would not be overrun with error; there would not be so many absurd and dangerous opinions propagated and pertinaciously defended. In one sense, indeed, they may be said to follow reason, for they are guided by a blinded, prejudiced, and perverted reason.[78]

In short, Alexander is convinced that the rational power of the soul is used in a right or proper fashion when it is exercised without partiality, and it is used in a wrong or improper fashion when its exercise is prejudiced by bias. What this means for Alexander, then, is that the distinguishing characteristic of the right use of reason is found in the impartial analysis of revealed truth, and reason is a reliable guide to truth when it leads us to assess what God has revealed with "an unbiased mind."[79]

"Right Reason" and the Inclination of the Heart

But what, specifically, does Alexander believe is entailed in the right or impartial use of reason? When he argues that "The defenders of the truth have ever been ready to meet their antagonists on the ground of impartial reason,"[80] what kind of partiality does he believe compromises the right use of the rational power of the soul? Does he believe that impartiality necessitates a commitment to epistemological neutrality? Is his understanding of impartiality ultimately grounded, in other words, in an endorsement of the Enlightenment myth of the

78. Ibid., 11.
79. Ibid., 15.
80. Ibid., 16.

disinterested knower? Or is his understanding indebted to larger, more consistently Reformed kinds of concerns? In one sense, Alexander's understanding of the right use of reason is clearly opposed, for example, to the tendentious nature of biblical scholarship that, while granting that the Bible contains a revelation from God, nevertheless insists on "the right of bringing the truths revealed to the test of human judgment and opinion, and reject[ing] them as unreasonable if they do not accord with this standard."[81] In an even more basic and fundamental sense, however, Alexander's understanding of the right use of reason is grounded in larger, more consistently Reformed kinds of concerns, for it emphasizes that the capacity for impartial analysis has much more to do with "the dispositions of the [knower's] heart"[82] or the "moral character" that "actuates" the knower's soul[83] than it does with the "preconceived opinions" or "narrow conceptions" that inform the knower's thinking.[84] That this is the case, and that Alexander's understanding of the right use of reason focuses more on the inclination of the knower's heart than on the actual contents of the knower's mind, will be clear after a brief examination of the impact of sin and regenerating grace on the knower's ability to see revealed truth more or less for what it objectively is, namely glorious.

The "Delusive Influence" of the Sinful Heart

Alexander argues that as a created being, man "has many things in common with the inferior animals," yet he is unique in that he has the potential for "a higher kind of life. He is endowed with reason and a moral faculty; and by these he is made capable of spiritual life."[85] According to Alexander, in his original state man possessed

81. Ibid., 14.

82. Archibald Alexander, "Deceitfulness of the Heart," in *Evangelical Truth: Practical Sermons for the Christian Home* (Birmingham: Solid Ground Christian Books, 2004; 1850), 164.

83. Alexander, *A Brief Compendium of Bible Truth*, 136–37.

84. Alexander, *Evidences*, 15. Note that for Alexander, "If men possessed good and honest hearts, they would search diligently for the truth, and would be disposed to judge impartially of its evidence; and, as was said, evidence being on the side of truth, and the truth congenial with the moral feelings of the upright mind, it would always be embraced." Alexander, "Deceitfulness of the Heart," 164.

85. Alexander, "The New Creation," in *Evangelical Truth*, 120.

this life without qualification, for he had "the very image of his Creator, delineated on his inmost soul."[86] In other words, his soul was clothed with "that clothing of moral excellence which was the beauty and glory of his nature," and thus he was both "holy and happy,"[87] for the "reason and conscience"[88] that governed his soul were actuated by "holy desires and affections,"[89] rather than by his "animal passions."[90] However, when "in a moment of inadvertency" he fell under the influence of his "lower propensities," "the moral excellence in which [he] was created" was "effaced," he became "destitute of any principle of true holiness,"[91] and his soul became "depraved and disordered" so that it was disposed "neither . . . to know [n]or love its Creator."[92] Indeed, when his "inferior passions and carnal appetites" usurped the control of "reason and conscience,"[93] he "lost that moral purity and perfection with which [his soul] was originally endued" and he died spiritually, for "the reins of [the] government"[94] of his soul were seized by the "corrupt dispositions"[95] of his sinful heart and he "turned with aversion from God and holiness, and [his] affections attached themselves to the creature."[96] In this fallen state, there is "perpetual discord" in the soul of man because "The regulator of the whole machinery of human agency is wanting. Man was made to love his Creator supremely, but in his fallen state, this principle is wanting; and its place has been usurped by *self*. Self is now the centre of all the affections and pursuits, so that the orderly and harmonious operations of the mind are destroyed."[97]

Why, though, are those who are "alienated from God" and thus inclined to making themselves the "centre around which . . . all things

86. Ibid., 119.

87. Alexander, *A Brief Compendium of Bible Truth*, 98, 82.

88. Alexander, "The New Creation," 119.

89. Alexander, *A Brief Compendium of Bible Truth*, 136.

90. Alexander, "The New Creation," 119.

91. Alexander, *A Brief Compendium of Bible Truth*, 97, 136, 83, 101.

92. Alexander, "Love to Christ," in *Evangelical Truth*, 234.

93. Alexander, "The New Creation," 117.

94. Archibald Alexander, "A Practical View of Regeneration," *BRTR* 8, 4 (1836): 477–78.

95. Archibald Alexander, "An Inquiry into that Inability under Which the Sinner Labours, and Whether It Furnishes Any Excuse for His Neglect of Duty," *BRTR* 3, 3 (1831): 362.

96. Alexander, "A Practical View of Regeneration," 478.

97. Alexander, "The New Creation," 117.

revolve"[98] without the ability to reason in a right or proper fashion? Why, in other words, is a mind that is not "rightly disposed"[99] to God and to his revelation "incapable of judging impartially of the nature and evidence of truth"?[100] The answer is found generally in Alexander's commitment to the unitary operation of the soul, and specifically in the "delusive influence"[101] that depraved dispositions have on the judgment of the understanding. In his occasional essays on Christian anthropology, Alexander makes it clear that he opposes a "philosophy of the mind" that "separates entirely between the intellect and the will, and maintains that the former in its operations is incapable of virtue or vice."[102] Such a "method of philosophizing" must be repudiated, he argues, because it is grounded in a "dissociation of the understanding and heart" that cannot be justified either by experience or by the teaching of Scripture.[103] The Scriptures, he insists,

> do often use the word *heart* for moral exercise, but not to the exclusion of the intellect. Indeed, this word in the Old Testament, where it most frequently occurs, is used for the whole soul. . . . We are required to love with the understanding; and "a wise and understanding heart" is a mode of expression which shows how little the inspired penmen were influenced by a belief of this modern theory. And, in the New Testament, to "believe with the heart" includes the intellect as much as what is called the will. It means to believe really and sincerely; so to believe, as to be affected by what we believe, according to its nature. But is not all moral exercise voluntary, or an exercise of the will? yes, undoubtedly; and so is all moral exercise rational, or such as involves the exercise of the intellect.[104]

98. Alexander, "A Practical View of Regeneration," 478.

99. Alexander, "An Inquiry into that Inability under Which the Sinner Labours," 362.

100. Archibald Alexander, "Why Halt Thou between Two Opinions?" in *Practical Truths* (Harrisonburg, VA: Sprinkle Publications, 1998; 1857), 68.

101. Alexander, "Deceitfulness of Sin," in *Practical Truths*, 59.

102. Alexander, "An Inquiry into that Inability under Which the Sinner Labours," 376, 365.

103. Ibid., 366. While Alexander insists the intellect takes logical priority in all rational/moral activity, he nonetheless acknowledges that the understanding and the heart always act as a single substance. According to Alexander, "There can be no exercise of heart which does not necessarily involve the conception of the intellect; for that which is chosen must be apprehended; and that which is loved and admired, must be perceived." Ibid.

104. Ibid., 367.

Given the organic nature of the relationship between the understanding and the heart in Alexander's philosophical psychology, it follows that the unregenerate cannot reason in a "right" or "impartial" fashion not, in the first place, because of the ideas that inform their thinking on one topic or another but, even more basically, because, "Under the influence of an evil heart, every thing appears in false colours."[105] According to Alexander, to a mind that is in bondage to depraved dispositions, things that are true appear to be false and things that are good appear to be "odious"[106] because the sinful heart—which "blinds" the mind and "perverts" reason[107]—"presents objects in a false light, or leads to a misconception of the nature of things within us and around us."[108] Indeed, a mind that is depraved by sin can have "no right apprehensions of God, no holy affections towards him, [and] no cheerful and habitual purpose to serve him"[109] not because it cannot know anything about God, but because it cannot know anything about God rightly. It is incapable, in other words, "of perceiving the beauty and sweetness of spiritual objects; and is, therefore, totally incapable of loving such objects."[110] While Alexander acknowledges that the evidence "is always on the side of truth," nevertheless he insists that a mind that "is strongly biased by inclination to sinful indulgence" cannot see this evidence "with sufficient clearness to give it efficacy"[111] because truth, "in order to produce its effect, requires a correspondent state or temper in the mind; so that even the brightest display of God's perfections to the understanding of a sinner, will only excite greater enmity, as in the devils."[112]

For Alexander, then, the explanation for why the unregenerate cannot reason in a "right" or "impartial" fashion is ultimately found not merely in "the opposition of the heart to the dictates of the understand-

---

105. Alexander, "Deceitfulness of the Heart," 167. Note that the appearance is more basic than the idea because it is the appearance that informs the idea.

106. Ibid.

107. Archibald Alexander, "Christ Our Wisdom, Righteousness, Sanctification, and Redemption," in *Evangelical Truth*, 197.

108. Alexander, "Deceitfulness of the Heart," 162.

109. Alexander, "A Practical View of Regeneration," 479.

110. Alexander, "An Inquiry into that Inability under Which the Sinner Labours," 365.

111. Alexander, "Why Halt Thou between Two Opinions?" 68.

112. Alexander, "Love to Christ," 235.

ing," as if the understanding and the heart really are distinct and the corrupt understanding really does have the capacity to "present truth in its true colours, to the heart," as many of Alexander's contemporaries were arguing.[113] It is found, rather, in "the depravity of the heart"[114] that prevents the unregenerate from seeing what God has revealed for what it objectively is, namely glorious. While Alexander concedes that the unregenerate can have a "speculative" understanding of what God has revealed and that this understanding "may be correct as far as it goes," nevertheless he insists that such an understanding cannot move the soul to embrace the truth with assurance and delight "simply because it is inadequate."[115] It "produces no effect," in other words, because "it does not penetrate the excellence and the beauty of any one spiritual object; and it may be averred, that the affections of the heart do always correspond with the real views of the understanding."[116] "If men are unaffected with the truth known," Alexander concludes,

113. Alexander, "An Inquiry into that Inability under Which the Sinner Labours," 365–66. Alexander notes that "there has been current with many, in our day, a theory which separates entirely between the intellect and will, and maintains that the former in its operations, is incapable of virtue or vice; and to corroborate this opinion, a distinction has been made of the powers of the soul itself, into natural and moral. By this division, the understanding or intellect belongs to the former class, the will and affections to the latter. According to this hypothesis, all sin consists in voluntary acts, or in the exercise of the will; and the understanding is incapable of moral obliquity, because it is not a moral faculty. They who have adopted this theory (and they are many) entertain the opinion that depravity consists very much in the opposition of the heart to the dictates of the understanding. In regeneration, according to them, there is no illumination of the understanding by the Holy Spirit. This, according to the theory under consideration, is altogether unnecessary. This work, therefore, consists in nothing else, than giving a new heart, or a new set of feelings. If the person has received correct doctrinal instruction, no other illumination is needed; and the whole difference in the conceptions of truth, between the regenerate and unregenerate, is owing to nothing else than a change in the feelings; for, as far as mere intellect is concerned, the views of the understanding are the same before regeneration as afterwards; except, that a renewed heart disposing the person to the impartial love of truth, he will be more careful to collect and weigh its evidences, and will thus be preserved from errors into which the unregenerate, through the corrupt bias produced by the affections, are prone to fall." Ibid.

114. Alexander, "Deceitfulness of the Heart," 163.

115. Alexander, "An Inquiry into that Inability under Which the Sinner Labours," 366. Note that the source of the inadequacy is not found in what God has revealed, for there is "light enough" in God's revelation and this light is objectively compelling. Archibald Alexander, *Thoughts on Religious Experience* (Edinburgh: The Banner of Truth Trust, 1989; 1844), 61. Rather, the source is found in the "blindness" of the mind of "the percipient being." Ibid.

116. Alexander, "An Inquiry into that Inability under Which the Sinner Labours," 366. Elsewhere, Alexander argues, "If there be a clear truth in the law of mental operation, it is that the affections are in exact accordance with the views of the understanding." Alexander,

it must be because they do not know it aright. . . . Did any man ever see an object to be lovely and not feel an emotion corresponding with that quality? And what unconverted man ever beheld in Christ, as represented in Scripture, the beauty and glory of God? Hence that doctrine is not true which confines depravity or holiness to the will, and which considers the understanding as a natural and the will as a moral faculty. The soul is not depraved or holy by departments; the disease affects it, as a soul; and of course all faculties employed in moral exercises must partake of their moral qualities.[117]

The Work of the Spirit

If it is therefore true that for Alexander, "True knowledge and pious affections are inseparably conjoined . . . [because] The views of the understanding and the purposes of the heart, from the constitution of the mind, must be in coincidence,"[118] then how do fallen sinners acquire the ability to reason "rightly"? How, in other words, do fallen sinners acquire the ability to see revealed truth more or less for what it objectively is, namely glorious? The answer is found in Alexander's understanding of the new birth, for it is in the new birth that the Spirit, through the "instrumentality" of the Word, does two things that foster the capacity for impartial analysis.[119] First, the Spirit regenerates fallen sinners by "introduc[ing spiritual] life into . . . depraved soul[s]."[120] In regeneration, which Alexander

---

Thoughts on Religious Experience, 63. Alexander's discussion of the nature of faith is grounded in his commitment to the logical priority of the intellect in faith. "If any thing is known of the order of exercises in the rational mind, the perception of the qualities on which an affection terminates, is, in the order of nature, prior to the affection. The soul, in an unregenerate state, is equally incapable of seeing and feeling aright in relation to spiritual objects. And, indeed, we hardly know how to distinguish between the clear perception of the beauty of an object, and the love of that object: the one might serve as a just description of the other. Not but that the intellect and heart may be distinguished; but when beauty, sweetness, excellence, and glory, or good in any of its forms, is the object of the understanding, this distinction, in experience, vanishes." Alexander, "An Inquiry into that Inability under Which the Sinner Labours," 366.

117. Alexander, *Thoughts on Religious Experience*, 63.

118. Alexander, "Obedience to Christ Gives Assurance of the Truth of His Doctrines," in *Evangelical Truth*, 22.

119. Alexander, "A Practical View of Regeneration," 481.

120. Alexander, "Christ the Believer's Life," in *Practical Truths*, 63.

insists cannot be produced "by any human efforts"[121] but requires "a peculiar work of God" because it necessitates "a 'new creation,' "[122] the Spirit changes the "moral character"[123] that actuates the soul and thereby grants fallen sinners "a capacity of being properly affected with truth when proposed."[124] The Spirit renders sinners "susceptible of impression from divine truth,"[125] in other words, neither by operating on the soul like "a mechanical force," nor by "doing violence to its free and spiritual nature."[126] Rather, the Spirit restores the "lost power of spiritual perception and susceptibility of holy feeling" by operating on the soul "in a way perfectly consistent with its nature, as a spirit, and a creature of understanding and will."[127] In short, the Spirit renders sinners "impressible"[128] by divine truth by implanting a "principle of holiness" that restores—at least in part—"the image of God, lost by the fall."[129] It is this "partial restoration of the lost image of God,"[130] then, that not only frees "the rational powers [of the soul] . . . from the misdirection of evil motives" so that they can "act more correctly,"[131] it is also that which disposes regenerated sinners to "a sincere love of the truth," the kind of love that informs the impartial analysis of what God has revealed.[132] According to Alexander, "The genuine love of truth makes its possessor willing to relinquish his most cherished opinions as soon as it shall be satisfactorily demonstrated that they are not true. The love of the truth

121. Alexander, "Love to Christ," 235. Note that the "human efforts" to which Alexander is referring include those of the self as well as those of others: "Not by the man himself, for he can only bring into action such principles as are within him. Nor by any other creature, for another can only address himself to the heart by objectively proposing truth to the understanding." Ibid.

122. Alexander, "A Practical View of Regeneration," 480.

123. Alexander, *A Brief Compendium of Bible Truth*, 136.

124. Alexander, "Love to Christ," 235.

125. Alexander, "A Practical View of Regeneration," 482.

126. Alexander, *Thoughts on Religious Experience*, 62. Note that examples of acting on the soul in a mechanical fashion would include changing "the substance of the soul," creating a "new faculty" in the soul, or giving "new strength to the faculties, which belong to human nature" as such. Alexander, "The New Creation," in *Evangelical Truth*, 111.

127. Alexander, *Thoughts on Religious Experience*, 62, 59.

128. Alexander, "Holding Forth the Word of Life," in *Evangelical Truth*, 451.

129. Alexander, *Thoughts on Religious Experience*, 62, 59.

130. Alexander, *A Brief Compendium of Bible Truth*, 137.

131. Alexander, "The New Creation," 112.

132. Alexander, "Love of the Truth," in *Practical Truths*, 80. Note that at the heart of the impartiality that Alexander is commending is not neutrality, but the "principle of holiness."

renders a man not only earnest in the pursuit of the beloved object, but impartial in his judgment of evidence."[133]

The first thing that the Spirit does in the new birth, then, is to create the capacity for impartial analysis by placing God again "on the throne of the human heart."[134] It is the communication of spiritual life in regeneration, Alexander insists, that gives fallen sinners the ability to see the "supreme excellence" of what God has revealed,[135] for it is the communication of spiritual life that frees the soul from its bondage to the blinding influence of sinful dispositions and enables it to function according to a holy rather than a depraved principle.[136] The second thing that the Spirit does in the new birth is to actually give a "just conception"[137] of what God has revealed by enlightening "the eyes of our mind"[138] to the "true nature" of revealed truth.[139] In illumination,

133. Ibid., 81.

134. Alexander, "The New Creation," 117–18.

135. Alexander, "Obedience to Christ Gives Assurance of the Truth of His Doctrines," 17.

136. Alexander argues that when God is placed again on the throne of the human heart in regeneration, the "disorder" of the mind begins to be "removed" and the "harmony" of the mind begins to be "restored." "The renewed man is no longer a selfish, sensual, and sordid creature. He is now spiritual in his prevailing desires. His affections are set on things above, and not on things on the earth, and he strives to keep a conscience void of offence to God and man, by taking pains to have it truly enlightened as to the rule of duty, and by obeying its dictates uniformly. The course which the renewed man pursues is approved by enlightened reason; and he endeavours more and more to bring all the thoughts and imaginations of his heart into obedience to the gospel of Christ." Alexander, "The New Creation," 118.

137. Ibid., 115.

138. Archibald Alexander, "Privileges of the Sons of God," in *Evangelical Truth*, 154.

139. Alexander, *Thoughts on Religious Experience*, 73. From the beginning of this discussion of illumination, note that for Alexander the "just conception" of truth that the Spirit gives to regenerated minds is not always and everywhere precisely the same, but varies to one degree or another, and this is the case for two reasons, both of which suggest that Alexander embraced a form of perspectivalism that takes seriously both the subjective condition and the situation of the knower. The first has to do with the varied nature of the Spirit's work in the lives of individuals. While Alexander insists that "The work of grace on the heart, is *in kind* the same in all," nevertheless "The *degrees* of light, and the *vigour* of life, communicated in regeneration, are very different in different converts." Alexander, "Privileges of the Sons of God," 155; emphasis added. The second reason has to do with the "diversity" of the "particular truths" that regenerated sinners "are led to contemplate when their eyes are first opened" by the Spirit. Alexander, *Thoughts on Religious Experience*, 64, 67. Speaking of the religious exercises of renewed sinners, Alexander argues that "as the field of truth is very wide, and divine things may be perceived under innumerable aspects and relations, and as there is no uniformity in the particular objects which may first occupy the attention of the enlightened mind, it is impossible to lay down any particular order of exercises which take place. . . . The case may be illustrated by supposing a great multitude of blind persons restored to sight by

which Alexander maintains is "the first effect of regeneration,"[140] the Spirit gives "a discernment of the true quality of spiritual objects"[141] by removing "the films of ignorance and unbelief and prejudice" from the eyes of the fallen mind.[142] When the Spirit works in this fashion, Alexander argues, fallen sinners begin to see "the very best evidence for the truth of Christ's doctrine,"[143] for they begin to see the truth "in its genuine and attractive colours."[144] They begin to see, in other words, not only "the mere verity and relative connexion of divine truth, but the beauty and glory of the truth" as well.[145] Alexander concludes,

> There is a wide and real distinction between merely intellectual ideas of divine things and those which are spiritual. The unregenerate man may be endowed with a powerful intellect, and he may exercise his reasoning powers on divine truth, and may draw just conclusions respecting them; but he can never by the mere exercise of reason attain to spiritual ideas, any more than the man born blind can attain to the knowledge of light and colours, by logical reasoning; or the deaf mute attain to the correct idea of sounds in some other way. The weakest Christian, even the mere child, by the illumination of the Spirit, possesses a species of knowledge, to which the philosopher can never attain, by the utmost exertion of unassisted reason. And

an act of divine power. Some of them would be so situated, that the first object seen would be the glorious luminary of day; another might receive the gift of sight in the night, and the moon and stars would absorb his wondering attention; a third might direct his opened eyes to a beautiful landscape; and a fourth might have but a ray of light shining into a dark dungeon without his knowing whence it came. Of necessity, there must be the same endless variety in the particular views of new converts; but still they all partake of new views of divine truth; and the same truths will generally be contemplated, sooner or later, but not in the same order, nor exhibited to all with the same degree of clearness." Ibid.

140. Alexander, *Thoughts on Religious Experience*, 62.

141. Archibald Alexander, "Faith's Victory Over the World," in *Evangelical Truth*, 417.

142. Alexander, "Privileges of the Sons of God," 155.

143. Alexander, "Obedience to Christ Gives Assurance of the Truth of His Doctrines," 19.

144. Alexander, "Holding Forth the Word of Life," 451.

145. Alexander, "Faith's Victory Over the World," 418. Alexander insists that when spiritual truth is seen, "the affections relinquish their hold of earthly things, and however strong the grasp by which they were embraced, they are now voluntarily resigned for the sake of those more excellent things which faith reveals to the soul. With these objects full in view, the glory of this world fades away, and all its grandest objects appear trivial, and little worthy of the pursuit of a rational and immortal mind. The riches, honours, and pleasures of the world, are to the person in the exercise of faith, like the toys of children to the man of mature age." Ibid., 419–20.

this knowledge is far more excellent, than that of any human science, however sublime or useful.[146]

The Right Use of Reason and Saving Faith

For Alexander, then, the new birth is at the foundation of the ability to "know . . . aright" for it is "nothing but the impression of divine truth on the mind, by the energy of the Holy Spirit."[147] It is, in other words, the means by which those who are "entirely destitute of any spark of true holiness" are enabled to see the "beauty, and glory, and sweetness . . . of divine things,"[148] for it is the means by which their eyes are opened to the "real nature"[149] of the truth that in one way or another is brought before their minds.[150] While interpreters such as Lefferts Loetscher would have us believe that Alexander's religious epistemology was compromised by "a dualism of mind and heart" that was grounded in the accommodation of Scottish Realism, Alexander's understanding of the new birth establishes, on the contrary, that he stood in the epistemological mainstream of the Reformed camp.[151] Indeed, it establishes that for Alexander, it is the work of the Spirit that not only brings the mind into a state in which it can perceive in the Word of God "*that* which it never saw before," namely, "a beauty and excellence, of which it had no conception until now,"[152] but it is also that which thereby

146. Ibid., 418.

147. Alexander, *Thoughts on Religious Experience*, 63, xviii.

148. Ibid., 17, 66.

149. Alexander, "Obedience to Christ Gives Assurance of the Truth of His Doctrines," 23.

150. On what is involved in bringing truth "fairly before the mind," cf. Alexander, *Thoughts on Religious Experience*, 59–61.

151. Lefferts Loetscher, *Facing the Enlightenment and Pietism: Archibald Alexander and the Founding of Princeton Theological Seminary* (Westport, CT: Greenwood, 1983), 168. Loetscher insists that although Alexander rejects "the old 'faculty psychology,'" he practically reinstates it by endorsing the primacy of the intellect in faith. Loetscher argues that "In his youthful sermons [Alexander] had at times reflected the fine blending of 'affections' and intellect seen in Jonathan Edwards's 'Treatise on Religious Affections,' but in more mature life he seems to have kept intellectual functions quite separate from the 'affections,' a pattern more obviously suited to mathematics and to natural science than to religion or to relations between persons divine or human." Ibid. In my estimation, the validity of this point is undermined by the blending of the affections and intellect that is found in *Thoughts on Religious Experience*, one of Alexander's more mature works.

152. Alexander, *Thoughts on Religious Experience*, 64.

excites "those exercises and affections in which the spiritual life essentially consists."[153]

That Alexander was consistently Reformed in this regard is clearly revealed in his endorsement of the distinction between "a merely rational, or historical faith" and "a true, [or] saving faith."[154] According to Alexander, the new birth not only opens the eyes of the mind to "a new heaven and a new earth"[155] so that "even natural objects, the visible heavens, and the earth appear clothed with new attributes,"[156] it also engenders the love of truth that is at the heart of "genuine faith."[157] While Alexander acknowledges a "species of faith"[158] that "is merely the offspring of man's reason,"[159] he insists that saving faith follows "as a thing of course"[160] from the "views of divine truth"[161] that are "produced by the illumination of the Holy Spirit," for he recognizes that it is impossible—given the organic nature of the relationship between the understanding and the will— "that the rational mind should see an object to be lovely, and not love it."[162] He recognizes, in other words, that it is the perception

153. Alexander, *A Brief Compendium of Bible Truth*, 136. Note that these affections are primarily focused on Christ. For elaboration on what this entails, see Archibald Alexander, "Excellency of the Knowledge of Christ," in *Evangelical Truth*, 437–46.

154. Alexander, "Obedience to Christ Gives Assurance of the Truth of His Doctrines," 21.

155. Alexander, "Privileges of the Sons of God," 154.

156. Alexander, "The New Creation," 116. According to Alexander, in the new birth we receive "a susceptibility of taking on lively impressions from objects which affected us not at all before. A new heaven and a new earth seem to be created; for the views of all nature are changed, by the new life which has been communicated." Alexander, "Privileges of the Sons of God," 154. Elsewhere, Alexander insists that God's special revelation is the key that opens the "book of nature" to regenerated sinners. "With the Bible in our hands," he argues, "the heavens shine with redoubled lustre," for through the "declarations" of Scripture, "the mind [is] enlarged and elevated, in contemplating the heavens and the earth!" Whereas the universe "to the atheist is full of darkness and confusion" and thus is "as a volume sealed," to the Christian it "is resplendent with light and glory." Indeed, "How grand, how beautiful, how wise, how harmonious, is the universe, when viewed through the medium of divine revelation." Archibald Alexander, "The Bible, A Key to the Phenomena of the Natural World," *Biblical Repertory. A Journal of Biblical Literature and Theological Science*, Conducted by an Association of Gentlemen New Series 5, 1 (1829): 107–8.

157. Alexander, "Faith's Victory Over the World," 417.

158. Alexander, "Receiving Christ by Faith," in *Evangelical Truth*, 141.

159. Alexander, "Faith's Victory Over the World," 417.

160. Alexander, "Love to Christ," 235.

161. Alexander, *Thoughts on Religious Experience*, 64. Please note that I removed the italics from this quote.

162. Alexander, "Faith's Victory Over the World," 417.

of the "moral fitness and beauty"[163] of what God has revealed that "is nothing else but saving faith,"[164] for it is the perception of "the intrinsic excellence of spiritual objects" that—given the constitution of the mind—"excites holy affections, which prompt [the soul] to good purposes," including the "good purpose" of faith.[165]

What this suggests, then, is that for Alexander, the difference between a "saving faith" and a "historical or merely rational faith" is ultimately found "not in the truths believed . . . , nor in the degree of assent given . . . , but in the evidence on which they are respectively founded."[166] Whereas historical faith is essentially inert because it rests

163. Alexander, *Evidences of the Authenticity, Inspiration, and Canonical Authority of the Holy Scriptures*, 189.

164. Alexander, *Thoughts on Religious Experience*, 64.

165. Alexander, "A Practical View of Regeneration," 489, 482. While Alexander insists that "In the order of causation life must precede action," he is convinced that "in the order of time the communication of life and the acts of the new creature are simultaneous." Ibid., 483. Note that for Alexander, "every good desire, every holy emotion, every exercise of faith, love, repentance, hope, and joy, are produced by the views of truth which the [regenerated] soul now enjoys." Alexander, "Holding Forth the Word of Life," 451. How, though, are the acts that are produced by spiritual knowledge related to one another? How, for example, are we to understand the relationship between repentance and saving faith? According to Alexander, "Repentance literally signifies a change of mind for the better. In our Shorter Catechism, it is defined as 'a saving grace, whereby a sinner out of a true sense of his sin, and apprehension of the mercy of God in Christ, doth, with grief and hatred of his sin, turn from it unto God, with full purpose of and endeavour after new obedience' [WSC 87]. In the same place, faith is defined as 'a saving grace, whereby we receive and rest upon him (Jesus Christ) for salvation as he is freely offered in the gospel' [WSC 86]. Whatever difference of opinion there may be as to the precise meaning of these scriptural terms, all sound Christians will admit that for popular and practical use no language could be selected which would more perspicuously and properly convey to the reader a true notion of these fundamental graces. As to the precedence of one before the other, it is a question as impertinent as whether a whole precedes one of its parts, or is preceded by it. No man can give a sound definition of evangelical repentance which will not include faith. But if the word repentance be used in a more restricted sense, for godly sorrow for sin and hatred of it, it must be preceded by a true faith, for seeing in a rational mind goes before feeling. There must be a perception of the holiness of the divine law, before the turpitude of sin can be so seen as to occasion hatred of it and grief on account of it. But if by faith be meant that cordial reception of Christ, which is mentioned in the words cited from the Catechism, then certainly, there must be some true sense of sin before we can appreciate Christ as a Savior from sin. But it is altogether wrong to perplex the minds of serious Christians with useless questions of this sort. Let the school-men discuss such matters to their heart's content, but let the humble Christian rest in the plain and obvious meaning of the words of Scripture. The effect of divine truth on the heart is produced by general views, and not by nice and metaphysical distinctions." Alexander, *A Brief Compendium of Bible Truth*, 139–40.

166. Alexander, *Thoughts on Religious Experience*, 66.

merely "on the prejudices of education, or the deductions of reason," saving faith embraces those exercises that theologians typically ascribe to the understanding as well as those that theologians typically ascribe to the will, for it rests on a perception of spiritual truth that constrains the soul to appropriate what it now regards as the object of its affection.[167] We must conclude, therefore, that for Alexander, spiritual knowledge and saving faith "involve each other," for saving faith

> is simply *a belief of the truth*, when viewed as distinct, and discriminated from all other mental acts. Some will be startled at this nakedness of faith; and many will be ready to object, that it is to make faith to be no more than a bare assent of the understanding to the truth. . . . But I deny that, as described, it is a naked assent of the understanding, as those words are commonly understood. The wide distinction between the understanding and will, which has very much confounded our mental philosophy, has come down to us from the schoolmen. But in making the distinction, they made simple verity the object of the understanding. And that is what we commonly mean by bare assent; it relates to the simple truth; but the will has respect, they said, to *good*—every species of good. Now the faith of which I have spoken, at the same time contemplates the truth, and the beauty, excellency, and goodness of the object, and also its adaptedness to our necessities: all these things are comprehended in the views which the Holy Spirit gives to the mind. Therefore, though faith be a simple uncompounded act, a firm belief or persuasion, it comprehends the objects ascribed both to the understanding and the will.[168]

Charles Hodge on "Right Reason" and Saving Faith

The Relationship between Moral Character and Moral Activity

When we turn our attention to Charles Hodge, whom we will encounter again in Part Two of this study, we discover that subjective and experiential factors play just as significant a role in his religious epistemology as they do in the epistemology of Archibald Alexander,

167. Ibid.
168. Ibid., 64–65. See Alexander's sympathetic treatment of Edwards's views on regeneration and conversion, 67–72.

for Hodge also recognizes that the soul is a single "unit" that acts in all of its functions—including cognition—as a single substance.[169] In his published writings on Christian anthropology, Hodge argues that human beings consist of two substances: the body, which is material or corporeal, and the soul or heart, which is immaterial or spiritual and comprised of two faculties or powers, namely, the understanding and the will,[170] which he defines broadly to include the power of self-determination and "all the desires, affections, and even emotions."[171] While Hodge insists that the soul or heart is distinct from the body,

169. On how the soul acts in all its functions as a single unit, see Charles Hodge, "Free Agency," *BRPR* 29 (January 1857): 115. At the heart of Hodge's critique of the theology of Edwards A. Park is his insistence that Park's distinction between the theology of the intellect and the theology of the feelings is "founded on a wrong psychology. Whatever doctrine the writer may actually hold as to the nature of the soul, his thoughts and language are evidently framed on the assumption of a much greater distinction between the cognitive and emotional faculties in man than actually exists. The very idea of a theology of feeling as distinct from that of the intellect, seems to take for granted that there are two percipient principles in the soul. The one sees a proposition to be true, the other sees it to be false. The one adopts symbols to express its apprehensions; the other is precise and prosaic in its language. We know indeed, that the author would repudiate this statement, and deny that he held to any such dualism in the soul. We do not charge him with any theoretic conviction of this sort. We only say that this undue dissevering the human faculties underlies his whole doctrine, and is implied in the theory which he has advanced. Both scripture and consciousness teach that the soul is an unit; that its activity is one life. The one rational soul apprehends, feels and determines. It is not one faculty that apprehends, another that feels, and another that determines. Nor can you separate in the complex states of mind of which we are every moment conscious, the feeling from the cognition. From the very nature of affection in a rational being, the intellectual apprehension of its object, is essential to its existence. You cannot eliminate the intellectual element, and leave the feeling. The latter is but an attribute of the former, as much as form or colour is an attribute of bodies. It is impossible therefore that what is true to the feelings should be false to the intellect." Hodge, "The Theology of the Intellect and That of the Feelings," *BRPR* 22, 4 (1850): 660–61; cf. 671. For a helpful explanation of why the debate between Hodge and Park is relevant to the history of theology in North America, see D. G. Hart, "The Critical Period for Protestant Thought in America," in *Reckoning with the Past*, 181–99.

170. While Hodge concedes, "The Scriptures do not formally teach any system of psychology," he argues that "there are certain truths, relating both to our physical and mental constitution, which they constantly assume. They assume . . . that the soul is a substance; that it is a substance distinct from the body, and there are two, and not more than two essential elements in the constitution of man." Charles Hodge, "The Nature of Man," *BRPR* 37 (January 1865): 112, cf. 111.

171. Hodge, "Free Agency," 113; cf. Charles Hodge, "Regeneration, and the Manner of Its Occurrence," *BRTR* 2 (1830): 289–90. For Hodge, in this broad sense, "All liking and disliking, all preferring, all inclination and disinclination, are . . . acts of the will." Hodge, "Free Agency," 113.

he recognizes that it is not distinct from the spirit, but *is* the spiritual substance of human nature. It is, in other words, that underlying force or power which constitutes the essence of who we are, and which manifests itself in thoughts, feelings, and volitions. As the aspect of the human person that is synonymous with the "self," Hodge concludes that the soul or heart is properly regarded as the source from which the intellectual, religious, and moral life of the moral agent emerges.[172]

What, though, determines the quality of the various exercises of the soul, including the quality of its cognitive exercises? The answer is found in an understanding of moral agency that is grounded in Hodge's insistence that the quality of moral activity—whether that activity has to do with an act of the will or an act of the mind—is determined by the disposition or "principle,"[173] i.e., the "character,"[174] from which it flows. That this is the case is clearly revealed in Hodge's understanding of free agency. Whereas Hodge is convinced that moral agents are genuinely free when they are the efficient causes of their own actions, he rejects that understanding of free agency that presupposes the will is itself free, for he recognizes that the will cannot operate independently of the mind. The will, he argues, is not an autonomous faculty or power that can operate in isolation from the views of the understanding, but it is a faculty or power that always acts in concert with the understanding, for it is always determined by the "strongest motive" in the mind, i.e., by what appears to be most preferable to the mind in

172. Hodge, "The Nature of Man," 118. Hodge often uses the word "heart" to refer to the "whole soul" of a moral agent. As such, the "heart" is that internal power which "drives the current of thoughts, feelings, affections, desires and volitions, all that constitutes our inward life." Charles Hodge, "My Son, Give Me Thy Heart," in *Conference Papers* (New York: Charles Scribner's Sons, 1879), 131; cf. Charles Hodge, *Systematic Theology*, 3 vols. (Grand Rapids: Eerdmans, 1989; 1871–73), 2:255.

173. "By principle is not meant any act or purpose or state of conscious feeling. It is something which is the source of acts, purposes and feelings, and which determines their character. It is a law in the sense of an abiding force." Hodge, "Mortify the Deeds of the Body," in *Conference Papers*, 150.

174. Hodge describes character as "the inward principles which control the inward and outward life." Charles Hodge, "Except Ye Be Converted and Become as Little Children, Ye Shall Not Enter into the Kingdom of Heaven," in *Conference Papers*, 125. Elsewhere, Hodge notes that "The character of an act is decided by the nature of the principle by which it is determined. . . . A good man, therefore, is one who is inwardly good: who has a good heart, or nature, something within him which being good in itself, produces good acts." Charles Hodge, *Systematic Theology*, 2:109; cf. Hewitt, *Regeneration and Morality*, 73.

the moment of acting or choosing.[175] Since Hodge is convinced that the activity of the will is always determined by "the last judgment of the understanding," he concludes that "a man is [genuinely] free"—and "his acts are the true products of the man, and really represent or reveal what he is"—"so long as his volitions are the conscious expression of his own mind; or so long as his activity is determined and controlled by his reason and feelings."[176]

How, though, are we to conceive of the motives that determine the activity of the will, and how are they related to the moral character of an acting agent? The answer reveals how the understanding and the will are related in Hodge's philosophical psychology, and it explains why the understanding always takes precedence in moral activity. According to Hodge, the word "motive" can be defined in both objective and subjective senses. In an objective sense, the word refers to something that is outside the self and which awakens

175. According to Hodge, to say that the will is determined by the strongest motive in the mind "only means that it is not self-determined, but that in every rational volition the man is influenced to decide one way rather than another, by something within him, so that the volition is a revelation of what he himself is." Hodge, "Free Agency," 114. Hodge opposes that understanding of human freedom that presupposes the will is a self-determining power because it "presupposes that the will can act independently of motive, and it thereby denies the unity of the soul. It supposes that our volitions are isolated atoms, springing up from the abyss of the capricious self-determination of the will, from a source beyond the control or ken of reason. They are purely casual, arbitrary, or capricious. They have no connection with the past, and give no promise of the future. On this hypothesis, there can be no such thing as character. It is, however, a fact of experience universally admitted, that there are such things as principles or dispositions that control the will. We feel assured that an honest man will act honestly, and that a benevolent man will act benevolently. We are moreover assured that these principles may be so strong and fixed as to render the volitions absolutely certain." Ibid., 131.

176. Ibid., 110, 134, 112. As a general principle, Hodge argues that the will "gets all its light from reason. It is necessarily determined by the intelligence; if it is not, and so far as it is not, it is irrational." Charles Hodge, "The Elements of Psychology," BRPR 28, 2 (1856): 382. When Hodge discusses this general principle elsewhere, he makes it clear that "the intelligence" he is affirming has to do with the whole soul, not with the rational faculty alone. "If I desire anything," he argues, "it is because I apprehend it as suitable to satisfy some craving of my nature. If I will anything because it is right, its being right is something for the understanding to discern. In other words, all the desires, affections, or feelings which determine the will to act must have an object, and that object by which the feeling is excited and towards which it tends, must be discerned by the understanding. It is this that gives them their rational character, and renders the determinations of the will rational. Any volition which does not follow the last dictate of the understanding, in this sense of the words, is the act of an idiot. It may be spontaneous, be just as the acts of brutes are, but it cannot be free, in the sense of being the act of an accountable person." Hodge, "Free Agency," 111.

desire and affection and thereby moves the agent to an action or a decision. In a subjective sense, the word refers to "those inward convictions, feelings, inclinations, and principles *which are in the mind itself*, and which impel or influence the man to decide one way rather than another."[177] When the word "motive" is defined in this subjective sense, i.e., the sense that explicitly denies the understanding and the will can act independently of one another in moral activity,[178] it becomes immediately clear that the moral quality of a voluntary act is determined by the character of the acting agent because it is the character of the acting agent that determines what is most preferable to the mind in the moment of acting or choosing. "There is no such thing," Hodge argues, "as a purely intellectual cognition of a moral truth. It is the exercise of a moral nature; it implies moral sensibility. It of necessity, involves feeling to a greater or less degree. It is the cognition of a being sensitive to moral distinctions, and without that sensibility there can be no such cognition."[179]

What this suggests, then, is that for Hodge a moral agent is genuinely free not just when his actions are determined by his will, but more precisely when "his volitions are truly and properly his own, determined by nothing out of himself, but proceeding from his own views, feelings, and immanent dispositions, so that they are the real, intelligent, and conscious expression of his character, or of what is in his mind."[180] This is how moral character is related to moral activity,

177. Ibid., 113–14. Emphasis added.

178. Recall Hodge's broad definition of the "will." According to this definition, "the term voluntary applies not only to . . . acts of choice, but to all exercises of the affections or desires preliminary thereto." Hodge, "Regeneration, and the Manner of Its Occurrence," 290; cf. 288–90. While Hodge concedes that "purely intellectual cognition" is possible "in the apprehension of speculative truths," he insists that the cognition involved in moral activity involves the whole soul, and as such is not a "purely . . . intellectual exercise." Hodge, "The Theology of the Intellect and that of the Feeling," 662.

179. Hodge, "The Theology of the Intellect and that of the Feeling," 662.

180. Hodge, "Free Agency," 108–9. Hodge distinguishes between moral *certainty* and moral *necessity* largely for semantic reasons having to do with the relationship between the will and the motives that determine the will to act. He argues that the motives that determine the will to act are not the "efficient cause" of moral activity, but the "ground or reason" for moral activity. On the basis of this distinction Hodge affirms both the efficiency of the agent in moral activity as well as the essential truth captured in the doctrine of moral necessity, namely that "motives are the reasons which determine the agent to exert his efficiency in one way rather than another."

Hodge argues, no matter how the dispositions and feelings that "constitute character" and determine the will come to be what they are, for the inclinations that inform the last judgment of the understanding "derive their morality or immorality from their nature, and not from their origin. Malignity is evil and love is good," Hodge insists, "whether concreated, innate, acquired or infused."[181]

Sin, Grace, and the Ability to Reason "Rightly"

The subtleties of Hodge's philosophical psychology—especially those having to do with the precise nature of the relationship between the understanding and the will—are particularly evident in his understanding of saving faith. Like Alexander before him, Hodge maintains that a mind that is depraved by sin is incapable of moving the soul to embrace God precisely because a mind that is destitute of holiness is blind to the spiritual significance of "the things which are freely given to [us] of God."[182] It cannot yield a true and compelling perception of what

---

Ibid., 114. As such, "Motives are not the efficient cause of the volition; that efficiency resides in the agent; but what we, 'by a necessary mental law,' must demand, is a sufficient reason why the agent exerts his efficiency in one way rather than another." Ibid., 133.

181. Ibid., 134. According to Hodge, "A man is responsible for his external acts, because they are decided by his will; he is responsible for his volitions, because they are determined by his principles and feelings; he is responsible for his principles and feelings, because of their inherent nature as good or bad, and because they are his own, and constitute his character. If you detach the outward act from the will, it ceases to have any moral character." Ibid., 130.

182. Charles Hodge, *The Way of Life* (Edinburgh: The Banner of Truth Trust, 1978; 1841), 15, 23. Hodge argues that Adam was created in the image of God with a moral nature that was genuinely holy. Charles Hodge, "The First and Second Adam," *BRPR* 32 (April 1860): 358. He was created, in other words, in a state of "original righteousness," and thus was pronounced by God to be exceedingly good not only because of the "perfect harmony and due subordination of all that constituted man," i.e., "His reason was subject to God; his will was subject to his reason; his affections and appetites to his will; the body was the obedient organ of the soul," but more importantly because "his moral perfection in which he resembled God, included knowledge, righteousness and holiness." Hodge, *Systematic Theology*, 2:99. When Adam fell, however, he lost his original righteousness and plunged his posterity into a state of original sin (on the "inherent corruption" that constitutes the state of original sin, cf. ibid., 2:227–56). At the heart of this fallen condition is the depravity of human nature. According to Hodge, the depraved condition is not the consequence of a "positive infusion of wickedness," but its essence is found in "The mere absence of a native tendency to God [that] leaves the soul in moral confusion and ruin." Hodge, "Regeneration, and the Manner of Its Occurrence," 293. While the "essential attributes and constitutional propensities" remain in fallen human beings, "they are there without a principle of moral order and subordination. There is no presiding spirit to turn them to the service of God. The result of this absence is

God has revealed, in other words, because it can neither "discern" the beauty nor "taste" the sweetness of the truth that it can rationally perceive.[183] But how can this be? Why would an otherwise rational moral agent remain indifferent to the force of the truth that God has revealed when the truth itself is objectively compelling? The answer is found in Hodge's insistence that "No truth can be *properly* apprehended unless there is a harmony between it and the mind to which it is presented."[184] While Hodge acknowledges that the unregenerate can appropriate the "external evidence" for the truth of what God has revealed and thus can exercise a speculative or historical faith, he insists that a saving faith is beyond their grasp not because there is "any deficiency in the evidence of the truth," but because the depraved mind does not have the moral capacity "to appreciate" the true significance of the truth that it can rationally perceive.[185] The last judgment of the depraved mind is incapable of determining the will to make the beauty of God's glory the focus of the affections, in other words, because a moral defect "in the organ of vision"[186]—"by which the reason or understanding is blinded, and the taste and feelings are perverted"[187]—prevents a "true" or "right" apprehension of the truth that is present to the understanding.[188]

---

all manner of evil, and a tendency to all this evil lies in this very state of the soul, and exists prior to any of its moral acts." Ibid.

183. Cf. Hodge, *Systematic Theology*, 2:261. For Hodge, the supreme manifestation of spiritual blindness is found in the refusal "to recognize and receive [Christ] as being who he claims to be. . . . This is the greatest of sins. It is the condemning sin. Its heinousness consists . . . in its opposition to the clearest light. He who cannot see the sun, must be stone blind. He who cannot see the glory of God in the face of Jesus Christ must be blinded by Satan. This blindness is moral, religious, and spiritual deadness." Hodge, "The Sin of Unbelief," in *Conference Papers*, 98; cf. Hodge, "Regeneration, and the Manner of Its Occurrence," 283–84.

184. Hodge, *The Way of Life*, 12. Emphasis added.

185. Ibid., 12, 18. According to Hodge "the scriptures . . . clearly teach that holiness is necessary to the perception of holiness. In other words, that the things of the Spirit must be spiritually discerned: that the unrenewed have not this discernment, and therefore, they cannot know the things which are freely given to us of God, i.e., the things which he has graciously revealed in his word. They may have that apprehension of them which an uncultivated ear has of complicated musical sounds, or an untutored eye of a work of art. Much of the object is perceived, but much is not discerned, and that which remains unseen, is precisely that which gives to these objects their peculiar excellence and power." Hodge, "The Theology of the Intellect and That of the Feelings," 671.

186. Hodge, *Systematic Theology*, 3:51.

187. Ibid., 2:261.

188. Cf. ibid., 2:234; Hodge, *The Way of Life*, 15; Charles Hodge, "The Necessity of the Spirit's Teaching in Order to the Right Understanding of the Scriptures," in *Conference Papers*, 75–77.

If, then, the ultimate cause of unbelief is found in "the want of power rightly to discern spiritual things, and the consequent want of all right affections toward them,"[189] how do those who are positively unrighteous and inclined not to God but "to self and sin"[190] acquire the ability to appreciate "the beauty, excellence, and suitableness of the things of the Spirit"?[191] The answer is found in Hodge's understanding of the new birth. While Hodge acknowledges that fallen sinners play an active role in their own conversion, he insists that they are totally "passive" in regeneration because "the state of mind" that enables them to see and love what God has revealed "is produced directly by the Spirit of God."[192] According to Hodge, the Spirit regenerates fallen sinners not by changing "the essence or essential properties" of their souls,[193] nor by urging them to attend more carefully to the "moral power" of the truth that they can already rationally perceive.[194] Rather, the Spirit breathes "new life" into souls that are dead in sin by sovereignly changing "that inward immanent disposition or spiritual state which is back of all voluntary or conscious activity, and which, in the things of God, determines that activity."[195] For Hodge, then, it is this "infusion

189. Hodge, *Systematic Theology*, 2:261.

190. Charles Hodge, *Commentary on the Epistle to the Romans* (Grand Rapids: Eerdmans, 1993; 1835), 185. For Hodge, the positive nature of sin "results from the active nature of the soul. If there is no tendency to the love and service of God, there is, from this very defect, a tendency to self and sin." Ibid. For a fuller discussion of "positive unrighteousness," see Hodge, *Systematic Theology*, 2:187–88.

191. Hodge, *Systematic Theology*, 2:262.

192. Hodge, "Regeneration, and the Manner of Its Occurrence," 295. According to Hodge, "It is the soul that repents, believes, hopes and fears, but it is the Holy Spirit that regenerates." Ibid.

193. Ibid., 255. Hodge insists that the change wrought by the Spirit in regeneration is "a moral and not a physical change; and . . . it takes place without any violence being done to the soul or any of its laws." Ibid., 261.

194. Ibid., 261. Regeneration, Hodge argues, "is not effected by mere moral suasion; . . . there is something more than the simple presentation of truth and urging of motives. The idea of Calvinists uniformly was, that the truth, however clearly presented or forcibly urged, would never produce its full effect without a special influence of the Holy Spirit. This influence they maintained was supernatural, that is, above the mere moral power of the truth, and such as infallibly to secure the result, and yet . . . did the soul no more violence than demonstration does the intellect, or persuasion the heart." Ibid.

195. Charles Hodge, "Evidences of Regeneration," in *Conference Papers*, 137–38; cf. Hodge, *Systematic Theology*, 3:35. As the previous notes indicate, Hodge is convinced that the regenerating work of the Spirit does not violate the integrity of the fallen soul in any sense. He reinforces

of a new spiritual principle"[196] that enables the regenerate to see revealed truth more or less for what it objectively is, for it is this "renovat[ion] of the corrupted nature of man"[197] that gives them the ability "to see and love the beauty of holiness."[198] "Regeneration secures right knowledge as well as right feeling," Hodge argues, "and right feeling is not the effect of right knowledge, nor is right knowledge the effect of right feeling. The two are inseparable effects of a work which affects the whole soul."[199]

Having established that the inclination of the heart plays a decisive role in Hodge's philosophical psychology, we must conclude our consideration of Hodge's religious epistemology by reflecting on his understanding of the relationship between "right reason" and saving faith. If it is indeed true that for Hodge there is an intimate relationship between moral character and moral activity because the soul is a single "unit" that acts in all its functions as a single substance, then might there be grounds for expecting that the inclinations that inform the perception of the regenerated mind will also "fit and dispose" the regenerated agent to "holy acts"?[200] Might there be grounds for expecting, in other words, that because of the "constitut[ion]" of the mind,[201] the inclinations that inform a "right" understanding of what God has revealed will also lead the regenerated agent "to embrace [the truth] with assurance and delight"?[202] Indeed there are. Hodge argues that the genesis of saving faith is found in the new birth because it is

this point with the following quotation from the Puritan Stephen Charnock: "His grace is so sweet and so strong, that he neither wrongs the liberty of his creature, nor doth prejudice his absolute power. As God moves necessary causes, necessarily; contingent causes, contingently; so he moves free agents freely, without offering violence to their natures. The Spirit glides into the heart by sweet illapses [sic] of grace, and victoriously allures the soul . . . not by crossing, but changing the inclination, by the all conquering and alluring charms of love." Charnock, quoted in Hodge, "Regeneration, and the Manner of Its Occurrence," 264.

196. Charles Hodge, "Regeneration," in *Conference Papers*, 136.

197. Hodge, "The First and Second Adam," 341.

198. Hodge, "Regeneration, and the Manner of Its Occurrence," 285.

199. Hodge, *Systematic Theology*, 3:36. For concise summaries of Hodge's understanding of regeneration, cf. ibid., 2:69–70; Hodge, "Regeneration," 136–38.

200. Hodge, "Regeneration, and the Manner of Its Occurrence," 267. See also Hodge's sympathetic treatment of Edwards's understanding of the relationship between regeneration and the spiritual sense that fosters holy acts. Ibid., 268–69.

201. Hodge, *The Way of Life*, 16.

202. Hodge, *Systematic Theology*, 3:71.

in the new birth that the Spirit imparts "a discernment not only of the truth, but also of the holiness, excellence, and glory of the things discerned."[203] It is this perception of the truth in its true or "right" nature, then, that is "inseparably connected" with saving faith, for it is this "opening of the eyes on the certainty, glory, and excellence of divine things" that engenders the "delight" that directs "all the energies of the new-born soul" toward the pursuit of that which is spiritual and eternal rather than toward that which is "seen and temporal."[204] What this suggests, then, is that when "the excellence of spiritual objects" is revealed by the Spirit "to the intelligence" of a regenerated sinner, there is a sense in which it is entirely right to say that this knowledge "is . . . eternal life,"[205] for the "delight" that determines the will to embrace what the sinner now discerns to be glorious is itself "the necessary consequence of spiritual illumination; and with delight come satisfaction and peace, elevation above the world, or spiritual mindedness, and such a sense of the importance of the things not seen and eternal, that all the energies of the renewed soul are . . . devoted to securing them for ourselves and others."[206]

Conclusion

If the foregoing analysis of the religious epistemologies of Archibald Alexander and Charles Hodge articulates the epistemological context within which the "intellectualism" of Old Princeton must be interpreted, then two conclusions—both of which call for a reassessment of the consensus of critical opinion—are in order regarding how we should approach Old Princeton's emphasis on "science," "facts," and the primacy of the intellect in faith. First, if it is indeed true that

203. Ibid., 3:69.
204. Ibid., 3:34–35.
205. Hodge, "The Theology of the Intellect and That of the Feelings," 672.
206. Hodge, *Systematic Theology*, 3:34; cf. ibid., 2:263; Hodge, "Regeneration, and the Manner of Its Occurrence," 295–96; Hewitt, *Regeneration and Morality*, 57. On the delight that determines the soul to embrace what God has revealed, cf. Charles Hodge, "Delighting in the Law of God," in *Conference Papers*, 249–50; Hodge, "Living by Faith," in *Conference Papers*, 152.

subjective and experiential factors play a critical role in Old Princeton's religious epistemology because the soul is a single unit that acts in all of its functions as a single substance, then it would be a serious mistake to conclude that the Princeton Theology in general and the Princeton apologetic in particular are grounded in a form of Enlightenment rationalism rather than in faithfulness to the epistemological assumptions of the Reformed tradition. Indeed, if we can account for the "intellectualism" of Old Princeton by pointing to emphases that are standard components of the Reformed tradition, then a reconsideration of Old Princeton's orthodox bearings is in order because in that case, its emphasis on "science," "facts," and the primacy of the intellect in faith is not "*ipso facto* evidence of an intellectualized faith."[207]

Second, given the plausibility of the claim that the "intellectualism" of Old Princeton in fact is moral rather than merely rational, there is warrant for concluding that despite what the consensus of critical opinion would have us believe, the Princeton Theology was driven by subjective rather than objective, theological rather than philosophical concerns. There is warrant for concluding, in other words, that the Princeton theologians were not indifferent to the subjective and experiential components of a consistently Reformed religious epistemology, nor were they exceedingly optimistic about the epistemic competence of the unregenerated mind. Rather, like those in the mainstream of the Reformed tradition before them, they recognized that even in cognition, the quality of the operation of the soul is always determined by the disposition or character of the acting agent. If these conclusions hold water, then what this suggests is not that the Princeton theologians were so indebted to the assumptions of the Enlightenment that they passed on to their descendants a bastardized version of Calvinism. What this suggests, rather, is that they were more or less consistently Reformed scholars who responded to the modern era's relocation of the divine-human nexus not only by insisting that the Christian religion entails the rational appropriation of objective truth, but also by maintaining that the ability to see this truth for what it objectively is presupposes the work of the Holy Spirit on the "whole soul" of a moral agent.

207. Dowey, *The Knowledge of God in Calvin's Theology*, 3.

2

A "Rather Bald Rationalism"?

Consistently Reformed?

In the first chapter I considered the work of Archibald Alexander and Charles Hodge, and suggested that Old Princeton's religious episte-mology is compatible with the assumptions of the Reformed tradition because its emphasis on "right reason" is moral rather than merely rational. I suggested, in other words, that Old Princeton's epistemo-logical commitments are grounded not in the accommodation of one form of Enlightenment rationalism or another, but in the endorsement of the classical Reformed distinction between a merely speculative and a spiritual understanding of what God has revealed.

Beginning in this chapter and concluding in the next, I consider the work of Benjamin B. Warfield and show how the Princeton apologetic and the understanding of Christian scholarship that follows from it are also grounded in epistemological assumptions that are consistently Reformed.[1] While critics would have us believe Warfield's insistence that the Christian religion has been placed in the world "to *reason*

---

1. For the purposes of this study, Warfield's views on apologetics and Christian scholarship are representative of those of the best thinkers at Old Princeton Seminary.

its way to its dominion"[2] is a particularly egregious example of Old Princeton's "rather bald rationalism,"[3] these chapters establish that such a conclusion cannot be justified because Warfield retained an important role for subjective and experiential factors in his evidentialist apologetic and in his approach to Christian scholarship. Whereas Warfield certainly affirmed that a saving apprehension of what God has revealed entails the rational appropriation of objective evidence, he nonetheless recognized that the "rightness" of this apprehension is determined neither by the scholarly prowess of the perceiving mind, nor by the objective sufficiency of the evidence that is presented to one's consciousness, but by the moral or ethical state of the knowing soul. In short, Warfield insisted that neither the labors of the apologist nor the investigations of the believing academic would lead anybody to embrace what God has revealed without the sovereign working of the Spirit of God, for he recognized that only the regenerate have the moral ability to see revealed truth more or less for what it objectively is, namely glorious.

As such, the forthcoming chapters challenge the consensus of critical opinion by establishing that Warfield's appeal to "right reason,"[4] and his insistence that the primary mission of the Christian apologist "is no less than to *reason* the world into acceptance of the 'truth,' "[5] are grounded not in the accommodation of an especially naïve formulation of Enlightenment humanism, but in the recognition that fallen sinners are absolutely dependent on the sovereign grace of God not only for salvation, but also for the "right" apprehension of revealed truth by which salvation is obtained and the kingdom of God is advanced. That this is the case, and that a reconsideration of how we should think about the role of reason in the Princeton apologetic is long overdue,

2. B. B. Warfield, "Introduction to Francis R. Beattie's *Apologetics*," in *Selected Shorter Writings of Benjamin B. Warfield*, ed. John E. Meeter (Phillipsburg, NJ: P&R Publishing, 2001), 2:98–99.

3. William Livingstone, "The Princeton Apologetic as Exemplified by the Work of Benjamin B. Warfield and J. Gresham Machen: A Study in American Theology 1880–1930" (PhD diss., Yale University, 1948), 186.

4. For this appeal, see Warfield, "Introduction to Francis R. Beattie's *Apologetics*," in *Shorter Writings*, 2:99–100, and B. B. Warfield, "A Review of *De Zekerheid des Geloofs*," in *Shorter Writings*, 2:120–21.

5. B. B. Warfield, "Christianity the Truth," in *Shorter Writings*, 2:213.

will be clear after a brief examination of how both objective and subjective factors—the head and the heart—are related in Warfield's religious epistemology.

The Knowledge of God and Religious Faith

The "Simplicity" of the Soul

Warfield argues that the proper context for thinking about the knowledge of God is that which is found in Augustine's ontology of "theistic Intuitionalism" and Calvin's conception of the *sensus deitatis*. Whereas Augustine maintains that "innate ideas" are "the immediate product in the soul of God the Illuminator, always present with the soul as its sole and indispensable Light, in which alone it perceives truth,"[6] Calvin insists that the knowledge of God, as a fact of self-consciousness that is quickened by the manifestations of God in nature and providence, "is given in the very same act by which we know self. For when we know self, we must know it as it is: and that means we must know it as dependent, derived, imperfect, and responsible being."[7]

Although Warfield concedes there are "some very interesting and some very significant differences" between the religious epistemologies of Augustine and Calvin, he argues that their doctrines of knowledge are essentially the same for two important reasons.[8] The first has to do with "the theistic conception of the constant dependence of the creature on God."[9] According to Warfield, both Augustine and Calvin acknowledge that human beings are absolutely dependent on

6. B. B. Warfield, "Augustine's Doctrine of Knowledge and Authority," in *Tertullian and Augustine*, vol. 4, *The Works of Benjamin Breckinridge Warfield* (Grand Rapids: Baker, 1991; 1930), 143–44.

7. B. B. Warfield, "Calvin's Doctrine of the Knowledge of God," in *Calvin and Calvinism*, vol. 5, *The Works of Benjamin Breckinridge Warfield* (Grand Rapids: Baker, 1991; 1931), 31. Cf. B. B. Warfield, "God and Human Religion and Morals," in *Shorter Writings*, 1:41–45.

8. Warfield, "Calvin's Doctrine of the Knowledge of God," 117. Warfield argues that "with Augustine's profound sense of dependence on God and his vital conviction of the necessity of grace for all that is good in man, in the whole circle of his activities, he could not fail to work out a general doctrine of the knowledge of God in all essentials the same as Calvin's. In point of fact, as we have already pointed out, he did so." Ibid.

9. Warfield, "Augustine's Doctrine of Knowledge and Authority," 145.

the sovereign grace of God not only for their enduring existence from one moment to the next, but also for everything that they know or will ever learn about what God has revealed. Indeed, both recognize that God is not only the source of all life and the ground of all truth, but—in one way or another—"the Light of all knowledge" as well.[10]

The second reason has to do with the relationship between the knowledge of God and the religious lives of those who are made in his image. According to Warfield, both Augustine and Calvin are convinced that the knowledge of God that is reflected into the soul and quickened by the manifestations of God in nature and providence is the source not just of what we know about God, but of religious expression as well. Indeed, both recognize that religious life is grounded not in the determination of a will that is presumed to have the ability to act independently of the understanding or even, more remarkably, of God, but in the religious reaction of the "whole man"[11] to the knowledge of God that is ours by way of revelation.

The justification for this contention is found in their realization "that knowledge is not a function of the intellect merely but involves the whole man."[12] According to Warfield, both Augustine and Calvin embrace a philosophical psychology that regards the soul as a single "unit"[13] that engages "as a whole in all its acts."[14] The "human spirit does not function . . . in sections"[15] but always acts as a single sub-stance, they argue, and this is why "the religious truth which impinges

10. Ibid., 143. Among the places where Augustine's and Calvin's doctrines of the knowledge of God appear to be more at odds than they in fact are, Warfield argues, is the following: "It is interesting to note . . . that where Calvin speaks of an innate *sensus deitatis* in man, as lying at the root of all his knowledge of God, Augustine, with a more profound ontology of this knowledge . . . speaks of a continuous reflection of a knowledge of Himself by God in the human mind. There is here, however, probably only a difference in fullness of statement, or at most only of emphasized aspect." Warfield, "Calvin's Doctrine of the Knowledge of God," 117.

11. Warfield, "Augustine's Doctrine of Knowledge and Authority," 150.

12. Ibid.

13. B. B. Warfield, "Authority, Intellect, Heart," in *Shorter Writings*, 2:668. This short yet extremely important essay clearly establishes that Warfield endorsed a bipartite, heart-centered psychology. In this regard, see also Warfield, "Augustine's Doctrine of Knowledge and Authority," 150–51.

14. Warfield, "Augustine's Doctrine of Knowledge and Authority," 151.

15. B. B. Warfield, review of *Van Den Eeuwigen Vrede Tusshen Wetenshap en Religie*, by H. Visscher, and *Professor Visscher's Rectorale Rede*, by H. W. van der Vaart Smit, in *CR*, vol. 10, *The Works of Benjamin Breckinridge Warfield* (Grand Rapids: Baker, 1991; 1932), 477.

upon [man] must affect him in all of his activities, or in none."[16] What this suggests, then, is that for Augustine and Calvin as well as for Warfield, the knowledge of God that is reflected into the soul and quickened by the manifestations of God in nature and providence is at the foundation not just of the conceptions that we have about God and about the world in which we live, but of religious expression as well, for the knowledge that is received by "the souls of men" can never— given what Warfield calls "the simplicity of the soul"[17]—"be otiose and inert; but must produce an effect in human souls, in the way of thinking, feeling, willing."[18] It must produce, in other words, an effect that manifests itself first in the conceptual formulation of perceived truth, i.e., in perception "ripening" into conception,[19] and second in the religious reaction of the will—which Warfield defines broadly to include not just the "faculty of determination" but the "whole voluntary nature" of the agent that knows[20]—to the conceptual content of this formulated perception. Among other things, this explains why Warfield insists that "as is the perception ripening into conception, so is the religion."[21]

The Knowledge of God and the "Ethical State" of the Knowing Soul

But if it is the knowledge of God that is reflected into the soul that "underlies" the religious reaction of the will,[22] then why, we must ask, are there so many forms of religious expression? Why, in other words, do not all rational agents respond to their consciousness of dependence on God and to the knowledge of God that is manifest in both nature and providence in the same fashion? The

16. Warfield, "Authority, Intellect, Heart," in *Shorter Writings*, 2:668.

17. Warfield, "Augustine's Doctrine of Knowledge and Authority," 150.

18. Warfield, "Calvin's Doctrine of the Knowledge of God," 37.

19. B. B. Warfield, review of *Foundations: A Statement of Christian Belief in Terms of Modern Thought*, by Seven Oxford Men, in *CR*, 325.

20. Warfield, "Augustine's Doctrine of Knowledge and Authority," 150n37.

21. Warfield, review of *Foundations*, 325; cf. B. B. Warfield, "The Idea of Systematic Theology," in *Studies in Theology*, vol. 9, *The Works of Benjamin Breckinridge Warfield* (Grand Rapids: Baker, 1991; 1932), 53–54; Warfield, "Calvin's Doctrine of the Knowledge of God," 37–38.

22. B. B. Warfield, "On Faith in Its Psychological Aspects," in *Studies in Theology*, 314.

answer is found in Warfield's warning against supposing that "the human mind is passive in the acquisition of knowledge, or that the acquisition of knowledge is unconditioned by the nature or state of the acquiring soul."[23] While Warfield insists the religious reaction of the will is determined by the conceptual formulation of perceived truth, he nonetheless recognizes that the conceptual formulation of perceived truth is itself conditioned by the moral or "ethical state,"[24] i.e., the "personality,"[25] of the knowing soul. It is the "ethical state" of the knowing soul that determines the religious reaction of the will, he argues, for it is the "ethical state" of the soul that conditions the purity or clarity of perception, and thereby the purity or clarity of the conception that informs religious expression.[26] Since knowledge is a function of the "whole man" rather than of the rational faculty alone, it follows that there is more than one form of religious expression, simply because the knowledge that engenders the religious reaction of the will is qualified and conditioned by the "whole voluntary nature" of the agent that knows.

How, though, is the conception of the mind related to the religious reaction of the will? Why, in other words, does Warfield believe that "the nature of our [theological] conceptions so far from having nothing, [has] everything, to do with religion"?[27] The answer is found in Warfield's understanding of the mental movement called faith.[28] In

23. Warfield, "Augustine's Doctrine of Knowledge and Authority," 149.
24. Ibid., 149n37. Cf. Warfield, "Calvin's Doctrine of the Knowledge of God," 31–32, 38; B. B. Warfield, "Augustine and the Pelagian Controversy," in *Tertullian and Augustine*, 295–96, 401–4.
25. Warfield, "On Faith in Its Psychological Aspects," 336. Hoffecker notes that "Alexander's and Hodge's concern for the content of faith plus the role of man's subjective aspect is maintained intact by Warfield." Andrew Hoffecker, *Piety and the Princeton Theologians: Archibald Alexander, Charles Hodge, and Benjamin Warfield* (Phillipsburg, NJ: P&R Publishing; and Grand Rapids: Baker, 1981), 117.
26. According to Warfield, "If the condition of all knowledge . . . is revelation, and therefore all knowledge is in its source divine; yet it is equally true that the qualification of all knowledge is rooted in the human nature that knows, and in the specific state of the human being whose particular knowledge it is. It is in this fact that the varying degrees of purity in which knowledge is acquired by men find their explanation." Warfield, "Augustine's Doctrine of Knowledge and Authority," 149–50.
27. B. B. Warfield, *The Power of God Unto Salvation* (Philadelphia: The Presbyterian Board of Publishing and Sabbath-School Work, 1903), 243–44.
28. Warfield suggests that the difference between convictions of *faith* and convictions of *knowledge* is found in the prominence of "trust" in convictions of faith. According to Warfield,

response to the notion that responsibility attaches to faith only when the act of faith is grounded in the "free volition" of an autonomous moral agent, Warfield argues that we are responsible for our faith, simply because faith—from its lowest to its highest forms—is an act of the mind, the subject of which is "the man in the entirety of his being as man."[29] While Warfield acknowledges that the mental movement called faith "fulfills itself" or is specifically "formed" in that voluntary movement of the sensibility called trust, he insists that the act itself includes—indeed is based on—"a mental recognition of what is before the mind, as objectively true and real, and therefore depends on the evidence that a thing is true and real and is determined by this evidence; it is the response of the mind to this evidence and cannot arise apart from it."[30] Since faith is a mental conviction that as such is "determined by evidence, not by volition," we must conclude that for Warfield the act of faith is best defined as that "forced consent" in which "the movement of the sensibility in the form of trust is what is thrust forward to observation."[31]

Faith as a "Forced Consent"

In what sense, though, is faith a "forced consent"? While Warfield insists that the fulfillment of faith in the movement of trust is determined or "forced" by the substance of what is rationally perceived, he never suggests that the "consent" of the mind is "the mechanical result of the adduction of the evidence."[32] "There may stand in the

---

"trust" is "the active expression of that sense of dependence in which religion largely consists." Warfield, "On Faith in Its Psychological Aspects," 331–32. In other words, it is the active expression of that sense "which always abides as the innermost essence of the whole crowd of emotions which we speak of as religious, the lowest and also the highest." B. B. Warfield, "God and Human Religion and Morals," in *Shorter Writings*, 1:42. For a brief discussion of both the difference between and the interdependence of "faith" and "knowledge," see Warfield, "On Faith in Its Psychological Aspects," 325–30.

29. Warfield, "On Faith in Its Psychological Aspects," 341.

30. Ibid., 315, 342.

31. Ibid., 317, 331.

32. Ibid., 314, 336. In reflections on John 5:44, Warfield asks, "Is it not plain to you that it is not evidence alone that produces faith? Did the abundant evidence of the Divine mission of Christ convince the Jews; who sought His life the more vindictively for every item of evidence they could not resist; who answered His demonstration of deity by hanging Him on the tree? Nay, be the evidence never so perfect, we cannot believe who have evil hearts of unbelief. Never

way of the proper and objectively inevitable effect of the evidence," he argues, "the subjective nature or condition to which the evidence is addressed."[33] But how can this be? If faith is indeed a "forced consent," then how can Warfield deny that there is an "exact correlation" between the "objective adequacy" of the evidence that is rationally perceived and the "subjective effect" that the evidence will have on those who perceive it?[34]

The answer is found in Warfield's insistence that faith "does not follow the evidence itself . . . but the judgment of the intellect on the evidence."[35] According to Warfield, the "judgment of the intellect" does not have to do with an act of the rational faculty alone, but with an act of the "whole man" in which the "complex of emotions" that reflects the "ethical state" of the soul and forms the "concrete state of mind" of the perceiving agent plays the decisive or determining role.[36] What role, then, does the "complex of emotions" play in the assessment of what God has revealed, and why is the "judgment of the intellect" therefore the most prominent element in the movement of assent, the "central movement in all faith"?[37] In short, Warfield argues that the "complex of emotions" plays the decisive role in the "judgment of the intellect" because it determines both the "accessibility" of the mind to the objective force of the evidence in question, and the religious reaction of the will—broadly understood to include the "whole voluntary nature" of the agent that knows—to the substance of what is rationally perceived.[38] Given Warfield's emphasis on the unitary operation of the soul, what this suggests is that the "judgment of the intellect"

---

until that Divine voice, freighted with supernatural power, which said to the impotent man, Arise, take up thy bed and walk, has sounded with a personal message to our souls, do we gain the power to believe, though Moses himself and the law written in our hearts pronounce us inexcusable." B. B. Warfield, "Looking to Men," in *Faith and Life* (Edinburgh: The Banner of Truth Trust, 1974; 1916), 98–99.

33. Warfield, "On Faith in Its Psychological Aspects," 336.

34. Ibid., 318.

35. Ibid.

36. Ibid., 314, 331.

37. Ibid., 341. The movement of assent is the central movement in faith because it "must depend" on a prior movement of the intellect, and the movement of the sensibilities in the act of "trust" is the "product" of assent. Thus assent unites the intellectual and the volitional components of faith. Cf. ibid., 341–42.

38. Ibid., 336–37; cf. Warfield, review of *The Christian Faith: A System of Dogmatics*, by Theodore Haering, in *CR*, 412.

is at the foundation of the moral agent's religious response to what God has revealed because the "complex of emotions" that reflects the "ethical state" of the soul and forms the "concrete state of mind" of the perceiving agent also determines the activity of the will, broadly understood. As such, when the evidence that is being perceived has the objective capacity to "force" the "consent" of the mind, it follows that the "consent" of the mind in fact will be "forced"—and the moral agent will embrace what God has revealed in saving faith—if the perceiving mind is "accessible" to the objective force of the evidence in question. For Warfield, then, it is this understanding of faith as a "simple" act of the "whole man" that explains why human beings are responsible for their faith even though faith—in all its manifestations—is a "forced consent." Faith, he argues,

> is not merely a question of evidence but of subjectivity; and subjectivity is the other name for personality. Our action under evidence is the touchstone by which is determined what we are. If evidence which is objectively adequate is not subjectively adequate the fault is in us. If we are not accessible to musical evidence, then we are by nature unmusical, or in a present state of unmusicalness. If we are not accessible to moral evidence, then we are either unmoral, or, being moral beings, immoral. The evidence to which we are accessible is irresistible if adequate, and irresistibly produces belief, faith. And no belief, faith can arise except on the ground of evidence duly apprehended, appreciated, weighed.[39]

39. Warfield, "On Faith in Its Psychological Aspects," 336. Note that it is Warfield's emphasis on subjectivity—which grounds his contention that "our action under evidence is the touchstone by which is determined what we are"—that accounts for his insistence that "parabolic teaching" is "the test of men. Whether men understand or do not understand the teaching veiled in the parable," he argues, "is the revelation of their state of mind and heart, or, as it is fashionable nowadays to call it, of their receptivity. Parabolic teaching then comes into the world as a rock of decision; those who are open to the truth understand, those not open to the truth do not understand. . . . [In fact,] All teaching as to divine and heavenly things is, in a measure, parabolic; we can reach above the world and ourselves only by symbols. All such teaching comes to us, then, as a test, and the proximate account of its varied reception may be found in the condition of the ears that hear it. Have we ears to hear this music? Or does it beat a vain jangling discord only in our ears? The philosophy of the progress of the Kingdom in the world rests on the one fact—the condition of the hearer. He that has ears to hear, hears; he that has no ears to hear this music, remains unmoved." B. B. Warfield, "Light and Shining," in *Faith and Life*, 62–63.

Merely Rational versus Saving Faith

The foregoing analysis has established that for Warfield, faith is both the vital effect of the knowledge of God in the human soul and the necessary product of the natural sense of dependence because it is the response of the "whole man" to the knowledge of God that is reflected into the soul and quickened by the manifestations of God in nature and providence. The question that we must now consider has to do with the nature of "saving" faith. If it is indeed true that "no man exists, or ever has existed or ever will exist, who has not 'faith,'"[40] then what for Warfield sets the faith that saves apart from the faith that cannot save? The forthcoming discussion answers this question by examining the nature of faith in sinners who are regenerate and sinners who are unregenerate. What it suggests is that sinners who are regenerate form their consciousness of dependence in a manner that saves because they have what unregenerated sinners will never have apart from an outpouring of the special grace of God, namely, the moral ability to see revealed truth more or less for what it objectively is, namely glorious.

The Faith of "Abnormal Man"

Again following Augustine and Calvin, Warfield maintains that "it is knowledge, not nescience, which belongs to human nature as such."[41] Had human nature not been disordered by the "abnormal" condition of original sin, he argues, all moral agents—"by the very necessity of [their] nature"[42]—not only would have known God in the fullest creaturely sense of the term, but they would have entrusted themselves to his care because their consciousness of dependence would have taken "the 'form' of glad and loving trust."[43] When

40. Warfield, "On Faith in Its Psychological Aspects," 338.
41. Warfield, "Augustine's Doctrine of Knowledge and Authority," 158.
42. Warfield, "Calvin's Doctrine of the Knowledge of God," 36, 43.
43. Warfield, "Review of *De Zekerheid des Geloofs*," in *Shorter Writings*, 2:116; cf. Warfield, "On Faith in Its Psychological Aspects," 338. On the relationship between "the disease of sin" and Warfield's contention that "Man as we know him is not normal man," see Warfield, "Augustine's Doctrine of Knowledge and Authority," 156–58; Warfield, "Calvin's Doctrine of the Knowledge of God," 32, 70.

Adam fell and lost his original righteousness, however, this capacity for true knowledge and loving trust was lost, for Adam's sin plunged his posterity into a state of spiritual death.[44] Why, then, does spiritual death prevent the unregenerate from responding to the knowledge of God that is reflected into their souls in a loving and trusting fashion? The answer has to do with the "noetic as well as thelematic and ethical effects" of the fall.[45] Warfield argues that the unregenerate remain indifferent—indeed hostile—to the truth of what God has revealed because the knowledge of God that is reflected into their souls is "dulled," "deflected," and twisted by the power of sin.[46] Whereas "unfallen man" had an intimate knowledge of God because the truth of God was reflected in his consciousness with clarity, the unregenerate are incapable of such knowledge and love because the sinful heart "refracts and deflects the rays of truth reflected into it from the divine source, so rendering the right perception of the truth impossible."[47] While "abnormal man" thus remains conscious of his dependence on God and believes in God in an intellectual or speculative sense, he can neither "delight" in this dependence nor can he place his trust in the God on whom he knows he is dependent because the truth of God is deflected by a corrupt nature "into an object of distrust, fear, and hate."[48]

Since the unregenerate remain conscious of their dependence on God yet form this consciousness by fear and hate rather than by loving trust, it follows—given the intimate nature of the relationship between the conception of the mind and the religious reaction of the will—that they are unable to respond to their consciousness of

44. On the nature of Adam's federal headship, see, for example, B. B. Warfield, "Imputation," in *Studies in Theology*, 301–9; B. B. Warfield, "Repentance and Original Sin," in *Shorter Writings*, 1:278–82.

45. Warfield, "Augustine's Doctrine of Knowledge and Authority," 158.

46. Warfield, "Calvin's Doctrine of the Knowledge of God," 32; cf. Warfield, "Augustine's Doctrine of Knowledge and Authority," 155–56.

47. Warfield, "Augustine's Doctrine of Knowledge and Authority," 155. According to Warfield, "The sole cause of the failure of the natural revelation is to be found . . . in the corruption of the human heart." Warfield, "Calvin's Doctrine of the Knowledge of God," 44. On the failure of general revelation, see ibid., 39–45.

48. Warfield, "On Faith in Its Psychological Aspects," 338–39; Warfield, "God and Human Religion and Morals," in *Shorter Writings*, 1:42; cf. Warfield, "Review of *De Zekerheid des Geloofs*," in *Shorter Writings*, 2:116.

dependence in glad and loving trust because they do not have the moral ability to do so. Herein lies the heart of the depravity that constitutes the fallen condition. While the unregenerated sinner cannot escape the knowledge that he is and always will be dependent on God for the entirety of his existence, he is morally incapable of entrusting himself to God because "he loves sin too much,"[49] and thus cannot use his will—which in the narrower sense is "ready, like a weathercock, to be turned whithersoever the breeze that blows from the heart ('will' in the broader sense) may direct"[50]— for believing. As such, the unregenerated sinner neither will nor can trust in God, not because there is an objective deficiency in the substance of what God has revealed, nor because there is a physical defect in the constitution of his being that prevents him from seeing clearly or from doing what he truly desires, but because his sinful heart lacks the moral ability to "explicate" its sense of dependence and obligation "on right lines."[51] It lacks the moral ability to form its consciousness of dependence in glad and loving trust, in other words, because it is blind to the true significance of what it can rationally perceive.[52]

The Work of the Spirit

What hope is there, then, for fallen sinners who are blind to the true significance of what they can rationally perceive? Does the fallen condition prevent the descendants of Adam from ever delighting in the knowledge of God that is theirs by way of revelation? According to Warfield, there is hope for fallen sinners because God has rescued them from their "intellectual imbecility"[53] by giving them a supernatural revelation that "supplements" and "completes" the

49. B. B. Warfield, "Inability and the Demand of Faith," in *Shorter Writings*, 2:725; cf. Warfield, "On Faith in Its Psychological Aspects," 339.

50. Warfield, "Augustine and the Pelagian Controversy," 403–4.

51. Warfield, "God and Human Religion and Morals," in *Shorter Writings*, 1:44.

52. For a more comprehensive discussion of the relationship between the inability to see revealed truth for what it objectively is and the "infinite variety" of "religions and moralities" that are produced by "reprobate minds," cf. ibid., 1:42–44.

53. Warfield, "Augustine's Doctrine of Knowledge and Authority," 159–60; cf. Warfield, "Calvin's Doctrine of the Knowledge of God," 47.

truth that he has given them in general revelation.[54] Whereas God reveals himself in a more general sense in the natural constitution of the moral agent as well as in nature and providence, this general revelation "is insufficient that sinful man should know Him aright" because it is not reflected clearly in minds that are blinded by sin.[55] In order to remedy this inability to know God aright, God therefore reveals himself to fallen sinners in a fashion that is adapted to their needs. It is this special revelation, the purpose of which is to "neutralize" the noetic effects of sin by providing a "mitigation for the symptom," that then serves as the primary reference point for the "proper assimilation" of the knowledge of God that is manifest in general revelation.[56] "What special revelation is, therefore—and the Scriptures as its documentation—is very precisely represented by the figure of the spectacles. It is aid to the dulled vision of sinful man, to enable it to see God."[57]

While special revelation as such is "the condition of all right knowledge of higher things for sinful man,"[58] it is clear that this revelation alone—its objective adequacy notwithstanding—will not yield true and compelling knowledge of God if the soul to which it is addressed is morally incapable of discerning the wisdom of what it teaches. What this suggests, then, is that sinners who are at enmity with God need more than external aid to see what God has revealed for what it objectively is; they need "the power of sight."[59] They need, in other words, a remedy for their spiritual blindness so that "the light of the Word itself

54. B. B. Warfield, "Christianity and Revelation," in *Shorter Writings*, 1:27.

55. Warfield, "Calvin's Doctrine of the Knowledge of God," 32; cf. Warfield, "Augustine's Doctrine of Knowledge and Authority," 222.

56. Warfield, "Augustine's Doctrine of Knowledge and Authority," 159, 222.

57. Warfield, "Calvin's Doctrine of the Knowledge of God," 69. Warfield suggests that general and special revelation together form an "organic whole" that includes all that God has done to make himself known. As such, special revelation was not given to supersede general revelation, but to meet the altered circumstances occasioned by the advent of sin. Cf. B. B. Warfield, "Christianity and Revelation," in *Shorter Writings*, 1:28.

58. Warfield, "Augustine's Doctrine of Knowledge and Authority," 161. Note that Warfield's reference to "higher things" in this quotation ought not to be interpreted as referring merely to "spiritual" or "supernatural" kinds of things. The discussion in the preceding paragraph, as well as the discussion in the forthcoming chapter and in Part Two of this study, suggests that the "right knowledge" made possible by special revelation has to do with "all things," including "scientific" or "natural" kinds of things.

59. Warfield, "Calvin's Doctrine of the Knowledge of God," 70.

can accredit itself to them as light."[60] Wherein, then, is this remedy found? According to Warfield, it is found generally in the work of the Spirit in the new birth, and specifically in the testimony of the Spirit to the truthfulness of what God has revealed in his Word.[61] While the subjective corruption of the fallen sinner prevents the truth of God from being "hospitably received" by the unregenerated mind and heart,[62] the work of the Spirit makes it possible for fallen sinners to see what God has revealed with more or less clarity by inclining the powers of their souls "in the love of God."[63] Indeed, the Spirit enables the regenerate to "feel, judge, and act differently from what [they] otherwise should,"[64] for the Spirit renews their moral natures and thereby alters the certain operation of their souls. As a consequence, those who have been born again "recognize God where before [they] did not perceive Him; [they] trust and love Him where before [they] feared and hated Him; [and they] firmly embrace Him in His Word where before [they] turned indifferently away."[65]

60. Ibid., 32.

61. Please note that at this point Warfield is following Calvin's understanding of the remedy rather than that of Augustine. According to Warfield, "it is highly significant that, instead of Calvin's doctrine of the testimony of the Spirit, Augustine, in conformity with the stress he laid upon the 'Church' and the 'means of grace' in the conference of grace, speaks of the knowledge of God as attainable only 'in the Church.' Accordingly, in him also and his successors there are to be found only such anticipations specifically of the doctrine of the testimony of the Spirit as are afforded by the increased frequency of their references to the dependence of man for all knowledge of God and divine things on grace and the inward teaching of the heavenly Instructor. The voice of men may assail our ears, says Augustine, for instance, but those remain untaught 'to whom that inward unction does not speak, whom the Holy Spirit does not inwardly teach': for 'He who teaches the heart has His seat in heaven.' Moses himself, yea, even if he spoke to us not in Hebrew but in our own tongue, could convey to us only the knowledge of what he said: of the truth of what he said, only the Truth Himself, speaking within us, in the secret chamber of our thought, can assure us though He speaks neither in Hebrew nor in Greek nor in Latin, nor yet in any tongue of the barbarians, but without organs of voice or tongue and with no least syllabic sound. Further than this men did not get before the Reformation. . . . But such occasional remarks as this could not fail wherever the Augustinian conception of grace was vitally felt; and show only that the doctrine of the testimony of the Spirit was always implicit in that doctrine." Warfield, "Calvin's Doctrine of the Knowledge of God," 117–19.

62. Cf. Warfield, "God and Human Religion and Morals," in *Shorter Writings*, 1:43.

63. Warfield, "On Faith in Its Psychological Aspects," 339. On the relationship between regeneration and the "habits or dispositions" that govern the activity of the soul, cf. B. B. Warfield, "Regeneration," in *Shorter Writings*, 2:323; B. B. Warfield, "New Testament Terms Descriptive of the Great Change," in *Shorter Writings*, 1:267–77.

64. Warfield, "Calvin's Doctrine of the Knowledge of God," 111.

65. Ibid.

The Faith of "Renewed Man"

Yet how, specifically, does the work of the Spirit ensure that fallen sinners will embrace what God has revealed in saving faith? Why, in other words, is the work of the Spirit effectual? According to Warfield, the work of the Spirit is effectual because it implants—or rather restores—"a spiritual sense in the soul by which God is recognized in His Word."[66] It is this restoration of susceptibility to spiritual truth, he argues, that then has two immediate effects on the regenerated agent. In the first place, it enables the regenerated agent to reason "rightly." Although Warfield acknowledges that the testimony of the Spirit is not revelation in the strict sense of the term, he insists that it "is just God Himself in His intimate working in the human heart, opening it to the light of the truth, that by this illumination it may see things as they really are and so recognize God in the Scriptures with the same directness and surety as men recognize sweetness in what is sweet and brightness in what is bright."[67] Despite the fact that the work of the Spirit thus "presupposes the objective revelation and only prepares the heart to respond to and embrace it," nevertheless it is the source of all our "right knowledge" of God because it is the means by which regenerated sinners are enabled to "see" through the spectacles of Scripture, i.e., to discern not only the truthfulness, but also the beauty and excellence of what God has revealed.[68]

If the work of the Spirit is effectual in the first place because it is the means by which the regenerate are enabled to see and know things "as they really are," it is so in the second because it is the less direct though no less effectual means to the rise of saving faith in the regenerated soul. The justification for this contention is found in the subtleties of Warfield's philosophical psychology (which, it should be clear, is very similar to that of Alexander and Hodge). Because he recognizes that there is an intimate relationship between the conception of the mind and the religious reaction of the will, Warfield insists that a "right" apprehension of what God has revealed will immediately and irresistibly manifest itself in an act of saving faith because the sense that informs

66. Ibid., 33.
67. Ibid., 32, 79, 111–12.
68. Ibid., 32, 70, 79, 121.

the perception of the mind is the same sense that determines the activity of the will, broadly understood. Since the knowledge of God that is communicated to the regenerated soul via the "conjoint divine action" of Word and Spirit is a "vital and vitalizing knowledge of God" that "takes hold of the whole man in the roots of his activities and controls all the movements of his soul,"[69] we must conclude that the testimony of the Spirit renders both true knowledge and saving faith absolutely certain because it is the implanted sense of the divine that "forces" the regenerated sinner to see and pursue that which he perceives (rightly) to be both true and trustworthy. It follows, therefore, that

> If sinful man as such is incapable of the act of faith, because he is in-habile to the evidence on which alone such an act of confident resting on God the Saviour can repose, renewed man is equally incapable of not responding to this evidence, which is objectively compelling, by an act of sincere faith. In this its highest exercise faith thus, though in a true sense the gift of God, is in an equally true sense man's own act, and bears all the character of faith as it is exercised by unrenewed man in its lower manifestations.[70]

The Task of Apologetics and the Appeal to "Right Reason"

Having established that the "keystone" of Warfield's doctrine of the knowledge of God is found in the "conjoint divine action" of Word and Spirit,[71] the question that we must finally consider has to do with how we should interpret his apologetical appeal to "right reason." Must we conclude, along with the consensus of critical opinion, that Warfield was a rationalist whose approach to apologetics was grounded in an almost "Pelagian confidence"[72] in the epistemic competence of the human mind? Must we conclude, in other words, that Warfield's apologetic was indebted to epistemological assumptions that are diametrically

69. Ibid., 31, 75.
70. Warfield, "On Faith in Its Psychological Aspects," 337–38. On the essential correspondence between faith in "renewed man" and faith in "unfallen man," see 340.
71. Warfield, "Calvin's Doctrine of the Knowledge of God," 113; cf. 82–83.
72. Jack Rogers and Donald McKim, *The Authority and Interpretation of the Bible* (San Francisco: Harper & Row, 1979), 290.

opposed to those of the Reformed tradition? The remainder of this chapter argues that we must not, unless we want to seriously misrepresent Warfield's understanding of the task of apologetics.

The Character of Warfield's "Intellectualism"

Before we unpack this argument, however, let us suggest a plausible conclusion to what we have learned thus far about Warfield's religious epistemology, for doing so will help us understand the true character of Warfield's "intellectualism." To this point we have seen that both objective and subjective factors are of critical importance in Warfield's religious epistemology because the soul is a single unit that acts in all of its functions as a single substance. Given Warfield's philosophical psychology, we may plausibly conclude that his "intellectualism" finds its likely genesis not in the accommodation of one form of Enlightenment rationalism or another, but in the desire to preserve two important elements of the Reformed tradition in an increasingly subjectivistic age. The first has to do with the classical Reformed distinction between a merely speculative and a spiritual understanding of what God has revealed. Because he recognizes that the "ethical state" of the soul determines the quality of an agent's perception and conception, Warfield maintains there is "a shallower and a deeper sense of the word 'knowledge'—a purely intellectualistic sense, and a sense that involves the whole man and all his activities."[73] While he concedes that all moral agents are religious beings because all moral agents "know God" in at least an intellectual or speculative sense, he insists that the regenerate alone know God in a spiritual or saving sense, because it is only in the souls of the regenerate that there is "perfect interaction" between the objective and subjective factors that inform religious epistemology and underlie religious belief and practice.[74] Since Warfield is convinced that "real" knowledge of God involves the "whole soul," and as such "is inseparable from movements of piety towards Him,"[75] it is clear that

73. B. B. Warfield, "Theology a Science," in *Shorter Writings*, 2:210.
74. Warfield, "Authority, Intellect, Heart," in *Shorter Writings*, 2:669; cf. Warfield, "Review of *De Zekerheid des Geloofs*," in *Shorter Writings*, 2:115ff.
75. Warfield, "Calvin's Doctrine of the Knowledge of God," 37. Note that for Warfield, the kind of knowledge that Paul desires for his readers in Eph. 3:14–19 "is not merely external

the charge of rationalism cannot be sustained because there is more in his thought to a saving apprehension of what God has revealed than the rational appropriation of objective evidence.

If Warfield's "intellectualism" is inspired on the one hand by the desire to safeguard the enduring relevance of the distinction between a merely speculative and a spiritual understanding of what God has revealed, it is driven on the other by the eagerness to uphold the foundational principle of Augustinian and Reformed piety in an increasingly anthropocentric age, namely that "It is God and God alone who saves, and that in every element of the saving process."[76] Whereas the vast majority of Warfield's contemporaries were reducing the Christian religion to a natural phenomenon by bending Scripture "into some sort of conciliation" with the latest pronouncements of modern science, philosophy, and scholarship,[77] Warfield was eager to champion both the objective foundation of the Christian faith and the absolute sovereignty of God in salvation by grounding the gift of saving faith in the ability to reason "rightly." "Christianity is not," he argues, "a distinctive interpretation of a religious experience common to all men, much less is it an indeterminate and constantly changing interpretation of a religious experience common to men; it is a distinctive religious experience begotten in men by a distinctive body of facts known only to or rightly apprehended only by Christians."[78] Since Warfield was convinced that saving faith—as an act with "cognizable ground in right reason"—is both a "moral act and the gift of God,"[79] we must conclude

---

mind-knowledge, but the real knowledge of full feeling and apprehension; knowledge not of the mere head but of the heart. And for this, something more is needed than the mere proclaiming of the Gospel, which may be grasped in its propositions by the mere mechanical action of the intellect: even a new heart, Spirit-made and Spirit-determined." B. B. Warfield, "The Fullness of God," in *Faith and Life*, 284. For more on how objective and subjective factors are related in "sound religion" and "true religious thinking," and on how there is a symbiotic relationship between religion and theology because of the unitary operation of the soul, cf. Warfield, "Authority, Intellect, Heart," in *Shorter Writings*, 2:668–71; Warfield, "Theology a Science," in *Shorter Writings*, 2:210; Andrew Hoffecker, "Benjamin B. Warfield," in *The Princeton Theology*, Reformed Theology in America, no. 1, ed. David Wells (Grand Rapids: Baker, 1989), 67.

76. B. B. Warfield, *The Plan of Salvation* (Philadelphia: Presbyterian Board of Publications, 1915), 59.

77. B. B. Warfield, "Heresy and Concession," in *Shorter Writings*, 2:675.

78. Warfield, review of *Foundations*, 325–26.

79. B. B. Warfield, "Apologetics," in *Studies in Theology*, 15.

that he was neither an overt nor a covert rationalist who undermined the sovereignty of God in salvation by emptying saving faith of its subjective and experiential components. Rather, he was a consistently Reformed scholar who recognized that because the operation of the intellect involves the "whole soul" rather than the rational faculty alone, the "taste for the divine" that informs the ability to reason "rightly" and leads to the fulfillment of faith in the movement of trust "cannot be awakened in unbelievers by the natural action of the Scriptures or any rational arguments whatever, but requires for its production the work of the Spirit of God *ab extra accidens.*"[80]

The Appeal to "Right Reason"

Given Warfield's clear stand within the epistemological mainstream of the Reformed camp, what, then, are we to make of his apologetical response to the modern era's relocation of the divine-human nexus? What are we to make, in other words, of his apologetical appeal to "right reason"? An important indication of how we should approach this question is suggested by Warfield's definition of the term "apologetics." Whereas "apologies" for Warfield are defenses of Christianity "against either all assailants, actual or conceivable, or some particular form or instance of attack," "apologetics" is "a positive and constructive science" that undertakes "not the defense, not even the vindication, but the establishment . . . of that knowledge of God which Christianity professes to embody and seeks to make efficient in the world."[81] While "apologies" thus derive their value from that which is incidental to the propagation of the Christian religion, namely the defense of Christianity against "opposing points of view," "apologetics" is of the essence of propagation because it

> finds its deepest ground . . . not in the accidents which accompany
> the efforts of true religion to plant, sustain, and propagate itself in
> this world . . . but in the fundamental needs of the human spirit. If it
> is incumbent on the believer to be able to give a reason for the faith

80. Warfield, "Calvin's Doctrine of the Knowledge of God," 124n99.
81. Warfield, "Apologetics," 3.

that is in him, it is impossible for him to be a believer without a reason for the faith that is in him; and it is the task of apologetics to bring this reason out in his consciousness and make its validity plain.[82]

When we approach Warfield's appeal to "right reason" with the positive and constructive nature of apologetics in mind, it becomes immediately clear that whatever we make of his appeal must give due consideration to the inherently offensive orientation of the apologetical task. It is this realization, then, that brings us to a critical interpretive juncture. Is the appeal that plays a primary role in the Christianizing of the world addressed to the regenerated reason of the Christian apologist, i.e., to the believer who is laboring in the public square to establish the "objective validity" of what God has revealed?[83] Or, is the appeal addressed to the potential targets of apologetical science, i.e., to unbelievers who are analyzing the grounds of faith that are being established by the Christian apologist? Whereas the consensus of critical opinion would have us believe that the appeal to "right reason" is an appeal "to the *natural man's* 'right reason' to judge of the truth of Christianity,"[84] our analysis of the relationship between the objective and the subjective components of Warfield's religious epistemology suggests a different conclusion. We have seen that the ability to reason "rightly" presupposes the regenerating activity of the Holy Spirit on the "whole soul" of a moral agent because the soul is a single unit that acts in all of its functions as a single substance. When we consider the appeal to "right reason" in this light, it follows that the appeal was not, in the first place, an invitation to unbelievers to judge the truth of what God has revealed, but a call to "the men of the palingenesis" to establish the integrity of "the Christian view of the world" by urging their " 'stronger and purer thought' continuously, and in all its details, upon the attention of

82. Ibid., 4, 15. The apologist must validate the truth that has been established, simply because faith, although it is a moral act and the gift of God, "is yet formally conviction passing into confidence." Validation is necessary, therefore, because an intellectual conviction of the truth of the Christian religion is "the logical *prius* of self-commitment to the Founder of that religion." Warfield, "Review of *De Zekerheid des Geloofs*," in *Shorter Writings*, 2:113.

83. Warfield, "Introduction to Francis R. Beattie's *Apologetics*," in *Shorter Writings*, 2:99.

84. Jack Rogers, "Van Til and Warfield on Scripture in the Westminster Confession," in *Jerusalem and Athens: Critical Discussions on the Philosophy and Apologetics of Cornelius Van Til*, ed. E. R. Geehan (Phillipsburg, NJ: Presbyterian and Reformed, 1980), 154.

men."[85] This interpretation not only does justice to the context of the appeal,[86] but more importantly it explains how Warfield could insist that the Christian religion would "*reason* its way to the dominion of the world"[87] without being a "rather bald rationalist." In short, Warfield argued that the Christian religion would bring the "thinking world"[88] into subjection to the gospel of Christ not because he had "unbounded confidence in the apologetic power of the rational appeal to people of common sense,"[89] but because he recognized that "the Christian view of the world" is true and capable of vindication "in the forum of pure reason" through the superior science of redeemed thought.[90]

> The Christian, by virtue of the palingenesis working in him, stands un-doubtedly on an indefinitely higher plane of thought than that occupied by sinful man as such. And he must not decline, but use and press the advantage which God has thus given him. He must insist, and insist again, that his determinations, and not those of the unilluminated, must be built into the slowly rising fabric of human science. Thus will he serve, if not his own generation, yet truly all the generations of men.[91]

85. Warfield, "Introduction to Francis R. Beattie's *Apologetics*," 2:102–3. While Warfield acknowledges that there "do exist . . . 'two kinds of men' in the world" who give us "two kinds of science," he insists that the difference between the science of the regenerate and the science of the unregenerate is not "a difference in *kind*," but a difference in "perfection of performance." The science of the regenerate is of a higher quality than that of the unregenerate, he argues, not because the regenerate are producing "a different kind of science," but because the entrance of regeneration produces "the better scientific outlook" and thereby "prepares men to build [the edifice of truth] better and ever more truly as the effects of regeneration increase intensively and extensively." Ibid., 2:100–2. For further discussion of this point, please see the next chapter.

86. Just as the soldier in combat appeals to his sword as the means to advance the objectives of the commander in chief, so too the Christian apologist appeals to his "right reason" as the means to bringing the "thinking world" into subjection to the gospel of Christ. To conceive of "right reason" as anything other than the offensive weapon of the Christian apologist—for instance, as the "self-established intellectual tool" of the autonomous natural man (Cornelius Van Til, "My Credo," in *Jerusalem and Athens*, 11)—is to fundamentally misconstrue the word picture being painted in the context of the appeal. It is to make Warfield guilty, moreover, of reducing the Christian religion to a natural phenomenon, and of endorsing what he elsewhere describes as "autosoterism." Cf. B. B. Warfield, "How to Get Rid of Christianity," in *Shorter Writings*, 1:60.

87. Warfield, "Review of *De Zekerheid des Geloofs*," in *Shorter Writings*, 2:120.

88. Ibid.

89. George Marsden, *Fundamentalism and American Culture: The Shaping of Twentieth-Century Evangelicalism 1870–1925* (New York: Oxford University Press, 1980), 115.

90. Warfield, "Introduction to Francis R. Beattie's *Apologetics*," in *Shorter Writings*, 2:103.

91. Ibid. Thus, the efforts of the apologist are not directed toward arguing the unregenerate into the kingdom of God, but toward establishing the "objective validity" of the Christian view

Conclusion: Warfield and the Task of Apologetics

This chapter has called the prevailing historiographical consensus into question by interpreting Warfield's "intellectualism" in a fashion that is compatible with the assumptions of the Reformed tradition. Whereas the consensus of critical opinion would have us believe that Warfield was a rationalist whose epistemology was compromised by the assumptions of Enlightenment philosophy, this chapter has demonstrated that such a conclusion cannot be justified because Warfield's "intellectualism" was moral rather than merely rational. This is historically significant not only because it challenges the rather tenuous claim that Warfield and his colleagues at Old Princeton failed to take the subjective and experiential components of a consistently Reformed religious epistemology as seriously as they should have,[92] but also because it gives us a clear understanding of why Warfield was eager to engage in the task of apologetics. While Warfield was convinced that "rational argumentation does, entirely apart from that specific operation of the Holy Ghost which produces saving faith, ground a genuine exercise of faith," nevertheless he acknowledged that "rational arguments can of themselves produce nothing more than 'historical faith.' "[93] Of what use is apologetics, then, if it can produce

---

of the world. The apologetical task, therefore, is focused primarily on the labor of the apologist, and only secondarily on the mind of the unregenerate.

92. For example, see Ernest Sandeen, "The Princeton Theology: One Source of Biblical Literalism in American Protestantism," *CH* 31 (1962): 307–19. Again, for the purposes of this chapter, I am suggesting that Warfield's epistemological assumptions are representative of those of the best thinkers at Old Princeton Seminary.

93. Warfield, "Review of *De Zekerheid des Geloofs*," in *Shorter Writings*, 2:115; cf. Hoffecker, *Piety and the Princeton Theologians*, 101–3, 108–9. While some will likely suggest that Warfield's endorsement of even the possibility of "historical faith" is evidence that he accommodated epistemological assumptions that find their genesis in the Enlightenment, Warfield insisted that the possibility of "historical faith" in fact is grounded in the objective rationality of the Christian religion. For Warfield, "The question here is not whether this *fides humana* is of any great use in the spiritual life; the question is whether it is possible and actual. We may argue that it is not worthwhile to awaken it—though opinions may differ there—but how can we argue that it is a thing inherently impossible? To say this is not merely to say that reason cannot save, which is what Calvin said and all his followers; it is to say that salvation is intrinsically unreasonable—which neither Calvin nor any of his true followers could for a moment allow. Sin may harden the heart so that it will not admit, weigh, or yield to evidence, but sin, which affects only the heart subjectively and not the process of reasoning objectively, cannot alter the relations of evidence to conclusions. Sin does not in the least degree affect the cogency of any

only "historical" and not "saving" faith? In short, Warfield insisted that "historical faith" is "of no little use in the world" because what the Holy Spirit does in the new birth is not to work "a ready-made faith, rooted in nothing and clinging without reason to its object," but "to give to a faith which naturally grows out of the proper grounds of faith, that peculiar quality which makes it saving faith."[94] Since the Holy Spirit "does not produce faith without grounds,"[95] it follows that Warfield engaged in the task of apologetics—and did so, as we will see in the next chapter, by laboring to establish the integrity of the Christian view of the world—not to argue the unregenerate into the kingdom of God, but to facilitate their engagement in the most basic activity of human existence, namely, reaction to the truth of God that is reflected into their souls and quickened by the manifestations of God in nature and in providence. As Andrew Hoffecker has incisively argued, the underlying assumption of this approach to apologetics—and, as we will see in the next chapter, to Christian scholarship—is of course that the Spirit—who blows where he wills—will enable the elect to see revealed truth more or less for what it objectively is, thereby ensuring that they will embrace what God has revealed in saving faith.[96]

---

rightly constructed syllogism. No man, no doubt, was ever reasoned into the kingdom of heaven; it is the Holy Spirit alone who can translate us into the kingdom of God's dear Son. But there are excellent reasons why every man should enter the kingdom of heaven, and these reasons are valid in the forum of every rational mind, and their validity can and should be made manifest to all." Warfield, "Calvin's Doctrine of the Knowledge of God," 124–25n99.

94. Warfield, "Review of *De Zekerheid des Geloofs*," in *Shorter Writings*, 2:115. With respect to the work of the Spirit, Warfield cites the following quote from J. Pannier with sympathy: "What we deny is that our reason—moral consciousness, religious consciousness, the term is of no importance—can, of itself, *make us see* the divinity of the Scriptures. It is this which *sees* it; but it is the Holy Spirit which *makes us see it*. He is not the inner eye for seeing the truth which is outside of us, but the supernatural hand which comes to open the eye of our consciousness—an eye which is, no doubt, divine in the sense that it too was created by God, but which has been blinded by the consequences of sin." Pannier, quoted in Warfield, "Calvin's Doctrine of the Knowledge of God," 112n79.

95. Warfield, "Review of *De Zekerheid des Geloofs*," 2:115.

96. Cf. Hoffecker, *Piety and the Princeton Theologians*, 109; Warfield, "Introduction to Francis R. Beattie's *Apologetics*," in *Shorter Writings*, 2:99. Note that this is the understanding of apologetics that informs Warfield's optimism with respect to the salvation of the whole world at the end of the age. For example, see Warfield, "God and Human Religion and Morals," in *Shorter Writings*, 1:43–44; Warfield, *The Plan of Salvation*, 125–33.

3

The Task of Christian Scholarship

A Place at the Academic Table

In *The Outrageous Idea of Christian Scholarship*, the sequel to his highly acclaimed *The Soul of the American University: From Protestant Establishment to Established Nonbelief*,[1] George Marsden proposes that "mainstream American higher education should be more open to explicit discussion of the relationship of religious faith to learning."[2] There is no compelling reason to relegate religious perspectives to the periphery of academic life, he argues, because the postmodern critique of Enlightenment standards of objectivity has neutralized the intellectual rationale for suppressing perspectives that are considered by many to be "unscientific."[3] Since the contemporary academy "on its own terms" has no consistent grounds for rejecting perspectives that "are ultimately

1. New York: Oxford University Press, 1994.
2. George Marsden, *The Outrageous Idea of Christian Scholarship* (New York: Oxford University Press, 1997), 3.
3. Ibid., 30.

grounded in some faith or another," Marsden submits that there ought to be room at the academic table for explicitly religious points of view "so long as their proponents are willing to support the rules necessary for constructive exchange of ideas in a pluralistic setting."[4] In such a setting, i.e., one where the *modus operandi* is informed by strict adherence to the ideals of the liberal pragmatic academy, the idea of self-consciously Christian scholarship will be anything but outrageous because the rules that govern the life of the academy will be applied "equally to religious and nonreligious views."[5]

While Marsden's proposal is commendable because it urges believing academics to take part in the life of the academy and to transform university life by working to improve those rules that marginalize the Christian perspective, nevertheless it may be critiqued for encouraging Christian scholars to accommodate rules of academic comportment that relegate the teaching of the Bible to the status of a mere "background belief."[6] Christians can reflect on the implications of special revelation within the bounds of the mainstream academy, Marsden contends, but they can do so only "by talking about them conditionally."[7] They cannot "argue on the basis of their special or private revelations," in other words, for such revelations are "ultimately mysterious, rather than scientific," and as such they are inaccessible to those who do not share the Christian worldview.[8]

Although such accommodation would certainly afford the Christian scholar a hearing in the postmodern academy, some are concerned that it may do so at the cost of equating—albeit unintentionally—the authority of Scripture with the authority of classic texts from other religious traditions. For many believing academics, such an approach would leave something to be desired not only because it seems to offer

4. Ibid., 30, 45.
5. Ibid., 57.
6. Ibid., 48–51. Obviously, this is not the only way that Marsden's proposal may be critiqued. For an interesting critique from a Reformed perspective that is significantly different from the assessment I am offering here, cf. D. G. Hart, "Christian Scholars, Secular Universities, and the Problem with the Antithesis," *CSR* 30, 1 (Summer 2001): 383–402. See also the thoughtful response to Hart by William C. Davis, "Contra Hart: Christian Scholars Should Not Throw in the Towel," *CSR* 34, 2 (Winter 2005): 187–200.
7. Marsden, *The Outrageous Idea of Christian Scholarship*, 52.
8. Ibid., 48, 50.

little of substance to prevent academic give and take from degenerating into mere "dialogue" (which Marsden rejects),[9] but more importantly because it could leave its practitioners open to the charge that they are covert, if not overt, "perspectivalists." According to Bruce Kuklick, "perspectivalism" is an essentially postmodern form of analysis that is problematic for the Christian scholar because believing academics do not begin "from the conceptually dubious starting point of the perspectivalist."[10] Whereas committed perspectivalists take part in the life of the academy because they suppose, as outspoken defenders of the modern distinction between religious truth and scientific truth, that there is "no rational way" of adjudicating between the competing truth claims of various ways of seeing the world,[11] the Christian takes part because he is convinced that when all is said and done, the Christian perspective and the authority upon which it is based are true, as J. Gresham Machen would say, "in the plain man's sense of the word 'truth.'"[12]

9. Cf. ibid., 45, 57–58.

10. Bruce Kuklick, "On Critical History," in *Religious Advocacy and American History*, ed. Bruce Kuklick, D. G. Hart (Grand Rapids: Eerdmans, 1997), 59–61.

11. Ibid., 59.

12. J. Gresham Machen, "The Creeds and Doctrinal Advance," in *God Transcendent*, ed. Ned Stonehouse (Edinburgh: The Banner of Truth Trust, 1982; 1949), 165. The word "perspectivalism" may be used in both benign and pernicious senses. In the benign sense, it refers to that view of epistemology that simply acknowledges that all truth claims are grounded in metaphysical perspectives or "worldviews." In the pernicious sense—the sense in which I am using the word above—it refers to that far more foundational view of epistemology that denies even the possibility of objective knowledge by reducing the worldviews that inform truth claims to the level of subjective preference. Such perspectivalism is the kiss of death to Christian scholarship, I contend, not only because it finds its genesis in a naturalistic understanding of knowledge, but more importantly because it eradicates the basis for claiming that the Christian worldview is superior—both objectively and subjectively—to all others. Let me be clear at this point that I am in no way suggesting that Marsden is a perspectivalist in this sense of the term. At the level of method, though, I wonder whether his opposition to "tendentious" scholarship lends itself to asking Christians to act *as if* they are perspectivalists in this sense of the term. Given the truthfulness of the Christian faith commitment, how do Christians in the postmodern academy go about affirming the truthfulness of the Christian worldview when doing so necessarily involves engaging in "tendentious" scholarship, which Marsden insists has no place in the academy? While I am not now proposing an answer to this question, it is difficult for me to see what strategic benefit there is in playing by rules that deem claims to absolute truth out of bounds from the start. See Marsden's discussion of "Christian schizophrenia" in *The Outrageous Idea of Christian Scholarship*, chapter 3.

The Exemplary Nature of Warfield's Apologetic

How, then, should Christians who are reluctant to relegate the authority of Scripture to the status of a "control belief" go about integrating faith and learning?[13] What posture should Christians who do not want to empty Scripture of its objective significance assume, in other words, when interacting with scholarship that is neither exclusively theological nor overtly Christian? The purpose of this chapter is neither to argue about the role of the Christian in the secular academy nor to debate the manner in which Christian commitments should be defended in a pluralistic setting. It is, rather, to place the apologetic nature of B. B. Warfield's response to the modern era's relocation of the divine-human nexus in its proper historical context, and thereby to set Warfield up as an example of an evangelical scholar who responded to the problem of the relationship between Christianity and culture in the correct fashion.[14] Whereas the vast majority of Warfield's contemporaries insisted that Christians should integrate faith and learning by bending Scripture "into some sort of conciliation" with the "latest pronouncements" of modern science, philosophy, and scholarship, Warfield countered with the orthodox contention that "The condition of right thinking . . . is . . . that the Christian man should look out upon the seething thought of the world from the safe standpoint of the sure Word of God."[15] Christians, he argued, should not adopt the "very prevalent" yet heretical tendency of looking at the teachings of God's Word "from the standpoint of the world's speculations."[16] Rather, they should repudiate the "habit of 'concession'" manifest in modern reconstructions of religious thinking and assimilate modern learning to Christian truth on the basis of "the fundamental fact of

13. Marsden, *The Outrageous Idea of Christian Scholarship*, 50.

14. In this chapter and the next, "the problem of the relationship between Christianity and culture" is being defined as the problem that centers on the question of how the Christian theologian is to reconcile the tension between the competing truth claims of Christianity and culture. According to this definition, the problem has to do with the methodological question of how biblical and extra-biblical truth claims should interact with one another in our doing of theology and in our thinking about faith.

15. B. B. Warfield, "Heresy and Concession," in *Selected Shorter Writings of Benjamin B. Warfield*, 2 vols., ed. John E. Meeter (Phillipsburg, NJ: P&R Publishing, 2001), 2:676–77, 674–75.

16. Ibid., 2:675.

Christianity—that we have a firmer ground of confidence for our religious views than any science or philosophy or criticism can provide for any of their pronouncements."[17]

While the forthcoming discussion only anticipates the more extensive analysis of Warfield's theological method in Part Two of this study, it proposes that the apologetic nature of his response to the problem of the relationship between Christianity and culture is exemplary not only because it encourages Christians to "seek" and "embrace" truth wherever it is found, but also because it tempers this encouragement with the realization that the seeking and embracing of truth must not be compromised by the pagan tendency to erect " 'Modern discovery' and 'modern thought' . . . into the norm of truth."[18] "No one should greet truth from whatever source with more readiness and more enthusiasm than [the Christian scholar]," Warfield argued,

> for the believing academic has in his hands the norm of truth, in the Word of God. This is the Ariadne clue by means of which he can thread his way through the labyrinths of the world's thought; this is the touchstone by the art of which he may choose the good and refuse the evil. So long as he clings to it he will build up the temple of truth, whencesoever he quarries the stones. When he loses hold of it, however, he descends into the arena and takes his hap with other men; and going his own way, it is not strange that he is often found with his back turned to God.[19]

Truth versus Experience

The Essence of Christianity and the Nature of Theology

Warfield's views on the nature of Christian scholarship were formed in an intellectual environment that was being overwhelmed by controversy over what ideals and values would gain cultural supremacy

17. Ibid., 2:675, 677. Assimilating modern learning to Christian truth involves sifting "the good" and " 'discarding whatever is at variance with the gospel.' " Cf. 2:675, 672.
18. Ibid., 2:674, 676–77.
19. Ibid., 2:674.

and dominate in the public square. Gary Scott Smith suggests that "in the years between the Civil War and World War I, a battle for cultural supremacy broke out on many fronts in America. Humanism, the claims of scientism, and intellectual disdain for the Bible wrestled with theism, both Christian and Jewish, for control of American public life."[20] This cultural battle did not arise in a vacuum, however, but was the immediate consequence of the crisis of religious authority manifest in the nineteenth-century debate over the essence of Christianity, particularly as it impinges on the nature of theology and its relationship to religious belief and practice. Whereas orthodox scholars insisted that religion and theology are the parallel products of the objective truth of God "operative in the two spheres of life and thought,"[21] more progressive scholars were compelled by their accommodation of culture to abandon to science the whole realm of objective truth, and consequently to regard religion and theology as distinct rather than as intimately related entities.[22] Theology, they argued, must not be regarded as that

20. Gary Scott Smith, *The Seeds of Secularization: Calvinism, Culture, and Pluralism in America 1870–1915* (Grand Rapids: Christian University Press, 1985), 39. See especially Chapter 3, "The Clash of Worldviews: Secularism vs. Calvinism."

21. B. B. Warfield, "Authority, Intellect, Heart," in *Shorter Writings*, 2:668; cf. B. B. Warfield, review of *Foundations: A Statement of Christian Belief in Terms of Modern Thought*, by Seven Oxford Men, in *CR*, vol. 10, *The Works of Benjamin Breckinridge Warfield* (Grand Rapids: Baker, 1991; 1932), 325.

22. Cf. John William Stewart, "The Tethered Theology: Biblical Criticism, Common Sense Philosophy, and the Princeton Theologians, 1812–1860" (PhD diss., University of Michigan, 1990), 79. The developments of the modern era that led to the separation of the epistemological realms of religion and science include: (1) The epistemological skepticism of Kant (cf. William Livingstone, "The Princeton Apologetic as Exemplified by the Work of Benjamin B. Warfield and J. Gresham Machen: A Study of American Theology, 1880–1930" [PhD diss., Yale University, 1948], 117–18; Andrew Hoffecker, *Piety and the Princeton Theologians: Archibald Alexander, Charles Hodge, and Benjamin Warfield* [Phillipsburg, NJ: Presbyterian and Reformed; Grand Rapids: Baker, 1981], 103); (2) The anti-intellectualism of Schleiermacher and the Romantic tradition (cf. Livingstone, "The Princeton Apologetic," 68; Stewart, "The Tethered Theology," 77–79; Lloyd Averill, *American Theology in the Liberal Tradition* [Philadelphia: The Westminster Press, 1967], 37); (3) The Absolute Idealism of Hegel, the naturalistic standards of evolutionary theory, and the relativizing influence of the historical consciousness (cf. Kenneth Cauthen, *The Impact of American Religious Liberalism* [New York: Harper & Row, 1962], 8–12; Averill, *American Theology in the Liberal Tradition*, 22–24; Ferenc Morton Szasz, *The Divided Mind of Protestant America, 1880–1930* [Tuscaloosa, AL: University of Alabama Press, 1982], 17); and (4) The progressive developments within American evangelicalism (cf. Averill, *American Theology in the Liberal Tradition*, 69; William Hutchison, *The Modernist Impulse in American Protestantism* [Cambridge, MA: Harvard University Press, 1976], 13, 48; George Marsden, *The Evangeli-*

"science of God" that systematizes the objective truths that underlie and produce religious expression.[23] Rather, it must be conceived of as that "science of faith" or "science of religion" that supplies—at the behest of the "provisional findings" of modern science, philosophy, and scholarship—merely "the intellectual interpretation" of a really inexpressible subjective experience for a particular time and place.[24] If theology is to sustain vital rather than sterile religious life in each successive age, progressive scholars reasoned, then it must articulate religious truth in a manner that is attuned to the *zeitgeist*, i.e., to the progressive activity of the divine within nature, history, and culture.

The Crisis of Religious Authority

While orthodox scholars were not unaware of the potential advantages of switching the *discrimen* in theology (or that "imaginative

---

cal Mind and the New School Presbyterian Experience [New Haven: Yale University Press, 1970]; Iain H. Murray, *Revival and Revivalism: The Making and Marring of American Evangelicalism, 1750–1858* [Edinburgh: The Banner of Truth Trust, 1994]). According to Kenneth Cauthen, these developments fostered the formulation of three principles that together characterize the template of the modern mind. These principles, the endorsement of which led to the emergence of the New Theology, are *continuity* (because of evolutionary theory and Hegel's Absolute Idealism), *autonomy* (the adoption of an internal rather than an external source of authority), and *dynamism* (because of continuity, all external standards of religious authority are provisional because all things are in the process of dynamic change). He suggests that the dominating motif of the era—the motif responsible for the critical importance of the other two—was that of continuity. Continuity, he contends, manifests itself "in every area of thought and permeates all liberal theology" (Cauthen, *The Impact of American Religious Liberalism*, 9). That Warfield would have agreed with Cauthen at this point is clear. For Warfield's take on how the concept of evolution fostered the virtual obliteration of "a distinguishable supernatural," cf. B. B. Warfield, "Christianity and Revelation," in *Shorter Writings*, 1:26–27; Warfield, "Christian Supernaturalism," in *Studies in Theology*, vol. 9, *The Works of Benjamin Breckinridge Warfield* (Grand Rapids: Baker, 1991; 1932), 28–33.

23. Orthodox scholars are convinced that just as systematic theology forms "the crown and head" of theological science, so too theology forms "the apex of the pyramid of the sciences by which the structure [of truth] is perfected." Since the subject matter of genuinely theological science "indirectly" includes "all the facts of nature and history," orthodox scholars conclude that the scope of theological science ought never to be restricted to that which is merely the subjective product of the human soul. In short, orthodox scholars are convinced that the modern distinction between religious truth and scientific truth is invalid. Cf. B. B. Warfield, "The Idea of Systematic Theology," in *Studies in Theology*, 64, 71, 72–74. On the relationship between the "parts" that constitute the organism of "theology," cf. B. B. Warfield, "The Task and Method of Systematic Theology," in *Studies in Theology*, 91–92.

24. Warfield, review of *Foundations*, 322–24.

construal" of how God is authoritatively present among the faithful)[25] from an objective to a subjective base, nevertheless they were convinced that anti-intellectualism of any kind was problematic for two important reasons.[26] It was problematic, they argued, not only because it confounds the objective subject matter of genuinely theological science with "the subjective experiences of the human heart,"[27] but more importantly because it reduces the Christian religion to a natural phenomenon by "casting . . . men back upon their 'religious experience,' corporate or individual, as their sole trustworthy ground of religious convictions."[28] Although orthodox scholars acknowledged that natural religion is valid religion insofar as it expresses the natural religious tendency of the human heart, they claimed that it is inadequate to the

25. David Kelsey, *The Uses of Scripture in Recent Theology* (Philadelphia: Fortress Press, 1975), 205–6.

26. One of the potential benefits is the elimination of the need to integrate faith and learning. If it is indeed true that religious truth is merely subjective, then there is no compelling need to relate it to the "objective" conclusions of modern scholarship. Warfield clearly believes that such anti-intellectualism is "the indirect product of unbelief, among men who would fain hold their Christian profession in the face of an onset of unbelief, which they feel too weak to withstand." Cf. B. B. Warfield, "Evading the Supernatural," in *Shorter Writings*, 2:681. On the rise of anti-intellectualism in American culture, cf. Richard Hofstadter, *Anti-Intellectualism in American Life* (New York: Vintage Books, 1962, 1963), 55–141; Ann Douglas, *The Feminization of American Culture* (New York: The Noonday Press, 1998; 1977), 3–13, 17–43, 12–64.

27. B. B. Warfield, "Apologetics," in *Studies in Theology*, 7; cf. Warfield, "The Idea of Systematic Theology," 56. Obviously, this confusion is the logical consequence of abandoning the whole realm of objective truth to science.

28. B. B. Warfield, "Mysticism and Christianity," in *Studies in Theology*, 658. The attack on the principle of external authority was waged on two fronts: the metaphysical side, "in general, a neo-Kantianism mediated through Albrecht Ritschl"; and the "mystical" side, which stressed "subjective religious experience as the norm and authority of Christian faith" (cf. Livingstone, "The Princeton Apologetic," 175–80; Warfield, "Apologetics," 14–15). On the value judgments that cultivate the religious life of the Christian community, cf. B. B. Warfield, "The Latest Phase of Historical Rationalism," in *Studies in Theology*, 591–605; B. B. Warfield, review of *Mystik und Geschichtliche Religion*, by Wilhelm Frensenius, in *CR*, 357–58; B. B. Warfield, "Introduction to Beattie's *Apologetics*," in *Shorter Writings*, 2:94. On how the mystic substitutes "his religious experience for the objective revelation of God recorded in the written Word," cf. Warfield, "Mysticism and Christianity," 651, 655. For a good summary of the relationship between Christianity, mysticism, and historical rationalism, cf. Warfield, review of *Mystik*, 362–65. On the ontology that calls the *semen deitatis* into action, cf. 359. On the relationship between the adoption of an internal standard of authority and *autonomy*, cf. Cauthen, *The Impact of American Religious Liberalism*, 12ff; and Averill, *American Theology in the Liberal Tradition*, 36ff. On the relationship between an internal standard of authority and natural religion, cf. B. B. Warfield, review of *Mysticism in Christianity*, by W. K. Fleming, and *Mysticism and Modern Life*, by John W. Buckham, in *CR*, 366–67; B. B. Warfield, "Recent Reconstructions of Theology," in *Shorter Writings*, 2:291, 293; Warfield, "The Idea of Systematic Theology," 57; Warfield, "Mysticism and Christianity," 656, 658.

needs of fallen sinners because it lacks the power to save. Whereas Christianity can save precisely because it is based on a supernatural act of God in history, natural religion cannot meet the supernatural need of the sinful soul because it supplies merely the "natural foundation" for Christianity's "supernatural structure."[29] That is to say, it is simply the creature's response to the perception of God in nature and conscience, and as such it is "unequal" to the "unnatural" conditions brought about by the fall of Adam.[30] Since orthodox scholars were convinced that external, supernatural truth "is the very breath of Christianity's nostrils,"[31] it follows that they repudiated the progressive solution to the problem of the relationship between Christianity and culture not simply because it transformed the Christian religion into "a veritable nose of wax, which may be twisted in every direction as it may serve our purpose,"[32] but more importantly because it emptied the Christian religion of its ability to save fallen sinners from the consequences of sin by throwing them "back on what we can find within us alone."[33] When natural religion in any form "pushes itself forward as an adequate religion for sinners," orthodox scholars such as Warfield maintained, "it presses beyond its mark and becomes, in the poet's phrase, 'procuress to the lords of hell.'"[34]

In light of the crisis of religious authority manifest in the modern debate over the nature of theology and its relationship to religious belief

29. Warfield, "Mysticism and Christianity," 661.

30. Ibid., 659–61; cf. B. B. Warfield, "Faith and Life," in *Shorter Writings*, 1:366; Warfield, review of *Mystik*, 362. On how "Christianity is superinduced upon and presupposes natural religion and forms with it the one whole which is the only sufficing religion for sinful man," cf. 362–63; see also Robert Swanton, "Warfield and Progressive Orthodoxy," *RTR* 23 (October 1964): 76–77. On the inherent "moralism" of natural religion and how it deteriorates into a salvifically ineffectual religion of works, cf. B. B. Warfield, "What Is Calvinism?" in *Shorter Writings*, 1:391; cf. also Warfield's chapter titled "Autosoterism," in B. B. Warfield, *The Plan of Salvation* (Philadelphia: Presbyterian Board of Publication, 1918; 1915), 37–63. On the inherent moralism of all who tend "to reduce to the vanishing-point the subjective injury wrought by Adam's sin on his posterity" (B. B. Warfield, "Imputation," in *Studies in Theology*, 304), cf. B. B. Warfield, "On the Doctrine of the Holy Spirit," in *Shorter Writings*, 1:216–18.

31. Warfield, "Christian Supernaturalism," in *Studies in Theology*, 29.

32. Warfield, review of *Foundations*, 322. On the explicit meaning of the word "Christianity," cf. B. B. Warfield, "'Redeemer' and 'Redemption,'" in *Biblical Doctrines*, vol. 2, *The Works of Benjamin Breckinridge Warfield* (Grand Rapids: Baker, 1991; 1929), 396.

33. Warfield, "Mysticism and Christianity," 659.

34. Ibid., 661; cf. Warfield, "Christian Supernaturalism," in *Studies in Theology*, 38–41.

and practice, it follows that modernity's relocation of the divine-human nexus not only had a tremendous impact on basic understandings of the subject matter of theological science, but it thereby had a revolutionary impact on what the goal of the entire theological enterprise was thought to be. Whereas orthodox scholars were committed to the systematic explication of a body of truth that they regarded as the ultimate authority in all matters of faith, learning, and living, more progressive scholars resolved to adapt theology to the modern *zeitgeist* because they presumed that traditional standards of external authority had been largely discredited by the theological, philosophical, and scientific developments of the modern era. The crisis of religious authority that blossomed into the fundamentalist-modernist controversy of the 1920s must be regarded, therefore, as that struggle marked on the one hand by orthodox theologians' opposition to theological "progress" and change, and on the other by liberal or modernist theologians' accommodation of Christianity to modern culture.[35] Whereas orthodox

---

35. Hutchison, *The Modernist Impulse in American Protestantism*, 2. According to Kenneth Cauthen, the New Theology was occasioned by the perceived need "to adjust the ancient faith to the modern world." Cauthen, *The Impact of American Religious Liberalism*, 5. The New Theologians insisted that "The repetition of old answers can serve no purpose. New answers must be framed, and these answers must be couched in the 'terms of modern thought.'" Warfield, review of *Foundations*, 322. As such, the agenda of theological liberalism was driven by the notion that a living faith must come to terms with the modern world. While there is a general consensus about how to characterize the primary elements of the liberal program, there is no consensus on how to classify the purveyors of theological liberalism. Should "liberals" and "modernists" be lumped together into one category as I have done? Or, should they be differentiated according to the relative priority of their methodological starting point, i.e., according to their starting point in revelation (evangelical liberals) or in science (modernist liberals)? Although many interpreters embrace the distinction between evangelical and modernist liberals—for example, cf. Averill, *American Theology in the Liberal Tradition*, 100ff; Cauthen, *The Impact of American Religious Liberalism*; and Martin Marty, *The Irony of It All, 1893–1919* (Chicago: University of Chicago Press, 1986), 13–80—William Hutchison's insights on the matter, which I find compelling, deserve thoughtful consideration. Hutchison maintains that "Such a differentiation [makes] sense as embodying an opinion about the theological *consequences* of varying modes of liberal advocacy; [but] it [is] not very helpful in clarifying what liberals themselves had *intended*." Few liberals, he contends, denied that Christian revelation is normative in some sense, and as a consequence few intended to repudiate the essential substance of Christianity. "The deeper difficulty in any sharply drawn distinction between liberals who built on revelation and those who allegedly began with science or culture," he argues, "was that it could not deal with the liberals' crucial contention that this distinction is, from the start, largely invalid. The antinomies that such a system of classification presupposes—between sacred and secular, between a starting point in revelation and a starting point in reason or in science—were precisely what proponents of this movement . . . sought to minimize." Hutchison, *The Modernist Impulse in America*, 8.

theologians insisted that the modern preoccupation with theological reconstruction was part and parcel of a reduction of the Christian religion to a merely natural phenomenon, liberal or modernist theologians argued that orthodoxy's stubborn refusal to make theology relevant to the thought-world of the modern era manifested nothing less than gross insensitivity to the immanent activity of the divine within nature, history, and culture, as well as an implicit relegation of the Christian religion to the realm of impotence and meaninglessness. The orthodox refusal to state Christian belief in terms of modern thought could be viewed as nothing less, they maintained, than the kiss of death to the religious life of the Christian community.

The Authority of Scripture and the Posture of the Christian Scholar

The Ideal in Christian Scholarship

B. B. Warfield's involvement in this cultural as well as theological controversy was inspired by his determined opposition to liberalism's heretical attempt not to assimilate modern learning to Christian truth, but to "desupernaturalize" Christianity so as to make it more palatable to the modern mind.[36] Christians should have an attitude "of eager hospitality toward the researches of the world,"[37] he argues, not so they can determine when a reconstruction of religious thinking is in order,[38] but so they can "*reason* the world into acceptance of the 'truth'" through the superior science of redeemed thought.[39] "The Christian," he maintains,

> by virtue of the palingenesis working in him, stands undoubtedly on an indefinitely higher plane of thought than that occupied by sinful

36. Warfield, "Christian Supernaturalism," in *Studies in Theology*, 29.

37. Warfield, "Heresy and Concession," in *Shorter Writings*, 2:674.

38. According to Warfield, "No one will doubt that Christians of to-day must state their Christian beliefs in terms of modern thought. Every age has a language of its own and can speak no other. Mischief comes only when, instead of stating Christian belief in terms of modern thought, an effort is made, rather, to state modern thought in terms of Christian belief." Warfield, review of *Foundations*, 322.

39. B. B. Warfield, "Christianity the Truth," in *Shorter Writings*, 2:213.

man as such. And he must not decline, but use and press the advantage which God has thus given him. He must insist, and insist again, that his determinations, and not those of the unilluminated, must be built into the slowly rising fabric of human science. Thus will he serve, if not obviously his own generation, yet truly all the generations of men.[40]

40. Warfield, "Introduction to Beattie's *Apologetics*," in *Shorter Writings*, 2:103. Please note two important points suggested by this quotation and articulated with more or less clarity elsewhere in Warfield's writings. First, Warfield clearly recognizes that science is not a "neutral" enterprise involving the exercise of "pure" rationality alone, for he recognizes that the "determinations" of scientific investigation are related in one way or another to the moral character of the investigating agent. Indeed, as Mark Noll and David Livingstone incisively observe, Warfield consistently acknowledges that "science is as subjective as theology." Warfield, *Evolution, Science and Scripture, Selected Writings*, ed. Mark A. Noll, David N. Livingstone (Grand Rapids: Baker, 2000), 321. That this is the case is perhaps nowhere more clearly revealed than in Warfield's critical analysis of Hugo Visscher's rectoral address at the celebration of the University of Utrecht's 284th anniversary. According to Warfield, "the science with which Prof. Visscher proclaims religion to be eternally at peace, has never, whether in the limitations which he puts upon it, or in the perfection which he ascribes to its deliverances, existed on sea or land. He is not unaware of course of the subjective side of science; but he appears to neglect it in the prosecution of his discussion, and to identify the science of which he speaks with the objective system of realities itself, which he apparently imagines to be perfectly reflected in the human intellect. Thus he seems to think of science as the pure product of the pure intellect of a pure humanity working purely. We shall get no such science as that until the world or reality is reflected in the consciousness of the perfected humanity of the completed palingenesis. The science and religion of perfected humanity will of course be in harmony. What we have in the meantime, however, is only the distorted reflection of reality in warped intellects, dimmed by imperfections and clouded by prepossessions. Could we listen to the teaching of that 'beautiful Maiden bearing the torch of enlightenment,' to whom Prof. Visscher introduces us, we should of course yield to it instant and complete obedience. But this 'calm-eyed Science' is not to be encountered in the Market-place, and is not to be met with in the Rialto. She speaks to us only in the voices of her servants, and each of them has his own—well, say personal equation. After all is said, the voices of the scientists are not the voice of Science. And no inability which religion—the Christian religion—may show to live in peace with the one can argue disharmony with the other." B. B. Warfield, review of *Van Den Eeuwigen Vrede Tusschen Wetenshap en Religie*, by H. Visscher, and *Professor Visscher's Rectorale Rede*, by H. W. van der Vaart Smit, in *CR*, 481.

Second, this quotation also suggests that for Warfield, it is not only the "determinations" of scientific investigation that are related to the subjectivity or moral character of the investigating agent, but the quality of those "determinations" as well, for it is the moral character of the investigating agent that determines the "plane of thought" that the investigating agent is able to do his investigation from. As we will see in the forthcoming discussion—and as is indicated in both the paragraphs above and in the preceding chapter—Warfield argues that the moral renovation associated with the work of the Spirit in regeneration informs scholarship that is not only different from, but qualitatively superior to, the scholarship of those who remain dead in their sins, for he recognizes that science, like religion, is the product "of the human spirit and the human spirit does not function . . . in sections." Ibid., 477. What the quotation above finally suggests, then, is that it is this typically Reformed emphasis on the work of the Spirit in regeneration that grounds Warfield's optimism with respect to "the slowly rising fabric of human science," not a rationalistic or Pelagian confidence in the epistemic competence of the human mind.

While the consensus of critical opinion would have us believe that the aggressive nature of this response to the problem of the relationship between Christianity and culture is evidence that Warfield accommodated the rationalistic assumptions of Enlightenment philosophy, in fact it represents the ideal in Christian scholarship for three reasons. It represents the ideal, first, because it is based on the conviction that the "source and norm of truth"—"the only really solid basis of all . . . thinking"—is found in the Word of God.[41] Although Warfield acknowledges that there are "other sources of knowledge from which [the Christian] may learn what is true," nevertheless he insists that "there is no source of knowledge which will rank with [the Christian] in authority above the written Word of God, or to which he can appeal with superior confidence."[42] When the Christian comes into contact with "modes of thought and tenets originating elsewhere than in the Scriptures of God," therefore, "the teachings of God's word" must be esteemed as authoritative "over against all the conjectural explanations of phenomena by men."[43] To do otherwise, i.e., to yield authority to the provisional conclusions of modern scholarship by modifying the teachings of God's Word "at the dictation of any 'man-made opinion,'" he argues, is to fall prey to "the fruitful mother of heresy."[44]

If Warfield's response is ideal in the first place because it refuses to give "decisive weight" to modes of thought originating elsewhere than in the Word of God, it is so in the second because it acknowledges that esteeming Scripture as the norm of truth compels the believing

41. Warfield, "Heresy and Concession," in *Shorter Writings*, 2:674–75.
42. Ibid., 2:674.
43. Ibid., 2:677, 679.
44. Ibid., 2:677, 675. "It is very plain," Warfield insists, "that he who modifies the teachings of the Word of God in the smallest particular at the dictation of any 'man-made opinion' has already deserted the Christian ground, and is already, in principle, a 'heretic.' The very essence of 'heresy' is that the modes of thought and tenets originating elsewhere than in the Scriptures of God are given decisive weight when they clash with the teachings of God's Word, and those are followed to the neglect or modification or rejection of these." Ibid., 2:677. Note that for Warfield, the heretical eagerness to yield authority to the provisional conclusions of modern scholarship is grounded in an implicit appeal to our own authority. This is because what is typically meant by modern scholarship "is our own 'science, philosophy, and scholarship'—which seems to be only a naïve way of transferring the claim of infallibility from 'Christianity' and 'its theology' to ourselves." Warfield, review of *Foundations*, 322.

academic to "seek and embrace" truth wherever it is found.[45] As a Reformed scholar, Warfield was convinced that "zeal in investigation" is one of the "marked characteristics" of Christian scholarship because Christians alone have the moral ability to handle correctly the "touchstone" of truth—Scripture.[46] In the context of the current discussion, this means at least two things. First, it means that Christians zealously pursue truth "in every sphere"[47] because they recognize that the Word of God is not "a substitute for general revelation, but only . . . a preparation for its proper assimilation."[48] Special revelation was not given, they maintain, "to supplant a strictly natural knowledge [of God] by a strictly supernatural knowledge," but "so that the general revelation of God may be reflected purely in minds which now are blinded to its reflection by sin."[49] Second, it means that Christians engage aggressively in the life of the mind because they are confident they have the moral ability to reason "rightly," i.e., to "see" through the "spectacles" of Scripture.[50] Whereas progressive scholars bend Scripture into conciliation with the latest pronouncements of modern scholarship because they look at the teachings of God's Word from the standpoint of the world's speculations, the regenerate assimilate modern learning to Christian truth because their investigations are informed by "the better scientific outlook," i.e., by the ability to see revealed truth more or less for what it objectively is, namely glorious.[51] What this suggests, then, is that believing academics should stand calmly "over against the world" not only because "the Christian view of the world"

45. Warfield, "Heresy and Concession," in *Shorter Writings*, 2:677, 674.

46. Ibid., 2:674.

47. Ibid.

48. B. B. Warfield, "Augustine's Doctrine of Knowledge and Authority," in *Tertullian and Augustine*, vol. 4, *The Works of Benjamin Breckinridge Warfield* (Grand Rapids: Baker, 1991; 1930), 222.

49. Ibid.; cf. Warfield, "Christianity and Revelation," in *Shorter Writings*, 1:27–28.

50. Warfield, "Augustine's Doctrine of Knowledge and Authority," 222.

51. Warfield, "Introduction to Beattie's *Apologetics*," in *Shorter Writings*, 2:100–2. Recall from the previous chapter that for Warfield: (1) there "do exist . . . 'two kinds of men' in the world" who give us "two kinds of science"; and (2) the difference between the science of the regenerate and the science of the unregenerate is not "a difference in *kind*," but a difference in "perfection of performance." The science of the regenerate is of a higher quality than that of the unregenerate, he argues, not because the regenerate are producing an altogether "different kind of science," but because the entrance of regeneration "prepares men to build [the edifice of truth] better and ever more truly as the effects of regeneration increase intensively and extensively." Ibid.

is true, but more importantly because they have no reason to fear the "contention of men."[52] They have the truth, they have the ability to discern the truth in all things, and they are confident that everything they encounter will be assimilated to the truth by sifting the good and rejecting the bad.

Finally, Warfield's response represents the ideal in Christian scholarship because it recognizes that assimilating modern learning to Christian truth is the means to moving the church of God forward in her apologetic task. As we saw in the last chapter, Warfield distinguishes between the giving of an "apology" and the task of "apologetics." Whereas an "apology" is a defense of Christianity "against either all assailants, actual or conceivable, or some particular form or instance of attack," "apologetics" is "a positive and constructive science" that undertakes "not the defense, not even the vindication, but the establishment . . . of that knowledge of God which Christianity professes to embody and seeks to make efficient in the world."[53] While "apologies" thus derive their value from that which is incidental to the propagation of the Christian religion, namely the defense of Christianity against "opposing points of view," "apologetics" is of the essence of propagation because it concerns itself with both the setting forth and the justification of the truth that the Christian worldview is believed to entail.[54] In short, apologetics

> finds its deepest ground . . . not in the accidents which accompany the efforts of true religion to plant, sustain, and propagate itself in this world . . . but in the fundamental needs of the human spirit. If it is incumbent on the believer to be able to give a reason for the faith that is in him, it is impossible for him to be a believer without a reason for the faith that is in him; and it is the task of apologetics to bring this reason out in his consciousness and make its validity plain.[55]

52. Ibid., 2:100, 103.
53. Warfield, "Apologetics," 3.
54. Ibid., 15.
55. Ibid., 4. The apologist must validate the truth that is being established, simply because faith, although it is a moral act and the gift of God, "is yet formally conviction passing into confidence." Validation is necessary, therefore, because an intellectual conviction of the truth of the Christian religion is "the logical *prius* of self-commitment to the Founder of that religion." Warfield, "Review of *De Zekerheid des Geloofs*," in *Shorter Writings*, 2:113. From this it follows

The Apologetic Nature of Christian Scholarship

When Warfield's response to the problem of the relationship between Christianity and culture is seen in this light, it becomes immediately clear that assimilating modern learning to Christian truth does not merely sustain the task of apologetics; it *constitutes* the task of apologetics. We must conclude, therefore, that for Warfield "the men of the palingenesis" ought to engage in the life of the mind not to argue the unregenerate into the kingdom of God, but to establish the integrity of "the Christian view of the world" by urging their "'stronger and purer thought' continuously, and in all its details, upon the attention of men."[56] When they do this, they bring the "thinking world" into subjection to the gospel of Jesus Christ, and thereby lay the groundwork for the Spirit to work saving faith where he sovereignly chooses, i.e., to "give to a faith which naturally grows out of the proper grounds of faith, that peculiar quality which makes it saving faith."[57] Despite the fact that some scholars will continue to object that such an approach owes more to Enlightenment philosophy than it does to a consistently Reformed epistemology, Warfield's position in fact is incomprehensible apart from his clear stand within the epistemological mainstream of the Reformed camp. Indeed, such an approach is virtually unintelligible apart from Warfield's forthright endorsement of the classical Reformed distinction between a merely speculative and a spiritual understanding of what God has revealed, and for this reason we ought not to conclude that it is grounded in the accommodation of the anthropocentric assumptions of Enlightenment philosophy.[58]

---

that the apologetical task is focused primarily on the labor of the apologist, and only secondarily on that which is beyond the apologist's control, namely the mind of the unregenerate.

56. Warfield, "Introduction to Beattie's *Apologetics*," in *Shorter Writings*, 2:102–3; cf. 2:104–5.

57. Warfield, "Review of *De Zekerheid des Geloofs*," in *Shorter Writings*, 2:120, 115. What is supplied by the "creative energy" of the Holy Spirit in the new birth is not, Warfield argues, "a ready-made faith, rooted in nothing and clinging without reason to its object; nor yet new grounds of belief in the object presented; but just a new ability of the heart to respond to the grounds of faith, sufficient in themselves, already present to the understanding." Warfield, "Introduction to Beattie's *Apologetics*," in *Shorter Writings*, 2:99.

58. Cf. George Marsden, "The Evangelical Love Affair with Enlightenment Science," in *Understanding Fundamentalism and Evangelicalism* (Grand Rapids: Eerdmans, 1991), 122–52. Marsden clearly believes that Kuyperians (who "emphasize that any discipline is built on starting assumptions and that Christians' basic assumptions should have substantial effects on many of their theoretical conclusions in a discipline") are less indebted to Enlightenment categories of

The Relationship between Warfield and Kuyper

Was Warfield a Disciple of Kuyper?

To this point we have seen that Warfield's response to the problem of the relationship between Christianity and culture represents the ideal in Christian scholarship for three reasons: It esteems Scripture as the norm of truth; it acknowledges that this esteem compels believing academics to seek and embrace truth wherever it is found; and it insists that the seeking and embracing of truth is the means to moving the church of God forward in her apologetic task. Having thus distinguished between the assimilation of modern learning to Christian truth on the one hand and the accommodation of Christianity to modern culture on the other, we must now consider how to account for the Kuyperian and quasi-Kuyperian pronouncements that pervade Warfield's writings. Given the intensity of the contemporary debate over how Christians should go about integrating faith and learning, such an accounting will amplify the genius of Warfield's conception of Christian scholarship, for it will demonstrate that the aggressive nature of his response to the cultural challenges of his day was informed not by an implicit rationalism, but by his unambiguous affirmation of the supremacy of the Christian worldview in all things.[59]

In his analysis of six lectures delivered by Abraham Kuyper at Princeton Theological Seminary in the fall of 1898, Peter Heslam suggests that despite the apparent differences between Warfield and Kuyper on key issues of religious epistemology, Warfield's conception of Calvinism "was . . . indebted to Kuyper's exposition of it at

---

thought than are Warfieldians ("those who believe in one science or rationality on which all humanity ought to agree"). As we have seen in preceding chapters, while defenders of Warfield and Old Princeton must concede that the Scottish philosophy had a marked impact on the theological method of the Princeton theologians, they need not concede that Old Princeton's emphasis on objective truth and the primacy of the intellect in faith is *ipso facto* evidence that the Princetonians embraced the categories of Enlightenment thought. Interestingly, the charge of accommodation to Enlightenment categories has also been made against Kuyperians. In this regard, see Donald Fuller and Richard Gardiner, "Reformed Theology at Princeton and Amsterdam in the Late Nineteenth Century: A Reappraisal," *Presbyterion* 21, 2 (1995): 89–117.

59. For an overview of the broad outline of the methodological debate between Warfieldians, Kuyperians, and hybrids in between, see Marsden, "The Evangelical Love Affair with Enlightenment Science," 149–52.

Princeton" in at least four ways.[60] According to Heslam, Kuyper's Stone Lectures helped Warfield understand that Calvinism "represented a broad movement in society and culture, not restricted to the church or doctrine; that it emanated outwards from its central source in the religious consciousness; that this religious consciousness represented the purest and most advanced stage in the development of religion; and that Calvinism offered the best prospects for the future of Christianity."[61] Heslam goes on to cite the following quotation as evidence that Kuyper's influence on Warfield was so profound that Warfield eventually acquiesced even in Kuyper's insistence "on the radical influence of worldview on [the] scientific enterprise."[62] Commenting on the publication of a series of lectures delivered by James Orr at Princeton Seminary in 1905, Warfield enthusiastically and, as Heslam would have us believe, uncharacteristically insists that,

> Their publication . . . will carry to a wider audience their fine exposition of the fundamentals of Christian anthropology and their vigorous protest against a tendency, apparently growing among us, "to wholesale surrender of vital aspects of Christian doctrine at the shrine of what is regarded as 'the modern view of the world' " (p. vi). What renders this protest most valuable is that it is particularly directed against weak evasions of the issue raised by the conflict between the Christian view of the world and that "congeries of conflicting and often mutually irreconcilable views" which is commonly spoken of as the "modern view." Dr. Orr has the courage to recognize and assert the irreconcilableness of the two views and the impossibility of a compromise between them; and to undertake the task of showing that the Christian view in the forum of science itself is the only tenable one. This task he accomplishes with distinguished success: and this is the significance of the volume.[63]

60. Peter S. Heslam, *Creating a Christian Worldview: Abraham Kuyper's Lectures on Calvinism* (Grand Rapids: Eerdmans; Carlisle: Paternoster, 1998), 255. See also Peter S. Heslam, "Architects of Evangelical Intellectual Thought: Abraham Kuyper and Benjamin Warfield," *Themelios* 24, 2 (fall 1999): 3–20.

61. Heslam, *Creating a Christian Worldview*, 255.

62. Ibid.

63. B. B. Warfield, review of *God's Image in Man, and Its Defacement, in the Light of Modern Denials*, by James Orr, in *CR*, 136–37.

While Heslam's comprehensive examination of Kuyper's *Lectures on Calvinism* is noteworthy for its incisive treatment of the Dutch theologian's wide-ranging brilliance, his assessment of the significance of the above quotation leaves something to be desired because it presumes that Warfield and Kuyper in fact disagreed on key issues of religious epistemology prior to 1898. According to Heslam, Warfield and his colleagues at Old Princeton were at epistemological odds with their more consistently Reformed brethren from the Netherlands because the Princetonians were rationalists whose "infatuation" with Enlightenment categories of thought left them without the epistemological wherewithal to affirm the scientific superiority of the Christian view of the world.[64] Warfield's "glowing" review of Orr is regarded as evidence, therefore, not of continuity with the assumptions of the Princeton tradition, but of a deviation from those assumptions, and thus as evidence that Warfield was won over—in principle if not in fact—to the more consistently Reformed views of the Renaissance man from Amsterdam.[65] Although Heslam concedes that Warfield's more mature writings continue to affirm the value of apologetics, he nonetheless insists that these writings manifest a "less triumphalistic" and perhaps domesticated Warfield, chastened by the realization that there is more to religious epistemology than the cold analysis of brute facts.[66]

The Continuity between Old Princeton and Amsterdam

What, then, should we make of Heslam's assessment? Are Warfield's Kuyperian and quasi-Kuyperian pronouncements in fact evidence that he was inspired by Kuyper to move away from the epistemological assumptions of Old Princeton in a more presuppositional direction? Two factors, both of which can be found in Warfield's pre-1898 writings, suggest an answer to this question. The first has to do with Warfield's insistence that only the regenerate have the moral ability to see revealed truth more or less for what it objectively is, namely glorious. Whereas the consensus of critical opinion would have us believe

---

64. Heslam, *Creating a Christian Worldview*, 190; cf. chapters 5 and 7, especially 123–32 and 176–92.
65. Ibid., 256.
66. Ibid.

Warfield stood outside the epistemological mainstream of the Reformed camp because he was indifferent to the subjective and experiential components of religious epistemology, Warfield, in fact, was authentically Reformed because these concerns were of critical significance to his religious epistemology despite its apparently rationalistic rigor. As we saw in the last chapter, the justification for this contention is found in the moral, rather than the merely rational nature of his thought. Like his predecessors at Old Princeton Seminary, Warfield was convinced that the operation of the intellect involves the "whole soul"—mind, will, and emotions—rather than the rational faculty alone. He concluded, therefore, that the regenerate alone could see revealed truth more or less for what it objectively is, because it is only in the souls of the regenerate that there is "perfect interaction" between the objective and subjective factors that impinge upon religious epistemology and underlie religious belief and practice.[67]

One of the principal texts that substantiate this claim is an extremely significant yet largely overlooked essay titled, "Authority, Intellect, Heart" (1896). In this article, published two and a half years before Kuyper delivered his Stone Lectures in the fall of 1898, Warfield outlines the anthropological context within which his epistemological views must be interpreted. The key passage, which grounds his endorsement of the classical Reformed distinction between a merely speculative and a spiritual understanding of revealed truth in his unambiguous commitment to the unitary operation of the soul, reads as follows:

> Authority, intellect, and the heart are the three sides of the triangle of truth. How they interact is observable in any concrete instance of their operation. Authority, in the Scriptures, furnishes the matter which is received in the intellect and operates on the heart. The revelations of the Scriptures do not terminate upon the intellect. They were not given merely to enlighten the mind. They were given through the intellect to beautify the life. They terminate on the heart. Again, they do not, in affecting the heart, leave the intellect untouched. They cannot be fully understood by the intellect, acting alone. The natural man cannot receive the things of the Spirit of

67. Warfield, "Authority, Intellect, Heart," in *Shorter Writings*, 2:669.

God. They must first convert the soul before they are fully comprehended by the intellect. Only as they are lived are they understood. Hence the phrase, "Believe that you may understand," has its fullest validity. No man can intellectually grasp the full meaning of the revelations of authority, save as the result of an experience of their power in life. Hence, that the truths concerning divine things may be so comprehended that they may unite with a true system of divine truth, they must be: first, revealed in an authoritative word; second, experienced in a holy heart; and third, formulated by a sanctified intellect. Only as these three unite, then, can we have a true theology. And equally, that these same truths may be so received that they beget in us a living religion, they must be: first, revealed in an authoritative word; second, apprehended by a sound intellect; and third, experienced in an instructed heart. Only as the three unite, then, can we have vital religion.[68]

What this text suggests, among other things, is that it might not be so easy to dismiss Warfield as a rationalist as it might at first appear to be, for his epistemological views are far more sophisticated—indeed far more consistently Reformed—than interpreters such as Heslam have been willing to grant to this point.

If Heslam's assessment cannot account for Warfield's epistemological assumptions on the one hand, it fails to address his pre-1898 opposition to defending the "minimum" of Christianity on the other. In "Heresy and Concession," an article that was published in early 1896, Warfield announces that he is opposed to any approach to doing apologetics that is based on the assumption that the "minimum" of Christianity is all "that is worth defending, or all that is capable of defense."[69] What he means by this opposition is later made clear in his "Introduction to Francis R. Beattie's *Apologetics*" (1903), perhaps his most sustained critique of the Kuyperian approach to apologetics. The apologist's function, he argues, "is not to vindicate for us the least that we can get along with, and yet manage to call ourselves Christians; but to validate the Christian 'view of the world,' with all

68. Ibid., 2:671.
69. Warfield, "Heresy and Concession," in *Shorter Writings*, 2:677.

that is contained in the Christian 'view of the world,' for the science of men."[70] Apologetics, Warfield explains,

> does not concern itself with how this man or that may best be approached to induce him to make a beginning of Christian living, or how this age or that may most easily be brought to give a hearing to the Christian conception of the world. It concerns itself with the solid objective establishment, after a fashion valid for all normally working minds and for all ages of the world in its developing thought, of those great basal facts which constitute the Christian religion; or, better, which embody in the concrete the entire knowledge of God accessible to men, and which, therefore, need only explication by means of the further theological disciplines in order to lay openly before the eyes of men the entirety of the knowledge of God within their reach.[71]

But what, we must ask, is at the heart of this opposition to defending the "minimum" of Christianity? Why was Warfield so opposed, in other words, to reducing the all-encompassing task of "apologetics" to the level of a bare "apology"? The answer goes to the core of the matter and is found in "Heresy and Concession," the pre-1898 essay in which Warfield articulates the methodological assumptions that inform his aggressive response to the problem of the relationship between Christianity and culture. In short, Warfield was opposed to defending the "minimum" of Christianity because he recognized that the ability to see revealed truth more or less for what it objectively is extends beyond the scope of Scripture itself to all truth, be it scientific or religious. The justification for this contention is found in his understanding of the authority of Scripture. Scripture, Warfield argues, is not only the "source and norm" of religious truth, but it is the "interpreter" and "corrector" of modern thought as well.[72] It is the standard for measuring "right thinking" of all kinds, and as such it is "superior in point of authority" to the provisional conclusions of modern scholarship.[73] Since

70. Warfield, "Introduction to Beattie's *Apologetics*," 2:104.
71. Ibid., 2:105.
72. Warfield, "Heresy and Concession," in *Shorter Writings*, 2:674, 679.
73. Ibid.

Warfield was convinced that the view of the world mediated through Scripture is objectively true as opposed to merely subjectively true, he urged believing academics to engage aggressively in the life of the mind not so they could impose a merely subjective interpretation of reality on an unsuspecting public, but so they could establish the integrity of the only view of the world that accords with what is objectively true, i.e., with the way things objectively are.

In light of Warfield's pre-Stone Lectures inclination to affirm the supremacy of the Christian view of the world in all areas of learning, it follows that the presence of Kuyperian elements in Warfield's writings is evidence not that Warfield was inspired by Kuyper to move away from the assumptions of Old Princeton in a presuppositional direction, but that there was perhaps more in common between the epistemological views of Warfield and Kuyper, of Old Princeton and Amsterdam, than has hitherto been acknowledged. If this revisionist interpretation has any merit, it indicates that the epistemological assumptions that have typically been regarded as the coin of the realm in the Kuyperian camp were in fact always present in the Princeton tradition. More importantly, it explains why Warfield was confounded by Kuyper's reluctance to engage in an offensive apologetic. Given the likely continuity between Warfield and Kuyper on key issues of religious epistemology, we may plausibly conclude that Kuyper's approach to apologetics was "a standing matter of surprise" to Warfield not because Kuyper refused to advance the kingdom by appealing "to the *natural man's* 'right reason' to judge of the truth of Christianity,"[74] as the consensus of critical opinion would have us believe. It was a matter of surprise, rather, because he was reluctant to do what Warfield believed the Christian must of necessity do even when there is "no opposition in the world to be encountered and no contradiction to be overcome,"[75] namely, establish the integrity of the grounds of faith by urging " 'his stronger and purer thought' continuously, and in all its details, upon

74. Jack Rogers, "Van Til and Warfield on Scripture in the Westminster Confession," in *Jerusalem and Athens: Critical Discussions on the Philosophy and Apologetics of Cornelius Van Til*, ed. E. R. Geehan (Phillipsburg, NJ: Presbyterian and Reformed, 1980), 154.

75. Warfield, "Apologetics," 4.

the attention of men."[76] It is entirely possible, therefore, that it was Kuyper's perceived indifference to the necessity of establishing the grounds of faith, i.e., his perceived tip of the hat to an astonishing fideistic tendency, that led Warfield to conclude that

> no mistake could be greater than to lead them [the men of the palin-genesis] to decline to bring their principles into conflict with those of the unregenerate in the prosecution of the common task of man. It is the better science that ever in the end wins the victory; and palingenetic science is the better science; and to it belongs the victory. How shall it win its victory, however, if it declines the conflict? In the ordinance of God, it is only in and through this conflict that the edifice of truth is to rise steadily onwards to its perfecting.[77]

Conclusion: Implications for Christian Scholarship

The Contemporary Relevance of Warfield's Response to the Modern Era's Relocation of the Divine-Human Nexus

Having proposed a plausible explanation for the presence of Kuyperian and quasi-Kuyperian pronouncements in Warfield's response to the modern era's relocation of the divine-human nexus, it remains to be seen how Warfield's response is relevant to ongoing discussions in the evangelical camp about the goal and task of Christian scholarship. I would suggest that Warfield's response is relevant for three reasons. In the first place, it is relevant because it encourages Christian scholars to engage zealously in the life of the mind without embracing what Nancy Pearcey and others have called the "two-story view of truth."[78]

76. Warfield, "Introduction to Beattie's *Apologetics*," in *Shorter Writings*, 2:103. This statement will be misunderstood if it is not interpreted in light of Warfield's clear endorsement of the distinction between a merely speculative and a spiritual understanding of the gospel.

77. Ibid.

78. Cf. Nancy Pearcey, *Total Truth: Liberating Christianity from Its Cultural Captivity* (Study Guide Edition) (Wheaton, IL: Crossway Books, 2005). According to this view of truth, "the concept of truth itself has been divided. . . . In the lower story are science and reason [and fact], which are considered public truth, binding on everyone. Over against it is an upper story of noncognitive experience, which is the locus of personal meaning [and value]. This is the realm of private truth, where we hear people say, 'That may be true for you, but it's not true for me.'" Ibid., 21.

Pearcey argues that this view of truth "is the single most potent weapon for delegitimizing the biblical perspective in the public square today" (ibid.) because it precludes religious truth

Although Warfield acknowledges that "all truth is God's"[79] and that "men of all sorts . . . work side by side at the common task" of building up the temple of truth,[80] he nonetheless insists that true interpretations of reality—indeed the best interpretations of reality—are possible only when general revelation is looked at through the spectacles of special revelation.[81] Despite what the consensus of critical opinion would have us believe, Warfield's epistemology here shows remarkable continuity with that of consistently Reformed scholars such as Jonathan Edwards.[82] Like Edwards before him, Warfield was convinced that genuinely Christian

---

claims from being regarded as having to do with genuine knowledge. "Most secularists," Pearcey contends, "are too politically savvy to attack religion directly or to debunk it as false. So what do they do? They consign religion to the *value* sphere—which takes it out of the realm of true and false altogether." Ibid. Note two relevant matters at this point: First, Warfield's insistence that theology is a science is grounded in his rejection of this way of thinking about truth. "Theology is as truly a science as physical science; it is as truly a product of the intellect; it deals as truly with facts; it is as truly a knowledge. It is theology, the science, not religion, the life, which should be set in comparison with physical science. The thrusting of 'religion,' so understood, into its place has the effect of depriving it of—or at least of obscuring—its fact-content. Of 'religion' it may be possible to say—what could not be said of theology—that it is only a manner—perhaps only an emotional manner—of looking at facts with which as facts 'science' alone has to do, so that 'science' and 'religion' cannot possibly come into conflict. It is 'science' alone that determines facts while it is the sole function of 'religion' to suffuse these facts, given to it by 'science,' with a glow of transcendental emotion. . . . The effect [of this view] is that [it] seems to require Christianity to surrender to natural science . . . all question of facts, while it confines itself to a 'valuation of them in relation with God.' This appears to abolish all supernaturalism from the fact-basis and fact-content of Christianity. For the 'science' to which is assigned the determination of the facts that will be allowed actually to have occurred, is defined not only as a science that cannot know anything of God . . . but a science that can take cognizance of nothing that does not proceed mechanically." Warfield, review of *Van Den Eeuwigen Vrede Tusschen Wetenshap en Religie*, and *Professor Visscher's Rectorale Rede*, 477–78.

Second, Warfield repudiates the modern distinction between religious truth and scientific truth—the distinction that "places science as the only organ of objective reality and religion as moving in a purely subjective sphere"—because he recognizes that "that religion which is Christianity is inseparably bound up with its 'facts,' and stands or falls with their objective reality. Any science which leaves no place for these facts, as such, is not neutral but antagonistic to Christianity; and between that science and this religion there must be not eternal peace but eternal war." Ibid., 479–80.

79. Warfield, "Heresy and Concession," in *Shorter Writings*, 2:674.

80. Warfield, "Introduction to Beattie's *Apologetics*," in *Shorter Writings*, 2:102.

81. Recall Warfield's understanding of the relationship between general and special revelation, discussed in the previous chapter, and his insistence earlier in this chapter that "palingenetic science is the better science; and to it belongs the victory." Warfield, "Introduction to Beattie's *Apologetics*," in *Shorter Writings*, 2:103.

82. The claim of epistemological continuity between Warfield and scholars such as Edwards is grounded in Warfield's endorsement of an Augustinian understanding of "right reason." For elaboration of this continuity, see the forthcoming discussion in Part Two of this study.

scholarship depends on the new birth. The regenerate alone can see revealed truth more or less for what it objectively is, he argues, because they alone can discern the spiritual excellence of what is rationally perceived by looking at it through the spectacles of Scripture. Since Warfield was convinced that only believing academics have the moral ability to—as John Piper expresses it in another context—"see and savor God in every branch of learning,"[83] he concludes that they must engage aggressively the life of the mind not so that they can, as Phillip Johnson puts it, "find a place for theology within the picture of reality defined by scientific naturalists,"[84] but so they can assimilate modern learning to Christian truth through the superior science of redeemed thought, and thereby lay the groundwork for the Spirit to work saving faith where he sovereignly chooses by opening the eyes of unbelieving minds to the integrity of the Christian view of the world.[85]

If Warfield's response is relevant in the first place because it is fundamentally opposed to both methodological naturalism on the one hand and all forms of anti-intellectualism on the other, it is relevant in the second because it suggests that the contemporary debate between Warfieldians and Kuyperians finds its genesis, at least in

83. John Piper, *God's Passion for His Glory: Living the Vision of Jonathan Edwards* (Wheaton, IL: Crossway Books, 1998), 43. With respect to Edwards's (and, I would add, Warfield's) distinction between speculative rationality (that which grasps "natural things") and spiritual rationality (that which grasps "divine things"), Piper anticipates the predictable objection: "One might object that the subject matter of psychology or sociology or anthropology or history or physics or chemistry or English or computer science is not 'divine things' but 'natural things.' But that would miss the first point: to see reality in truth we must see it in relation to God, who created it, and sustains it, and gives it all the properties it has and all its relations and designs. To see all these things in each discipline is to see the 'divine things'—and in the end, they are the main things." Ibid.

84. Phillip E. Johnson, *Reason in the Balance: The Case against Naturalism in Science, Law & Education* (Downers Grove, IL: InterVarsity Press, 1995), 97. For an incisive response to evangelicals who "accept not just the particular conclusions that [naturalistic] scientists have reached but also the naturalistic methodology that generated those conclusions," see Johnson's response to Nancey Murphy, "Phillip Johnson on Trial: A Critique of His Critique of Darwin," in *Perspectives on Science & Christian Faith* 45, 1 (March 1993): 26–36, in *Reason in the Balance*, 97–110, 235. According to Johnson, "Theists who accept a naturalistic understanding of knowledge fatally undercut their own intellectual position," for in so doing they unwittingly endorse the naturalistic distinction between religious truth and scientific truth, and thereby abandon to "science" the whole realm of objective truth.

85. For more on this understanding of the Princeton apologetic, please see the discussion in the previous chapter.

part, in the unresolved and misunderstood tension between Warfield and Kuyper. When we consider the contemporary debate in light of Warfield's clear stand within the epistemological mainstream of the Reformed camp, it becomes immediately clear that at the heart of the tension between Warfieldians and Kuyperians is the unresolved question of the relationship between regeneration and scholarly activity. Do the regenerate simply see revealed truth differently than do the unregenerate, and are the views of the unregenerate thus just as viable as those of the regenerate? Or, do the regenerate see revealed truth more or less for what it objectively is, and as a consequence do they have a rational basis for claiming that the views of the unregenerate are out of accord with the way reality objectively is despite the fact that their views follow logically from their starting premises? While it is certainly true that precisely how general and special revelation should interact in the minds of the regenerate is a question that warrants ongoing consideration in the evangelical camp, to suggest that the regenerate and the unregenerate look at general revelation in essentially the same manner—to suggest, in other words, that the views of the unregenerate are, in a certain sense, just as viable as those of the regenerate—is to suggest that the ability to see revealed truth more or less for what it objectively is will have little or no impact on the work of the Christian scholar. It is to suggest, moreover, that the Christian worldview is only subjectively or pragmatically true, and thus of no more epistemological significance than the worldviews of unbelieving academics.[86]

Finally, Warfield's response to the modern era's relocation of the divine-human nexus is relevant because it calls attention to the inher-

---

86. In this regard, I like the following statement by Phillip Johnson because it presents a challenge to believing academics who for one reason or another are reluctant to acknowledge that the Christian worldview makes any appreciable difference in the doing of academic work. Speaking of the contradiction between theism in religion and naturalism in science, Johnson writes: "If evidence of divine action in the history of the universe is conspicuous by its apparent absence, then we may still choose to believe that the universe would disappear if God did not constantly uphold it with his mighty (but scientifically undetectable) word of power. Wise metaphysical naturalists will smile at these transparent devices, but they will not openly ridicule them. Why should they—when theists implicitly comply with the naturalistic doctrine that 'religion' is a matter of faith not reason?" Johnson, *Reason in the Balance*, 101.

ently slippery nature of the enterprise that we will examine more closely in Part Two of this study, namely the enterprise that Warfield refers to as "progressive orthodoxy."[87] Although Warfield was convinced that he lived in an age in which the primary responsibility of believing academics was to establish the integrity of the biblical worldview over and against the critical reconstructions of those who "cheerfully give up the substance, but never the name of Christianity,"[88] he nonetheless "had no quarrel . . . with the notion that men's understanding of Christianity will advance as their understanding of both natural and special revelation is corrected and enlarged."[89] Indeed, he refused to equate the "construction" of theology with the "destruction" of theology,[90] and as a consequence he insisted that the science of theology should proceed into the future "on the basis of the already ascertained truth of the past."[91] Whereas scholars such as Mark Noll applaud Warfield and his colleagues at Old Princeton for holding, among other things, "that the findings of science should be enlisted to help discover proper interpretations of Scripture,"[92] others such as David Hall are convinced that Warfield jettisoned the authority of Scripture because he allowed science to have "at least *theoretical* preeminence over Scripture, at

87. Warfield, "The Idea of Systematic Theology," 78.

88. Warfield, review of *Foundations*, 324.

89. Samuel G. Craig, introduction to *Biblical and Theological Studies*, by B. B. Warfield, Samuel G. Craig, ed. (Philadelphia: Presbyterian and Reformed, 1952), xliii.

90. Warfield, "The Idea of Systematic Theology," 78.

91. Swanton, "Warfield and Progressive Orthodoxy," 86. "Progressive orthodoxy," Warfield argues, "implies that first of all we are orthodox, and secondly that we are progressively orthodox, that is, that we are ever growing more and more orthodox as more and more truth is being established. . . . In any progressive science, the amount of departure from accepted truth which is possible to the sound thinker becomes thus ever less and less, in proportion as investigation and study result in the progressive establishment of an ever increasing number of facts. . . . It is of the very essence of our position at the end of the ages that we are ever more and more hedged around with ascertained facts, the discovery and establishment of which constitute the very essence of progress. Progress brings increasing limitation, just because it brings increasing knowledge. And as the orthodox man is he that teaches no other doctrine than that which has been established as true, the progressively orthodox man is he who is quick to perceive, admit, and condition all his reasoning by all the truth down to the latest, which has been established as true." Warfield, "The Idea of Systematic Theology," 78–79.

92. Mark A. Noll, "Charles Hodge and B. B. Warfield on Science, the Bible, Evolution, and Darwinism," *ModRef* 7, 3 (May/June 1998): 18–22; see also Mark A. Noll, *The Scandal of the Evangelical Mind* (Grand Rapids: Eerdmans, 1994), 177–208.

least as an intermediate hermeneutic."[93] He was willing to suggest, in other words, "that if an 'indisputable' result of thorough induction manifestly contradicted an existing doctrine of the church, the theologian *must reconsider* his interpretation of God's word, and see if he has not misunderstood it."[94]

A Call to Methodological Integrity

While the question of whether Noll or Hall is correct in his assessment of Warfield is beyond the scope of this chapter, what is of immediate relevance is the question of how those who affirm that "all truth is God's truth" should distinguish "God's truth" from "Satan's error."[95] How, specifically, should those who have been given the ability to reason "rightly" interact with the conclusions of naturalistic scholarship, and, more importantly, when does their attempt to sift the good and reject the bad cross the almost imperceptible line that separates assimilation from accommodation?[96] Commenting on the inherently conflicted nature of

93. David W. Hall, "Holding Fast the Concession of Faith: Science, Apologetics, and Orthodoxy," A Paper Presented to the 47th Annual Meeting of the Evangelical Theological Society, November 1995, Philadelphia, 10.

94. Theodore Dwight Bozeman, *Protestants in an Age of Science* (Chapel Hill, NC: University of North Carolina Press, 1977), 118. While I agree with Hall that evangelicals "ought to be leery" of surrendering aspects of historical orthodoxy to what he incisively calls "idea-fads of modernity" (Hall, "Holding Fast the Concession of Faith"), I am not entirely convinced that allowing accepted *interpretations* of Scripture to be challenged by the *indisputable* conclusions of scientific investigation necessarily entails setting the authority of science over that of Scripture *itself*. Certainly, all but the most progressively inclined will agree that accepted interpretations of Scripture should not be jettisoned cavalierly, if at all. But does it therefore follow that accepted interpretations should never be challenged? Does it follow that Christians should discount scientific findings even if those findings will establish *conclusively* that an accepted interpretation of Scripture was never truly scriptural, i.e., true, at all? These kinds of questions, which will be explored more fully in Part Two of this study, go to the core of the debate between scholars such as Noll and Hall.

95. I am indebted to Rev. Ian Hewitson for framing the question in this fashion.

96. These questions are admittedly troublesome in part because no matter how they are resolved the potential for accommodating to the spirit of the age—and thereby endorsing, either explicitly or implicitly, what J. Gresham Machen calls "one of the chief shibboleths of modern skepticism," namely the notion that religious truth is distinct from scientific truth (Machen, "The Relation of Religion to Science and Philosophy," PTR 24 [1926]: 50)—appears very real. Those who insist on reading Scripture in light of the latest conclusions of modern scholarship are clearly in danger of bending Scripture into conciliation with conclusions that are not *really* true but merely what Hall calls "idea-fads of modernity." As such, they are in danger of acting as if the Christian religion is merely a subjective phenomenon that must be brought into conformity

Christian scholarship that makes Scripture "potentially nonfalsifiable" by reading the Bible "through the lens of empirical science," John Mark Reynolds and Paul Nelson articulate the point that all who are concerned about the ultimate authority of Scripture would be wise to consider.[97] "There is something troubling," they argue,

> about the fact that there is no built-in limit to the amount of accommodation possible. What is meant by the statement "The Bible is true" if accommodation proceeds past a certain point? People holding this view, or any view like it, would need to clarify how far they are willing to stretch language before giving up the initial premise. As the

with the prevailing thought of the day, and therefore of thinking like those who are convinced that scientific truth and religious truth occupy different epistemological realms. Certainly this is one reason why arguments that are critical of Old Princeton's alleged openness to certain aspects of evolutionary theory are so forceful. See, for example, Hall, "Holding Fast the Concession of Faith," and David W. Hall, "Angels Unaware: The Ascendancy of Science over Orthodoxy in Nineteenth Century Reformed Orthodoxy," unpublished paper. On Old Princeton's attitude toward science in general and evolutionary theory in particular, cf. Charles Hodge, *What Is Darwinism? And Other Writings on Science and Religion*, ed. Mark A. Noll, David N. Livingstone (Grand Rapids: Baker, 1994); B. B. Warfield, *Evolution, Scripture, and Science: Selected Writings*, ed. Mark A. Noll, David N. Livingstone; Bradley John Gundlach, "The Evolution Question at Princeton, 1845–1929" (PhD diss., University of Rochester, 1995); David N. Livingstone, "Science, Region, and Religion: The Reception of Darwinism in Princeton, Belfast, and Edinburgh," in *Disseminating Darwinism: The Role of Place, Race, Religion, and Gender*, ed. Ronald L. Numbers, John Stenhouse (Cambridge: Cambridge University Press, 1999), 7–38.

But if believers who read Scripture in light of modern scholarship are in danger of accommodating what Hall calls the "idea-fads" of the present day, it is entirely possible that those who refuse to bring the non-"idea-fads of modernity" to bear on the interpretation of Scripture are in danger of enshrining the "idea-fads" of an earlier day. They are in danger, in other words, of regarding as true a previous generation's inability to look at general revelation through the spectacles of special revelation, and thus they too are in danger of treating the Christian religion as little more than an essentially subjective phenomenon. How, then, should Christians proceed? Perhaps we should begin by proceeding patiently and cautiously, allowing accepted interpretations of Scripture to be challenged *only* after generations of those who have the mind of Christ and hold the norm of truth in their hands have sorted truth from error on the basis of careful scholarly analysis that is informed and guided by sound exegesis. I would suggest, moreover, that when we are having difficulty determining which conclusions of modern scholarship are "provisional" and which ones are "indisputable," we would be wise to assume a posture that defers to orthodox interpretations of Scripture. For when we do not assume this posture we act as if the scientific enterprise always and everywhere yields facts instead of interpretations of facts, which is to prejudice believing academics against orthodoxy.

97. John Mark Reynolds and Paul Nelson, "Young Earth Creationism," in *Three Views on Creation and Evolution*, ed. J. P. Moreland, John Mark Reynolds (Grand Rapids: Zondervan, 1999), 69.

argument stands now, the Bible could theoretically be made to say the opposite of its "plain sense" and still be defended as "scientifically accurate." This is disconcerting.[98]

While no participant in the contemporary discussion has any intention of undermining either the integrity or the authority of Scripture, the controversial nature of Warfield's solution to the problem of the relationship between Christianity and culture is a reminder to scholars on both sides of the divide that the line between assimilation and accommodation—between "progressive orthodoxy" and what Warfield calls "retrogressive heterodoxy"[99]—is razor thin and difficult to discern. As such, Warfield's apologetical response to the modern era's relocation of the divine-human nexus is finally relevant because, as we will see in Part Two of this study, it is a call to those who have the mind of Christ and hold the norm of truth in their hands to integrate faith and learning with wisdom, i.e., to engage in the task of Christian scholarship in a manner that self-consciously accords with presuppositions that are consistently Christian. Before we move on to a more extensive analysis of Warfield's theological method, however, we must first consider the relevance of my proposal to J. Gresham Machen's critique of theological liberalism.

98. Ibid., 69–70.
99. Warfield, "The Idea of Systematic Theology," in *Studies in Theology*, 78.

4

The Critique of Theological Liberalism

Machen's Relationship to Warfield

In an essay titled "Machen, Van Til, and the Apologetical Tradition of the OPC," Greg Bahnsen addresses two questions that are of critical importance to the apologetical identity of the Orthodox Presbyterian Church. These questions, which are related to the perceived tension between the Old Princeton and New Westminster approaches to apologetics, can be stated as follows: Is J. Gresham Machen's approach to apologetics conceptually opposed to the presuppositionalism of Cornelius Van Til? And are there, therefore, two apologetical traditions in the Orthodox Presbyterian Church that are diametrically opposed to one another? While most interpreters either have or will conclude that Machen's apologetic was conceptually at odds with the presuppositional approach of Van Til, Bahnsen insists such a conclusion is unfounded. Indeed, while he acknowledges that the approaches of Machen and Van Til are not identical, he nonetheless argues that there is a "harmony of perspective" between the two because Machen "moved away from the old Princeton conception of apologetics in a presuppositional direction."[1] According to Bahnsen, whereas we might expect Machen "to have had the same old Princeton conception of, and goal for, his historical apologetic; namely, to reason his way to dominion . . . by using historical evidence which is compelling in itself to the unbeliever's neutral reasoning," he actually conceived of his work in historical apologetics "as requiring and resting on Christian presuppositions, as Van Til taught."[2]

Although I, like Bahnsen, suspect there might be more in common between the apologetical approaches of Machen and Van Til than most of their students have been willing to grant, I disagree with Bahnsen as to why compatibility is possible because I disagree with his assessment of Machen's relationship to Old Princeton in general and B. B. Warfield in particular. Whereas Bahnsen insists that compatibility is likely because Machen conceived of apologetics much like Van Til did, namely as a *defensive* task that is directed, "quite contrary to Warfield, mainly to *believers*,"[3] I am persuaded that if the methods of Machen and Van Til are compatible they are so *only* because Machen conceived of apologetics much like Warfield did, namely as an *offensive* task that is directed mainly to *unbelievers*. While this chapter leaves it to others to determine whether or not there is in fact a "harmony of perspective" between the approaches of Machen and Van Til, it demonstrates—via an examination of the correspondence between Machen's understanding of the task of apologetics and his solution to the problem of the relationship between Christianity and culture—that apologetics for Machen was an *offensive* rather than a *defensive* task. As such, it suggests that if there is a "harmony of perspective" between the approaches of Machen and Van Til it is not because Machen moved away from Old Princeton, but because he stood squarely in the tradition of Old Princeton, at least insofar as I am describing that tradition

1. Greg Bahnsen, "Machen, Van Til, and the Apologetical Tradition of the OPC," in *Pressing Toward the Mark: Essays Commemorating Fifty Years of the Orthodox Presbyterian Church*, ed. Charles Dennison, Richard Gamble (Philadelphia: The Committee for the Historian of the Orthodox Presbyterian Church, 1986), 262–63.

2. Ibid., 277–78.

3. Ibid., 280.

in this study. In so doing, it reinforces the fact of Machen's continuity with Warfield, and outlines the context within which his critique of theological liberalism—which we will examine in some depth at the end of this chapter—is properly understood. It also establishes, in keeping with the thesis of this study, that this critique was driven not by a philosophical commitment to a kind of Enlightenment rationalism, but by a theological commitment to epistemological assumptions that are consistently Reformed.

The Problem of the Relationship between Christianity and Culture: Two Anti-Intellectual Solutions

The "Worldly" Solution

Machen was convinced that there is no greater problem facing the modern church than that which has to do with the relationship between Christianity and culture. "What," he asks, "is the relation between Christianity and modern culture; may Christianity be maintained in a scientific age?"[4] Machen's answer is clearly articulated in an address delivered to the Philadelphia Ministers' Association in the fall of 1912, an address that was intended to be "a defense of 'scientific theological study.' "[5] In this address, originally titled "Scientific Preparation of the Minister" but published later under the heading "Christianity and Culture," Machen argues that the problem of the relationship between Christianity and culture may be settled in one of three ways. It may be settled in the first place by accommodating Christianity to modern culture and the conclusions of

4. J. Gresham Machen, *Christianity and Liberalism* (Grand Rapids: Eerdmans, 1990; 1923), 6. Also cf. J. Gresham Machen, "Christianity and Culture," in *Selected Shorter Writings of J. Gresham Machen*, ed. D. G. Hart (Phillipsburg, NJ: P&R Publishing, 2004), 401. In this chapter the word "culture" refers generally to everything in human civilization that is related to the life of the mind, and specifically to those "intellectual forces which are rampant in the world [that] are grievously perplexing the Church." J. Gresham Machen, *The New Testament: An Introduction to Its Literature and History*, ed. W. John Cook (Edinburgh: The Banner of Truth Trust, 1990), 377. In this regard, see Harry Emerson Fosdick, "Shall the Fundamentalists Win?" *The Christian Century* 39 (June 8, 1922): 713–14.

5. D. G. Hart, " 'Doctor Fundamentalis': An Intellectual Biography of J. Gresham Machen, 1881–1937" (PhD diss., Johns Hopkins University, 1988), 63. Cf. J. Gresham Machen to Minnie Gresham Machen, 3 March 1912, Machen Archives, Montgomery Memorial Library, Westminster Theological Seminary, Philadelphia.

modern science. The religious needs of people in each successive generation will be satisfied, advocates of this solution insist, not by clinging to outmoded expressions of religious truth, but by blending "the old faith" and "the new knowledge" into "a new combination."[6] This solution, which Machen believes is grounded in the assumption that the Christian religion is a mystical or moral rather than a supernatural historical phenomenon, is perhaps nowhere more succinctly articulated than in the writings of Machen's contemporary Harry Emerson Fosdick.[7] "We must be able to think our modern life clear through in Christian terms," Fosdick argues, "and to do that we also must be able to think our Christian life clear through in modern terms."[8]

The "Obscurantist" Solution

The second solution goes to the opposite extreme. While the "worldly solution" seeks to preserve the Christian religion by subordinating it to modern culture and the conclusions of modern science, the "obscurantist solution" seeks to save the Christian religion from the devastating conclusions of modern scholarship by withdrawing from the world "into a sort of unhealthy, modernized, intellectual monastery."[9] "Some men in the Church are inclined to choose a simple way out of the difficulty," Machen argues, "they are inclined to reject the whole of modern culture as either evil or worthless; this wisdom of the world, they maintain, must be deserted for the divine 'foolishness' of the gospel."[10] Although advocates of this solution recognize correctly that salvation is a gift that flows entirely from the grace of God, they conclude wrongly that "the culture of this world must be a matter at least of indifference to the Christian."[11] Indeed, while they concede that the Christian must

6. Fosdick, "Shall the Fundamentalists Win?" 713–14.
7. Cf. J. Gresham Machen, "The Modern Use of the Bible," in *What Is Christianity? And Other Addresses*, ed. Ned Stonehouse (Grand Rapids: Eerdmans, 1951), 199. See also Machen, "Christianity and Culture," 401.
8. Fosdick, "Shall the Fundamentalists Win?" 713–14.
9. J. Gresham Machen, *The Literature and History of New Testament Times, Teachers Manual*, The Westminster Departmental Graded Series, ed. John T. Faris (Philadelphia: The Presbyterian Board of Publication and Sabbath School Work, 1916), 277–78.
10. Ibid., 277.
11. Machen, "Christianity and Culture," 401.

live in and be a part of human culture, they regard this participation "as a necessary evil—a dangerous and unworthy task necessary to be gone through with under a stern sense of duty in order that thereby the higher ends of the gospel may be attained."[12]

The "Epistemological Error" of the Modern Era

While Machen was not oblivious to the potential advantages of these solutions to the problem of the relationship between Christianity and culture,[13] nevertheless he was convinced that they pose a serious threat to the enduring integrity of the Christian religion because they are grounded in what he regarded as the "epistemological error" of the modern era, namely the notion that there is discontinuity—perhaps even antagonism—between the epistemological realms of religion and science.[14] Based on their post-Kantian aversion to metaphysical speculation, and inspired by their accommodation of a more or less secular view of the universe, advocates of these solutions presumed that the Christian religion is an inherently anti-intellectual phenomenon that can be preserved in the modern era only "by divorcing it from science."[15] Indeed, the Christian religion is not based, they argued, on the rational appropriation of something that is considered to be objectively true.[16] Rather, it is based on an ineffable experience that is the natural manifestation of the universal human effort to "tap" into and thereby order life according to the vital moral force that pervades and actuates what Machen calls "the mighty world process itself."[17]

12. Ibid., 402.

13. For example, cf. J. Gresham Machen, "Christianity in Conflict," in *Contemporary American Theology*, vol. 1, ed. Vergilius Ferm (New York: Round Table Press, 1932), 255–57; J. Gresham Machen, "Christianity and Liberty: A Challenge to the 'Modern Mind,' " *The Forum* (March 1931): 165.

14. J. Gresham Machen, "The Relation of Religion to Science and Philosophy," *PTR* 24 (1926): 62.

15. J. Gresham Machen, "Religion and Fact," *The Real Issue* 1 (April 15, 1924): 3.

16. J. Gresham Machen, "The Gospel and Modern Substitutes," in *God Transcendent*, ed. Ned Stonehouse (Edinburgh: The Banner of Truth Trust, 1982; 1949), 102.

17. Machen, *Christianity and Liberalism*, 63. On the mystical and moral ways of tapping into this force, cf. J. Gresham Machen, "Faith and Knowledge," *Fourth Biennial Meeting of the Conference of Theological Seminaries and Colleges in the United States and Canada: Bulletin* 4 (August 1924): 14–15. Note that it is in this effort to "tap" into what is considered to be divine that the defining characteristic of theological liberalism—"naturalism"—is found. According to Machen,

Since religion, according to these solutions, is little more than that individual or corporate effort to live in accord with those values of love and good will that the Ultimate Reality has woven into the processes of the cosmos, advocates conclude that the conflict between Christianity and culture will be settled as soon as people realize that religion and science occupy autonomous epistemological realms. Religion, they maintained, "may hold to a realm of [religious and ethical] ideals; but science must be given the entire realm of facts."[18] It is herein, then, i.e., in this abandonment to science of "the whole realm of objective truth,"[19] that the threat posed by these solutions to the problem of the relationship between Christianity and culture is found.

The Task of Consecration

The "True Solution" to the Problem

Despite Machen's willingness to acknowledge that these solutions seem at first to offer promising responses to the problem of the relationship between Christianity and culture, he insists that they need to be rejected

---

"naturalism" is "the denial of any entrance of the creative power of God, as sharply distinguished from his works in nature, at the beginnings of Christianity." J. Gresham Machen, "Christianity vs. Modern Liberalism," *Moody Bible Institute Monthly* 13 (April 1923): 349. While this naturalism is *implicitly* manifest in theology that affirms the transcendence of God yet denies the sovereignty of God in salvation (as in much of contemporary evangelicalism), it is *explicitly* manifest in the work of those who conceive of God not as the personal, transcendent yet immanent "Creator and Ruler of all" (Machen, "The Relationship of Religion to Science and Philosophy," 39), but as "the universe itself, conceived of not in its individual manifestations but as a mighty whole." J. Gresham Machen, "God, the Creator," in *The Christian Faith in the Modern World* (Grand Rapids: Eerdmans, 1936), 113. For examples of scholars who conceived of God in this explicitly naturalistic fashion, see Harry Emerson Fosdick, *The Modern Use of the Bible* (New York: Macmillan, 1924), 161, 266; Shailer Mathews, *The Faith of Modernism* (New York: Macmillan, 1924), 100, 115, 119, 148, 174–75; and Shailer Mathews, *New Faith for Old* (New York: Macmillan, 1936), 225, 233, 237. Note that it is this common grounding in some form of naturalism that substantiates D. G. Hart's claim that Machen's critique of theological liberalism cannot be understood "simply on the binary categories of conservative and liberal. For all his conservatism . . . Machen approached any number of issues in ways that today's conservatives might think liberal. Meanwhile, for all his antipathy to liberalism, Machen's defense of historic Christianity was not dependent on recent views of biblical authority or novel ideas about creation or Christ's return; instead, it was thoroughly in the mainstream of Augustinian Christianity." D. G. Hart, "The Forgotten Machen?" in *Selected Shorter Writings of J. Gresham Machen*, 4.

18. Machen, "The Relation of Religion to Science and Philosophy," 46.

19. J. Gresham Machen, *What Is Faith?* (Edinburgh: The Banner of Truth Trust, 1991; 1925), 242.

precisely because they cannot satisfy the religious needs of fallen sinners.[20] Nothing but something that is objectively true can meet the supernatural need of the sinful soul, he reasons, and objective truth is abandoned by "the epistemological By-Path Meadow which is found in the separation of religion from science."[21] Because he recognizes that all truth—be it religious or scientific—is God's truth, he concludes that Christians will resolve the conflict between Christianity and culture not by destroying "one or the other of the contending forces," but by "transforming the unwieldy, resisting mass of human thought until it becomes subservient to the gospel."[22] "Instead of obliterating the distinction between the Kingdom and the world, or on the other hand withdrawing from the world into a sort of modernized intellectual monasticism," Christians must "go forth joyfully, enthusiastically to make the world subject to God."[23]

The Assimilation of Modern Culture to Christianity

How, then, should believing scholars go about making the world subject to God? How, in other words, do "the soldiers of the cross" move the church of God forward "to joyous conquest"?[24] According to Machen, believing scholars accomplish this end neither by appealing to the natural moral capacities of fallen sinners, nor by waging social and political warfare against the perceived forces of cultural disintegration.[25]

20. Machen, "Christianity and Liberty," 165.

21. Machen, "The Relation of Religion to Science and Philosophy," 66; see also Machen, "Isaiah's Scorn of Idolatry," in *God Transcendent*, 27. Machen repudiates the "fatal" anti-intellectualism of the first two solutions (J. Gresham Machen, "What Is the Gospel?" *USR* 38 [1927]: 170), because he recognizes that human beings who are dead in sin and "totally unable to please God" (J. Gresham Machen, *The Christian View of Man* [Edinburgh: The Banner of Truth Trust, 1984; 1937], 241) need salvation "from the awful wrath of a righteous God" rather than an ineffable experience. Machen, *What Is Faith?* 58. In other words, they need an object that is outside them that can save them from their sin. In this regard, D. G. Hart incisively notes that "Machen's high regard for the role of the intellect in faith . . . was tied to his defense of the historical basis of Christianity. Without an objective and external reality upon which individuals could trust, salvation was impossible." Hart, "'Doctor Fundamentalis,'" 217.

22. Machen, "Christianity and Culture," 402, 405. On the unity of truth, see J. Gresham Machen, *The Virgin Birth of Christ* (Grand Rapids: Baker, 1967; 1930), 219.

23. Machen, "Christianity and Culture," 402.

24. J. Gresham Machen, "Rejoice with Trembling," Unpublished Sermon, Machen Archives, 2.

25. D. G. Hart argues that Machen is critical of theological liberalism because he is convinced the true identity of the church is found in its confession of correct doctrine rather than in its "social utility." According to Hart, Machen not only rejects the idea of a "Christian

Rather, Christians make the world subject to God by cultivating the arts and sciences "with all the enthusiasm of the veriest humanist, but at the same time consecrat[ing] them to the service of our God."[26] "Patient study should not be abandoned to the men of the world," he argues, but those "who have really received the blessed experience of the love of God in Christ must seek to bring that experience to bear upon the culture of the modern world, in order that Christ may rule, not only in all nations, but in every department of human life."[27] In short, elements of modern culture that are hostile to the gospel must be "refuted and destroyed," the rest must be "made subservient," but nothing can be "neglected."[28] It is in this fashion, then, i.e., by assimilating modern culture to Christianity, that Christians set modern culture apart for the service of the kingdom.[29]

Why Consecration Is Necessary

Why, though, does Machen insist that Christians must pursue the consecration—rather than the destruction or accommodation—of modern culture? Why does he argue, in other words, that the "true solution" to the problem of the relationship between Christianity and culture is found in the assimilation of modern learning to Christian truth?[30] He

---

America," but he also insists that the involvement of the church in social and political affairs undermines the witness of the church to Christian truth. Indeed, it fosters the substitution of social and political warfare for the proclamation of the gospel. Cf. D. G. Hart, "Christianity and Liberalism in a Postliberal Age," *WTJ* 56 (1994): 329–44; D. G. Hart, *Defending the Faith: J. Gresham Machen and the Crisis of Conservative Protestantism in Modern America* (Grand Rapids: Baker, 1995; 1994).

26. Machen, "Christianity and Culture," 402.
27. Machen, *The Literature and History of New Testament Times, Teachers Manual*, 278.
28. Ibid.
29. Machen, "Christianity and Culture," 404–6; cf. Machen, *The Literature and History of New Testament Times, Teachers Manual*, 278. Machen is convinced that only believing scholars can set modern culture apart for the service of the kingdom because only believing scholars: (1) know what Christianity "really is" (Machen, "What Is Christianity?" 18); and (2) are capable of "true science." While he concedes that unbelieving scholars "are doing useful work in detail, in Biblical philology, in exegesis, in Biblical theology, and in other branches of study," he insists that they are not consecrating modern culture to Christianity "because they are without that experience of God's power in the soul which is of the essence of Christianity. . . . Modern thought they know, but Christianity is really foreign to them" (Machen, "Christianity and Culture," 405–6). On the relationship between "true science" and the joy that empowers the task of consecration, see the forthcoming discussion as well as "Rejoice with Trembling," 1–11. Note that my take on Machen's understanding of Christian cultural involvement is different from that of Hart, "The Forgotten Machen?" 13–14.
30. Machen, *The Literature and History of New Testament Times, Teachers Manual*, 278.

does so for two reasons, both of which will be clear after a brief consideration of the two factors that together make the consecration of modern culture necessary. The first factor has to do with Machen's insistence that saving faith is grounded in the rational appropriation of objective evidence rather than the ineffable religious experience of fallen moral agents.[31] While Machen acknowledges that in the temporal order of faith the experience of regeneration precedes the embracing of what God has revealed by the mind, nevertheless he insists that "what the Holy Spirit does in the new birth is not to make a man a Christian regardless of the evidence, but on the contrary to clear away the mists from his eyes and enable him to attend to the evidence"[32] that is "thoroughly reasonable" in itself.[33] Since saving faith "is always a conscious condition of the soul"[34] that as such necessarily involves a movement of the mind, it follows that the need for consecration is related to the fact that "A man can believe only what he holds to be true."[35] "Obviously," Machen argues, "it is impossible to hold on with the heart to something that one has rejected with the head, and all the usefulness of Christianity can never lead us to be Christians unless the Christian religion is true."[36]

If the first factor concerns the logical priority of the intellect in faith, the second is closely related in that it has to do with what Machen regards as the primary obstacle to the advancement of the kingdom of God in the modern era, namely the hostility of the mod-

31. For example, see Machen, *The New Testament*, 375; Machen, *What Is Faith?* 174, 197–98, 202–4.

32. J. Gresham Machen, "Shall We Defend the Bible?" in *The Christian Faith in the Modern World*, 63.

33. J. Gresham Machen, review of *Apology and Polemic in the New Testament*, by Andrew D. Heffern, *Presbyterian* 93 (September 13, 1923): 10. According to the classical notion of faith, experience "cannot jump the rational gun" because people can believe only what they know to be both true and trustworthy. John Gerstner, "The Contributions of Charles Hodge, B. B. Warfield, and J. Gresham Machen to the Doctrine of Inspiration," in *Challenges to Inerrancy: A Theological Response*, ed. Gordon R. Lewis, Bruce Demarest (Chicago: Moody Press, 1984), 374–75; cf. Machen, *What Is Faith?* 48. On the logical vs. the temporal order of faith, see Machen, "The Relation of Religion to Science and Philosophy," 43, 59; Machen, *Christianity and Liberalism*, 56; D. G. Hart, "The Princeton Mind in the Modern World and the Common Sense of J. Gresham Machen," *WTJ* 46 (1984): 23. For Machen's analysis of the "strange epistemology of the Barthian school," see J. Gresham Machen, "Forty Years of New Testament Research," *USR* 40 (1929): 9; J. Gresham Machen, "Karl Barth and 'The Theology of Crisis,'" *WTJ* 53 (1991): 197–207.

34. Machen, *What Is Faith?* 197.

35. Machen, "Christianity and Culture," 403; cf. Machen, *What Is Faith?* 94.

36. Machen, "Christianity in Conflict," 261.

ern mind to the "gospel *about* Jesus," i.e., "the message upon which salvation depends."[37] According to Machen, many people reject the gospel, simply because their thinking is dominated by ideas that are "profoundly opposed to Christianity, or at least—what is nearly as bad—. . . out of all connection with Christianity."[38] But why is their thinking dominated by such ideas, and why do they therefore believe that the "gospel *about* Jesus" is absurd?[39] Machen insists that the answer is found in the pervasive antisupernaturalism of the modern era.[40] In short, many people can no longer believe that the gospel is true, not because the gospel has been demonstrated to be false, but because their thinking is attuned to the naturalism of the age.[41] As such, they reject Christianity not because the Christian religion is absurd, but because their thinking is controlled "by ideas which, by the resistless force of logic, prevent Christianity from being regarded as anything more than a harmless delusion."[42]

If it is therefore true that saving faith is grounded in the kind of conviction that seems foolish to those whose thinking is controlled by ideas that make the acceptance of the gospel "logically impossible,"[43] it follows that the consecration of modern culture to Christianity is necessary for two reasons. It is necessary not only because the Christian religion "must justify its place, despite all that that may cost, in the world of facts,"[44] but more importantly because this justification, i.e., this creation of "those favorable conditions for the reception of the gospel,"[45] is really necessary for the "external advancement" of the kingdom of God.[46] For Machen, then, "Intellectual conquests are just as necessary for the progress of the gospel as are conquests in the

37. J. Gresham Machen, "Christian Scholarship and Evangelism," in *What Is Christianity?* 123. See also Machen, "Christianity and Culture," 406–7; Machen, *The Literature and History of New Testament Times, Teachers Manual*, 278.
38. Machen, "Christianity and Culture," 404.
39. Cf. J. Gresham Machen, "Christian Scholarship and the Defence of the Faith," in *What Is Christianity?* 129; Machen, "Christianity in Conflict," 245.
40. Machen, "Christianity and Culture," 401, 406–8.
41. Machen, "Christian Scholarship and the Defence of the Faith," 126; cf. 136.
42. Machen, "Christianity and Culture," 404.
43. Machen, *The New Testament*, 378; cf. Machen, *Christianity and Liberalism*, 142.
44. Machen, "Faith and Knowledge," 20.
45. Machen, "Christianity and Culture," 404.
46. Machen, *The New Testament*, 378.

external world"[47] because people can believe only what they know to be both true and trustworthy.

The Epistemological "Breadth" of "True Science"

A Rationalistic Solution?

To this point we have seen that of the three solutions to the problem of the relationship between Christianity and culture that Machen discusses, only the third—the one that he commends—repudiates the "epistemological error" of the modern era by insisting that saving faith is grounded in the rational appropriation of objective evidence rather than in the ineffable religious experience of fallen moral agents. It is likely at this point, however, that some will challenge the viability of Machen's solution, for they will suggest that his preoccupation with the rational nature of faith and his apparent indifference to the subjective and experiential components of a consistently Reformed religious epistemology betray an implicit endorsement of precisely those modern tendencies that he ostensibly rejects.[48] The effort to extend the kingdom by consecrating modern culture to Christianity is ultimately informed, they will likely suggest, not by faithfulness to the assumptions of the Reformed tradition, but by the accommodation of assumptions that find their genesis in some form of Enlightenment humanism. Indeed, these critics will likely conclude that the effort to extend the kingdom by establishing the integrity of the Christian view of the world is ultimately informed not by an epistemology that acknowledges the supremacy of God in all things, but by an epistemology that is covertly if not overtly rationalistic.

While it is altogether clear that the ultimate objective of the task of consecration is the advancement of the kingdom of God through the assimilation of modern learning to Christian truth, it is just as clear that

47. Ibid., 376; cf. Machen, *Christianity and Liberalism*, 174.

48. Those who endorse the standard interpretation of Old Princeton's religious epistemology will likely draw such a conclusion. For example, see George Marsden, "J. Gresham Machen, History, and Truth," *WTJ* 42 (1979–80): 157–75; George Marsden, "Understanding J. Gresham Machen," *PSB* 11 (1990): 46–60; Mark A. Noll, "The Princeton Theology," in *The Princeton Theology*, Reformed Theology in America, no. 1, ed. David Wells (Grand Rapids: Baker, 1989; 1985), 29.

the task itself is not a rationalistic enterprise, but one that acknowledges the import of the subjective and the centrality of experience in religious epistemology. That this is the case is perhaps nowhere more clearly manifest than in Machen's insistence that the task of consecration is based on and appeals to "true science." According to Machen, we ought not to define "science" in a manner that narrows the scope of what is regarded as "fact" to the conclusions of "those methods of research that operate merely with the doctrine of 'physical causation,' "[49] for such a definition explicitly endorses the "epistemological error" of the modern era. Rather, we ought to define "science" in a manner that is "true" because it recognizes that the sphere in which science moves is broad enough to include even the knowledge of God that he has given of himself "in nature and in His Word."[50]

The Work of the Spirit and "True Science"

What, then, determines how broadly or narrowly science is defined? What determines, in other words, whether the science of the consecrating scholar "is really scientific or not"?[51] One of the central contentions of this chapter is that the answer to this question will elude us if we fail to recognize that Machen endorsed the philosophical psychology of his predecessors at Old Princeton Seminary. Like Hodge and Warfield before him,[52] Machen insisted that

49. Machen, "The Relation of Religion to Science and Philosophy," 51.
50. Ibid., 52.
51. Machen, *What Is Faith?* 130. According to Machen, scientific investigation has to do with the collection and analysis of all the facts that are germane to a particular topic. As such, scientists who "ignore" relevant facts in their investigations are not engaging in "true" or "real" science, but their efforts are being compromised by things such as "neglect" and "presumption." Ibid., 130–32. When it comes to the analysis of the "claims of Christianity," Machen argues: "If a man were truly scientific, we think, he would be convinced of the truth of Christianity whether he were a saint or a demon; since the truth of Christianity does not at all depend upon the state of the soul of the investigator, but is objectively fixed. But the question is whether a method which ignores the consciousness of sin is really scientific or not; and the answer must be, we think, that it is not. If you take account of all the facts, you will be convinced of the truth of Christianity; but you cannot take account of all the facts if you ignore the fact of sin. You cannot take account of all the facts if, while searching the heavens above and the earth beneath, you neglect the facts of your own soul." Ibid., 130–31; cf. Machen, "The Relation of Religion to Science and Philosophy," 64.
52. Machen's indebtedness to the anthropological commitments of Charles Hodge and B. B. Warfield is stated explicitly in *The Christian View of Man*, 228.

the soul is a single unit whose unitary activity is certainly determined by that which "lies far deeper than individual actions," namely the moral character or personality of the "whole man."[53] There "is no such thing," Machen argues, "as the will, considered as a separate something-or-other inside of a man; but what we call the will is just the whole man willing, as what we call the intellect is the whole man thinking and what we call the feelings is the whole man feeling."[54] But does this rejection of the "faculty psychology" extend to the realm of scientific investigation? Does Machen regard the practice of science, in other words, as a form of human activity that is engaged in by the "whole man," and which, as a consequence, is conditioned by the moral character or personality of the investigating agent? He clearly does, for while he insists that all science rests on presuppositions that are determined by the perception and conception of the intellect, he nonetheless recognizes that the perception and conception of the intellect are themselves conditioned by the moral character or personality of the investigating agent.[55] That this is the case, and that both the breadth and the quality of scientific investigation are determined by the moral character of the "whole man," will be clear after a brief examination of the scientific capacities of moral agents in their unregenerated and regenerated states.

Following Hodge, Warfield, and the Westminster divines, Machen argues that Adam was created in the image of God and thus "was like God not only in that he was a person but also in that he was good."[56] His likeness to God did not consist, in other words, merely in the possession of one personal attribute or another, but "there was [also] a moral likeness between man and God."[57] It was this moral likeness, however, that Adam lost for himself and for his posterity when he sinned in the garden, for when he sinned "God withdrew His favour" and the souls of "all mankind became spiritually dead" and fell "into an estate

53. Ibid., 146. On the certain relationship between moral character and the activity of the "whole man," see 26–29, 125, 138, 234–39.

54. Ibid., 236.

55. Cf. Machen, "The Relation of Religion to Science and Philosophy," 53. On the relationship between presuppositions and science, cf. Machen, *The Virgin Birth of Christ*, 219.

56. Machen, *The Christian View of Man*, 149.

57. Ibid.

of sin and misery."[58] According to Machen, one of the primary characteristics of this fallen estate is that those who are dead in sin do not have the moral ability to attend to what God has revealed in a "truly scientific" fashion. But how can this be? The answer gets to the heart of the relationship between moral character and the presuppositions that inform and condition scientific investigation. In short, Machen insists that the power of sin precludes the possibility of "true science" because it makes it impossible for fallen sinners to "see clearly," and thus to engage in scientific investigation in a fashion that is informed by "a sound metaphysic," i.e., by presuppositions that correspond with the way God and reality more or less objectively are.[59]

How, then, do those who are dead in sin come to "see clearly" so they can attend to what God has revealed in a "truly scientific" fashion? Machen insists that those who are dead in sin come to "see clearly" only through the "regenerating power of the Spirit of God."[60] It is the work of the Holy Spirit in regeneration that makes the intellect a "trustworthy instrument for apprehending truth," Machen argues, for it is the regenerating power of the Spirit of God that raises the chosen agent from spiritual death to spiritual life by applying to the soul the saving benefits of the redeeming work of Christ.[61] While the specific consequences of this supernatural act will be clear after the forthcoming consideration of the task of consecration's appeal to Christian experience as the means to advancing the kingdom of God, for now it is evident that the work of the Spirit is at the foundation of the task of

58. Ibid., 218, 214, 215. On the "profound corruption of man's whole nature" and the moral inability that constitutes the state of total depravity, cf. 220, 241–43.

59. Machen, "The Relation of Religion to Science and Philosophy," 59–60. My justification for contending that the fall into sin entails the loss of communion with God as well as the loss of the ability to be "truly scientific" is found in the correlation between the origin of the presuppositions that condition "true science" and the origin of the convictions that foster "real" communion with God, i.e., "true religion." The presuppositions that condition "true science" and the convictions that foster "true religion" are: (1) a genuine theism; and (2) a genuine awareness of the ontological as well as moral gulf that separates fallen sinners from the Creator. Ibid. On how the regenerate alone can endorse either of these presuppositions, cf. Machen, "Rejoice with Trembling," 1–11; Machen, *Christianity and Liberalism*, 54–68.

60. Machen, *The Christian View of Man*, 144.

61. Machen, *What Is Faith?* 135. On the benefits of Christ's redeeming death, cf. Machen, "The Active Obedience of Christ," in *God Transcendent*, 187–96. On the miraculous nature of the work of the Spirit, cf. Machen, *The Christian View of Man*, 102–4.

consecration because it is that "moral awakening of a soul dead in sin"[62] that makes fallen sinners "better philosophers"—and thereby better scientists—by enabling them "to see clearly where formerly [their] eyes were darkened."[63] "What the new birth does," Machen concludes, "is not to absolve men from being scientific in their defense of the faith, but rather to enable them to be truly scientific because a veil has been taken from their eyes."[64]

Summary Observations

Before we move on to our consideration of the role that Christian experience plays in the advancement of the kingdom of God, two summary observations are in order regarding the relationship between the work of the Spirit and the science that informs the task of consecration. The first is that we will never understand why the work of the Spirit plays a critical role in Machen's understanding of science if we fail to recognize that the veil that lies before the eyes of the unregenerated sinner's mind is moral rather than merely rational.[65] The foregoing discussion has established that for Machen, the metaphysical presuppositions that inform the breadth and quality of scientific investigation are reflections of the moral character of the "whole man," for it is the moral character of the "whole man" that conditions the perception and thereby the conception of the intellect. When we approach questions regarding the quality of scientific investigation with this in mind, it becomes immediately clear that the unregenerate do not have the ability to be "truly scientific" not merely because of rational weakness, but ultimately because of moral weakness. That is to say, they do not have the moral ability to see God more or less for who he objectively is, and as a consequence they do not have the moral ability to take account of "all of the facts" that impinge on the integrity of scientific investigation.[66]

62. Machen, *What Is Faith?* 144.
63. Machen, "The Relation of Religion to Science and Philosophy," 59.
64. Ibid., 63.
65. See, for example, Machen, *The Christian View of Man*, 83.
66. While Machen insists that the regenerating activity of the Spirit enables fallen sinners to see God more clearly, he never suggests that it enables them to see God perfectly. He never sug-

The second observation has to do with what the science that characterizes the task of consecration is like. When all is said and done, how are we to understand the difference between the science of the believing scholar and the science of the unbelieving scholar? In other words, exactly how is the science of the believing scholar, which is "true," different from the science of the unbelieving scholar, which is not "true"? Given Machen's insistence that the primary difference between the believing scholar and the unbelieving scholar is that the believing scholar has the moral ability to take account of all rather than merely some of the facts, it follows that the science of the believing scholar is different not because of one or another of its structural characteristics, but because it is informed by "a sound epistemology."[67] What this suggests, then, is that the science of the believing scholar is superior to that of the unbelieving scholar not because the believing scholar practices a kind of science that only believers can practice. Rather, it is superior because it is more "comprehensive" and therefore more truthful—and thus it is of a higher quality—than the science of those who because of spiritual blindness reject "a sound metaphysic."[68] As Warfield would say, the science of the believing scholar is different from the science of the unbelieving scholar not because there is "a difference in *kind*" between the two, but because there is a difference in terms of "perfection of performance."[69]

---

gests, in other words, that fallen sinners can have a perfect philosophy because: (1) mere mortals cannot see the face of God and live—"We are but finite creatures, and God has not destroyed us by showing us the full splendors of His being" (Machen, "Isaiah's Scorn of Idolatry," 25); and (2) no matter how good our metaphysic is, God is still shrouded in "mystery." Machen, "Rejoice with Trembling," 10–11. One of the important implications of these points is that no one—not even regenerated sinners—can practice science perfectly.

67. Machen, "The Relation of Religion to Science and Philosophy," 64–66.

68. Ibid. It goes without saying that "a sound metaphysic" and "a sound epistemology" are related in Machen's thought.

69. B. B. Warfield, "Introduction to Francis R. Beattie's *Apologetics*," in *Selected Shorter Writings of Benjamin B. Warfield*, 2 vols., ed. John E. Meeter (Phillipsburg, NJ: P&R Publishing, 2001), 2:100–3; see also B. B. Warfield, "A Review of *De Zekerheid Des Geloofs*," in *Shorter Writings*, 2:117–20. Note that Warfield's "temple of truth" analogy accurately characterizes Machen's understanding of science for two reasons: (1) Machen insists that Christians will bring modern learning into subjection to the gospel of Christ by meeting "non-Christian philosophers and non-Christian scientists on their own ground" (Machen, "The Relation of Religion to Science and Philosophy," 64); and (2) he believes there will be a time "when all of human thinking is permeated by the refining, ennobling influence of Jesus, when every thought has been brought into subjection to the obedience of Christ." Machen, "Christianity and Culture," 403.

The Appeal to "True Science"

The Place of Intellectual Labor

If the task of consecration is based on Christian experience because it demands that the consecrating scholar have the moral ability to assess what God has revealed in a "truly scientific" fashion, it also appeals to Christian experience because it attempts to advance the kingdom of God not by asking fallen sinners "to regard science and philosophy as without bearing upon religion, but on the contrary by asking them to become more scientific and more philosophic through attention to all, instead of to some, of the facts."[70] While some interpreters will likely conclude that this appeal is grounded in the anthropocentrism of the Enlightenment, in fact it is compatible with the assumptions of the Reformed tradition because it is informed by the realization that the ability to attend to "all of the facts," i.e., the ability to respond to the appeal of the consecrating scholar, presupposes the regenerating activity of the Holy Spirit on the "whole soul" of a moral agent. That this is the case, and that the external advancement of the kingdom of God is ultimately a divine rather than a human work, will be clear after a brief examination of the relationship of the intellectual labor of the believing scholar, the work of the Spirit, and the advent of saving faith.

While Machen insists that one of the primary responsibilities of the modern church is the task of transforming modern culture until it becomes subservient to the gospel, he nonetheless recognizes "that argument alone is quite insufficient to make a man a Christian. You may argue with him from now until the end of the world; you may bring forth the most magnificent arguments: but all will be in vain unless there be one other thing—the mysterious, creative power of the Holy Spirit in the new birth."[71] But if the decisive factor in the production of Christian conviction is the

---

70. Machen, "The Relation of Religion to Science and Philosophy," 64. Note that Machen's appeal to "true science," although it is grounded in the work of the Spirit on the "whole soul" of the consecrating scholar, nevertheless is directed to the unbeliever. In this respect, Machen's appeal to "true science" is different from Warfield's appeal to "right reason," which is directed to the believer.

71. Machen, "Christian Scholarship and the Defence of the Faith," 127; cf. Machen, *The New Testament*, 378.

regenerating power of the Spirit of God, does it follow—"as is so often assumed"—that the intellectual labor of the believing scholar is unnecessary?[72] Machen's answer must be understood within the context of his contention that the reason the "external proofs" of the Christian religion do not always elicit saving faith "is due not at all to any weakness of their own but only to a weakness in our minds."[73] While Machen argues that the believing scholar can elicit an "intellectual" or "theoretical" conviction of the truth of the Christian religion by presenting the standard proofs for its trustworthiness, he insists that a "saving" conviction cannot be produced, not because the arguments are insufficient, but because the veil that lies before the eyes of the fallen sinner's mind prohibits the apprehension, i.e., the "recognition," of that sufficiency.[74] If the arguments of the believing scholar are ultimately ineffectual, then, because the unregenerate are blind to the true significance of what is objectively present to their understanding, we must conclude that the work of the Spirit is of critical importance not because it makes fallen sinners Christians regardless of the evidence, but because it removes the veil from the eyes of their minds and enables them to attend to the evidence. It enables them to see, in other words, that the "probable" conclusions of the believing scholar, which are necessary precisely because they establish the integrity of the gospel and thereby "prepare" for the "gracious coming" of the Spirit of God, are indeed true and therefore trustworthy.[75]

72. Machen, "Christianity and Culture," 407; cf. Machen, *The Literature and History of the New Testament, Teacher's Manual*, 279; Machen, *What Is Faith?* 248–50.

73. Machen, *What Is Faith?* 248–49.

74. Machen's point will be lost if we forget that the veil before the eyes of the fallen sinner's mind is moral rather than merely rational. For Machen's endorsement of the classical Reformed distinction between a merely speculative and a spiritual understanding of the gospel, see Machen, *The New Testament*, 375; Machen, "The Relation of Religion to Science and Philosophy," 63–64; Machen, *What Is Faith?* 135, 202–4; Machen, *The Christian View of Man*, 150–51.

75. J. Gresham Machen, "History and Faith," in *What Is Christianity?* 182–83; Machen, *The New Testament*, 378. At this point, two important observations are in order. The first is that the historical and philosophical proofs for the trustworthiness of the Christian religion do not point to themselves, but to the trustworthiness of what God has revealed. As such, the faith of the believer does not focus on rational arguments about what God has revealed, but on the actual substance of what God has revealed. Second, if Machen did *not* endorse the classical Reformed distinction between a merely speculative and a spiritual understanding of the gospel, then statements such as the following—which presume the distinction—would pose a

The Law of God, "True Science," and the External Advancement of the Kingdom

How, then, does the Spirit of God enable fallen sinners to attend to the true significance of what they in their natural state can only rationally perceive, and how is the Spirit therefore responsible for the external advancement of the kingdom of God? According to Machen, the Spirit gives fallen sinners the capacity to see by bringing them into contact with the law of God and thereby enabling them to take "a truly scientific attitude towards the evidence."[76] Through the law, which Machen believes is grounded in the perfect righteousness of God, the Spirit opens the eyes of fallen sinners' minds to the supremacy of God in all things and thereby convicts them of "the guilt and misery of man in his sin."[77] It is this illumination of the mind to "the facts of the inner life of man"[78] that then does two things that ensure the external advancement of the kingdom. In the first place, it enables fallen sinners to "really lay hold upon the central message in the Bible,"[79] for it is the "sense of need"[80] that is produced by the consciousness of the holiness and "awful transcendence of God"[81] that suddenly makes "the words of Scripture glow with a heavenly light and burn in the hearts of men."[82] "When a man . . . comes under the conviction of sin,"

---

serious challenge to my thesis. "Thus even in order to exhibit the truth of Christianity at the bar of reason, it is necessary to learn the lesson of the law. It is impossible to prove first that Christianity is true, and then proceed on the basis of its truth to become conscious of one's sin, for the fact of sin is itself one of the chief foundations upon which the proof is based." Machen, *What Is Faith?* 134.

76. Machen, *What Is Faith?* 135.

77. J. Gresham Machen, "Christian Scholarship and the Building up of the Church," in *What Is Christianity?* 144. See also J. Gresham Machen, Address at the Second Annual Symposium on Religion at Columbia University, 2 April 1930, Machen Archives, 12; Machen, *Christianity and Liberalism*, 56; Machen, *The Christian View of Man*, 188.

78. Machen, "The Relation of Religion to Science and Philosophy," 64.

79. Machen, *The Christian View of Man*, 33. The central message in the Bible is the gospel, or that which has to do with "the redeeming work of Christ." Machen, "What Fundamentalism Stands for Now," in *What Is Christianity?* 259.

80. Machen, *What Is Faith?* 248.

81. Machen, *Christianity and Liberalism*, 62.

82. J. Gresham Machen, "Prophets False and True," in *God Transcendent*, 121. Note that the unregenerate can take account of all the facts except the fact that reveals the glory of the gospel, namely the fact of sin.

Machen argues, "his whole attitude toward life is transformed; he wonders at his former blindness, and the message of the gospel, which formerly seemed to be an idle tale, becomes now instinct with light."[83]

If the illumination of the mind to the "fact of sin"[84] enables fallen sinners in the first place to see that the gospel is true, it compels them in the second place not only to cling to Jesus "like a drowning person [who] will snatch at a plank that may save him from the abyss,"[85] but also to enlist in the campaign to conquer the world for Christ with "mighty enthusiasm."[86] The justification for this contention is found generally in the subtleties of Machen's philosophical psychology, and specifically in the broad understanding of the will that informs his thinking about the nature of saving faith. "The will of man is not free," Machen argues,

> in the sense that it operates independently of the feelings and the intellect. Indeed, if we regard the will as a sort of separate somewhat inside of a man, going about its business in its own way, capable of taking advice from other parts of man's nature but also capable of acting quite independently of such advice when the mood strikes it—if we think of the will thus, we are getting very far away from reality indeed. We are really making of something that we call the will a little separate personality; we are doing away with the unity of the man's personality. As a matter of fact, there is really no such thing as the will out of relation to the other aspects of the person. What we call the will is just the whole person making choices.[87]

83. Machen, *Christianity and Liberalism*, 67. Because he recognizes that the conviction of sin "cannot be obtained by ordinary methods of research," Machen concedes there is an "element of truth" to the notion that "religion possesses its own credentials and should be judged as religion and not as something else." Machen, "The Relation of Religion to Science and Philosophy," 63–64. Nevertheless, he insists that because Christian convictions are based on facts, e.g., the "fact of sin," the "attainment even of these convictions is not really to be separated from philosophy or from science. A man cannot be truly scientific if he neglects relevant facts; he cannot be truly scientific if he neglects the fact of sin." Ibid., 64.

84. Machen, "The Relation of Religion to Science and Philosophy," 64.

85. Machen, *What Is Faith?* 249. This clinging is the "immediate sign of . . . being born again." Machen, *The Christian View of Man*, 77; cf. Machen, *Christianity and Liberalism*, 140.

86. Machen, "Rejoice with Trembling," 2.

87. Machen, *The Christian View of Man*, 29.

When we consider the work of the Spirit in light of the philosophical psychology that is suggested by this comment,[88] it follows that the work of the Spirit is responsible for the external advancement of the kingdom because the "sense of need" that enables the regenerate to "really lay hold upon the central message in the Bible" is the same sense that determines the activity of the will, broadly understood. Whereas the unregenerate are "repelled by the stupendous nature of the thing that we ask them to believe"[89] because they are oblivious to the "fact of sin" and therefore blind to the true significance of what they can rationally perceive, the regenerate "rejoice,"[90] i.e., they "glory,"[91] in the message of the cross because they see that the gospel is true and that it alone will meet their supernatural need.

It is the joy of knowing the gospel is true, then, that not only compels regenerated sinners to cling to Jesus for their salvation from sin. It also drives them onto the battlefield of truth for the purpose of bringing all branches of earnest human endeavor "into *some* relation to the gospel."[92] In short, those who have been given eyes to see enter into combat with both joy and confidence not only because they know that Jesus has rescued them from the wrath of a God who is holy, but also because they recognize that they join the battle "armed with certain facts to a knowledge of which [the unregenerate] have not attained."[93] It follows, therefore, that the work of the Spirit is responsible for the external advancement of the kingdom of God because those who have been awakened to the glory of what God has revealed not only embrace Jesus in saving faith, but also enlist in the campaign to conquer the world for Christ, and they do both of these things because "in humanity as it is actually constituted, an intellectual conviction of the truth of Christianity [the kind of conviction that is produced by the work

88. For an understanding of how the Holy Spirit "determines the will" without dealing with moral agents as if they were "sticks or stones," see ibid., 44, 46–48, 62, 100. On the determining influence of motives, see 26–29.

89. Machen, *What Is Faith?* 248.

90. Machen, "Rejoice with Trembling," 10–11.

91. Machen, *Christianity and Liberalism*, 105–6.

92. Machen, "Christianity and Culture," 403; cf. Machen, "Rejoice with Trembling," 1–2.

93. Machen, "The Relation of Religion to Science and Philosophy," 64.

of the Spirit in the new birth] is always accompanied by a change of heart and a new direction for the will."[94]

The Offensive Nature of Machen's Apologetic

Apologetics: For Believers or Unbelievers?

Having established that the task of consecration is an offensive task that is ultimately directed to the external advancement of the kingdom of God, we must finally consider the question that was raised at the beginning of this chapter, the question of why Machen urged believing scholars to leave their "comfortable winter quarters" to do apologetical battle on the battlefield of truth.[95] Did Machen urge believers to do apologetics for the benefit of those who already have faith but are "troubled by hearing the scholarly objections against Christianity raised all around them,"[96] as Bahnsen insists? Or did Machen urge believers to do apologetics because he recognized that apologetics can perform "a kind of 'debris-clearing' function in the unbeliever's thinking,"[97] and can as a consequence be used as a means to the external advancement of the kingdom of God? Whereas I am convinced that Machen viewed apologetics much like Warfield did, namely as an offensive task that is ultimately directed to the production of Christian conviction and the external advancement of the kingdom of God, scholars such as Bahnsen contend that there is continuity between Machen's apologetic and the presuppositional approach of Van Til because Machen recognized that without "the enabling work of the Holy Spirit in their minds nothing like Warfield's 'right reason'" is at the disposal of the unregenerate.[98] In short, for scholars such as Bahnsen, Machen did apologetics not because he believed that the Christian religion must "*reason* its way to its dominion,"[99] but because he recognized that "Faith of a biblical sort . . . needs

---

94. Machen, *What Is Faith?* 249, 135.
95. Machen, "Christianity and Culture," 405.
96. Bahnsen, "The Apologetical Tradition of the OPC," 280.
97. Ibid., 293.
98. Ibid., 281.
99. Warfield, "Introduction to Francis R. Beattie's *Apologetics*," in *Selected Shorter Writings of Benjamin B. Warfield*, 2:98–99.

intelligent and detailed answers to the objections of modern critics, even when it already has the right presuppositions."[100]

What, then, are we to make of Bahnsen's conclusions? Did Machen really move "out of the Warfieldian camp and a long way toward Van Til's presuppositional conception of evidences"?[101] Did he believe, in other words, that evidences are useful primarily because they provide "intellectual reassurance"[102] to those who already have faith but are "troubled by hearing the scholarly objections against Christianity raised all around them"? The answer is found in an aspect of Machen's thought that Bahnsen apparently overlooks, namely the correspondence in Machen's thinking between the goal of the task of consecration and the goal of Christian apologetics.

The Correspondence between the Task of Consecration and Apologetics

In "Christianity and Culture" (1912), Machen's first published work on the problem of the relationship between knowledge and piety, or culture and Christianity, Machen argues that Christians must consecrate modern culture to Christianity so they can "mould the thought of the world in such a way as to make the acceptance of Christianity something more than a logical absurdity."[103] A remarkably similar statement can be found in an article titled "Christian Scholarship and the Defence of the Faith" (1932), an article that reflects what Bahnsen suggests is Machen's "most mature thinking" on the nature of Christian apologetics.[104] Referring not to the goal of consecration but to the goal of Christian apologetics, Machen insists that apologetics is useful "most of all in producing an intellectual atmosphere in which the acceptance of the gospel will seem to be something other than an offence against truth."[105] While both of these statements seem to indicate that believing scholars should pursue faithfulness to their callings for offensive rather

---

100. Bahnsen, "The Apologetical Tradition of the OPC," 280.
101. Ibid., 278–79.
102. Ibid., 280.
103. Machen, "Christianity and Culture," 404.
104. Bahnsen, "The Apologetical Tradition of the OPC," 279.
105. Machen, "Christian Scholarship and the Defence of the Faith," 129.

than for defensive reasons, might it be possible that these statements are actually referring to a service that believing scholars are called to provide for those who already have faith, as Bahnsen would have us believe? Might it be possible, in other words, that the production of an intellectual atmosphere in which acceptance of the gospel will seem to be something other than an offense against truth is actually a defensive enterprise that believers should undertake in order to strengthen the wavering faith of their brothers in Christ? The following statement, which Bahnsen addresses only tangentially in a footnote, establishes that such a conclusion cannot be justified. Despite his acknowledgment that the work of the Spirit is necessary for the production of Christian conviction, Machen nonetheless argues that although

> argument is insufficient, it does not follow that it is unnecessary. Sometimes it is used directly by the Holy Spirit to bring a man to Christ. But more frequently it is used indirectly. A man hears an answer to objections raised against the truth of the Christian religion; and at the time when he hears it he is not impressed. But afterwards, perhaps many years afterwards, his heart at last is touched: he is convicted of sin; he desires to be saved. Yet without that half-forgotten argument he could not believe; the gospel would not seem to him to be true, and he would remain in his sin. As it is, however, the thought of what he has heard long ago comes into his mind; Christian apologetics at last has its day; the way is open, and when he will believe he can believe because he has been made to see that believing is not an offense against truth.[106]

Since apologetics for Machen is directed to the same end as the task of consecration, namely the *creation* of an intellectual atmosphere in which the *acceptance* of the gospel will seem to be something other than an offense against truth, it follows that Machen did apologetics primarily for offensive rather than for defensive reasons. He did apologetics, in other words, not because he was convinced that faith needs answers to the objections of modern critics, but because he

106. Ibid., 128. For Bahnsen's treatment of this passage, see "The Apologetical Tradition of the OPC," 293n109. Interestingly, this statement immediately precedes and thus supplies the context for much of the evidence that Bahnsen cites in support of his thesis.

recognized that "False ideas are the greatest obstacle to the reception of the gospel,"[107] and that answers to the objections of modern critics are therefore needed for "faith of a biblical sort." That this is the case—and that any real or imagined harmony between the apologetical approaches of Machen and Van Til must acknowledge Machen's continuity with Old Princeton in general and B. B. Warfield in particular—is confirmed by a quotation from Machen's personal correspondence with a Dutch Calvinist by the name of Gerritt Hospers. "You will not take it amiss," Machen writes,

> that I still agree rather strongly with Dr. Warfield about the place of apologetics. It is quite true that the human reason because of the noetic effects of sin needs the Spirit of God in order to accept the truth of the reservation which God has given, but because the arguments for the truth of the Christian religion are insufficient to produce Christian conviction, it does not follow, I think, that they are unnecessary. On the contrary, it seems to me that they constitute one of the means which the Spirit of God uses in the production of Christian conviction and the conversion of the sinner.[108]

Van Til's Misreading of Warfield

If the foregoing analysis is correct and Machen did indeed view apologetics much like Warfield did, namely as an offensive task that is ultimately directed to the production of Christian conviction and the external advancement of the kingdom of God, then how do we account for Bahnsen's misunderstanding of the relationship between Machen and Old Princeton? It seems that Bahnsen was mistaken in his understanding of this relationship because he based his analysis on an endorsement of Van Til's misreading of Warfield. According to Van Til, "right reason" for Warfield "is not the reason of the Christian. It is the reason that is confronted with Christianity and possesses some criterion apart from Christianity with which to judge of the truth of Christianity."[109] Given

107. Machen, "Christianity and Culture," 404.

108. Machen to Rev. Gerrit H. Hospers, Ontario, New York, 27 December 1924, Machen Archives. See also Machen to Hospers, 11 December 1924.

109. Cornelius Van Til, *The Defense of the Faith*, 3rd ed. (Philadelphia: Presbyterian and Reformed, 1972), 264.

that such an understanding of "right reason" does in fact accommodate "the non-Christian principle of the rational autonomy of man,"[110] Van Til concludes that Warfield's approach must be rejected because it attempts to operate in "neutral territory" by appealing to the natural man's "right reason" to judge of the truth of Christianity.[111] That is to say, it explicitly endorses "the correctness of the natural man's problematics," and thereby abandons the unbeliever to his unbelief because it cannot "remind" him "that Christianity alone is reasonable for men to hold."[112]

But is this assessment based on an accurate analysis of Warfield? Bahnsen clearly believes that it is, for he insists that Machen moved away from Old Princeton in a presuppositional direction because he recognized that the unregenerate "must have their eyes changed *so that* they can, at last, 'attend to the evidence' properly."[113] How, though, is this different from what Warfield believed? Did Warfield really believe that the unregenerate have the moral ability to reason "rightly," as Van Til suggests? Did he really believe, in other words, that "right reason" is "not the reason of the Christian," but the reason of the natural man?

Earlier in Part One of this study, I argued that such a conclusion cannot be justified when Warfield's "intellectualism" is interpreted in the proper context. When Warfield's emphasis on "right reason" is interpreted within a context that regards the soul as a single unit that acts in all of its functions as a single substance, it becomes clear that the ability to reason "rightly" is not a capacity that human beings possess apart from the work of the Spirit, but a capacity that presupposes the work of the Spirit on the "whole soul" of a moral agent. Whereas Warfield certainly affirms that a saving, i.e., a "right," apprehension of what God has revealed entails the rational appropriation of objective evidence, he nonetheless recognizes that the "rightness" of this apprehension is determined neither by the scholarly prowess of the

110. Cornelius Van Til, "My Credo," in *Jerusalem and Athens: Critical Discussions on the Philosophy and Apologetics of Cornelius Van Til*, ed. E. R. Geehan (Phillipsburg, NJ: Presbyterian and Reformed, 1980), 21.

111. Van Til, *The Defense of the Faith*, 264–65. Cf. Jack Rogers, "Van Til and Warfield on Scripture in the Westminster Confession," in *Jerusalem and Athens*, 154.

112. Van Til, "My Credo," 11, 21.

113. Bahnsen, "The Apologetical Tradition of the OPC," 281.

perceiving mind nor by the objective sufficiency of the evidence presented to one's consciousness, but by the moral or "ethical state" of the knowing soul. It is the renewed soul that has the ability to reason "rightly," Warfield insists, for it is the renewed soul that has the moral capacity to see revealed truth more or less for what it objectively is, namely glorious.

Since "right reason" for Warfield is the offensive weapon of the Christian apologist rather than the "self-established intellectual tool" of the autonomous natural man,[114] we must conclude that Bahnsen misinterpreted the relationship between Machen and Van Til because he misunderstood how Warfield conceived of "right reason." Had Bahnsen recognized that Warfield's "intellectualism" is moral rather than merely rational, he would have understood that what is "true science" for Machen is "right reason" for Warfield, and he would have realized, as David Calhoun argues, that "what [he] puts forth as Machen's views are in line with the Old Princeton tradition as a whole."[115] While Bahnsen is to be commended for recognizing that subjective and experiential concerns play a critical role in the religious epistemology that informs Machen's understanding of apologetics, he may be critiqued for failing to see that these same concerns play a critical role in the Old Princeton tradition more generally. What this suggests, then, is that those who acknowledge a "harmony of perspective" between Machen and Van Til would do well to allow the clear continuity between Warfield and Machen to serve as the catalyst for a reexamination of the epistemological orthodoxy of Old Princeton. Those who undertake such an examination will likely conclude that Old Princeton's approach to apologetics is "not as far from presuppositionalism as Van Til believed,"[116] for they will discover that many of the alleged epistemological distinctives of the

---

114. Van Til, "My Credo," 11.

115. David B. Calhoun, *The Majestic Testimony, 1869–1929*, vol. 2, *The History of Princeton Seminary* (Edinburgh: The Banner of Truth Trust, 1996), 529n49.

116. This phrase is taken from a question posed by Professor John Frame in his brief analysis of Bahnsen's "very interesting essay." Frame's question reads as follows: Is it possible, he asks, "that Old Princeton's apologetic was not as far from presuppositionalism as Van Til believed?" John Frame, *Cornelius Van Til: An Analysis of His Thought* (Phillipsburg, NJ: P&R Publishing, 1995), 450.

presuppositional approach in fact are essential to Old Princeton's understanding of "right reason."

Machen's Critique of Theological Liberalism

A Divergence of Heart and Mind

Having established that Machen's apologetic is best understood against the backdrop of Old Princeton's consistently Reformed religious epistemology, we must finally consider the relevance of my proposal to his critique of theological liberalism. What does my unorthodox proposal suggest, in short, for how we should think about Machen's repudiation of the liberal solution to the problem of the relationship between Christianity and culture? In his now classic work *Christianity and Liberalism*, Machen argues that liberalism's solution may be criticized on two grounds. "Modern liberalism may be criticized," he maintains, "(1) on the ground that it is un-Christian and (2) on the ground that it is unscientific."[117] How, then, should we conceive of the relationship between these grounds? Given Machen's insistence that science is a moral rather than a merely rational enterprise, and in light of his contention that in order to come to a saving knowledge of the gospel it is necessary only to be "truly scientific," we may plausibly conclude that for Machen, theological liberalism is un-Christian precisely *because* it is unscientific. It is the product, in other words, not of the ability to see what God has revealed "clearly," but of the moral inability to do theology with a mind that is open to all instead of just some of the facts.[118] That this is the case, and that Machen had grounds for arguing that the divergence between liberalism and Christianity is "a divergence of the heart fully as much as of the mind,"[119] will be

117. Machen, *Christianity and Liberalism*, 7. The apologetic nature of *Christianity and Liberalism* is clearly stated on page 16: "In setting forth the current liberalism, now almost dominant in the Church, over against Christianity, we are animated . . . by no merely negative or polemic purpose; on the contrary, by showing what Christianity is not we hope to be able to show what Christianity is, in order that men may be led to turn from the weak and beggarly elements and have recourse again to the grace of God."

118. Cf. Machen, *What Is Faith?* 130, 135, 240.

119. J. Gresham Machen to Rev. Charles H. Parkhurst, 28 February 1924, Machen Archives; see also Parkhurst, "Theology Is the Product of Intellect's Futile Effort to Reduce Religion to Forms of Thought," Machen Archives.

clear after a brief consideration of how committed liberals conceive
of doctrine, a consideration that will help us understand why Machen
would conclude that theological liberalism is a form of religious expression that is "anti-Christian to the core."[120]

120. Machen, *Christianity and Liberalism*, 160. Some will argue that I am misrepresenting
the nature of Machen's critique by suggesting that he considers theological liberalism to be
un-Christian precisely *because* it is unscientific. They will argue that Machen is not making
a moral critique in his classic work *Christianity and Liberalism*, but assessing theological
liberalism "as a comprehensive system" (for example, see Hart, " 'Doctor Fundamentalis,' "
157–61). In general, these arguments are compelling not only because they help explain the
judicious nature of Machen's critique (see, for example, *Christianity and Liberalism*, 160),
but also because they establish that Machen was not guilty of committing "the syllogistic
sin of the 'undistributed middle.' " Gerstner, "The Contributions of Hodge, Warfield, and
Machen," 379–80. For a good analysis of critiques of *Christianity and Liberalism* by Machen's
contemporaries, and for a fine treatment of the issue of caricature, cf. Hart, " 'Doctor Fundamentalis,' " 157–61.

While I find these arguments to be helpful, I remain convinced that we will never understand
the gravity of Machen's overall assessment of theological liberalism if we fail to recognize that
it includes an important moral component. While this component is largely held in check in
Christianity and Liberalism by the descriptive nature of the project—Machen clearly states
that he is using the term "un-Christian" in a descriptive sense, not "as a term of opprobrium,"
and that his purpose is not to examine the "unscientific" nature of theological liberalism
(cf. Machen, *Christianity and Liberalism*, 7–8, 147)—it is evident in his analysis of liberal
scholarship that takes liberal ideas to their logical conclusions and consequently "abuse[s]
and ridicule[s] the things dearest to the heart of every Christian man." Ibid., 173. This moral
component is evident in the following quotation from an address in which Harry Emerson
Fosdick is named as a representative of "naturalistic, or agnostic modernism": "The question
is whether the advocates of agnostic modernism are 'brethren' or not. *I do not think they are.*
They are fellow citizens, they are human beings with immortal souls, whom we ought to love,
and try to win for Christ, but 'brethren' in the Christian sense they are not. On the contrary,
they are what Paul calls 'false brethren, privily brought in,' and the first step toward the unity
of the church is the exclusion of these men from the teaching ministry." Machen, "An Earnest
Plea for Christian Freedom—and Honesty!" *The Lookout: Magazine of Christian Education*
36 (March 2, 1924): 6, emphasis added. If there is indeed a certain relationship between the
moral character and the activity of an acting agent, and if it is indeed reasonable to conclude
that theology is a human activity in which the character of an acting agent is fully on display,
then it would be surprising—given Machen's commitment to the unitary operation of the soul
and his understanding of the relationship between the work of the Spirit and "true science"—if
he did not insist at some point that committed liberals are not brothers in Christ.

While the quotation above is sobering, note that Machen never suggests that all liberal believers take liberal ideas to their logical conclusion. Theological liberalism, he insists, "constitutes,
in essentials, a unitary system of its own. That does not mean that all liberals hold all parts of
the system, or that Christians who have been affected by liberal teaching at one point have been
affected at all points. There is sometimes a salutary lack of logic which prevents the whole of a
man's faith being destroyed when he has given up a part. But the true way in which to examine
a spiritual movement is in its logical relations; logic is the great dynamic, and the logical implications of any way of thinking are sooner or later certain to be worked out." Machen, *Christianity
and Liberalism*, 172.

The "Paganism" of Theological Liberalism

According to Machen, the liberal solution to the problem of the relationship between Christianity and culture poses a serious threat to the enduring integrity of the Christian religion because it subverts the biblical foundation of religious life by substituting religious experience for the Bible as the seat of authority in religion.[121] This subversion of the Bible "with the exaltation in the place of it of the feelings or of the will"[122] is perhaps nowhere more clearly manifest, he argues, than in the conception of "doctrine" that is at the heart of the liberal response to culture. While both liberal and conservative scholars acknowledge that theology plays a critical role in the religious life of the believing community, liberals reject the notion that religious life is based on the rational appropriation of doctrines that are considered to be objectively true,[123] for they are convinced that doctrines are merely the "functional patterns" that express the experience of religion in the thought forms of a particular age.[124] Indeed, since doctrines are merely the "symbolic intellectual expressions" of an

121. By "substituting religious experience for the Bible as the seat of authority in religion" I mean that "substitution of experience, whether individual or corporate, for the Word of God as the source of authoritative information" for religious life and practice. Machen, "What Is the Gospel?" 170. Machen suggests that it is this adoption of "an inner criterion of truth" (J. Gresham Machen to Edward Holder, 28 January 1925, Machen Archives) that "underlies the mysticism of Schleiermacher and his many successors; it underlies the Ritschlian rejection of 'metaphysics'; it underlies the popular exaltation of 'abiding experiences' at the expense of the mental categories in which they are supposed to be expressed; and in general it is at the roots of the entire separation between religion and theology, experience and doctrine, faith and knowledge, which is so marked a characteristic of the religious teaching of the present day." J. Gresham Machen, "My Idea of God," in My Idea of God: A Symposium of Faith, ed. Joseph Fort Newton (Boston: Little, Brown, and Company, 1926), 41.

122. Machen, What Is Faith? 23.

123. J. Gresham Machen, "A Debate: Is the Teaching of Dr. Harry Emerson Fosdick Opposed to the Christian Religion? Yes," The Christian Work 117 (December 13, 1924): 686. Machen insists that the word "doctrine" can be used in "broader" and "narrower" senses. In the broader sense, which is how the word is being used in the discussion above, "doctrine" does not have to do with the technical differences that distinguish one creedal statement from another, but with the interpretation of the historical facts at the foundation of the Christian religion. Cf. Machen, Christianity and Liberalism, 45–47. Since "doctrine" in its broadest sense concerns the interpretation of the facts at the basis of the Christian religion, it follows that "doctrine," broadly understood, "is itself the gospel." Machen, "The Relation of Religion to Science and Philosophy," 43. According to Machen, "What many men despise today as 'doctrine' the New Testament calls the gospel; and the New Testament treats it as the message upon which salvation depends." Machen, "Christian Scholarship and Evangelism," 123; cf. Machen, "What Is the Gospel?" 164–65.

124. Cf. Machen, "What Fundamentalism Stands for Now," 254.

ineffable religious experience for a particular time and place,[125] liberals insist that the integrity of a doctrine is not found in the accuracy with which it communicates the objective substance of biblical teaching, but in the degree to which it facilitates the subjective experience of religion for those who are living at a particular time and in a particular place.[126] When a doctrine can no longer facilitate the experience of religion for people who are living in one sociohistorical context or another, then that doctrine, liberals believe, must be modified or abandoned.[127]

While Machen was clearly aware of the potential advantages of conceiving of doctrine as the "managed currency"[128] of the religious

125. Machen, "What Is Christianity?" 20. See also Machen, "Faith and Knowledge," 12; Machen, *What Is Faith?* 31.

126. Cf. Machen, *What Is Faith?* 30.

127. Fosdick argues that because "All doctrines spring from life," they are properly regarded as the "mental categories" in which "abiding [religious] experiences" are expressed. Fosdick, *The Modern Use of the Bible*, 185; on the distinction between "experiences" and the "categories" in which those experiences are expressed, cf. chapter 4. While he is convinced that the "abiding experiences" remain constant, he insists that the "mental categories" in which those experiences are expressed must change when they are no longer able to facilitate the development of personality. Cf. Kenneth Cauthen, *The Impact of American Religious Liberalism* (New York: Harper & Row, 1962), 69. For Fosdick, if a doctrine no longer facilitates the experience that leads to the cultivation of personality, then it must be revised or abandoned.

While doctrines for Fosdick are the "mental categories" that facilitate the cultivation of personality, for Shailer Mathews they are the "functional patterns" that articulate the values of that religious/social movement called Christianity for a particular time and place. Since Mathews is convinced that the essence of the Christian movement is found in convictions and values that facilitate "a personal co-operation with cosmic activities," he suggests that the truthfulness of one doctrine or another is not found in the words of the patterns themselves, but in the functional significance of the patterns. Mathews, *New Faith for Old*, 237. Doctrines, Mathews insists, are simply conceptual patterns that "attempt to relate persons positively to the personality-producing factors in the world process." Cf. Cauthen, *The Impact of American Religious Liberalism*, 149. Doctrines, in other words, are not wooden expressions of metaphysical truth, but "analogies and social patterns raised by common usage and group authority into symbols of convictions"—"symbols of convictions" that are significant because they facilitate the ordering of individual and communal life in a particular way. Mathews, *The Faith of Modernism*, 59. Because theology "is not a philosophy but the result of a group's utilization of unquestioned ideas and practices of contemporary social life as patterns by which to describe adjustment with cosmic activities upon which men feel they are dependent" (Mathews, *New Faith for Old*, 285), Mathews insists that theologians must distinguish "permanent Christian convictions from their doctrinal expression." Mathews, *The Faith of Modernism*, 15. In short, Mathews is convinced that doctrines remain valid as functional patterns as long as they are able to sustain the convictions and values of the Christian movement in a particular time and place. These patterns must be abandoned, however, when their functional significance has been invalidated by the advent of a new social mind and practice.

128. J. Gresham Machen, "The Bible Versus Human Authority," in *The Christian Faith in the Modern World*, 78–79.

life, nevertheless he remained critical of liberalism's solution to the problem for two primary reasons. In the first place, he was critical of the effort to sustain religious life by depreciating the objective significance of doctrine because it presumes a form of pragmatism that reduces theologizing to "the most useless form of trifling in which a man could possibly engage."[129] Whereas Machen insists that the Christian religion is based on the acceptance of doctrines that are considered to be true "in the plain man's sense of the word 'truth,'"[130] advocates of theological liberalism—who presuppose the modern distinction between religious truth and scientific truth—are convinced that doctrines are "true" not because of what they say about the substance of what God has revealed, but because they facilitate the experience of religion for a particular time and place.[131]

If Machen was critical of theological liberalism in the first place because its pragmatic conception of truth is grounded in "the most bottomless skepticism which could possibly be conceived,"[132] he was critical in the second because it devolves into a form of religious expression that is "sub-Christian" because it cannot provide salvation from sin.[133] The justification for this contention is found in what Machen refers to as the "imperative mood" of liberal religion.[134] While Machen insists that the Christian religion can meet the supernatural needs of those who are dead in sin because it is grounded in the "triumphant

129. Machen, *What Is Faith?* 29.

130. J. Gresham Machen, "The Creeds and Doctrinal Advance," in *God Transcendent*, 165.

131. Cf. Machen, *What Is Faith?* 32–35; Machen, "Christianity vs. Modern Liberalism," 351; George Marsden, "Understanding J. Gresham Machen," *PSB* 11 (1990): 51. Machen maintains that the modern drive for theological relevance is based on a false conception of "progress." Genuine progress, Machen insists, "involves something to progress *to* as well as something to progress *from*." Since progress presupposes the "possibility of attaining truth and of setting it forth ever more completely," Machen argues that liberalism's rejection of the possibility of objective doctrinal truth actually destroys the possibility of genuine doctrinal advance. Machen, *What Is Faith?* 32–33; cf. J. Gresham Machen, "The Progress of Christian Doctrine," *Guardian* 7 (January 10, 1940): 1–2, 8–9; Machen, "The Creeds and Doctrinal Advance," 157–67.

132. Machen, *What Is Faith?* 31. With respect to Machen's insistence that the liberal conception of doctrine is grounded in pragmatism, D. G. Hart notes that "A comparison of *What Is Faith?* with John Dewey's thoughts on religion, appearing a few years later in *A Common Faith* (1934), substantiates Machen's analysis." Hart, "'Doctor Fundamentalis,'" 199–200. On the pragmatism of theological liberalism, cf. J. Gresham Machen to Rev. Ralph W. Nelson, 2 April 1924, Machen Archives.

133. Machen, *Christianity and Liberalism*, 8.

134. Ibid., 47.

indicative" of the gospel, he contends that liberalism offers no hope for fallen sinners because it finds the "highest goal" of human existence not in submission to a source of salvation that is *extra nos*, but in "the healthy and harmonious and joyous development of existing human faculties."[135] Whereas Christianity "begin[s] with the broken heart" and "announces, first, a gracious act of God," liberalism is inherently "pagan," Machen argues, for it is really nothing more than a form of religious expression that is grounded in "that same indefinite type of religious aspiration which was in the world before Christianity came upon the scene."[136]

How, then, do we account for this "substitution of paganism for Christianity" by those who profess to be believers?[137] The answer to this question—which is grounded in the intimate connection between the work of the Spirit, the conviction of sin, and the ability to be "truly scientific"—reveals the incisive and consequential nature of Machen's critique. According to Machen, liberal scholars find the ideal of Christian existence in the development of existing human faculties because they have lost all sense of "the consciousness of sin."[138] Indeed, they have lost "all sense of the gulf that separates the creature from the Creator,"[139] and as a consequence they regard the Christian religion

135. Ibid., 47, 65.

136. Ibid., 66, 47, 65, 7. Cf. J. Gresham Machen, "The Real Issue Stated: What Evangelical Christians Stand For," *The Bible for China* 22 (October 1925): 14.

137. Machen, *Christianity and Liberalism*, 65. Note that Machen uses the word "pagan" in the same way he uses the word "un-Christian," i.e., in a descriptive sense rather than as "a term of reproach." Ibid. In this descriptive sense, a pagan is one who finds the highest goal of human existence in the cultivation and development of existing human faculties because he has not been convicted of his sin.

138. Machen, *Christianity and Liberalism*, 64; cf. Machen, *What Is Faith?* 58. But is it true that *only* the regenerate can possess a genuine consciousness of sin? According to Machen, it is. Cf. J. Gresham Machen, "Liberalism or Christianity?" *PTR* 20 (1923): 103; Machen, *Christianity and Liberalism*, 67.

139. Machen, *Christianity and Liberalism*, 64. Machen suggests that the loss of a sense of the ontological as well as moral gulf that separates creatures from the Creator "follows naturally" from an "*anima mundi* view of God." Machen, "Is the Teaching of Dr. Harry Emerson Fosdick Opposed to the Christian Religion? Yes," 687. According to Fosdick, "The background of abysmal distance between the divine and the human which the [Westminster] Confession had perforce to bridge, is no longer in our minds. The presupposition of all our thinking is the conviction, not that there is a vast distance between God and man, but that God and man belong together and in each other are fulfilled." Fosdick, *The Modern Use of the Bible*, 267. On the relationship between the consciousness of sin and the Christian religion, cf. Machen, *Christianity and Liberalism*, 62, 65, 106.

as the means to "uplift" or "betterment" rather than as the source of salvation from sin.[140] It is ultimately for this reason, then, i.e., because liberals reduce the Christian religion to a natural phenomenon by ignoring the "yawning chasm" that separates creatures from the Creator,[141] that Machen concludes that "if liberalism is to return into the Christian communion there must be a change of heart fully as much as a change of mind."[142] Without such a change, he argues, and without the ability to take account of all of the facts that impinge on the integrity of the gospel message, liberal theologians will continue to promote a kind of religious life that is "anti-Christian to the core," for without the conviction of sin that empties fallen sinners of confidence in their own resources, the good news of the gospel *about* Jesus will forever seem to them to be "an idle tale."[143]

Conclusion

We conclude this chapter and Part One of this study by insisting that neither Machen's approach to apologetics nor his critique of theological liberalism will ever be understood correctly if the subjective and experiential components of his thought are presumed to play a secondary role in his religious epistemology. While Machen clearly believed that saving faith is based on the rational appropriation of objective evidence, nevertheless he was not a rationalist because he recognized that without the work of the Spirit in regeneration, fallen sinners do not have the moral ability either to attend to the substance of what God has revealed in a "truly scientific" fashion or to embrace the substance of this revelation in saving faith. What this suggests, then, is that Christian experience did not play a merely peripheral role in Machen's religious epistemology, but it played

140. Machen, *What Is Faith?* 58.
141. Machen, "Rejoice with Trembling," 10. Note that indifference to this "chasm" is evidence that the scholar in question does not have the moral ability to take account of all of the facts that impinge on the integrity of the gospel message. Cf. Machen, "Christianity and Culture," 406–7.
142. Machen, *Christianity and Liberalism*, 173; cf. Machen, "The Separateness of the Church," in *God Transcendent*, 113.
143. Machen, *Christianity and Liberalism*, 106, 160.

a central—indeed a defining—role, despite what the consensus of critical opinion would have us believe. In short, much like his predecessors at Old Princeton Seminary, Machen recognized that the soul is a single unit that always acts as a single substance, and this is why we must conclude that his apologetical efforts—including those that are manifest in his critique of theological liberalism—were driven by subjective rather than objective, theological rather than philosophical concerns.

PART 2

"RIGHT REASON" AND THE POSTCONSERVATIVE CRITIQUE OF CONSERVATIVE EVANGELICALISM

The knowledge of Christ . . . is not the apprehension of what he is, simply by the intellect, but also a due apprehension of his glory as a divine person arrayed in our nature, and involves not as its consequence merely, but as one of its elements, the corresponding feeling of adoration, delight, desire and complacency.[1]

1. Charles Hodge, "The Excellency of the Knowledge of Christ Jesus our Lord," in *Conference Papers* (New York: Charles Scribner's Sons, Paternoster Row, 1879), 214.

5

"Reimagining" the Princeton Mind

The Historiographical Consensus

It has become something of an article of faith in the historiography of North American Christianity that the theologians at Old Princeton Seminary were committed rationalists whose doctrine of Scripture was shaped by the Scottish Common Sense Realism of the "Didactic Enlightenment" in America.[1] "The standard line," Roger Schultz notes, "is that in battling the skeptics of the Enlightenment, Scottish realists demanded an extreme (and unbiblical) standard of authority and certainty, and that the Princetonians incorporated this rationalistic element in their inerrantist doctrine of scripture."[2] According to the accepted wisdom, then, Old Princeton's doctrine of inerrancy—

1. As we saw in Chapter One, the Didactic Enlightenment was in part a counter-Enlightenment because it espoused "a variety of thought which was opposed both to skepticism and revolution, but tried to save from what it saw as the debacle of the Enlightenment the intelligible universe, clear and certain moral judgments, and progress." Henry May, *The Enlightenment in America* (New York: Oxford University Press, 1976), xvi.
2. Roger Schultz, "Evangelical Meltdown: The Trouble with Evangel*histoire*," *Contra Mundum* 2 (Winter 1992), 45–46.

the taproot of what is considered to be its rather immodest dogmatism—"is not a Biblical doctrine, but rather a bastard ideology of the Enlightenment"[3] that was woven into the fabric of its highly innovative yet thoroughly modern and epistemologically naïve response to "an increasingly secular culture, on the one hand, and a rising liberal Christianity, on the other."[4]

The Postconservative Endorsement of the Historiographical Consensus

While a growing body of scholarship is establishing that Old Princeton's indebtedness to the naïve realism of the Scottish philosophy is more imagined than real, many evangelicals nonetheless endorse the broad outline of the standard critique.[5] Among those who concur with the historiographical consensus are those ostensibly irenic individuals who presume that the essence of evangelicalism is found not in "propositional truths enshrined in doctrines," but in "a narrative-shaped experience"[6] that "is more readily 'sensed' than described theologically."[7] Believing that Christianity is primarily a life and only secondarily a doctrine, these evangelicals lament what Gary Dorrien calls "the fundamentalist evangelical establishment['s]"[8] enduring preoccupation with "questions of propositional truth,"[9] for such preoccupation, they contend, is evidence that much of evangelicalism has yet to

3. Ibid.

4. Stanley J. Grenz, *Renewing the Center: Evangelical Theology in a Post-Theological Era* (Grand Rapids: Baker, 2000), 73; cf. Gary Dorrien, *The Remaking of Evangelical Theology* (Louisville: Westminster John Knox, 1998), 13–47.

5. See the literature cited in Part One of this study.

6. Roger E. Olson, "Postconservative Evangelicals Greet the Postmodern Age," *The Christian Century* 112 (May 3, 1995): 481.

7. Stanley J. Grenz, *Revisioning Evangelical Theology: A Fresh Agenda for the 21st Century* (Downers Grove, IL: InterVarsity Press, 1993), 31; Stanley J. Grenz, "Concerns of a Pietist with a Ph.D.," *WesTJ* 36 (Fall 2002): 60–64, 70; Robert E. Webber, *The Younger Evangelicals: Facing the Challenges of the New World* (Grand Rapids: Baker, 2002), 27, 31, 37.

8. Dorrien, *Remaking of Evangelical Theology*, 10; cf. Grenz, *Revisioning Evangelical Theology*, 21–35.

9. Grenz, *Revisioning Evangelical Theology*, 26.

move beyond the mind-set engendered by the wrenching struggles of the fundamentalist-modernist controversy of the early twentieth century. Indeed, having wed themselves to Old Princeton's doctrine of inerrancy and thereby to the more divisive tendencies of a scholasticized theology,[10] conservative evangelicals, these postconservatives maintain, "have exaggerated the rationalistic dimension of Christian belief"[11] and thus have fallen prey to a kind of theological hubris—even bigotry—that threatens to plunge evangelicalism "back toward fundamentalism."[12]

Because they are convinced that all cognitive expressions of Christian experience *"reflect the particular cultural grid in which they were originally articulated,"*[13] and because they consequently agree with Alfred Lord Tennyson that "Our little systems have their day . . . and thou, O Lord, are more than they,"[14] postconservative evangelicals therefore advocate a "revisioning" of the theological task along

10. According to Jack Rogers and Donald McKim, the Princetonians developed a doctrine of Scripture "that would engender continuing strife on the American religious scene." Jack Rogers and Donald McKim, *The Authority and Interpretation of the Bible: An Historical Approach* (San Francisco: Harper & Row, 1979), 247.

11. Dorrien, *Remaking of Evangelical Theology*, 195.

12. Olson, "Postconservative Evangelicals Greet the Postmodern Age," 480, 482. The word "fundamentalism" is used in this chapter in the largely negative sense that it is used by Roger E. Olson in, "The Future of Evangelical Theology," *Christianity Today* 42 (February 9, 1998): 40–48. As such, it is used in the sense that has less to do with the affirmation of particular doctrines than it does with the dogmatic manner in which those doctrines are affirmed, for it describes a way of thinking about and doing theology that leads to a kind of gratuitous arrogance, i.e., to unwarranted "triumphalism, elitism, and separatism" (ibid., 47). On the "religious bigotry" of those who insist on drawing distinct boundaries between theological views that are thought to be acceptable and unacceptable, see the comments of Robert Webber in James R. and Elizabeth Newby, *Between Peril and Promise* (Nashville: Thomas Nelson, 1984), 111. Interestingly, Webber's remarkably harsh intimation that evangelicals who are "enmeshed in modern categories of thought" (Webber, *The Younger Evangelicals*, 79) articulate the faith in a more or less bigoted fashion itself borders on bigotry. It is, moreover, a fine example of special pleading. Unlike their modern counterparts who have an ahistorical understanding of the faith, the younger evangelicals, Webber argues, "are humbled by the complexity of truth, and they are gentle and generous toward those who differ. The younger evangelicals are not fighters intent on splitting churches. They are not dogmatic zealots or mean-spirited close-minded bigots. They seek to hold that which has always been held by all and affirm affection for those with whom they differ. Their love of the ancient and their return to tradition has given them this 'catholic spirit.'" Ibid., 81.

13. Alan F. Johnson and Robert E. Webber, *What Christians Believe: A Biblical and Historical Summary* (Grand Rapids: Zondervan, 1989), ix-x, emphasis original.

14. Alfred Lord Tennyson, "In Memoriam."

the lines of "the postliberal research program."[15] Evangelicalism will become something more than "fundamentalism with good manners,"[16] they contend, only when evangelicals recognize that doctrines are not "timeless and culture-free" summaries of biblical truth that form the cognitive foundation of faith.[17] Rather, they are "reflection[s] on the faith of the converted people of God whose life together is created and shaped by the paradigmatic narrative embodied in scripture."[18] Doctrines, as such, are not to be afforded the same exalted status as the experiential "ethos" that unites the disparate elements of the evangelical community into a single body of faith.[19] Rather, they must be treated as those secondary reflections on Christian experience "that reflect and guide the converted community of God's people."[20]

The Unsustainability of the Historiographical Consensus and the Crumbling Foundation of Non-Foundational Theology

Whatever the merits of postconservatism's move away from a "propositionalist understanding of the theological enterprise"[21] toward a "narrativist-communitarian model" of theology might be,[22] there is no disputing that postconservatives justify this transition in part by rejecting what they regard as the "Enlightenment foundationalist rationalism" of the Princeton Theology.[23] "Beneath and behind the postconservatives' approach to theology," Roger Olson argues, "lies a growing discontent with evangelical theology's traditional ties to what [former] Wheaton historian Mark Noll describes as the

15. Cf. F. LeRon Shults, "Truth Happens? The Pragmatic Conception of Truth and the Postliberal Research Program," *PTR* 4 (February 1997): 26–36.

16. Dorrien, *Remaking of Evangelical Theology*, 9.

17. Grenz, *Revisioning Evangelical Theology*, 67.

18. Olson, "Postconservative Evangelicals Greet the Postmodern Age," 481.

19. Grenz, *Revisioning Evangelical Theology*, 30–35.

20. Olson, "Postconservative Evangelicals Greet the Postmodern Age," 481.

21. Grenz, *Revisioning Evangelical Theology*, 67.

22. Dorrien, *Remaking of Evangelical Theology*, 195.

23. Grenz, *Renewing the Center*, 70; cf. Rodney Clapp, "How Firm a Foundation: Can Evangelicals Be Nonfoundationalists?" in *The Nature of Confession: Evangelicals and Liberals in Conversation*, ed. Timothy Phillips, Dennis Okholm (Downers Grove, IL: InterVarsity, 1996), 83–84.

'evangelical Enlightenment,' especially common-sense realism."[24] While most postconservatives acknowledge that the Princeton theologians were not fundamentalists themselves,[25] they nonetheless argue that Old Princeton's naïve rationalism—itself the necessary byproduct of the Princetonians' somewhat credulous endorsement of Scottish Realism[26]—was "mediated" to contemporary evangelicalism through the fundamentalism of the early twentieth century.[27] Turn-of-the-century fundamentalists endorsed Old Princeton's doctrine of inerrancy and thereby accommodated the legacy of Protestant scholastic rationalism, postconservatives contend, and this legacy has been passed on to all those whose decidedly cognitive concerns lead them to seek "an invulnerable foundation for theology in an error-free Bible, viewed as the storehouse for divine revelation."[28] "Nowhere is neo-evangelicalism's genesis in fundamentalism more evident," Grenz concludes, "than in its theology. The fundamentalist acceptance of the Princeton understanding of inspiration . . . gave a particular nineteenth-century cast to neo-evangelicalism's emphasis on biblical authority."[29]

It is the contention of this chapter that however warranted postconservativism's repudiation of "evangelical propositionalism"[30] might be for any one of a number of different reasons, it cannot be justified by appealing to the naïve rationalism of Old Princeton,

24. Olson, "Postconservative Evangelicals Greet the Postmodern Age," 481; cf. Grenz, *Renewing the Center*, 71; Mark A. Noll, *The Scandal of the Evangelical Mind* (Grand Rapids: Eerdmans, 1994), 83–107.

25. For example, see Roger E. Olson, *The Story of Christian Theology: Twenty Centuries of Tradition and Reform* (Downers Grove, IL: InterVarsity, 1999), 556–61; Grenz, *Renewing the Center*, 79. For a notable exception, see Webber, *The Younger Evangelicals*, 81.

26. For example, see Grenz, *Renewing the Center*, 73; Olson, *The Story of Christian Theology*, 558; Dorrien, *Remaking of Evangelical Theology*, 23–28.

27. Grenz, *Revisioning Evangelical Theology*, 65–72; cf. Grenz, "Concerns of a Pietist with a Ph.D.," 65–68; Webber, *The Younger Evangelicals*, 31, 37.

28. Grenz, *Renewing the Center*, 70; cf. Ibid., 70–84.

29. Ibid., 83. For a noteworthy response to this contention, see Kenneth J. Stewart, "That Bombshell of a Book: Gaussen's *Theopneustia* and Its Influence on Subsequent Evangelical Theology" (paper presented at the Wheaton Theology Conference, Spring 2001), 15–18. Stewart suggests that since 1950, "Evangelical thinking about the Bible has, without our realizing it, been in process of necessary recovery [*not* from the influence of Warfield and Old Princeton, but] from the exaggerated emphases of [Gaussen's] *Theopneustia*."

30. Grenz, *Revisioning Evangelical Theology*, 65.

simply because the Princeton theologians were not naïve rationalists. While they certainly were the methodological disciples of Francis Turretin and consequently conceived of theology as that "science" having to do with God,[31] nevertheless they were not beholden for their epistemology either to the humanism of the scholastic tradition or to the rationalism of the Enlightenment in a formative sense. For not only did they recognize that objective as well as subjective factors are of critical importance to the life of the mind, but they also based their theology on that combination of head and heart, of "cognitive-doctrinal" and "practical-experiential" factors that postconservatives themselves insist is of defining significance to the mainstream of the evangelical tradition.[32]

31. Cf. Francis Turretin, *Institutes of Elenctic Theology*, 3 vols., trans. George Musgrave Giger, ed. James T. Dennison Jr. (Phillipsburg, NJ: P&R Publishing, 1992), 1:1–3.

32. Grenz, *Renewing the Center*, 84; cf. 44–47; Grenz, *Revisioning Evangelical Theology*, 22–26; Grenz, "Concerns of a Pietist with a Ph.D.," 71–76; Olson, "The Future of Evangelical Theology," 42. In a recent article, Mark Noll insists, "the difficulty with [Charles] Hodge's view of the spiritual life was not a neglect of lived religious experience, of the person, or of the affections. It was rather his predilection for affirming Christianity both as a set of scriptural doctrines and as a living connection with Christ, while yet never finding a way to bring these two affirmations into cohesive unity." Mark Noll, "Charles Hodge as an Expositor of the Spiritual Life," in *Charles Hodge Revisited: A Critical Appraisal of His Life and Work*, ed. John W. Stewart, James H. Moorhead (Grand Rapids: Eerdmans, 2002), 191–92). It is the contention of this chapter that both of these affirmations are more or less unified in Hodge's understanding of "right reason." If this contention is essentially correct, it follows that: (1) the weaknesses Noll cites in his analysis of Hodge's exposition of the spiritual life (cf. ibid., 205) are significantly less troublesome than they might otherwise appear to be; and (2) postconservatives who cite Hodge's alleged shortcomings as justification for advancing new theological methodologies or epistemologies must be on guard lest they fall prey to a kind of iconoclasm that pressures evangelicals to make what Richard Mouw calls, in this regard, "some false choices." With respect to this second point, Mouw worries about what he regards as "an iconoclastic spirit that often manifests itself in evangelical calls for new constructive theological initiatives." In short, he is not confident that recent evangelical efforts "to clear the way for new theological paths" will accomplish "much that is good," in part because these efforts appear to be based on misrepresentations of the evangelical heritage. He suggests that, "What some of my evangelical friends seem to be after in calling for such new moves [including the moves toward a theological interpretation of the text and a combination of head and heart in religious epistemology] seems already to be there in past evangelical thinkers who have helped me in my theological journey." Richard J. Mouw, "Comments on Grenz Paper and 'The Word Made Fresh'" (presented at the annual meeting of the American Academy of Religion, Toronto, November 2002), 2; cf. Richard J. Mouw, "How Should Evangelicals Do Theology? Delete the 'Post' from 'Postconservative,'" *Books and Culture* (May/June 2001): 21–22. For an example of iconoclasm, note that Robert Webber writes as if virtually all traditional evangelicals neglected the importance of the heart in religious epistemology. Cf. Webber, *The Younger Evangelicals*, 52–53, 103.

Thus, in order to challenge the viability of a major component of postconservatism's justification for repudiating the "evangelical establishment's" conception of the theological task, what I undertake in the forthcoming discussion is an analysis of important scholarship that buttresses the point I attempted to make in Part One of this study, the point that calls into question the presumed connection between Scottish Common Sense Realism and the Princeton Theology. That point, in short, is that Old Princeton's emphasis on "right reason" and the primacy of the intellect in faith is not evidence that the Princeton theologians were covert—if not overt—rationalists, and the purveyors of a theology that was scholasticized by an "alien philosophy."[33] It is evidence, rather, that they stood in the epistemological mainstream of the Reformed tradition, and thereby in the epistemological mainstream of the evangelical tradition.[34] As such, the forthcoming discussion is a call of sorts for evangelicals to *"reimagine"* the standard interpretation of the Princeton mind so that false conclusions are corrected and potentially troublesome consequences are avoided.[35] When evangelicals

33. This is the general theme of John Vander Stelt's *Philosophy and Scripture: A Study of Old Princeton and Westminster Theology* (Marlton, NJ: Mack, 1978). The Dutch and Neoorthodox branches of the Reformed camp generally agree with this critique of Old Princeton, as do the postconservative scholars with whom I am familiar.

34. Obviously, I think the Reformed interpretation of the history of evangelicalism is largely correct. I recognize, however, that the issues involved are complex, which is why I like what Douglas A. Sweeney has to say about the matter: "When the historiographical wrangling ends and the dust settles, it may well be seen that 'Reformed' and 'Holiness' themes, indeed Calvinist/forensic/confessional and Arminian/realistic/revivalist themes, have been functioning dialectically all along (for better and for worse) in both evangelical history and evangelical historiography. In evangelical history, Arminianism and Wesleyanism (even Pentecostalism, although less directly) have arisen not in seclusion, but from within Reformed Protestantism. They were not intended as radically new alternatives but as correctives to trends prevalent among other, more established members of the Reformed family. Likewise in recent evangelical historiography, [Donald] Dayton and the Holiness camp have offered criticisms of and provided helpful correctives to trends prevalent within the more established Reformed paradigm." Douglas A. Sweeney, "Historiographical Dialectics: On Marsden, Dayton, and the Inner Logic of Evangelical History," *CSR* 23, 1 (1993): 52.

For an overview of the debate over the essential character of evangelicalism, see the entire issues of the *CSR* 23, 1 (1993), and *ModRef* 10, 2 (March/April 2001). See also the "Reflection and Response" involving Michael S. Horton and Roger E. Olson in *CSR* 31, 2 (2001): 131–68.

35. Just as the "Reimagining God" conference was convened in Minneapolis in 1993 so that progressive scholars could rethink how to conceive of "god" in our day based on the conviction that traditional conceptions of "god" were stifling the religious vitality of "communities of faith" (cf. Peter Jones's description of the festive atmosphere in *Spirit Wars: Pagan Revival in Christian America* [Mukilteo, WA: WinePress Publishing, and Escondido, CA: Main Entry Editions, 1997],

undertake such an examination they will discover that a "superficial reading" of the Princetonians will make them appear "considerably more rationalistic" than they really were.[36] They will also likely conclude, as I do in the concluding section of this chapter, that conservatism's postconservative critics—having rejected a caricature of Old Princeton rather than the views of the Princetonians themselves—are themselves guilty of some of the worst characteristics that they perceive in their conservative brethren.[37]

Reassessing the Princeton Mind: The Augustinian Nature of "Right Reason"

The Rogers and McKim Thesis: Simply False

Any attempt to reassess the standard interpretation of the Princeton mind must demonstrate at least a basic awareness of the Rogers and McKim thesis, in part because recent critiques—including those of postconservative and Neoorthodox theologians—cite their conclusions favorably.[38] In *The Authority and Interpretation of the Bible: An Historical Approach*, Jack Rogers and Donald McKim argue that the Princeton theologians were not the genuine heirs of the central Chris-

---

142–45), so too evangelicals must *reimagine* the standard interpretation of the Princeton mind so that the voice of the Princetonians is given a fair hearing in our day.

36. Peter Hicks, *The Philosophy of Charles Hodge: A 19th Century Evangelical Approach to Reason, Knowledge and Truth* (Lewiston, NY: Edwin Mellen, 1997), 115.

37. Among these is the kind of dogmatism that breeds both fundamentalism and an inability to engage in genuine dialogue with those with whom they have serious theological disagreements. One of the more exasperating aspects of life under the "big tent" of contemporary evangelicalism is the tendency of postconservatives to call for dialogue with their conservative brethren without acknowledging that the kind of dialogue they are encouraging can take place only if conservatives concede from the start that postconservative assumptions are correct. See, for example, Michael Horton's "Response to Roger Olson's Reply," *CSR* 31, 2 (2001): 165–66, in which Horton, a confessional Protestant, chastises Olson for doing the very thing he (Olson) deplores in others, namely claiming the evangelical tent for his party. According to Horton, "By making his own heritage, which emphasizes the individual's experience, definitive for the whole of evangelicalism, [Olson] has pushed the rest of us to the margins." Obviously, the same could be said of many conservatives. The point, though, is that while the conservative has an epistemological basis for affirming a kind of dogmatism, the postconservative, as far as I can tell, does not. For a brief explanation of how the word "fundamentalism" is being used in this chapter, please see note 12 above.

38. For example, cf. Grenz, *Renewing the Center*, 77; Olson, *The Story of Christian Theology*, 566, 639n23; Dorrien, *Remaking of Evangelical Theology*, 215n19.

tian tradition that they claimed to be, in part because their distinctively Reformed commitments were jettisoned by their philosophical assumptions. While the Princetonians were convinced their view of the Bible was that of orthodox believers throughout the history of the church, in fact their doctrine of Scripture was shaped by their reverence for Turretin and their "uncritical acceptance" of the Scottish philosophy.[39] These factors not only led them to adopt "wholeheartedly the naïve inductive method of Bacon," but they also conspired to reverse in their thinking the Augustinian approach of "faith seeking understanding as a theological method."[40] Indeed, they had an "unbounded confidence" in the competence of human reasoning powers,[41] yet they failed to recognize that this confidence was fundamentally at odds with the theological commitments of the central Christian tradition.

> Despite the constant profession of faithfulness to Calvin and the Augustinian tradition, the Princeton theologians seemed never to fear that their minds had been affected by sin. Their later followers worked out the full implications of this faculty psychology. The Princeton men were sure that sin had made the emotions unreliable. But they held an almost Pelagian confidence that the mind was essentially undisturbed by sin's influence.[42]

According to Rogers and McKim, then, Old Princeton's understanding of the place of Scripture in the central Christian tradition was informed not by sound scholarly analysis, but by tendentious historical scholarship that was colored by the assumptions of Enlightenment philosophy. This philosophy lent itself to Old Princeton's narrow apologetical concerns, which culminated, as Rogers suggests in a later essay, in B. B. Warfield's rationalistic appeal "to the *natural man's* 'right reason' to judge of the truth of Christianity."[43] It also subverted the Princetonians'

39. Rogers and McKim, *The Authority and Interpretation of the Bible*, 289.

40. Ibid., 289, 296; cf. 269, 289–90.

41. Ibid., 245; see also Lefferts Loetscher, *The Broadening Church: A Study of Theological Issues in the Presbyterian Church Since 1869* (Philadelphia: University of Pennsylvania, 1957), 70.

42. Rogers and McKim, *The Authority and Interpretation of the Bible*, 290.

43. Jack Rogers, "Van Til and Warfield on Scripture in the Westminster Confession," in *Jerusalem and Athens: Critical Discussions on the Philosophy and Apologetics of Cornelius Van Til*, ed. E. R. Geehan (Phillipsburg, NJ: Presbyterian and Reformed, 1980), 154, emphasis original.

standing in the Augustinian tradition, for it turned them into naïve rationalists who were largely indifferent to the role that subjective and experiential factors play in religious epistemology, and who, as a consequence, "self-consciously and carefully followed the Thomistic order that reason had to precede faith."[44]

An important piece of scholarship that challenges the assumptions behind this line of argumentation is the examination by Peter Hicks of Charles Hodge's philosophy. Although Hicks's analysis has yet to make much of an impact on the historiography of the Princeton Theology, it makes a number of important points that call into question prevailing assumptions about Old Princeton, and as such it is relevant to the thesis of this chapter.[45] In *The Philosophy of Charles Hodge: A 19th*

44. Rogers and McKim, *The Authority and Interpretation of the Bible*, 296. In personal correspondence that is cited with permission, Stanley Grenz suggests that Old Princeton's theological method is problematic not primarily because of its "dependence" on the Scottish philosophy ("although this is not to be discounted"), but because of its "indebtedness to the method of empirical science . . . inherited from the Enlightenment, which led [the Princetonians] . . . to model theology on the pattern of the natural sciences. This legacy in turn was passed on to neo-evangelicalism via fundamentalism," and neo-evangelicals then elevated this program "to normative status." Stanley J. Grenz to Paul Kjoss Helseth, November 21, 2001. While I welcome Grenz's eagerness to downplay the significance of Scottish Common Sense Realism, I wonder whether taking the focus off the Scottish philosophy and placing it on Old Princeton's inductive method hurts rather than helps his critique. According to the historiographical consensus, the Princetonians "modeled theology on the pattern of the natural sciences" *precisely because* their accommodation of Scottish Common Sense Realism jettisoned their commitment to the distinctive emphases of Reformed orthodoxy, including the noetic effects of sin. Although I disagree with this consensus, I nonetheless acknowledge that if the Princetonians in fact were "dependent" on the Scottish philosophy, then their employment of an inductive method was extremely problematic, because it was then simply the practical outworking of warmed-over humanism. Thus, by downplaying the significance of Scottish Common Sense Realism, I wonder whether Grenz is downplaying the primary reason for being opposed to an inductive method in the first place. As far as I can tell, the problem is not an inductive method *per se*, but an inductive method that has been bastardized by humanistic philosophical assumptions. What I am trying to establish in this chapter is that since the Princetonians themselves were not unduly influenced by such assumptions, one cannot repudiate their approach to doing theology by repudiating the methodological indiscretions of those who in fact have sacrificed the theological integrity of Old Princeton's method to the assumptions of an essentially humanistic philosophy. To state the matter clearly, I would suggest that if there is a problem with "a propositionalist understanding of the theological enterprise," it is not to be found in the consistently Reformed understanding of the Princetonians, but in the latent humanism of their later-day supporters, especially their later-day Arminian supporters. For Richard Mouw's rather sympathetic comments on induction, cf. "Comments on Grenz Paper and 'The Word Made Fresh.'"

45. According to John W. Stewart, Hicks's work addresses three important "lacunae" in the current scholarship about Hodge: first, "the degree to which Hodge may be characterized properly as a rationalist"; second, the nature of Hodge's relationship to Schleiermacher and

Century Evangelical Approach to Reason, Knowledge and Truth, Hicks argues that although the Princeton theologians used ideas and expressions that were "influenced by" the Scottish philosophy, "there is no indication in their writings that they saw it as in any way binding, or that they saw [Thomas] Reid, for instance, as the 'pure' form by which subsequent deviations were to be tested."[46] Indeed, while they agreed with the Scottish philosophers that truth exists objectively, that truth is a unity, and that we can have real, although partial, knowledge of the way reality is, "it would seem from the evidence that the Princetonians did not hold this position because Reid and his followers taught it; rather, they accepted the Scottish philosophy because it concurred with their fundamental epistemology."[47] At the foundation of their thinking about knowledge, Hicks suggests, was the conviction that "the basis of epistemological realism" is "theological rather than philosophical."[48] That is to say, while the Princetonians "[were] able to agree with the Scottish philosophers that 'it is universally admitted that we have no foundation for knowledge or faith, but the veracity of consciousness' [their] own conviction went one stage deeper: 'The ultimate ground of faith and knowledge is confidence in God.' "[49] God, the Princetonians argued, is not only "the creator and controller of the world and so guarantor of its ontological stability and epistemological coherence."[50] More importantly, he is the author of our nature who has made us "capable of accurate belief about the external world and who would not let us be deceived."[51] For Hicks, therefore, the Princeton theologians endorsed certain elements of the Scottish philosophy neither for purely speculative nor for merely apologetical reasons, but because those elements were "a useful means of expressing principles that had their origin in [the Princetonians'] theological convictions."[52] The

---

other nineteenth-century romantic thinkers; and third, "Hodge's understanding—and eventual dismissal—of Immanuel Kant." John W. Stewart, review of *The Philosophy of Charles Hodge* by Peter Hicks, in *JPH* 77 (Spring 1999): 64–65.

46. Hicks, *The Philosophy of Charles Hodge*, 206, 26.

47. Ibid., 28.

48. Ibid., 166.

49. Ibid.

50. Ibid., 167; cf. 206.

51. Ibid., 168.

52. Ibid. 167.

Princeton theologians were "sophisticated theological realists" rather than "naïve theological realists," Hicks concludes, and as such they were convinced that we can have real knowledge of God and of the world in which we live because God has condescended to make himself and the contents of his mind known "in his works, in our nature, in the Bible, and in Christ," and because "we have been made deliberately by the creator of the world, and have been endowed with means of obtaining accurate information about that world."[53]

The Epistemological Context: The Unitary Operation of the "Whole Soul"

How, then, has God made us, and why can we plausibly conclude that Old Princeton's epistemological assumptions—"especially in the sphere of religion"[54]—in no way betray an accommodation of some form of human-centered rationalism? One of the most important aspects

53. Ibid., 191, 167. According to Hicks, "Naïve theological realism is the position of most unphilosophical people, past and present. If truth about God exists it may be known in essentially the same way as truth about anything else. Though it may be harder to believe, the statement 'God loves you' is not radically different from the statement 'John loves Mary.' We know how to use the words involved. We accept God is different from John and that his love will be appropriately different, but the logic of the two sentences appears to be identical. In a parallel way our knowledge of God is accepted by the naïve theological realist as on the same model as our knowledge of John, or of the 'numinousness' of a Gothic cathedral. We know what we mean by John, or the numinous, or God, and we know what we mean by saying we know, whether it is in the sense of being acquainted with, or being aware of, John, the numinous, or God.

"Sophisticated theological realism would agree that there is a close relationship between ordinary knowledge and religious knowledge. But it would want to reverse the direction of the presentation. Granted, it would claim, that in experience our knowledge of ordinary things provides the model for our knowledge of the divine, nevertheless in reality the reverse is the case. We can have knowledge because knowledge is something that has prior existence in God. Our knowledge is modeled on his knowledge. He is a God who knows, and he has created us able to know. We might cite as a parallel the case of divine love. For us experientially, human love is primary. We learn of it from our human parents, and then only later learn to project what we know on the human level on to God. But in reality love is primary in God; it can be experienced on the human level because the creator has chosen to incorporate into his creation aspects of what already existed in the divine being. So while our knowledge of love starts with the human and rises to the divine, the true movement is in the other direction. Our experience of love moves not from the real to the metaphysical, but from the copy or the derived to the original. The love of God is the reality that lies behind and the fulfilling of all that we have tasted in the lesser loving of our human experience." Ibid., 191–92.

54. Ibid., 107.

of Hicks's analysis is his repeated assertion that Hodge did not divide the soul "into various faculties or aspects," but conceived of the soul as a whole or integrated "unit" that acts in all of its functions—its thinking, its feeling, and its willing—as a single substance.[55] While this "unified anthropology" was "very much at odds with the current faculty concepts that were based on two centuries of rationalism and Scottish Common Sense Philosophy," Hodge nonetheless insisted, following Scripture, that our intellects and our wills "are not detachable parts of us which can operate in isolation from each other," but faculties or powers that act as a single unit in response to the governing disposition of the soul.[56] "The Scriptures do not contemplate the intellect, the will, and the affections, as independent, separable elements of a composite whole," he argued. "These faculties are only different forms of activity in one and the same subsistence."[57]

It is this rejection of the "faculty psychology," then, i.e., this conviction that our intellects and our wills "are neither independent nor distinct"[58] but are both expressions of an integrated whole which is "the thinking, feeling, and willing subject in man,"[59] that suggests at least three factors that are of critical importance to our analysis of the Princeton mind. In the first place, Hodge's unified anthropology suggests that he conceived of reason in a "broad" and not in a narrow sense,[60] and that he consequently acknowledged that a true or "right" understanding of whatever is apprehended by the mind involves more than just a movement of the rational faculty alone. Indeed, he recognized that since "[t]here is always an exercise of will in thought, and an exercise of feeling in cognition," a true or "right" understanding of what is rationally perceived involves "not mere intellectual apprehension. . . . It includes also the proper

55. Ibid., 174–5; see, for example, Charles Hodge, "Free Agency," *BRPR* 29 (January 1857): 115; Charles Hodge, "My Son, Give Me Thy Heart," in *Conference Papers* (New York: Charles Scribner's Sons, 1879), 131; Charles Hodge, *Systematic Theology*, 3 vols. (Grand Rapids: Eerdmans, 1982; 1872–73), 2:255.

56. Hicks, *The Philosophy of Charles Hodge*, 175, 17.

57. Hodge, *Systematic Theology*, 3:16; cf. Hicks, *The Philosophy of Charles Hodge*, 173.

58. Hodge, "The Excellency of the Knowledge of Christ Jesus our Lord," in *Conference Papers*, 214.

59. Hodge, *Systematic Theology*, 2:46.

60. Hicks, *The Philosophy of Charles Hodge*, 99.

apprehension . . . [of an object's] qualities; and if those qualities be either esthetic or moral, it includes the due apprehension of them and the state of feeling which answers to them."[61] That Hodge conceived of cognition as an activity involving the whole soul is perhaps nowhere more succinctly manifest than in a sermon on knowing Christ. "The knowledge of Christ," he argued, "is not the apprehension of what he is, simply by the intellect, but also a due apprehension of his glory as a divine person arrayed in our nature, and involves not as its consequence merely, but as one of its elements, the corresponding feeling of adoration, delight, desire and complacency."[62]

If Hodge's emphasis on the unitary operation of the soul suggests that cognition is an activity involving both the intellect and the will, it also suggests that it is a moral rather than a merely rational enterprise. It also suggests that the extent to which truth is apprehended by the mind and then followed in life is ultimately determined not by the rational power of the intellect alone, but by the moral character of the knowing agent. That this is the case, and that Hodge "combined both intellectual apprehension and moral response in the notion of knowledge,"[63] is clearly revealed in his endorsement of the classical Reformed distinction between a merely "speculative" and a "spiritual" understanding of the gospel, the distinction that grounds his insistence that the teaching of the Spirit is necessary "in order to the right understanding of the Scriptures."[64] While Hodge was convinced that the unregenerate can entertain "correct intellectual convictions"[65] about the truth of Scripture because they can apprehend that truth in a "speculative" or merely rational sense, he nonetheless insisted that they cannot "come to the knowledge of the truth"[66] because they "cannot

61. Hodge, "The Excellency of the Knowledge of Christ Jesus Our Lord," 214; cf. Charles Hodge, "The Necessity of the Spirit's Teaching in Order to the Right Understanding of the Scriptures," in *Conference Papers*, 75–77; Hicks, *The Philosophy of Charles Hodge*, 100, 107–8, 206.

62. Hodge, "The Excellency of the Knowledge of Christ Jesus our Lord," 214.

63. Hicks, *The Philosophy of Charles Hodge*, 175.

64. Hodge, "The Necessity of the Spirit's Teaching in Order to the Right Understanding of the Scriptures," 75–77; Hodge, "The Excellency of the Knowledge of Christ Jesus our Lord," 214–15.

65. Charles Hodge, "The Indwelling of the Spirit," in *Conference Papers*, 77.

66. Hodge, "The Necessity of the Spirit's Teaching in Order to the Right Understanding of the Scriptures," 76–77.

know the things of the Spirit."[67] That is to say, they can neither discern the beauty nor taste the sweetness of the truth that they can rationally perceive[68] because a moral defect "in the organ of vision"[69] prevents a "true" or "right" apprehension of the truth that is presented to their consciousness.[70]

The regenerate, on the other hand, can discern the "spiritual excellence"[71] of what is apprehended by their minds because they have the moral ability to "see and love the beauty of holiness."[72] Indeed, they can "know the things of the Spirit"[73] because they were infused with "a new spiritual principle" in the new birth,[74] and as a consequence they "embrace [the truth] with assurance and delight"[75] because they "see truth to be truth, to be excellent, lovely and divine."[76] That "right knowledge as well as right feeling . . . are inseparable effects of a work that affects the whole soul" and that certainly leads to saving faith is made clear in a sermon on delighting in the Law of God.[77] Delighting in the Law of God, Hodge argued,

67. Charles Hodge, "Delighting in the Law of God," in *Conference Papers*, 249.

68. Cf. Hodge, *Systematic Theology*, 2:261–62.

69. Ibid., 3:51.

70. Cf. Charles Hodge, *The Way of Life*, introduction by Mark A. Noll (Mahwah, NJ: Paulist, 1987; 1841), 60; Hodge, *Systematic Theology*, 2:234.

71. Hodge, "The Necessity of the Spirit's Teaching in Order to the Right Understanding of the Scriptures," 76.

72. Charles Hodge, "Regeneration, and the Manner of Its Occurrence," *BRPR* 2 (1830): 285.

73. Hodge, "Delighting in the Law of God," 249.

74. Charles Hodge, "Regeneration," in *Conference Papers*, 136.

75. Hodge, *Systematic Theology*, 3:71.

76. Charles Hodge, "Evidences of Regeneration," in *Conference Papers*, 138. Note that there is a certain relationship between seeing and believing in Hodge's thought because of the work of the Spirit on the "whole soul" of a moral agent (cf. Chapter One above). Note as well that while Hodge clearly affirms the primacy of the intellect in faith, he is unyielding in his insistence that the whole soul is the subject of the Spirit's influence. As such, he rejects "what has been called the 'light system,' which teaches that men are regenerated by light or knowledge, and that all that is needed is that the eyes of the understanding should be opened. As the whole soul is the subject of original sin the whole soul is the subject of regeneration. A blind man cannot possibly rejoice in the beauties of nature or art until his sight is restored. But, if uncultivated, the mere restoration of sight will not give him the perception of beauty. His whole nature must be refined and elevated. So also the whole nature of apostate man must be renewed by the Holy Ghost; then his eyes being opened to the glory of God in Christ, he will rejoice in Him with joy unspeakable and full of glory. But the illumination of the mind is indispensable to holy feelings, and is their proximate cause." Hodge, *Systematic Theology*, 2:263.

77. Ibid., 3:36.

is peculiar to the spiritual man, and is due to the influence of the Spirit. This influence is twofold, or produces a twofold effect. *First,* a subjective change in the state of the mind analogous to opening the eyes of the blind. It is such a change as imparts the power of spiritual vision, i.e., the vision of the spiritual excellence of divine things. . . . *Second,* it produces a revelation of the truth, a presentation of it to the mind in its true nature and relations. This is a special work of the Spirit. . . . The effect of these operations of the Spirit is delighting in the law of God, which includes,

1. An apprehension of its truth and consequent conviction of its divine origin.

2. An apprehension of its excellence, of its purity, of its justice, and its goodness. It is seen to be right, to be morally glorious.

3. An experience of its power to convince, to sanctify, to console, to guide, to render wise unto salvation; an experience of its appropriateness to our necessities. It is seen to suit our nature as rational beings, as moral beings, as sinners.

4. An acquiescence in it, and rejoicing in it, as an exhibition of the character of God, of the rule of duty, of the plan of salvation, of the person and work of Christ, and of the future state. The Scriptures, therefore, are the treasury of truth; the store-house of promises; the granary of spiritual food; the never-failing river of life.[78]

Finally and most importantly, Hodge's emphasis on the unitary operation of the soul suggests that he conceived of reason in an Augustinian rather than in a scholastic or an Enlightenment sense, and thus is not properly regarded as either a scholastic or an Enlightenment rationalist. Although this contention certainly challenges the historiographical consensus, nevertheless it is largely confirmed by an unlikely source, namely the historical analysis by Jack Rogers of the Westminster Confession of Faith. In *Scripture in the Westminster Confession: A Problem of Historical Interpretation for American Presbyterianism,* Rogers argues that the Princeton theologians "did not develop an historically valid interpretation of Scripture in the Westminster Confession," in part because they failed to interpret the Confession in light of "the distinctively British background which . . . informed the thinking of the Westminster Divines and which

78. Hodge, "Delighting in the Law of God," 249–50.

created the context in which they thought and wrote."[79] Whereas the Princetonians interpreted the Confession in light of the "Aristotelian and Scholastic" assumptions of "later Continental Reformed orthodoxy" and thus underemphasized "the witness of the Spirit and the saving purpose of Scripture in their formulation of the doctrine of Scripture," the Westminster Divines, being "both Puritans and Calvinists," "placed primary emphasis" on these "motifs" because they drew heavily on "an anti-Aristotelian Augustinianism"[80] that was "a deep-rooted tradition carried on in the Puritan party."[81]

One of the "principal threads" in this "anti-Aristotelian Augustinianism," Rogers argues, and thus one of the primary influences that distinguished the Westminster Divines from their more scholastic counterparts both in England and on the Continent, was "the presence of an Augustinian conception of 'right reason.'"[82] While those who

79. Jack B. Rogers, *Scripture in the Westminster Confession: A Problem of Historical Interpretation for American Presbyterianism* (Grand Rapids: Eerdmans, 1967), 448, 438.

80. Ibid., 438, 449, 220, 449.

81. Rogers and McKim, *The Authority and Interpretation of the Bible*, 202.

82. Rogers, *Scripture in the Westminster Confession*, 82, 438. According to Robert Hoopes, the author of the most extensive study on the concept of "right reason" to date, the concept of "right reason" was born in classical Greece when Socrates advanced the notion that "virtue and knowledge are identical." Robert Hoopes, *Right Reason in the English Renaissance* (Cambridge: Harvard University Press, 1962), 1. As an epistemological concept that was "assimilated by the early Church Fathers and redefined in the Christian context of sin and grace" (ibid.), the concept was controlled by two formative convictions. Not only did it advance the notion that there is a realm of truth that "includes both intellectual and moral truths" (ibid., 4), but more importantly it recognized that in order for men to know this truth "they must themselves *become* good" (ibid., 6). According to Hoopes, "wherever classical and Christian humanists speak of the achievement of true knowledge . . . they invariably speak of a certain transformation that must take place in the character of the knower before that knowledge can be attained. . . . Since Truth in its totality is at once intellectual and moral in nature, the conditions of wisdom are for men both intellectual and moral. True knowledge, i.e., knowledge of Truth, involves the perfection of the knower in both thought and deed." Ibid., 5.

How, though, do men become good so they can know what is true? In his incisive analysis of Hoopes's work, Rogers correctly notes that the concept of "right reason" developed along two lines in the Christian world, in large measure because differing anthropologies led to different answers to this question. Rogers, *Scripture in the Westminster Confession*, 84. While those who followed Aquinas emphasized the "essential goodness" of man and consequently conceived of "right reason" as a faculty that all possess, Augustine took seriously the reality of original sin and the need for regenerating grace and thus insisted that the regenerate alone can reason "rightly." For further analysis of this concept, see the forthcoming discussion in Chapter Six. For a more recent examination of the relationship between regeneration and knowing, see William J.

followed Aquinas conceived of "right reason" as a faculty that "was implanted by God in all men, Christian and heathen alike, as a guide to truth and conduct,"[83] those who followed Augustine insisted that the regenerate alone "may rise to an understanding of the truth"[84] because the regenerate alone have the moral ability to see revealed truth more or less for what it objectively is, namely glorious. Although those who followed Augustine acknowledged that there is a logical priority of the intellect in faith and thus were not "irrationalists" in any sense of the term, nevertheless they refused to give reason "a sphere of primary authority . . . in religious matters" because they recognized that the intellect and the will work together as a single substance in response to the governing inclination of the soul.[85] Indeed, they recognized that there is an intimate connection between the unitary operation of the soul and the quality of the reception of revealed truth, and as a consequence they insisted that the ability to apprehend what God has revealed in something more than a speculative or merely rational sense necessitates that the depravity "of both intellect and will" be taken away "by the power of God."[86]

For the followers of Augustine, therefore, "right reason" is not a faculty all human beings possess that forms the epistemological foundation for a natural theology and a naïve approach to evidentialist apologetics. Rather, it is an epistemological ability of the regenerated soul "which acknowledges the authority of God and which functions for moral, not [merely] speculative ends."[87] Whereas Rogers and McKim[88] would have us believe that Hodge's assimilation of the Scottish philosophy subverted his commitment to an Augustinian understanding of "right reason" and turned him into a rationalist who afforded reason "an independent sphere of operation prior to faith," in fact his understanding of "right rea-

---

Wainwright, *Reason and the Heart: A Prolegomenon to a Critique of Passional Reason* (Ithaca, NY, and London: Cornell University Press, 1995).

83. Douglas Bush, *Paradise Lost in Our Time* (Ithaca, NY: Cornell University Press, 1945), 37; cf. Hoopes, *Right Reason*, 3.

84. Hoopes, *Right Reason*, 64; cf. Rogers, *Scripture in the Westminster Confession*, 83.

85. Rogers, *Scripture in the Westminster Confession*, 230, 86, 85.

86. Ibid., 232.

87. Ibid., 231.

88. Cf. Rogers and McKim, *The Authority and Interpretation of the Bible*, 296.

son" is remarkably similar to that of the Westminster Divines.[89] For not only did he recognize that reasoning itself is an inherently moral enterprise involving all the powers of the soul, but he also acknowledged that the extent to which truth is apprehended by the mind and then followed in life is ultimately determined by the moral character of the knowing agent. What this suggests, in short, is that "it [is] inappropriate to categorize Hodge as a doctrinaire rationalist or a curmudgeonly scholastic,"[90] for he stood with the Westminster Divines in the mainstream of an epistemological tradition that was, as Rogers himself insists, "quite clearly" opposed both to the humanism of the scholastic tradition and to the rationalism of the Enlightenment.[91]

Postconservative Evangelicalism's Misunderstanding of the Princeton Mind

If we assume, for the purposes of this chapter, that Hodge's epistemological assumptions are representative of those of the best thinkers in the Princeton tradition, then we have grounds for concluding that postconservatism's repudiation of Old Princeton's "propositionalist understanding of the theological enterprise" is based on at least two profound misunderstandings of the Princeton mind. The first has to do with the alleged rationalism of the Princeton theologians. Whereas postconservatives follow the consensus of critical opinion and thus presume that the theologians at Old Princeton Seminary were naïve rationalists who were indifferent to the subjective and experiential components of a consistently Reformed religious epistemology, in fact the Princetonians were committed Augustinians who conceived of reason in a moral rather a merely rational sense. They recognized, in other words, that the reception of what God has revealed is an activity involving the "whole soul" rather than the rational faculty alone, and as a consequence they insisted, the allegations of Rogers and McKim

89. Rogers, *Scripture in the Westminster Confession*, 85.
90. Stewart, Review of *The Philosophy of Charles Hodge*, 65.
91. Rogers, *Scripture in the Westminster Confession*, 87n226. For Rogers's full discussion of "right reason" and related matters, cf. 82–87, 222–53.

notwithstanding,[92] that the regenerate alone could apprehend this truth in a "right" or saving sense. As Iain Murray has incisively argued:

> The *use* of the mind is not "rationalism"; it all depends on whether that use is right or wrong. Rationalism is a use of the mind which trusts in its own ability to arrive at truth about God *without* his aid and *apart* from revelation: it treats the mind as a source of knowledge rather than as a channel. The Enlightenment was a classic demonstration of innate human pride in the exaltation of the human intellect. To equate that spirit with the teaching of the Princeton men, who believed that it is the grace of God alone which sets men free to understand, is to stand truth on its head.[93]

The second misunderstanding follows from the first and has to do with the nature of Old Princeton's opposition to the rise of theological liberalism. While the Princeton theologians certainly were convinced that those who are "taught by God" articulate their thoughts about the things of God in an "orthodox" fashion,[94] nevertheless their opposition to the rise of theological liberalism was grounded in more than just a stubborn reluctance to allow "more light and truth to break forth from God's Word" (after all, even B. B. Warfield, as we shall see in the next chapter, was a proponent of "progressive orthodoxy").[95] The

92. Cf. Rogers and McKim, *The Authority and Interpretation of the Bible*, 290; Rogers, "Van Til and Warfield on Scripture in the Westminster Confession," 154.

93. Iain H. Murray, *Evangelicalism Divided: A Record of Crucial Change in the Years 1950 to 2000* (Edinburgh: The Banner of Truth Trust, 2000), 197.

94. For example, see Hodge, "The Indwelling of the Spirit," 77; cf. John 6:44–45.

95. John Robinson, quoted in Dorrien, *Remaking of Evangelical Theology*, 11. Theologians such as Roger Olson employ this phrase to help them distinguish between evangelicals who are "reformists" and evangelicals who are "traditionalists." Whereas "reformists" are open to "new light," "traditionalists" apparently are "unwilling" to modify their positions. Olson, "The Future of Evangelical Theology," 42, 47. While this rather strained distinction certainly packs a rhetorical punch, it is grossly unfair to both past and present members of the "traditionalist" camp. Warfield, for example, believed in "progressive orthodoxy" (cf. Robert Swanton, "Warfield and Progressive Orthodoxy," *RTR* 23 [October 1964]: 76–77), and today traditionalist evangelicals such as Ardel Caneday and Thomas Schreiner are challenging accepted understandings of perseverance and assurance in a constructive rather than a destructive fashion. Cf. Ardel B. Caneday and Thomas R. Schreiner, *The Race Set Before Us: A Biblical Theology of Perseverance and Assurance* (Downers Grove, IL: InterVarsity, 2001). This suggests, among other things, that the categories of commentators such as Olson have become sufficiently hardened to warrant immediate revision. For an interesting discussion of "hardening of the categories," which apparently is a condition that

Princetonians were opposed to the rise of theological liberalism, in short, not simply because liberals advanced interpretations of doctrine that differed from their own dogmatic assertions, but more specifically because liberals conceived of doctrines in an "anti-intellectual" or "feminized" sense.[96] Whereas the Princetonians conceived of doctrines as foundational summaries of biblical truth that must be believed in order for there to be faith, liberals conceived of doctrines as little more than expressions of an ineffable religious experience for a particular time and place. They considered doctrines to be true, in other words, not because they corresponded to real states of affairs in the external world, but because they captured the subjective experience of religion in the thought forms of a particular age.[97]

Although this pragmatic conception of truth certainly allowed for a broadening of theological boundaries along intra- and even intertextual lines, it needed to be opposed, the Princetonians reasoned, because it left fallen sinners without access to a source of salvation outside of their own (or their community's) experience. Indeed, it presumed an experiential orientation that emptied the Christian religion of enduring cognitive substance, and as a consequence it engendered a progressive inclination that confounded the stating of Christian belief "in terms of modern thought" with the stating of modern thought "in terms of Christian belief."[98] While the denominational heirs of classical theological liberalism have milked this progressive tendency for practically all it is

---

cripples even the most irenic of evangelicals, see Olson, *The Story of Christian Theology*, 554–69; Roger Olson, *How to Be Evangelical without Being Conservative* (Grand Rapids: Zondervan, 2008), 29–42.

96. Cf. Richard Hofstadter, *Anti-Intellectualism in American Life* (New York: Vintage Books, 1962, 1963), 55–141; Ann Douglas, *The Feminization of American Culture* (New York: Noonday, 1998; 1977), 3–13, 17–43, 121–64.

97. See, for example, Shailer Mathews, *The Faith of Modernism* (New York: Macmillan, 1924), 100, 115, 119, 148, 174–75, and *New Faith for Old* (New York: Macmillan, 1936), 225, 233, 237. Please note that this way of conceiving of doctrine is one of the evidences that substantiate what Douglas calls the feminization of American culture. According to Douglas, an intellectually rigorous Calvinism was displaced in the Victorian era "by an anti-intellectual sentimentalism." Douglas, *The Feminization of American Culture*, 13.

98. B. B. Warfield, review of *Foundations: A Statement of Christian Belief in Terms of Modern Thought*, by Seven Oxford Men, in *CR*, vol. 10, *The Works of Benjamin Breckinridge Warfield* (Grand Rapids: Baker, 1991; 1932), 322. On the definite meaning of the word "Christianity," cf. B. B. Warfield, "'Redeemer' and 'Redemption,'" in *Biblical Doctrines*, vol. 2, *The Works of Benjamin Breckinridge Warfield* (Grand Rapids: Baker, 1991; 1929), 396.

worth,[99] it is unfortunately enjoying something of a renaissance in certain quarters of the evangelical camp, albeit in a strangely nuanced form.[100] That this is the case, and that a new kind of fundamentalism is rising within the ranks of those who are searching for a "generous orthodoxy" with a large, forgiving center,[101] is manifest in the baldly imperialistic tendencies of postconservative evangelicals such as Robert Webber.

Paradigm Thinking and the Postconservative Evangelical

The Postconservative Project

According to Robert Webber, former professor of ministry at Northern Seminary and an erstwhile leader in the postconservative evangelical movement, the thinking of the evangelical community has been shaped by the "paradigm" of the modern era for too long, and thus it is high time for evangelicals to "rethink" the faith for a postmodern age. His ground-breaking offering, *Ancient-Future Faith: Rethinking Evangelicalism for a Postmodern World*, is intended for precisely this purpose. Evangelicals will liberate themselves from their bondage to the rationalistic assumptions of Enlightenment thought and faithfully

---

99. Cf. Jones, *Spirit Wars: Pagan Revival in Christian America*.

100. With respect to this renaissance of theological liberalism within the evangelical camp, note the interesting—and profoundly ironic and sad—remarks of B. A. Gerrish in "The New Evangelical Theology and the Old: An Opportunity for the Next Century?" http://www.union-psce.edu/news/Publications/archive/aisit-gerrish.html. Commenting on postconservative evangelicalism in general and Grenz's attempt to conceive of theology as a second-order discipline in particular, Gerrish notes that, "I couldn't agree more. But I can't help thinking that I've heard it before. Grenz does not seem to recognize, or perhaps he prefers not to say, that his theological program for the twenty-first century is pretty much the program that the supposed arch-liberal Friedrich Schleiermacher proposed for the nineteenth century. Differences there may be. But the threefold emphasis on experience, community, and context was precisely Schleiermacher's contribution to evangelical dogmatics. Successive waves of neoorthodox and postmodernist attacks on him have submerged his contribution beneath an ocean of misunderstandings. He never renounced his evangelical-pietistic experience: rather, his theology at its center was reflection upon this experience from within the believing community in its new situation. He was certain that his experience must point to something constant since the time of the apostles, yet always to be conveyed in language that is historically conditioned. No less a critic of his doctrines than Karl Barth correctly perceived in Schleiermacher's faith 'a personal relationship with Jesus that may well be called "love."'"

101. For example, see Grenz, *Renewing the Center*, 325–51; Olson, "The Future of Evangelical Theology," 42. For a brief explanation of how the word "fundamentalism" is being used in this chapter, please see note 12 above.

"re-present" the faith in our postmodern world, he suggests, neither by "preserving the Christian faith in its modern form," nor by running "headlong into the sweeping changes that accommodate Christianity to postmodern forms."[102] They will "re-present" the faith "in a fresh way," rather, by recovering the insights of an age very similar to our own, namely that of classical Christianity (A.D. 100–600).[103] "The fundamental concern of this book," Webber writes,

> is to find points of contact between classical Christianity and post-modern thought. Classical Christianity was shaped in a pagan and relativistic society much like our own. Classical Christianity was not an accommodation to paganism but an alternative practice of life. Christians in a postmodern world will succeed, not by watering down the faith, but by being a countercultural community that invites people to be shaped by the story of Israel and Jesus.[104]

At first glance, the basic thrust of Webber's proposal will undoubtedly resonate with thoughtful members of the "evangelical establishment." After all, both Luther and Calvin were indebted to the insights of classical Christianity, and even B. B. Warfield, the "lion of strict Presbyterian orthodoxy,"[105] insisted that Christians must state their beliefs in terms of the thought of the age in which they live.[106] More critical readers will quickly recognize, however, that Webber's approach to the Christian faith is altogether different from "the Book-oriented approach" of Luther, Calvin, and Warfield.[107] Indeed, whereas evangelicals such as Warfield emphasize "the foundational nature of Scripture" and consequently acknowledge that the Christian

---

102. Robert E. Webber, *Ancient-Future Faith: Rethinking Evangelicalism for a Postmodern World* (Grand Rapids: Baker, 1999), 14.

103. Ibid., 16.

104. Ibid., 7.

105. George M. Marsden, *Fundamentalism and American Culture: The Shaping of Twentieth-Century Evangelicalism 1870–1975* (New York: Oxford University Press, 1980), 98.

106. Cf. Warfield, review of *Foundations*, 320–34. Recall Warfield's comment: "No one will doubt that Christians of to-day must state their Christian beliefs in terms of modern thought. Every age has a language of its own and can speak no other. Mischief comes only when, instead of stating Christian belief in terms of modern thought, an effort is made, rather, to state modern thought in terms of Christian belief." Ibid., 322.

107. Webber, *Ancient-Future Faith*, 45.

faith can be "rationally explained and defended," Webber insists that the authoritative nexus of both faith and truth is found in an inherently mysterious, "event-oriented perception of the world" that is handed down from age to age in "the community of God's presence," the church.[108] As such, Webber argues that the responsibility of the church in the postmodern world is not to recover an articulation of this perception that was "incarnated" in an earlier age.[109] It is rather to "construct a theology that will be consistent with historic Christianity yet relevant to our new time in culture."[110] What is needed, he contends, is a faithful application of the essence of the Christian faith "to a postmodern worldview."[111]

Paradigm Thinking and the Continuity of the Christian Tradition

At the heart of Webber's attempt "to interface historic Christian truths into the dawning of a new era" is his insistence that evangelicals will "face the changing cultural situation with integrity" only if they allow themselves to think paradigmatically.[112] According to Webber, there have been six discernible "paradigms of time" throughout the history of the church in which believers have struggled to articulate the essence of the faith in response to the prevailing cultural circumstances of the day.[113] While the circumstances have changed from age to age and the "incarnations" of the faith have thus varied according to "the specific cultural context in which [they were] expressed (e.g., medieval Roman versus sixteenth-century Reformation)," what has remained constant throughout the ages, Webber contends, is a "transcultural framework of faith . . . that has been blessed by sociocultural particularity in every period of church history."[114] Since the "multiplicities of faith expressions"

108. Ibid., 45, 18, 78, 46.
109. Ibid., 17.
110. Ibid., 20–21.
111. Ibid., 12; cf. Webber, *The Younger Evangelicals*, 14–17.
112. Webber, *Ancient-Future Faith*, 14, 17.
113. Ibid., 13.
114. Ibid., 17.

reflect merely the "attempts within a particular cultural moment and geographical place to express the faith in a fresh way," those who would "incarnate the historic faith in the emerging culture" will do so only by recovering "the framework of faith that is common to the diversity."[115] It follows, therefore, that if we would faithfully "re-present" the faith in the postmodern context we must not "root" or "freeze" our understanding of the faith in a particular "incarnation" of the faith from the past (that of the Reformation, for example).[116] Rather, we must "affirm the whole church in all its previous manifestations" by retrieving

> the universally accepted framework of faith that originated with the apostles, was developed by the Fathers, and has been handed down by the church in its liturgical and theological traditions. . . . Our calling is not to reinvent the Christian faith, but, in keeping with the past, to carry forward what the church has affirmed from its beginning. We change . . . "not to be different, but to remain the same."[117]

While there is little doubt that most conservative readers will be intrigued by Webber's call for theological reconstruction, they likely will wonder whether the call sounds plausible only because religious language has been emptied of objective significance. After all, they might ask, is it not possible that one theological formulation differs from another because the framers of the two formulations were actually talking about different religious realities? In other words, if the words that are used in theological formulations are significant precisely because the framers presume the words they use correspond in some sense to extralinguistic realities, and if as a consequence the framers of those formulations are convinced of the extralinguistic truthfulness of the particular "incarnation" they affirm, then can it really be true that "while we are all Christians, some of us are Roman Catholic Christians, Eastern Orthodox Christians, Reformation Christians,

115. Ibid., 16–17.
116. Ibid., 16.
117. Ibid., 16–17. On the process of "deconstruction and reconstruction" that accompanies the re-presentation of the faith in each new age, cf. Webber, *The Younger Evangelicals*, 17.

twentieth-century evangelical Christians, or some other form of modern or postmodern Christians"?[118]

It can and indeed it must be true, Webber assures us, if all genuine expressions of the faith share a common core. What, then, might this unifying core be? The answer is found in the assumptions that inform "the hermeneutic of paradigm thinking."[119] In the first place, Webber insists that religious truth is found in subjective encounter with the classical origins of the Christian tradition. Following the postmodern theorist Hans-Georg Gadamer, Webber argues that it is possible for one paradigm of history to speak to another because it is possible for an individual living in one historical "horizon" to "fuse" with the "horizon" that is the source of the tradition.[120] In Webber's thinking, this "fusion" takes place in the life and worship of the church, the "body of Christ" that is the living sign of *Christus Victor*, "the community of people where the victory of Christ over evil becomes present in and to this world."[121]

In the second place, Webber contends that a "fusion of horizons" is possible in the community of faith because the truth-value of the religious utterances that sustain the community—be they the propositions of Scripture or of historical confessions—is not found in some kind of correspondence between the words themselves and the extralinguistic realities to which they refer, but in the religious function those words

118. Webber, *Ancient-Future Faith*, 17. Conservative readers will remain baffled by postconservative proposals as long as they fail to recognize that conservative and post-conservative evangelicals have significant disagreements over theological method. Webber describes this disagreement as follows: "The method of the traditionalists is to treat theology as a science, subject, as all other sciences are, to the empirical method. Through an analysis of the data of revelation, one could be brought to propositional truth. Theology, the traditionalist says, is a system of objective truth understood by the mind." Webber, *The Younger Evangelicals*, 91–92. Postconservative evangelicals, on the other hand, see theology "as the way to understand the world. It is an understanding based on the biblical narrative. This is the approach to faith that has captured the postmodern mind. Postmoderns have abandoned the modern worldview in which the supremacy of interpretation is given to science. In this context younger evangelicals are calling us to see the world primarily through the Christian story. . . . Theology [they contend] is not a science but a reflection of God's community on the narrative of God's involvement in history as found in the story of Israel and Jesus." Ibid., 92.

119. Webber, *Ancient-Future Faith*, 16.

120. Ibid., 24, 29; cf. Hans-Georg Gadamer, *Truth and Method* (London: Sheed & Ward, 1995).

121. Webber, *Ancient-Future Faith*, 81, 77.

perform. Following the "cultural-linguistic" approach of postliberal theologian George Lindbeck, Webber insists that the truth-value of religious utterances is "intratextual" rather than "extratextual."[122] That is to say, religious utterances are true because they form a perspective on life that is consistent with the perspective of a particular tradition, not because they correspond to "extratextual" reality as such.[123] Since the perception of the world that is characteristic of the Christian tradition was articulated by the apostles and summarized by the early church in the "rule of faith" (the classical summary of the apostolic interpretation of the Christ event that is embodied in the ecumenical creeds), it follows that the religious utterances of Christians from various "frame[s] of reference" are true to the extent that they form a "framework of thought" that is shaped by the central component of that "rule," namely the cosmic reality of *Christus Victor*.[124] The theme of *Christus Victor*, Webber insists, is "central to the classical Christian vision of reality. It does not stand alone, but is connected to all other aspects of the Christian faith as the central thread to the entire tapestry."[125]

When we consider Webber's call for unity within diversity in light of these hermeneutical assumptions, the justification for his reluctance to make one expression of the faith the "standard" by which all other expressions are measured suddenly comes into clearer focus.[126] The church is the community of faith in which the perception of the world that is grounded in the reality of *Christus Victor* and summarized in the "rule of faith" is "handed over" from one

122. Ibid., 30, 185; cf. Webber, *The Younger Evangelicals*, 74–75; George A. Lindbeck, *The Nature of Doctrine: Religion and Theology in a Postliberal Age* (Philadelphia: Westminster, 1984).

123. Webber, *Ancient-Future Faith*, 30, 46, 182–85; cf. Webber, *The Younger Evangelicals*, 90–92. According to William Placher, "A good Lindbeckian, postliberal theologian will . . . operate less like a philosophically oriented apologist and more like a sensitive anthropologist, who tries to describe the language and practice of a tribe in terms of how they function in the life of that community and how they shape the way that community sees the world, rather than trying to defend these people's way of talking by the standards of some universal rationality or experience." William Placher, *Unapologetic Theology: A Christian Voice in a Pluralistic Conversation* (Louisville: Westminster John Knox, 1989), 163.

124. Webber, *Ancient-Future Faith*, 180–86, 196.

125. Ibid., 31.

126. Ibid., 16.

generation of believers to another in the life and worship of the body, the "fellowship in faith."[127] The task of the church in each successive age and in every sociocultural context, then, is not to explain and defend a specific incarnation of the faith (for the essence of faith is found in a perspective on life rather than in submission to propositions that correspond to objective reality as such). It is, rather, first to express the faith "within the context of history and culture" through "the critical use of human methods of thought," and then to beckon "seekers" into the ongoing fellowship of the community so that their perspective on life can be shaped by that which is shared by all genuine expressions of the faith, namely the perception of the world that is embodied in the Word, liturgy, and symbolism of the "people of the Event."[128] "The goal of the church," Webber contends,

> is to be a divine standard, a sign of God's incarnational presence and activity in history. In a postmodern world the most effective witness to a world of disconnected people is the church that forms community and embodies the reality of the new society. People in a postmodern world are not persuaded to faith by reason as much as they are moved to faith by participation in God's earthly community.[129]

127. Ibid., 180–83, 79.

128. Ibid., 196, 163; Robert E. Webber, "Out with the Old," *Christianity Today* (February 19, 1990): 17.

129. Webber, *Ancient-Future Faith*, 72, 79. Postconservative evangelicals such as Webber advocate an "embodied" or "incarnational" apologetic because they are convinced that the believing community has the power not only "to communicate the reality of the gospel," but also "to lead people into conversion." Webber, *The Younger Evangelicals*, 95, 101, 220. The gospel, they contend, is a "story" that must be experienced; it is "not a noncontradictory, rationally defended, logically consistent fact [to be] apprehended by cognitive acquiescence." Ibid., 49. Since postconservative evangelicals are convinced that gospel truth is "embodied by individuals and by the community known as the church," they insist that this truth is "known" not when it is "proven," but when an individual "step[s] inside the community and into the stream of its interpretation and experience of reality." Ibid., 101, 104. From this it follows that faith "is not born outside the church" in submission to propositions that are presumed to be objectively true. Ibid., 104. Rather, faith involves "participation in truth embodied by the community," and as such it is born "within the church as individuals see themselves and their world through the eyes of God's earthed community. . . . In sum the community embodies the Christian narrative, the unchurched 'step into' the narrative, the narrative grasps them even as they grasp it, and eventually the individual embodies the reality of the church's story as he chooses to live his life from the standpoint of the community of faith." Ibid.

Say What? The Imperialism of Neo-Fundamentalism

No matter what one's initial reaction to Webber's proposal might be, even the harshest critic must concede that the typical author would kill for the kinds of reviews *Ancient-Future Faith* has received. Clark Pinnock, for example, not only suggests that *Ancient-Future Faith* presents a faith that has "the power to speak to the postmodern world," but more significantly he praises Webber in much the same way that the editors of major newspapers praise staunchly conservative politicians for voting in the "correct" fashion on conspicuous social issues.[130] Just as editors cite those votes as evidence that the politician in question has "grown" while in office, so too Pinnock cites *Ancient-Future Faith* as evidence of "Webber's own experience of growth as a hearer of God's Word."[131]

Most conservative readers will likely wonder, however, just what exactly it is that Webber has been hearing, for his proposal is marred by an ambivalence that undermines his attempt to move the evangelical camp out of the modern era and into the postmodern paradigm, an ambivalence that I would suggest is characteristic of the postconservative project. While Webber incisively critiques the deleterious influence that modern thought has had and continues to have on certain habits of the evangelical mind, nevertheless his own proposal is profoundly modern in three distinct yet interrelated senses.[132] In the first place, it is based on the assumption that Christianity is, as J. Gresham Machen used to say when critiquing theological liberalism, "a life, not a doctrine."[133] Postconservative evangelicals do not draw people into the kingdom of God by proclaiming propositions that articulate the objective foundations of the Christian life; rather they draw people into the corporate experience of the "fellowship in

---

For a helpful example of Webber's "embodied" apologetic, see Robert E. Webber, *Who Gets to Narrate the World? Contending for the Christian Story in an Age of Rivals* (Downers Grove, IL: InterVarsity, 2008).

130. Webber, *Ancient-Future Faith*, back cover.

131. Ibid.

132. Thus, I am challenging Webber's contention that postconservative evangelicals "are *not of the twentieth century and its mindset*." Webber, *The Younger Evangelicals*, 24.

133. J. Gresham Machen, *Christianity and Liberalism* (Grand Rapids: Eerdmans, 1990; 1923), 19. See, for example, Webber, *The Younger Evangelicals*, 102–5.

faith," and it is this experience that then moves seekers to embrace the "framework of faith" in some mysterious fashion.[134] As Machen makes clear in his classic work *Christianity and Liberalism*, such an approach not only has it backwards, but more importantly it can survive only because its advocates tragically presume that fallen sinners need an ineffable experience rather than a gospel that is proclaimed objectively.

If Webber's proposal is profoundly modern in one sense because it confounds the relationship between life and doctrine, it is so in another because it presumes that the *sine qua non* of the Christian religion is subjective rather than objective. This presumption, which is grounded in the modern era's relocation of the divine-human nexus, is perhaps nowhere more clearly manifest than in the "communal epistemology" that informs Webber's functional understanding of doctrine.[135] "Information," he contends, "is no longer something that can be objectively known and verified through evidence and logic. Knowledge is more subjective and experiential. Knowledge comes through participation in a community and in an immersion with the symbols and the meaning of the community."[136] When the relationship between life and doctrine is considered in light of this decidedly anti-intellectual understanding of religious epistemology, it becomes immediately clear that religious life precedes doctrine in Webber's thinking not because there is something substandard about doctrine itself, but because doctrines *qua* doctrines must be kept in their proper place. Doctrines are not important because they carry the " 'cognitive and informational meaningfulness' " that must be appropriated in order for there to be faith.[137] Rather, they are the expressions of faith that sustain the religious life of the community and mediate the "framework of faith" to those who are drawn into the corporate experience of the "fellowship in faith." As such, doctrines are

---

134. Webber, *Ancient-Future Faith*, 77–83.

135. Webber, *The Younger Evangelicals*, 104. I recognize that Webber would reject the notion that his subjectivism is grounded in the modern era's "retreat from the intellect into the heart." Cf. Webber, *Ancient-Future Faith*, 121–25. It is not entirely clear how he can avoid this charge, however, given his emphasis on the functional rather than the propositional significance of religious utterances in the corporate experience of the Christian community.

136. Webber, *Ancient-Future Faith*, 101.

137. Lindbeck, *The Nature of Doctrine*, 16, quoted in Webber, *Ancient-Future Faith*, 19.

of secondary—not primary—significance, because they simply express the "framework of faith" for a particular time and place.[138]

Finally, Webber's proposal is profoundly modern because his functional understanding of truth reduces to pragmatism. Not only does he insist that Scripture must be read "theologically" rather than propositionally, i.e., we read the text not to discover the foundational meaning of the text but to ask how "this book, this passage, this verse has been used in the history of the church" to form the life of the people of God.[139] He also contends that doctrines are true to the extent that they form a "framework of thought" consistent with the perspective of the Christian tradition.[140] The truth-value of the Nicene Creed, for example, "is not to be found in words that correspond with an exact reality, but in words that truthfully signify the religious reality of the Trinity in the system of thought (in this case, Hellenistic) in which it is articulated."[141] But as F. LeRon Shults has incisively argued, although

138. In personal correspondence, Grenz suggests it is wrong for me to argue that postconservatives such as Webber are subjectivists. I am misrepresenting theologians like Webber, he insists, because I am "reading these folks through Enlightenment lenses" (Grenz to Helseth, November 21, 2001). While I affirm with Stephen Nichols that "By basing truth in the interpretive community of the church and rejecting truth as grounded upon objectivity, one is left with a subjective faith and a subjective apologetic" (Stephen J. Nichols, "Contemporary Apologetics and the Nature of Truth" [paper presented at the annual meeting of the Evangelical Theological Society, Orlando, November 1998], 7), I have yet to be convinced that being critical of those who engage in an extended polemic against the concept of objective truth is necessarily evidence of indebtedness to Enlightenment categories of thought. Again, Nichols makes the crucial point. "While it is true that objectivity is a crucial part of the enlightenment, it is not true that the enlightenment is a crucial part of objectivity. In the enlightenment project, objectivity was predicated upon the autonomy of the individual. If, however, objectivity is predicated upon something different, can one affirm objectivity?" (Ibid., 6.). With Nichols and the Princetonians, I would argue that one can and indeed one must, since it is the objective content of faith—that which testifies to God's saving acts in history—that saves, not faith as a merely subjective phenomenon.

139. Webber, *Ancient-Future Faith*, 190.

140. Ibid., 19–20, 30, 189–90. Webber's understanding of the authority of Scripture is difficult to get a handle on. He insists that the text is inspired; yet he rejects *sola Scriptura*. He is less than enthused about the doctrine of inerrancy because it is grounded in "the notion of propositional truth." And he is convinced that "in the modern era biblical criticism has eroded the authority of Scripture." Such commitments, it seems, are difficult to square with what evangelicals have historically believed about Scripture. For a concise statement of how he uses the Bible in doing theology, see Robert E. Webber, "An Evangelical and Catholic Methodology," in *The Use of the Bible in Theology: Evangelical Options*, ed. Robert K. Johnston (Atlanta: John Knox, 1985), 150–58.

141. Webber, *Ancient-Future Faith*, 30. Despite his contention that postconservative evangelicalism is altogether different from the pragmatic evangelicalism of the twentieth century (cf.

the Nicene divines certainly developed doctrines in order to shape the life of the Christian community, they did so "because of certain things they thought were ontologically true."[142] Surely, to miss this point is to gut the creed of its truth content, to consign the believer to "a theological *cul-de-sac* of the worst kind, mired in the circular reasoning of fideism,"[143] and to raise the specter of religious imperialism. In an age when all truth claims are reduced to the level of subjective preference, any claim to universal truthfulness that is not grounded in an objective state of affairs in the external world will smack of precisely the kind of religious chauvinism that committed postmodernists rightly despise. While Webber repeatedly asserts that the Christian narrative is universally true, he fails to recognize that such an assertion is baldly imperialistic when it is grounded in nothing more than the experiential "ethos" of the believing community.[144] Indeed, we could say that it is in the inherently chauvinistic nature of truth claims that presume a functional understanding of truth, while simultaneously privileging the corporate experience of the Christian community, that the fundamentalism of postconservative evangelicalism is to be found.[145]

Webber, *The Younger Evangelicals*, 17–18, 54, 91–92), Webber's formulation of postconservatism reduces to pragmatism in at least two senses: Not only does his functional understanding of truth reduce to pragmatism—doctrines are true if they work, i.e., if they form what is thought to be a Christian perspective on life—but his version of embodied apologetics does so as well. In short, while Webber's approach to apologetics is commendable because it encourages believers to "get past rationalism" and engage unbelievers from "*inside* the [Christian] narrative," i.e., from a perspective that is grounded in the conviction that the Christian narrative stands "on its own" and doesn't need to be made "acceptable" by human rational effort (Webber, *Who Gets to Narrate the World?* 130, 128), it is difficult to imagine how inviting seekers to participate in the life of the believing community could take place in anything other than pragmatic terms when important questions about the extratextual truthfulness of Christianity are either begged or ignored at the start. Why should we look for "authentic spirituality" (cf. Webber, *The Younger Evangelicals*, 222) in the Christian community, realistic seekers will likely ask, and not in the Muslim, Bahai, or even homosexual communities? One does not have to be a rationalist, i.e., one who really does look to human reason "as the foundations of the Christian faith" (Webber, *Who Gets to Narrate the World?* 128), to acknowledge that there are compelling reasons to look for "authentic spirituality" in the Christian community as opposed to some other community. The Christian narrative, after all, is not irrational even though it should never be judged "by human reason or any other intellectual discipline." Ibid., 129.

142. Shults, "Truth Happens?" 35.

143. Ibid., 36.

144. Cf. Webber, *Ancient-Future Faith*, 93–115; cf. note 141 above.

145. For a brief explanation of how the word "fundamentalism" is being used in this chapter, please see note 12 above.

Conclusion

I have argued in this chapter that despite what the consensus of critical opinion would have us believe, the Princeton theologians should not be regarded as either scholastic or Enlightenment rationalists because they conceived of reason in a moral rather than a merely rational sense. They recognized, in other words, that cognition involves the "whole soul" rather than the rational faculty alone, and as a consequence they insisted that the regenerate alone could apprehend revealed truth in a "right" or saving sense. I have also suggested that since postconservatism's repudiation of Old Princeton's "propositionalist understanding of the theological enterprise" presumes the consensus of critical opinion, this repudiation, in short, is based upon a caricature of Old Princeton rather than the views of the Princetonians themselves. This is unfortunate, not simply because it severs postconservative evangelicals from the epistemological capital of Old Princeton's emphasis upon the unity of head and heart, but more significantly because it leaves them without the epistemological wherewithal to claim that the Christian worldview is universally true. Without the willingness to affirm that the regenerate are "taught by God," and without the eagerness to acknowledge that this teaching has reference to something more than merely subjective states of affairs, all claims to universal truthfulness—even those articulated by the most irenic among us—necessarily clank with the bigoted ring "of triumphalism, elitism, and separatism, which is the hallmark of fundamentalism."[146]

This, then, is what I take to be one of the more significant obstacles to the viability of postconservative evangelicalism's "narrativist-communitarian model" of theology. While postconservative evangelicals are convinced that the heart of Christian faith is found in an "identity-producing" experience that is facilitated by an "interpretive

---

146. Olson, "The Future of Evangelical Theology," 47; cf. note 12 above. According to Nichols, "by rejecting the possibility of asserting objective truth, one necessarily comments against the objective reality of the historical event that forms the basis of the faith and against the objective truths recorded about that event. The result of rejecting objective truth is that one cannot escape subjectivity in apologetics. In an increasingly pluralistic society, evangelicalism has no right to assert claims to exclusivity given this framework, and such may not be the healthiest for evangelical apologetics in any case." Nichols, "Contemporary Apologetics and the Nature of Truth," 6.

framework" that is shaped by an "identity-constituting narrative," they nonetheless acknowledge that different kinds of religious experiences are facilitated by different kinds of "interpretive frameworks."[147] But if all that sets one religious experience apart from another is the "interpretive framework" that facilitates the experience, on what basis can Christians claim that their experience is truer than another when the truth-value of the religious utterances that shape their "interpretive framework"—including the utterances of Scripture and of historic confessions—is functional rather than propositional, "intratextual" rather than "extratextual"? Postconservatives might suggest that the universal truthfulness of the Christian narrative is ultimately found in "the explicative power of the Christian faith," and in "the value of the Christian worldview for illuminating human experience, as well as our human understanding of our world."[148] Yet how can such claims be anything more than blatantly chauvinistic when they are grounded in utterances that can only be subjectively true? Although Grenz and Webber and their postconservative colleagues might imagine that the "explicative power" of the Christian faith surpasses that of other religious traditions, thinkers from other religious traditions—who are similarly convinced of the "explicative power" of their own "interpretive frameworks"—will certainly want to know why this contention is justified. A number of years ago, Millard Erickson zeroed in on this problem with characteristic clarity, and it is with his evaluation that I conclude this chapter.

> We now are aware of the claims of other religions, whose adherents are to be found even within what have previously been primarily Christian cultures. Many of them have the same sort of subjective certitude about the validity of their faith as do Christians. If indeed postconservative evangelicals hold that Christianity is the true religion, they must make some note of this phenomenon and offer a further reason for their conclusion. If not, this either looks like ethnocentrism or at least ignorance of the postmodern scene.[149]

147. Grenz, *Renewing the Center*, 202–3.
148. Ibid., 205.
149. Millard J. Erickson, *The Evangelical Left: Encountering Postconservative Evangelical Theology* (Grand Rapids: Baker, 1997), 84.

6

Theological Aesthetics at Old Princeton Seminary

Naïve Theological Realists?

In the last chapter I argued that postconservative evangelicalism's repudiation of Old Princeton's "propositionalist understanding of the theological enterprise" is based on at least two profound misunderstandings of the Princeton mind.[1] In the first half of this chapter I respond more fully to the second of these misunderstandings, which is theological and related to the nature of Old Princeton's opposition to the rise of theological liberalism, and in the second half I respond more fully to the first, which is historical and related to Old Princeton's alleged indebtedness to "habits of . . . mind spawned by the Enlightenment."[2] What I hope to establish in this chapter is not

1. On the "propositionalist understanding of the theological enterprise," cf. Stanley J. Grenz, *Revisioning Evangelical Theology: A Fresh Agenda for the Twenty-First Century* (Downers Grove, IL: InterVarsity, 1993), 67.
2. Roger E. Olson, "Postconservative Evangelicalism: An Update after a Decade," http://www.thedivineconspiracy.org/Z5209W.pdf.

only that the Princetonians were neither naïve theological realists nor rigid, uncompromising fundamentalists, but that they weren't rigid, uncompromising fundamentalists precisely because they weren't naïve theological realists, despite what the consensus of critical opinion would have us believe. As such, this chapter expands on my claim that the standard interpretation of the Princeton mind—which is now an essential component of postconservative evangelicalism's critique of the "received evangelical tradition"—cannot be sustained, and in the process it encourages readers to reconsider the "distinctive brand of conservatism" that postconservatives insist forms the "mythical evangelical magisterium" at the heart of "establishment evangelical theology."[3]

Theological Construction at Old Princeton Seminary

The Methodological Question

Thus far in Part Two I have argued, among other things, that the Princetonians were opposed to the rise of theological liberalism not simply because liberal theologians disagreed with their doctrinal formulations of revealed truth, but more specifically because liberals "reimagined" the essence of the faith and in the process emptied doctrinal formulations of real, enduring, objective substance.[4] Here is

3. Ibid. For a clear presentation of the postconservative approach to evangelical theology, see the recent works of Roger Olson, *Reformed and Always Conforming: The Postconservative Approach to Evangelical Theology* (Grand Rapids: Baker, 2007); Roger Olson, *How to Be Evangelical without Being Conservative* (Grand Rapids: Zondervan, 2008).

4. Recall that I am using the word "objective" in this study not in the sense of Enlightenment foundationalism, i.e., to suggest that neutral, comprehensive, mathematically indubitable knowledge is possible for finite human beings, but in the much less ambitious sense that affirms that at least some true knowledge of real states of affairs in the "world as it is" is possible for finite human beings, the influence of culture notwithstanding. In short, I am not convinced that the influence of culture is so profound that it precludes the Spirit from enabling believers to see reality more or less the way God would have his creatures see it. As far as I can tell, a text such as 1 Corinthians 1 and 2 gives us warrant for concluding that either the apostle Paul should have done some graduate work in the sociology of knowledge or that at least some measure of "objective, transcultural" knowledge in fact is possible for finite creatures, particularly for those who have the "mind of Christ." Yes, theology is an enterprise in which finite human beings who are constitutive members of particular cultures engage; but when properly understood is the theological enterprise a merely human enterprise? Is it not also, in its best sense, a spiritual enterprise requiring a regenerated nature and all the "stances" that

how I summarized the point in the last chapter, recalling the historical work of Richard Hofstadter and Ann Douglas:

> The Princetonians were opposed to the rise of theological liberalism . . . not simply because liberals advanced interpretations of doctrine that differed from their own dogmatic assertions, but more specifically because liberals conceived of doctrines in an "anti-intellectual" or "feminized" sense. Whereas the Princetonians conceived of doctrines as foundational summaries of biblical truth that must be believed in order for there to be faith, liberals conceived of doctrines as little more than expressions of an ineffable religious experience for a particular time and place. They considered doctrines to be true, in other words, not because they corresponded to real states of affairs in the external world, but because they captured the subjective experience of religion in the thought forms of a particular age.[5]

In the first half of this chapter I expand on this point by considering its implications for the practice of theology in general and the

---

entails? I don't see how we can conclude otherwise, and this is why I find it troubling when obviously gifted thinkers such as John Franke affirm that "We simply cannot escape from our particular setting and gain access to an objective, transcultural vantage point." John Franke, *The Character of Theology: An Introduction to Its Nature, Task, and Purpose* (Grand Rapids: Baker, 2005), 90. For a helpful critique of Christian postmodernists who have endorsed the prevailing assumption that objective knowledge is impossible because "there simply is no way [for human beings] to get 'outside' of the influence of language to know the real world as it actually is" (R. Scott Smith, *Truth and the New Kind of Christian: The Emerging Effects of Postmodernism in the Church* [Wheaton, IL: Crossway, 2005], 38), see the incisive works of R. Scott Smith, including: *Truth and the New Kind of Christian*, and R. Scott Smith, "Language, Theological Knowledge, and the Postmodern Paradigm," in *Reclaiming the Center: Confronting Evangelical Accommodation in Postmodern Times*, ed. Millard J. Erickson, Paul Kjoss Helseth, Justin Taylor (Wheaton, IL: Crossway, 2004), 109–33. For an impressive affirmation of the possibility of objective knowledge that grounds the possibility of such knowledge in the activity of God rather than in the self, either as an autonomous individual (following modernism) or as a constitutive member of a particular, narrative-shaped community (following postmodernism), see K. Scott Oliphint, *Reasons for Faith: Philosophy in the Service of Theology* (Phillipsburg, NJ: P&R Publishing, 2006).

5. Please note that I am using the words "anti-intellectual" and "feminized" much like Richard Hofstadter, *Anti-Intellectualism in American Life* (New York: Vintage Books, 1962, 1963) and Ann Douglas, *The Feminization of American Culture* (New York: Noonday, 1998; 1977) do, namely to refer to a kind of spiritual orientation that is focused almost exclusively on concerns that are subjective. For a helpful discussion of the difference between "classical" spirituality and "modern/postmodern" spirituality, see David F. Wells, *Losing Our Virtue: Why the Church Must Recover Its Moral Vision* (Grand Rapids: Eerdmans, 1998), 21–52.

possibility of progress in theology in particular. With respect to the question of what is involved in theological construction, I establish that the debate between conservative and postconservative evangelicals over the relative merits of the "propositionalist understanding of the theological enterprise" has less to do with whether or not believers should be open to progress in theology than it does with a disagreement about the kind of progress to which believers should be open. As this portion of the argument unfolds I challenge the notion that Old Princeton's understanding of the theological enterprise leads necessarily to an uncompromising, arrogant, and "rigid dogmatism"[6] by demonstrating that even though the Princetonians were eager to maintain the realistic nature of religious language and the objectivity of established doctrinal truth, they never insisted that genuine believers would or necessarily should walk in lockstep with every proposition contained in the Westminster Standards. Indeed, they allowed for a measure of doctrinal diversity even within their own communion, and they recognized that progress in theology is not only possible but—when properly conceived—necessary as well.

The Dogmatic Habit of Mind at Old Princeton Seminary

In a brief article published in 1894 titled "The Dogmatic Spirit," B. B. Warfield describes the dogmatic "habit of mind" that he believes should characterize the work of believing theologians who are approaching the task of theology in a biblically faithful fashion.[7] "What is called the dogmatic spirit," he argues,

> is not popular among men. It is characterized by an authoritative method of presenting truth; by an unwillingness to modify truth to fit it to current conceptions; by an insistence on what seem to many minor points; and above all by (what lies at the root of most of its other peculiarities) a habit of thinking in a system, and a consequent habit of estimating the relative importance of the separate items of truth by their logical relation to the body of truth, rather than by their

6. Olson, "Postconservative Evangelicalism: An Update after a Decade."
7. B. B. Warfield, "The Dogmatic Spirit," in *Selected Shorter Writings of Benjamin B. Warfield*, 2 vols., ed. John E. Meeter (Phillipsburg, NJ: P&R Publishing, 2001), 2:663.

apparent independent value. Such a habit of mind seems to be the only appropriate attitude toward a body of truth given by revelation, and committed to men only to embrace, cherish, preserve, and propagate. It seems to be, moreover, the attitude toward the body of revealed truth commended to those who were to be its "ministers" and not its masters, by the Lord and his apostles, when they placed it as a rich treasure in the keeping of stewards of the mysteries of God. But it is irritating to men. They would discuss rather than receive truth. And, if they must receive it, they would fain modify it here and there to fit preconceived opinions or permit cherished practices. Especially in a busy age in which Pilate's careless question, "what is truth?" represents the prevailing attitude of men's minds, the dogmatic habit is apt to fare somewhat badly.[8]

In 1897, three years after outlining his more basic views on the dogmatic nature of the theological task, Warfield then sharpened his understanding of the task of theology by pointing to the systematic interpretation of revealed truth that he believed should inform the labors of believing evangelicals who are approaching the task of theology in a biblically faithful fashion. In a short article in which he argues that "the Westminster Standards mark an epoch in the history of human reflection on the truths of the gospel—an epoch in the attainment and registry of doctrinal truth," Warfield asserts that

The significance of the Westminster Standards as a creed is to be found in the three facts that: historically speaking, they are the final crystallization of the elements of evangelical religion, after the conflicts of sixteen hundred years; scientifically speaking, they are the richest and most precise and best guarded statement ever penned of all that enters into evangelical religion and of all that must be safeguarded if evangelical religion is to persist in the world; and, religiously speaking, they are a notable monument of spiritual religion.[9]

It perhaps goes without saying that just as the "habit of mind" that is manifest in these quotations was not very popular in Warfield's

8. Ibid.
9. B. B. Warfield, "The Significance of the Westminster Standards as a Creed," in *Shorter Writings*, 2:661, 660.

day, neither is it very popular in ours, particularly when its focal point is a confession that is thought by many to be a rather narrow and exclusionary interpretation of revealed truth. Indeed, especially for those who adopt "a constructionist view of the world," this "habit of mind" smacks of an arrogance that is nothing short of alarming, for to them it betrays the kind of cocksure rigidity that is characteristic of those who credulously deny the creatureliness and "situatedness of all human thought" while simultaneously presuming that their doctrinal affirmations are just as authoritative as "the language of the biblical text," or, to use the language of postconservative nonfoundationalism, that their confessional commitments "constitute a first-order language of revelation."[10] Certainly, if the quotations above are taken in isolation from other things Warfield wrote on the approach to theology advocated at Old Princeton Seminary and adopted by thoughtful conservatives in the twentieth century—the approach that champions the collection and systematic organization of revealed truths into doctrines that are considered to be both objectively true and subjectively compelling[11]—then the postconservative conclusion that "the propositionalist understanding of the theological enterprise" is an inherently arrogant enterprise entailing both an uncompromising fundamentalism as well as the end to "constructive evangelical theology" could perhaps be justified.[12] But does wider reading in the primary sources of Old Princeton

10. Franke, *The Character of Theology*, 23, 78, 36, 35. According to Franke, "constructionists" maintain "that humans do not view the world from an objective or neutral vantage point but instead structure their world through the concepts they bring to it, particularly language. Human languages function as social conventions and symbol systems that attempt to engage and describe the world in a variety of ways that are shaped by the social and historical contexts and perceptions of various communities of discourse. No simple, one-to-one relationship exists between language and the world, and thus no single linguistic description can provide an objective conception of the 'real' world. Language structures our perceptions of reality and as such constitutes the world in which we live." Ibid., 23; cf. 23–26.

11. In "Admiring the Sistine Chapel: Reflections on Carl F. H. Henry's *God, Revelation and Authority*" (*Themelios* 25, 2 [2000]: 48–58), Carl R. Trueman makes a number of helpful observations about the nature of the propositionalist enterprise. For example, he suggests: "To argue that revelation is propositional is not, despite apparent popular opinion, to reduce the Bible to a series of statements of the kind represented by, say, Pythagoras' Theorem or some other mathematical formulae. This is the charge that is often levelled against Henry and the classic evangelical position by advocates of neo-orthodoxy and by those who press for the importance of the (often very useful) contributions of speech-act theory." Ibid., 56.

12. Olson, "Postconservative Evangelicalism: An Update after a Decade."

justify this conclusion? Were the Princetonians really convinced that the riches of God's revelation had been definitively exhausted in the Westminster Standards, and were they therefore opposed to the idea of more "light and truth" breaking forth from God's Word? Or, were they simply convinced that the "light and truth" that had yet to break forth needed to be in harmony with those doctrines that had already been "established" as true throughout the "slow but ever advancing process" of church history?[13]

Theological Construction at Old Princeton Seminary

The answer to these questions largely depends, of course, on what is meant by theological "construction." If our understanding of the task of theology is informed by the nonfoundationalist assumption that human language "does not represent reality as much as it constitutes reality," then yes, the propositionalist enterprise as practiced at Old Princeton was rigidly opposed to theological "construction," for the Princetonians were unwilling to grant what is essential to nonfoundationalist approaches to the task of theology, namely that in the process of contextualizing the language of Scripture in new social and historical settings "all . . . convictions and commitments, even the most long-standing and dear, [must] remain subject to ongoing critical scrutiny and the possibility of revision, reconstruction, or even rejection."[14]

13. B. B. Warfield, "The Idea of Systematic Theology," in *Studies in Theology*, vol. 9, *The Works of Benjamin Breckinridge Warfield* (Grand Rapids: Baker, 1991; 1932), 75.

14. Franke, *The Character of Theology*, 26, 78. The reason that all convictions and commitments must remain open to critical scrutiny is found in the second-order nature of theological discourse. According to Franke, "The creeds and confessions of the Christian church are second-order interpretive reflections on the primary stories, teachings, symbols, and practices of the Christian faith that, under the guidance of the Spirit, provide a hermeneutical trajectory in which the discipline of theology is pursued in conversation with the normative witness of Scripture and the contemporary cultural situation. From this perspective, we can summarize the second-order nature of church confessions as subordinate and provisional, open-ended, and eschatologically directed." Ibid., 111.

But does the second-order, provisional nature of theological discourse mean that all theological matters are up for grabs, so to speak? In other words, does "provisionality" promote a kind of "instability" (ibid.)? While Franke insists that it does not because creeds and confessions bear witness to gospel truth that will be objectively known in the eschaton (see Franke's discussion of "eschatological realism," ibid., 188–98), it seems to me that it cannot help but do so in the present without the willingness to affirm something close to what Warfield calls "progressive orthodoxy" (which presupposes that at least some measure of objective doctrinal knowledge

However, if our understanding of the task of theology is informed by the classically Protestant assumption that the Bible is "the sole foundation for theology" and that "objective, transcultural"[15] knowledge of its contents is possible for those who have been given the ability to discern the wisdom of its inexhaustible riches, then no, the propositionalist enterprise as practiced at Old Princeton was not opposed to theological "construction," for the Princetonians were convinced that progress in theology is possible not simply when "past achievements in theology" are "effectively spell[ed] out"[16] to a new generation of believers, but when the Spirit takes believers ever more deeply into the objective contents of God's Word as the history of Christian thought continues to unfold. The body of Christian truth that we now possess, Warfield argues,

> has come down to us in the form of an organic growth; and we can conceive of the completed structure as the ripened fruit of the ages, as truly as we can think of it as the perfected result of the exegetical discipline. As it has come into our possession by this historic process, there is no reason that we can assign why it should not continue to make for itself a history. We do not expect the history of theology to close in our own day. However nearly completed our realization of the body of truth may seem to us to be; however certain it is that the great outlines are already securely laid and most of the details

is possible for regenerated human beings; see the forthcoming discussion). For example, if it is true that objective theological knowledge is completely beyond the reach of finite human beings because of "the social context . . . and the historicity of all theological reflection" (ibid., 102), then how can even the ecumenical creeds of classical Christianity—which bind together and unite the various traditions of the universal church and serve as the consensual basis for the ongoing theological reflection that takes place in particular believing communities (ibid., 191, 41, 193)—be beyond critical scrutiny and potential rejection? Since it seems that even these creeds aren't immune to such scrutiny, then what becomes the basis for the "principled theological pluralism" that postconservatives want to promote? Franke suggests that "if we must speak of 'foundations' for the Christian faith and its theological enterprise, then we must speak only of the Triune God, who is disclosed in polyphonic fashion through Scripture, the church, and the world, albeit always in accordance with the normative witness to divine self-disclosure in Jesus Christ." Ibid., 78–79. But how can even "the Triune God" serve as the "foundation" for "a principled pluralism" when the doctrine of the Trinity is itself open to scrutiny given the contextual nature of all human thought?

15. Ibid., 88, 90.

16. Roger E. Olson, "The Future of Evangelical Theology," *Christianity Today* (February 9, 1998): 41.

soundly discovered and arranged; no one will assert that every detail is as yet perfected, and we are all living in the confidence so admirably expressed by old John Robinson, "that God hath more truth yet to break forth from His holy Word." Just because God gives us the truth in single threads which we must weave into the reticulated texture, all the threads are always within our reach, but the finished texture is ever and will ever continue to be before us until we dare affirm that there is no truth in the Word which we have not perfectly apprehended, and no relation of these truths as revealed which we have not perfectly understood, and no possibility in clearness of presentation which we have not attained.[17]

Thus, if we assume that Warfield is representative of his colleagues at Old Princeton Seminary, it follows that the Princetonians were open to more "light and truth" breaking forth from God's Word not because they were willing to jettison what had already been established as true as they attempted to "state their Christian belief in terms of modern thought,"[18] but because they recognized that "The progressive men in any science are the men who stand firmly on the basis of the already ascertained truth."[19] As such, although they were clearly open to theological "construction," they were zealous to distinguish the "construction" of theology from the "destruction" of theology, and it is this frank acknowledgment of the "increasing limitation" brought about by the establishment of theological truth that sets their view of progress apart from that of their contemporary nonfoundationalist critics.[20] "The prerequisite of all progress," Warfield argues,

> is a clear discrimination which as frankly accepts the limitations set by the truth already discovered, as it rejects the false and bad. Construction is not destruction; neither is it the outcome of destruction. There are abuses no doubt to be reformed; errors to correct; falsehoods to cut away. But the history of progress in every science

17. Warfield, "The Idea of Systematic Theology," 75–76.
18. B. B. Warfield, review of *Foundations: A Statement of Christian Belief in Terms of Modern Thought*, by Seven Oxford Men, in *CR*, vol. 10, *The Works of Benjamin Breckinridge Warfield* (Grand Rapids: Baker, 1991; 1932), 322.
19. Warfield, "The Idea of Systematic Theology," 76.
20. Ibid., 79.

and no less in theology, is a story of impulses given, corrected, and assimilated. And when they have been once corrected and assimilated, these truths are to remain accepted. It is then time for another impulse, and the condition of all further progress is to place ourselves in this well-marked line of growth.[21]

The Significance of Finitude and Fallenness at Old Princeton Seminary

But how is even this relatively modest understanding of theological construction compatible with the Princetonians' clear views on the significance of the Westminster Standards and the dogmatic nature of the theological task? In other words, how can we reconcile Old Princeton's dogmatic "habit of mind" with the notion that "as the orthodox man is he that teaches no other doctrine than that which has been established as true, the progressively orthodox man is he who is quick to perceive, admit, and condition all his reasoning by all the truth down to the latest, which has been established as true"?[22] The answer is informed by the Princetonians' endorsement of two commitments that lie close to the heart of the Reformed worldview, commitments that together suggest the Princetonians were open to progress in theology because they distinguished the essential truthfulness of the system of doctrine contained in the Westminster Standards from the truthfulness of every proposition that constitutes the Westminster Standards.

The first of these commitments has to do with the Creator-creature distinction in general, and the fact of creaturely-human finitude in particular. One of the more remarkable charges leveled by postconservative critics of the "propositionalist understanding of the theological enterprise" is that conservative theologians remain smugly indifferent to the "hermeneutics of finitude"[23] despite the thoughtful prodding of irenic postconservatives such as Roger Olson.[24] Conservative evangeli-

21. Ibid., 76–77.
22. Ibid., 79.
23. Franke, *The Character of Theology*, 27.
24. Olson, "Postconservative Evangelicalism: An Update after a Decade." Painting with strokes that some might suggest are entirely too generous, Olson asserts—but does not even attempt to demonstrate—that the critics of postconservative evangelicalism are "ultraconservatives" who are gripped by an "inquisitorial spirit." These critics are "uninformed"—perhaps

cals who claim to possess objective theological knowledge not only naïvely deny that the outlooks of human beings "are always limited and shaped by the particular circumstances in which they emerge,"[25] postconservative evangelicals contend, but more importantly they arrogantly presume a kind of godlike omniscience by elevating themselves "above the conditions of earthly mortality" and suggesting that their knowledge of God and of theological truth is unbiased and comprehensive and thus essentially the same as God's knowledge of himself and of his revelation.[26]

While there is perhaps some merit to this charge in the case of "naïve theological realists"[27] who insist that "words and concepts

even "dishonest"—and "have created a straw man . . . only to tear it down and burn it." They are "really fundamentalists" with "a knee-jerk preference for the most conservative answers to theological questions and a tendency to defend the status quo . . . uncritically," and they lack "intellectual humility." In fact, these critics have accommodated modernity, and this accommodation is evident "in their insistence on tying evangelical thought inextricably with epistemological realism and the correspondence theory of truth as well as their slavish adherence to deductive logic in developing and criticizing theological systems." Would any conservatives out there like another helping of "generous orthodoxy"?

25. Franke, *The Character of Theology*, 28.

26. Olson, "Postconservative Evangelicalism: An Update after a Decade." It is clear that critics such as Olson are primarily interested not in the qualitative difference between divine and human knowledge, but in the postmodern preoccupation with bias. While it is certainly true that the Princetonians would likely have been opposed to the frankly goofy notion of finitude that is daily on display in the ridiculous dramas of contemporary identity politics, it is also true that more than a few would likely have endorsed the chastened though no less robust "perspectivalism" of someone like Vern Poythress. In *Symphonic Theology: The Validity of Multiple Perspectives in Theology* (Phillipsburg, NJ: P&R Publishing, 2001; 1987), Poythress argues that the task of theology is enhanced by the contributions of theologians coming from a multiplicity of perspectives precisely because those contributions have the potential to enrich our understanding of objective, transcultural truths that are held in common. For evidence that Archibald Alexander was at least somewhat aware of the kinds of hermeneutical concerns that are of interest to postconservatives, see the notes in Chapter One. That Warfield was also sensitive to these kinds of concerns, see these examples: His acknowledgment that "the temple of God's truth . . . is a miracle of art to which *all* ages and lands bring their varied tribute" (Warfield, "The Idea of Systematic Theology," 77–78, emphasis added); his insistence that the "truest" systematic theology is "framed out of the mountains and plains of the *theologies* of the Scriptures" (ibid., 66–68; emphasis added); his recognition that in the providence of God, human "bias" serves to advance rather than obstruct "his gracious purposes" (B. B. Warfield, "God's Providence Over All," in *Shorter Writings*, 1:111–13); his opposition to the racism of segregation, believing that "in Christ Jesus there cannot be Greek and Jew, circumcision and uncircumcision, barbarian, Scythian, bondman, freeman." B. B. Warfield, "A Calm View of the Freedman's Case," in *Shorter Writings*, 2:741; B. B. Warfield, "Drawing the Color Line," in *Shorter Writings*, 2:748.

27. Peter Hicks, *The Philosophy of Charles Hodge: A Nineteenth-Century Evangelical Approach to Reason, Knowledge and Truth* (Lewiston, NY: Edwin Mellen, 1997), 191. According

must directly mirror the divine being, or they represent *untruth*,"[28] it is especially unfair to evangelicals who have been significantly influenced by the Princeton theologians, for the Princetonians endorsed, at least in principle, what J. V. Fesko calls "a hallmark teaching of the Reformed faith, namely the difference between *theologia archetypa* and *theologia ectypa*."[29] In short, the Princetonians were open to progress in theology in part because they recognized that there is a qualitative distinction between archetypal theology and ectypal theology, i.e., between "the knowledge of God which he has of himself" and the knowledge of God "which he has made available via revelation to humanity."[30] Whereas the Princetonians insisted that true theology is possible for finite human beings because God has condescended to make himself known to them in both general and special ways, they nonetheless would have agreed with Fesko's contention that "only God possesses *theologia archetypa*" because "only he is capable of knowing the object of theology, God Himself, perfectly."[31] Indeed, like the stalwarts of Protestant scholasticism before them, the Princetonians were convinced that although "true human theology" is possible, it is never more than what Richard Muller calls "an ectype or reflection resting on but not commensurate with the divine self-knowledge [or archetype],"[32] for they acknowledged a vast "epistemic gulf" separating creatures from the Creator.[33] As Warfield argues,

> Only in God's mind, of course, does [theological] science lie perfect— the perfect comprehension of all that is, in its organic completeness. In the mind of perfected humanity, the perfected ectypal science shall

---

to Hicks, "Naïve theological realism is the position of most unphilosophical people, past and present. If truth about God exists it may be known in essentially the same way as truth about anything else."

28. Michael S. Horton, *Covenant and Eschatology: The Divine Drama* (Louisville, KY: Westminster John Knox, 2002), 189.

29. J. V. Fesko, "The Legacy of Old School Confession Subscription in the OPC," *JETS* 46 (December 2003): 694; cf. Richard A. Muller, *Dictionary of Latin and Greek Theological Terms* (Grand Rapids: Baker, 1985), 298–301.

30. Trueman, "Admiring the Sistine Chapel," 58n12.

31. Fesko, "The Legacy of Old School Confession Subscription in the OPC," 695.

32. Richard A. Muller, *Post-Reformation Reformed Dogmatics*, vol. 1: *Prolegomena to Theology*, 2nd edition (Grand Rapids: Baker, 2003), 225.

33. Fesko, "The Legacy of Old School Confession Subscription in the OPC," 695.

lie. In the mind of sinful humanity struggling here below, there can lie only a broken reflection of the object, a reflection which is rather a deflection.[34]

If the Princetonians were open to progress in theology because they recognized that there is a qualitative distinction between God's knowledge of himself and human knowledge of his revelation, they were also open to progress because they acknowledged, as the preceding quotation suggests, that not even regenerated sinners do ectypal theology perfectly. According to Warfield, the task of theological construction in which systematic theologians are called to engage is a comprehensive enterprise involving all the facts "concerning God and His relations with the universe," including "all the facts of nature and history."[35] Indeed, all science finds "its completion and ground in Him,"[36] Warfield argues, and for this reason the knowledge of God is "indispensable" to a "right knowledge" of all things: "Without the knowledge of God it is not too much to say we know nothing rightly, so that the renunciation of the knowledge of God carries with it renunciation of all right knowledge."[37] Even the knowledge of God, however, although it enables the "men of the palingenesis" to reason "rightly" and thus to build the "edifice" of truth "better" than their unregenerate colleagues,[38] does not enable believing theologians to build perfectly, for the gift of regeneration neither raises them above

34. B. B. Warfield, "A Review of *De Zekerheid des Geloofs*," in *Shorter Writings*, 2:119. Recall and note the present relevance of Warfield's contention that "All teaching as to divine and heavenly things is, in a measure, parabolic; we can reach above the world and ourselves only by symbols. All such teaching comes to us, then, as a test, and the proximate account of its varied reception may be found in the condition of the ears that hear it." B. B. Warfield, "Light and Shining," in *Faith and Life* (Edinburgh: The Banner of Truth Trust, 1974; 1916), 63.

35. Warfield, "The Idea of Systematic Theology," 72.

36. Ibid., 70.

37. B. B. Warfield, "The Task and Method of Systematic Theology," in *Studies in Theology*, 97. Note that the comprehensive scope of the theological enterprise—which itself is based on the assumption "that all truth is God's. All truth comes forth from him; all truth leads back to him"—requires theologians to have "[a]n attitude of eager hospitality" for the truth claims of culture. B. B. Warfield, "Heresy and Concession," in *Shorter Writings*, 2:674. Thus it is not true, as John Franke claims, that the Princetonians avoided "the thorny issues surrounding the role of culture in theology" by "limiting the scope of theological reflection to the exposition of the biblical text." Franke, *The Character of Theology*, 89.

38. Warfield, "A Review of *De Zekerheid des Geloofs*," 119.

their creaturely status nor does it completely remove the effects of sin on their faculties; it simply restores their "old faculties" to "some measure" of their "proper functioning."[39] Since even "the regenerated man remains a sinner"[40] who is unable to lay hold of what God has revealed with absolute perfection, it follows that the Princetonians were open to progress in theology because they recognized that the ectypal theological task is an ongoing activity of "the whole church"[41] that ultimately depends for its completion on the sanctifying work of the Spirit throughout the progressively unfolding process of church history. It is the "intrusion" of regeneration and regeneration alone, they argued, that prepares believers "to build better, and ever more truly as the effects of regeneration increase intensively and extensively, until the end comes when the regenerated universe becomes the well-comprehended object of the science of the regenerated race."[42] For Warfield and his colleagues at Old Princeton, then,

> Systematic theology is thus . . . an attempt to reflect in the mirror of the human consciousness the God who reveals himself in his works and Word, and as he has revealed himself. It finds its whole substance in the revelation which we suppose God to have made of himself; and as we differ as to the revelation we suppose God to have made, so will

39. B. B. Warfield, "Introduction to Francis R. Beattie's *Apologetics*," in *Shorter Writings*, 2:101. Note that just as the gift of regeneration does not guarantee that the regenerated man will always be building the edifice of truth with perfection, so too it does not guarantee that he will always be seeking "heavenly things," i.e., ordering his life in a fashion that consistently acknowledges that God is the Lord not just of "all the earth" but of all our "affairs," with unflagging zeal: "There is a formal atheism of opinions and words and reasonings which declares that there is no God and seeks to sophisticate the understanding into believing that there is none. This the Bible describes as open folly. . . . But even when the lip and the mind behind the lip are true to right reason and confess that there is a God who rules the world and to whom we are responsible in our every thought and word and deed, there is often a practical atheism that lives as if there were no God. Formal atheism denies God; practical atheism is guilty of the possibly even more astounding sin of forgetting the God it confesses." B. B. Warfield, "This- and Other-Worldliness," in *Faith and Life*, 44–45.

40. Warfield, "A Review of *De Zekerheid des Geloofs*," 118.

41. Warfield, "The Idea of Systematic Theology," 81.

42. Warfield, "A Review of *De Zekerheid des Geloofs*," 119. Note that there is a postmillennial confidence that pervades Warfield's writings on science and apologetics. Here is another example: "We may assure ourselves from the outset that the palingenesis shall ultimately conquer to itself the whole race and all its products; and we may equally assure ourselves that its gradually increasing power will show itself only as the result of conflict in the free intercourse of men." Warfield, "Introduction to Beattie's *Apologetics*," 104.

our systematic theologies differ in their substance. Its form is given it by the greater or lesser perfection of the reflection of this revelation in our consciousness. It is not imagined, of course, that this reflection can be perfect in any individual consciousness. It is the people of God at large who are really the subject of that knowledge of God that systematic theology seeks to set forth. Nor is it imagined that even in the people of God at large, in their present imperfect condition, oppressed by the sin of the world of which they still form a part, the image of God can be reflected back to him in its perfection. Only the pure in heart can see God; and who, even of His redeemed saints, are in this life really pure in heart? Meanwhile God is framing the knowledge of himself in the hearts of his people; and, as each one of them seeks to give expression in the forms best adapted to human consciousness, to the knowledge of God he has received, a better and fuller reflection of the revealed God is continually growing up. Systematic theology is therefore a progressive science. It will be perfected only in the minds and hearts of the perfected saints who at the end, being at last like God, shall see him as he is. Then, the God who has revealed himself to his people shall be known by them in all the fullness of his revelation of himself. Now we know in part; but when that which is perfect is come that which is in part shall be done away.[43]

"System" Subscription at Old Princeton Seminary

How, then, do these commitments suggest that we ought to think about the relationship between the Princetonians' dogmatic "habit of

43. Warfield, "The Task and Method of Systematic Theology," 104–5. Recall Warfield's rejection of Hugo Visscher's rather idealistic conception of science. According to Warfield, Visscher "seems to think of science as the pure product of the pure intellect of a pure humanity working purely. We shall get no such science as that until the world of reality is reflected in the consciousness of the perfected humanity of the completed palingenesis. The science and religion of perfected humanity will of course be in harmony. What we have in the meantime, however, is only the distorted reflection of reality in warped intellects, dimmed by imperfections and clouded by prepossessions. . . . There is no conflict between science and religion: they are not only, as Prof. Visscher declares, two expressions of our spiritual life, but two revelations of God. But conflict between science and religion will continue so long as we toil and moil in the present distress; they are only expressions of our spiritual life, and in these days of our tribulation our spiritual life is faulty in all its expressions. It is only when that which is perfect is come, that here too imperfection shall put on perfection." B. B. Warfield, review of *Van Den Eeuwigen Vrede Tusschen Wetenshap en Religie*, by H. Visscher, and *Professor Visscher's Rectorale Rede*, by H. W. van der Vaart Smit, in *CR*, 481–82.

mind" on the one hand and their insistence that theological progress is not only possible but necessary on the other? Ought we to conclude that the Princetonians were hopelessly conflicted at this point? Or, ought we to acknowledge that both dogmatic certitude and openness to progress were compatible in their thinking? As far as I can tell we ought to acknowledge that both of these emphases could peacefully coexist in the Princetonians' minds, for the commitments above suggest that the Princetonians were "system" rather than "strict" subcription-ists with respect to the Westminster Standards, and thus eager to distinguish between their theological interpretations of God's revelation on the one hand and God's first-order revelation of himself on the other. According to William Barker, "system" subscriptionists affirm that the "system of doctrine" taught in the Westminster Standards is essentially the system of doctrine taught in Scripture itself.[44] "System" subscriptionists do not necessarily affirm, however, that every proposition contained in the Westminster Standards is essential to the system, and thus they allow "for an ordinand to take exception, not merely to wording, but to doctrinal teachings of the Standards."[45] Charles Hodge, for example, was convinced that "there are many propositions contained in the Westminster Confession which do not belong to the integrity of the Augustinian, or Reformed System. . . . [Thus] We do not expect our ministers should adopt every proposition contained in our Standards. This they are not required to do. But they are required to adopt the system; and that system consists of certain doctrines, no one of which can be omitted without destroying its identity."[46] If the Princetonians in fact were "system" rather than "strict" subscription-ists with respect to the Westminster Standards—a point that continues to be hotly contested in Reformed circles but which seems plausible

44. William Barker, "System Subscription," *WTJ* 63 (2001): 10.

45. Fesko, "The Legacy of Old School Confession Subscription in the OPC," 678. Note that for "system" subscriptionists whether or not an exception subverts the Reformed system is a matter for the elected officials of the covenant community to decide: "The candidate professing to adopt the *Westminster Standards* should declare any exceptions that he may have, and then the Presbytery should decide whether his exceptions are such that he cannot be deemed as sincerely taking his ordination vow." Barker, "System Subscription," 7.

46. Charles Hodge, "What Is Meant by Adopting the Westminster Confession?" in *The Confession of Faith*, by A. A. Hodge (Edinburgh: The Banner of Truth Trust, 1992; 1869), 420, 422.

to me[47]—then it follows that they were simultaneously dogmatic yet open to progress because they adopted the Standards in what Warfield calls a "liberal but conservative"[48] fashion: they did not require "the adoption of every proposition,"[49] thus allowing for progress as "the temple of God's truth" continues to be built throughout history,[50] but they required the adoption of "every doctrine essential to . . . [the Reformed] system,"[51] thus allowing for a kind of dogmatism that affirms essential, established truths. "There is, so far as we know," Warfield argues,

> no difference of opinion as to the import of the ordination vow in our Churches: it is everywhere understood and administered as binding those taking it merely to the system and not to the detailed manner of stating that system; but as binding them strictly to the system in its integrity and in its entirety. As such it has been justly lauded as combining in itself all reasonable liberty with all reasonable strictness—binding as it does to the great system of doctrine expressed in the Confession with absolute strictness, and yet leaving room for all possible individual preferences in modes of conceiving and stating this system. Under this combined strictness and liberty every genuine form of Calvinism has an equal right of existence under the Confession. . . . But beyond the limits of generic Calvinism the right of adoption ceases. Our vow of ordination is not a solemn farce: and the terms of our adoption of the Confession are not so phrased as to enable us to seem to adopt it while not adopting it at all.[52]

47. In addition to the essays already listed in the footnotes, a few of the other essays that lead me to support this conclusion include: Charles Hodge, "The Constitutional History of the Presbyterian Church in the United States of America," in *Paradigms in Polity: Classic Readings in Reformed and Presbyterian Church Government*, ed. David W. Hall, Joseph H. Hall (Grand Rapids: Eerdmans, 1994), 365–92; B. B. Warfield, "Presbyterian Churches and the Westminster Confession," *PR* 10, 40 (1889): 646–57; B. B. Warfield, "The Confession of Faith as Revised in 1903," in *Shorter Writings*, 2:370–410; J. Gresham Machen, "Premillennialism," *Guardian* (October 24, 1936): 21; J. Gresham Machen, "The Second General Assembly of the Presbyterian Church of America," *Guardian* (November 14, 1936): 41–45.

48. Warfield, "Presbyterian Churches and the Westminster Confession," 648–49.

49. Fesko, "The Legacy of Old School Confession Subscription in the OPC," 686.

50. Warfield, "The Idea of Systematic Theology," 77.

51. Barker, "System Subscription," 10.

52. B. B. Warfield, "The Proposed Union with the Cumberland Presbyterians," *PTR* 2 (1904): 314–15. Barker argues that there are four compelling reasons to endorse this form of subscription: (1) it "safeguards orthodoxy"; (2) it "promotes knowledge of the *Westminster*

Old Princeton and Second-Order Theological Discourse

A. B. Caneday has incisively argued that evangelical theologians "at their best" have always allowed for progress in theology because they have always distinguished between "first-order" and "second-order" theological discourse, i.e., "between *Scripture* as God's Word and *interpretation of Scripture* as entailing theological formulations."[53] This was certainly true of the theologians at Old Princeton Seminary, and for this reason it is simply wrong to suggest that the Princetonians were narrow-minded fundamentalists who challenged the spiritual integrity of those who refused to endorse every jot and tittle of the Westminster Standards. Indeed, fair-minded interpreters must acknowledge that the Princetonians allowed for a measure of doctrinal diversity even within their own communion not only because they recognized that there in fact is, as William Barker puts it, "a distinction between [the Westminster Standards] (which are subject to correction and revision) and Scripture (the very Word of God, the only infallible rule of faith and practice),"[54] but also because they conceded that even believing theologians are less than perfect interpreters of God's Word. Charles Hodge, for example, admits

> that theologians are not infallible, in the interpretation of Scripture. It may, therefore, happen in the future, as it has in the past, that interpretations of the Bible, long confidently received, must be modified or abandoned, to bring revelation into harmony with what God teaches in his works. This change of view as to the true meaning of the Bible may be a painful trial to the Church, but it does not in the least impair the authority of the Scriptures. They remain infallible; we are merely convicted of having mistaken their meaning.[55]

Standards"; (3) it "promotes honesty by avoiding mental reservations"; (4) it "promotes rule by Scripture." Barker, "System Subscription," 7.

53. A. B. Caneday, "Is Theological Language Functional or Propositional? Postconservatism's Use of Language Games and Speech-Act Theory," in *Reclaiming the Center*, 149. Note that conservative theologians such as Caneday refuse to elevate second-order interpretations of Scripture to the level of first-order theological discourse: "To the degree that evangelical theologians view their understanding of Scripture as fused into one with God's revelation, as if their knowledge of God and of his ways were already perfected and absolute, postmodern epistemological correctives are helpful." Ibid.

54. Barker, "System Subscription," 7.

55. Charles Hodge, *Systematic Theology*, 3 vols. (Grand Rapids: Eerdmans, 1982; 1872–73), 1:59.

It is also true, however, that the Princetonians were convinced that objective doctrinal knowledge is possible, and this raises the question of how they discerned the difference between truth and error and thus distinguished between "progressive orthodoxy" on the one hand and what Warfield calls "retrogressive heterodoxy" on the other.[56] As the preceding quotation suggests, the Princetonians were convinced that, given the unity of truth, Scripture must be interpreted in accordance with "established" or "ascertained facts," i.e., in accordance with what is known to be true from a variety of sources.[57] The difference between "progressive orthodoxy" and "retrogressive heterodoxy," then, is tied to the status of the truth claims being considered by the believing theologian as well as to the method of consideration. Whereas "progressive orthodoxy" is a constructive enterprise entailing the assimilation of modern learning to the established truths of Scripture, "retrogressive heterodoxy" is a destructive enterprise involving the accommodation of established doctrinal truths to truth claims that have yet to be established as true, or to truth claims that in fact are false.[58] "After all," Warfield asks,

> is it not enough to ask that "Christianity" and "its theology" shall be in harmony with truth? And if it is to be in harmony with truth, must it not be out of harmony with all the half-truths, and

56. Warfield, "The Idea of Systematic Theology," 78.

57. See Hodge, *Systematic Theology*, 1:56–59; Warfield, "The Idea of Systematic Theology," 76–79.

58. On the difference between assimilation and accommodation, see Warfield, "Heresy and Concession," in *Shorter Writings*, 2:672–79. Warfield was convinced that "the line of demarcation between the right-thinking and the willfully-thinking lies just here—whether a declaration of God is esteemed as authoritative over against all the conjectural explanations of phenomena by men, or whether, on the contrary, it is upon the conjectural explanations of phenomena by men that we take our stand as over against the declaration of God. In the sphere of science, philosophy, and criticism alike, it is the conjectural explanations of phenomena which are put forward as the principles of knowledge. It is as depending on these that men proclaim science, philosophy, and criticism as the norm of truth. We are 'orthodox' when we account God's declaration in his Word superior in point of authority to them, their interpreter, and their corrector. We are 'heretical' when we make them superior in point of authority to God's Word, its interpreter, and its corrector." Ibid., 679.

Some would argue that a plausible case can be made that not even Warfield himself was faithful to the methodological principle that he here sets forth. Whether or not that is the case, it is certainly true that this principle is at the conceptual foundation of his understanding of "progressive orthodoxy."

quarter-truths, and no-truths, which pass from time to time for truth, while truth is only in the making? A "Christianity" which is to be kept in harmony with a growing "science, philosophy, and scholarship," beating their way onward by a process of trial and correction, must be a veritable nose of wax, which may be twisted in every direction as it may serve our purpose.[59]

So how, finally, do believing theologians discern the difference between "God's truth and Satan's error," and how do they therefore know when an accepted interpretation of Scripture must be modified, abandoned, or retained?[60] The Princetonians' answer to this question, which will inform the discussion in the second half of this chapter, will likely disappoint those who are reluctant to acknowledge that the theologians at Old Princeton Seminary were something other than the credulous advocates of either scholastic or Enlightenment rationalism, for the answer makes clear that they regarded the science of theology as an aesthetic enterprise involving the work of the Spirit on the whole soul—the head as well as the heart—of a moral agent.[61] Indeed, the Princetonians acknowledged that the task of theology is concerned with more than "a bare series of intellectual propositions, however logically constructed,"[62] for they recognized that the "true" theologian needs to be "a divine."[63] By God's grace the true theologian needs to have, in other words, "a very sensitive religious nature, a most thoroughly consecrated heart, and an outpouring of the Holy Ghost upon him, such as will fill him with that spiritual discernment, without which all native intellect is in vain."[64] With this in mind, then, what I establish in the second half of this chapter is that the Princetonians sought to discern the difference between truth and error not by appealing to the modern canons of universal reason—as if epistemological neutrality were possible and absolute mathematical certitude

59. Warfield, review of *Foundations*, 322.
60. I am indebted to the Rev. Ian Hewitson for framing the question in this fashion.
61. On the unitary operation of the soul, cf. B. B. Warfield, "Authority, Intellect, Heart," in *Shorter Writings*, 2:668–71.
62. B. B. Warfield, "Theology a Science," in *Shorter Writings*, 2:211.
63. Warfield, "The Idea of Systematic Theology," 87.
64. Ibid.

could be attained through the inductive analysis of Scripture using autonomous reason—but by hearing the message of the text with "right reason," which for them was a biblically informed kind of theological aesthetic that presupposes the work of the Spirit on the whole soul of the believing theologian.

Theological Aesthetics at Old Princeton Seminary

Does Only the Mind Count?

Thus far in this study I have challenged an assessment of the Princeton Theology that has become an "article of faith" in historiography of North American Christianity. According to this assessment, the theologians at Old Princeton Seminary were naïve rationalists who compromised "the original spirit of the Reformation" by accommodating philosophical assumptions that fostered indifference to the subjective and experiential components of religious epistemology, thus engendering an exceedingly "wooden" approach to the task of theology both at Old Princeton and in conservative evangelicalism more generally.[65] As we have seen, this assessment is now an essential component of postconservative evangelicalism's religious historiography. Indeed, progressive evangelicals such as Carl Raschke are convinced that the Princetonians' repudiation of Reformation theology is manifest in a kind of gnostic tendency. For the Princetonians, Raschke argues, "The 'heart,' which Luther and Wesley regarded as the seat of spiritual discernment, is of little bearing [in religious matters]. It is the mind that counts."[66]

Throughout this study I have responded to this line of argumentation by insisting that despite what the consensus of critical opinion would have us believe, the Princetonians simply were not rationalists. Rather, they were committed Augustinians who

65. Carl Raschke, *The Next Reformation: Why Evangelicals Must Embrace Postmodernity* (Grand Rapids: Baker, 2004), 9. On theological "woodenness," see, for example, Mark A. Noll, "Charles Hodge as an Expositor of the Spiritual Life," in *Charles Hodge Revisited: A Critical Appraisal of His Life and Work*, ed. John W. Stewart, James H. Moorhead (Grand Rapids: Eerdmans, 2002), 191.

66. Raschke, *The Next Reformation*, 128.

conceived of reason in a moral rather than a merely rational sense, and as a consequence they insisted that the regenerate alone could apprehend what God had revealed "in a 'right' or saving sense." In the remainder of this chapter I expand on this argument by looking in more depth at the concept of "right reason" as it came to expression in the Christian tradition. After an overview of what the concept generally entails, I isolate the historical strain of "right reason" that more than likely was at the heart of Old Princeton's religious epistemology, and suggest that because the Princetonians were faithful to what Robert Hoopes calls the "antihumanistic" heritage of the Reformation,[67] a key premise in postconservative evangelicalism's critique of the "received evangelical tradition"— which presumes that the rationalistic bent of some conservatives represents a faithful appropriation of the Princeton Theology— cannot be sustained.

The Place of "Right Reason" in the Postmodern World

"Right reason" is a philosophical concept with roots "both in [ancient] Middle Eastern and biblical culture, as well as in Greco-Roman antiquity"[68] that was assimilated by the Christian church, and that in many respects is still at home in the postmodern world. If we conceive of postmodernism as "a mind-set" that, at its heart, "is tightly linked to . . . [the] denial that humans can know truth in any objective, universal sense" because they are thought to be "too historically situated and sociologically conditioned" to have anything approaching an unbiased, "God's-eye" view of reality,[69] "right reason" as a concept is remarkably at home in a postmodern world *not* because it lends credence to the truth-destroying notion that " 'Knowledge' is [nothing more than] a construction of one's social,

67. Robert Hoopes, *Right Reason in the English Renaissance* (Cambridge, MA: Harvard University Press, 1962), 97.

68. Brad Walton, *Jonathan Edwards, "Religious Affections" and the Puritan Analysis of True Piety, Spiritual Sensation and Heart Religion*, Studies in American Religion, vol. 74 (Lewiston, NY: Edwin Mellen, 2002), 166.

69. Stephen J. Wellum, "Postconservatism, Biblical Authority, and Recent Proposals for Re-Doing Evangelical Theology: A Critical Proposal," in *Reclaiming the Center*, 163.

linguistic structures,"[70] but because it acknowledges that both objective and subjective factors are involved in the process of knowing. To vastly oversimplify the matter, while modernists are convinced that objective truth can be known *only* when "personal and subjective factors . . . [are] eliminated from the knowing process,"[71] and while postmodernists are convinced that objective truth cannot be known *precisely because* personal and subjective factors are an essential component of each and every attempt to know, advocates of "right reason" recognize that although knowing does in fact involve the kinds of personal and subjective factors that many modernists naïvely presume have little if anything to do with our attempts to know, this does *not* mean that a more or less objective apprehension of reality is beyond our reach.[72]

The Concept of "Right Reason"

What, then, is "right reason"? In short, "right reason" is "not merely reason in our [modern] sense of the word; it is not a dry light, a nonmoral instrument of inquiry. . . . [Rather] It is a kind of rational and philosophic conscience which distinguishes man from the beasts and which links man with man and with God."[73] As a philosophical concept that was born in Ancient Greece and later assimilated "by the early Church Fathers and redefined in the Christian context of sin and grace," it denotes at once "a mode of knowing, a way of doing, and a condition of being" that is invested with "unique meaning" by two "controlling" assumptions.[74] In the first place, the concept assumes—in stark contrast with the fractured worldview that came to reign in the Age of Reason—that we live in a rationally ordered and organically integrated universe that is

70. J. P. Moreland and William Lane Craig, *Philosophical Foundations for a Christian Worldview* (Downers Grove, IL: InterVarsity, 2003), 146.

71. Millard J. Erickson, *Truth or Consequences: The Promise and Perils of Postmodernism* (Downers Grove, IL: InterVarsity, 2001), 74.

72. I qualify this statement with the words "more or less" simply to acknowledge that although none of us sees any aspect of reality perfectly, some of us see various aspects of reality more clearly than others, and we do so for a number of reasons, including theological reasons.

73. Douglas Bush, *Paradise Lost in Our Time* (Ithaca, NY: Cornell University Press, 1945), 37.

74. Hoopes, *Right Reason in the English Renaissance*, 1, 4.

comprised of truth that is simultaneously intellectual and moral as well as natural and supernatural in nature.[75] To put it differently, the concept affirms what Herschel Baker calls a "sacramental" as opposed to a "secular" view of the universe,[76] and thus it champions the notion that the right way for human beings to lay hold of the truth that comprises this organically integrated universe is through the use of an "organic epistemology."[77] Since "Beauty, goodness, [and] love" are according to this view "a part of truth," it follows that reasoning itself is rightly regarded as an act of the whole soul that includes "faith, intuition, [and] feeling, as well as the more strictly rational processes."[78]

75. S. L. Bethell, *The Cultural Revolution of the Seventeenth Century* (London: Dennis Dobson, 1951), 64, 63.

76. A "sacramental" as opposed to a "secular" view of the universe presupposes *not* that "truth and piety" belong "to quite different orders of reality which permit no interaction," but that "every element in man's experience . . . [is] an object of cognition that . . . leads ultimately to God" who is both the cause and the end "to which the whole creation inexorably and teleologically strives." Herschel Baker, *The Wars of Truth: Studies in the Decay of Christian Humanism in the Earlier Seventeenth Century* (Cambridge, MA: Harvard University Press, 1952), 305, 5.

77. Ibid., 124. Note that the transition from a "sacramental" to a "secular" understanding of reality at the dawn of the modern age is a central theme of *The Wars of Truth*. For Baker's initial discussion of the "sacramental" view, cf. 4–6. On this transition, see also Basil Willey, *The Seventeenth Century Background: Studies in the Thought of the Age in Relation to Poetry and Religion* (New York: Doubleday Anchor Books, 1955), 11–46. For helpful analysis of the intellectual history of the seventeenth century, see also: Gerald R. Cragg, *From Puritanism to the Age of Reason: A Study of Changes in Religious Thought within the Church of England 1660 to 1700* (Cambridge: Cambridge University Press, 1950); Gerald R. Cragg, *The Church in the Age of Reason, 1648–1789* (London: Hodder and Stoughton, 1960); Gerald R. Cragg, "Introduction," in *The Cambridge Platonists*, ed. Gerald R. Cragg (New York: Oxford University Press, 1968), 3–31; Perry Miller, *The New England Mind: The Seventeenth Century* (Boston: Beacon Press, 1961; 1939).

78. Bethell, *The Cultural Revolution of the Seventeenth Century*, 57. Note that this organic view of reason was largely rejected in the Age of Reason when the epistemological realms of faith and reason were disastrously separated. According to Bethell, in the modern world, "the pattern of reasoning was mathematical deduction, combined with the inductive but strictly quantitative reasoning necessary for physical science. It is a process that ideally ignores the human element, though a large degree of unconscious faith actuated its exponents. . . . But faith, though a precondition, was not a part of the process; intuition, though useful in suggesting hypotheses, had no function in their demonstration; feeling, even a sort of austere aestheticism, could accompany, but could not enter into, the methods of reasoning; and the whole great range of human experience knowable only through faith, intuition, and feeling—spiritual experience, human passion, the beauties of nature and art—was no longer proper material for rational thought. The universe that reason could properly explore had narrowed to the calculable aspects of material existence: this was the real, the rest was

In addition to this affirmation of a "reasoning process" that involves the whole soul as opposed to "the quasi-mathematical reason" alone,[79] the concept recognizes, secondly, that since truth is simultaneously intellectual and moral in nature, it follows that both the depth and quality of a particular agent's apprehension of reality are largely dependent on the kind of person that knowing agent is. According to Robert Hoopes, wherever advocates of "right reason"

> speak of the achievement of true knowledge . . . they invariably speak of a certain transformation that must take place in the character of the knower before that knowledge can be attained. . . . Since Truth in its totality is at once intellectual and moral in nature, the conditions of wisdom are for men both intellectual and moral. True knowledge, i.e., knowledge of Truth, involves the perfection of the knower in both thought and deed.[80]

In both its classical and Christian manifestations, then, "right reason" is a kind of moral reasoning that "unites truth and goodness"[81] while combining both "natural and supernatural . . . into one picture of total reality."[82] That is to say, it is a kind of theological aesthetic that affirms a rationally ordered, "theocratic universe"[83] while insisting that because truth is not only true but good, in order for human beings to know truth in a more or less true or right sense "they must themselves *become* good."[84]

"Right Reason" in the Tradition of "Christian Humanism"

How, then, do human beings become good so that they can then know what is true? In his incisive analysis of Robert Hoopes's *Right*

---

epiphenomenon, manageable in part . . . by a 'common sense' which aped the categorical exactitude of true reason, but in the main left to the incalculable caprice of 'enthusiasts' and sentimentalists." Ibid., 58.

79. Ibid., 55, 63.
80. Hoopes, *Right Reason in the English Renaissance*, 5.
81. Baker, *The Wars of Truth*, 235.
82. Bethell, *The Cultural Revolution of the Seventeenth Century*, 54.
83. Baker, *The Wars of Truth*, 5.
84. Hoopes, *Right Reason in the English Renaissance*, 4, 6.

Reason in the English Renaissance, Jack Rogers correctly notes that the concept of "right reason" developed along "humanist" and "anti-humanist" lines in the Christian church, in large measure because differing conceptions of philosophical psychology led to two different answers to this question.[85] Those who endorsed the "tripartite" psychology that originated in ancient Greece and was later accommodated by Christian humanists in the medieval and Renaissance eras viewed the human soul

> as an aggregate of autonomous functions ("faculties"), which were believed to operate discretely and in a prescribed order. Reason apprehended truth and recognized ultimate ends. The will, defined as a "rational appetite," sought the rationally defined good. [And] The affections, or passions, which constituted the "animal" part of human nature, followed sensually defined goods, such as food, sex or other sources of physical pleasure.[86]

85. Jack B. Rogers, *Scripture in the Westminster Confession: A Problem of Historical Interpretation for American Presbyterianism* (Grand Rapids: Eerdmans, 1967), 84.

86. Walton, *Jonathan Edwards, "Religious Affections" and the Puritan Analysis of True Piety, Spiritual Sensation and Heart Religion,* 15. Walton suggests that the Aristotelian analysis of human psychology (cf. *Eth. Nic.* 2, 3, 6, 7, 10 in *Ancient Philosophy*, 3rd edition, ed. Forrest Baird, Walter Kaufmann [Upper Saddle River, NJ: Prentice Hall, 2000]) "passed to Thomas Aquinas, who identified the concept of rational choice, or 'rational appetite,' with the Latin word *voluntas*, or 'will.'" Walton summarizes Aristotle's views in the following fashion: "For Aristotle, human moral excellence lies in the subordination of the nonrational aspects of the soul to prudence, or practical reason, operating through deliberation and rational choice. The objects of deliberation and choice are normally presented by the senses, which combine percipience with affectivity, and which represent the animal aspect of the soul. Choice is thus carried out within a psychological environment of emotion, of 'sensitive appetite' and 'desire.' Emotion, or desire, competes with rational deliberation, to determine action. The 'uncontrolled' person . . . is not moved to act by the command of reason, but by sensation and desire. The self-controlled person . . . while experiencing sensitive appetite and desire, is not moved to act, except by the determination of the intellect. In the self-controlled person, the emotions and desires have been brought, normally by an elaborate and lengthy process of education, to a state of such tranquility and equilibrium as permit rational choice to operate without interference. Thus, the affections contribute to human moral excellence only negatively, by being so carefully controlled as not to overpower rational choice." Walton, *Jonathan Edwards, "Religious Affections" and the Puritan Analysis of True Piety, Spiritual Sensation and Heart Religion,* 144.

On the nature of ancient Greek psychology, see also Norman Fiering, *Moral Philosophy at Seventeenth-Century Harvard: A Discipline in Transition* (Chapel Hill, NC: University of North Carolina Press, 1981), 147–48. For the primacy of reason in the thought of Aquinas, see, for example, *Summa Contra Gentiles* (Notre Dame, IN: University of Notre Dame Press, 1975), 3.1.25.

In short, those who endorsed this understanding of the "faculty psychology" conceived of reason as a power that "was implanted by God in all men, Christian and heathen alike, as a guide to truth and conduct,"[87] and they insisted that men become good and thus reason "rightly" when they learn to follow the dictates of reason rather than of passion, the dictates of the head rather than of the heart. That is to say, moral agents become wise—they become virtuous knowers—when the affections or passions are self-consciously subordinated to the appetites of the rational will, and reason—which, though fallen, is still able to discern the good, the beautiful, and the true—is thereby exalted as "the ruler of the soul."[88] Hoopes summarizes this "intellectualist" understanding of "right reason"—which sustained the medieval synthesis and empowered scholasticism's analogical investigation of reality[89]—as follows: "Right reason may thus be thought of as a faculty which fuses in dynamic interactivity the functions of knowing and being, which stands finally as something more than a proximate [or imme-

87. Bush, *Paradise Lost in Our Time*, 37; cf. Hoopes, *Right Reason in the English Renaissance*, 3; John Spurr, " 'Rational Religion' in Restoration England," *JHI* 49 (October-December 1988): 570.

88. Fiering, *Moral Philosophy at Seventeenth-Century Harvard*, 113. On the anthropological optimism that is at the heart of Christian humanism, cf. Baker, *The Wars of Truth*, 25–29, 90. Note that while classical and Christian humanists share a rather optimistic assessment of human nature, the assessment of Christian humanism is nowhere near as optimistic as that of classical humanism. According to Hoopes, whereas Christian humanists affirm the perpetual dependence of the creature on the Creator, classical thinkers assume that "man by his own efforts may realize whatever ideal of perfection he sets for himself. The omnipresence of this assumption is, or ought to be, the meaning of 'the classical ideal,' for it is the one element fundamental to the thought of all classical thinkers whose systems otherwise conflict." Hoopes, *Right Reason in the English Renaissance*, 65, 52; cf. 52–58. Thus, while classical humanists assert "man's essential independence" and insist that reason "possesses a potential infallibility *sui generis*," Christian humanists assert "man's everlasting dependence" (ibid., 57, 56) and insist that reason's pursuit of the end for which we were created is dependent not only on the law of God that is promulgated through and discerned by reason, but also on the infusion of the theological virtues that make the achievement of this end possible. On the significance of the theological virtues, see the helpful discussion in Jean Porter, *The Recovery of Virtue: The Relevance of Aquinas for Christian Ethics* (Louisville: Westminster John Knox, 1990). For a helpful discussion of how this understanding of "right reason" informed patristic and medieval ethical theory, see Vernon J. Bourke, *History of Ethics* (Garden City, NY: Doubleday & Company, 1968), 89–91.

89. On the relationship between analogical reasoning and the medieval synthesis of faith and reason, of natural knowledge and supernatural knowledge, cf. Baker, *The Wars of Truth*, 25–29, 309; Bethell, *The Cultural Revolution of the Seventeenth Century*, 53–58.

diate] means of rational discovery or 'a nonmoral instrument of inquiry,' *and which affirms that what a man knows depends upon what, as a moral being, he chooses to make himself.*"[90]

90. Hoopes, *Right Reason in the English Renaissance*, 5, emphasis added. The words "intellectualism" and "voluntarism" are being used in this chapter in the way that Richard Muller uses them in his analysis of Calvin's theology. According to Muller, "The terms refer to the two faculties of the soul, intellect and will, and to the question of which has priority over the other: intellectualism indicates a priority of the intellect; voluntarism, a priority of the will. In a technical theological and philosophical sense, however, intellectualism indicates a view of soul that denominates intellect the nobler of the two faculties because it is the intellect that apprehends the final vision of God as being and truth, whereas voluntarism denominates the will as the nobler faculty and assumes that its ultimate cleaving to God as the highest good . . . addresses the highest object of human love." Richard Muller, *The Unaccommodated Calvin: Studies in the Formation of a Theological Tradition* (New York: Oxford University Press, 2000), 162.

Muller argues that for Calvin the problem with the "intellectualism" of the Aristotelian-Thomistic psychology "is that its entirely correct definition of the relationship of intellect and will applies only to the prelapsarian condition of humanity. The philosophers did not understand grasp [sic] the problem of sin and therefore did not perceive the degree to which sin subverts the right ordering of the faculties." Ibid., 165. Muller therefore insists that what we find in Calvin is "not a philosophical but a soteriological voluntarism that not only recognizes the necessity of grace to all good acts of the will but also recognizes that, in the soul's present sinful condition, the will [which "determines even the extent of our knowledge of any given object"] most certainly stands prior to the intellect." Ibid., 166.

In his incisive analysis of Calvin's philosophy, Paul Helm amplifies the significance of the fall for understanding the basic differences between Calvin and Aquinas on issues relating to natural law and natural theology: "Calvin holds that there is an under-estimation of the noetic effects of sin possibly in the likes of Aquinas and certainly in the case of the classical philosophers more generally. He thinks that the idea that sin is solely a matter of sensuality prevails with them whereas for Calvin sin affects the understanding, not by destroying it but by depraving it. In particular the moral understanding is not completely wiped out, but it is choked with ignorance and prejudice, as a result of which without divine grace the will cannot strive after what is right." Paul Helm, *John Calvin's Ideas* (Oxford: Oxford University Press, 2004), 375.

For elaboration of Helm's point, see James K. A. Smith, *Introducing Radical Orthodoxy: Mapping a Post-Secular Theology* (Grand Rapids: Baker, 2004), 164–66. For helpful discussions of the "intellectualism" of the Aristotelian-Thomistic psychology, cf. Fiering, *Moral Philosophy at Seventeenth-Century Harvard*, 110–14; Walton, *Jonathan Edwards, "Religious Affections" and the Puritan Analysis of True Piety, Spiritual Sensation and Heart Religion*, 143–47.

Please note that one of the primary differences between the "intellectualist" view of "right reason" and the Augustinian view discussed below centers on disagreement over the effects of sin on our ability to know. Whereas advocates of the "intellectualist" view presume the "essential goodness" of man (Bush, *Paradise Lost in Our Time*, 39; cf. William J. Bouwsma, *The Culture of Renaissance Humanism* [Washington, D.C.: American Historical Association, 1973], 5–6) and affirm the ability of even unregenerated sinners to know rightly, advocates of the Augustinian view insist that the unregenerate are dead in sin and thus cannot know rightly without regenerating grace. In her analysis of Augustine's anthropology, Carol Harrison summarizes the basic difference between Augustine's assessment of the moral agent and that of classical philosophy. While it would be unfair to suggest that Christian humanists endorsed the classical Greek view without qualification—please see note 88 above—we can say that

"Right Reason" in the Tradition of "Christian Antihumanism"

While the affections or passions in this "intellectualist" view of the soul are separated from and thus are often at odds with the appetites of the rational will, the affections or passions are regarded as "an aspect" of the will in the psychology of "Augustinian voluntarism," the "bipartite, heart-centered psychology"[91] that Norman Fiering suggests is the "most enduring and persistent antagonist to intellectualism in [the history of] Western thought."[92] According to those who stand in the Augustinian tradition—the tradition that, in matters epistemological, came to be

they shared, at least in some measure, the optimistic view of human nature that prevailed in ancient Greece. "The Christian doctrine of the fall, with its denial of man's capacity to attain the good through his own unaided efforts, of his inability to know or to do the good without God's grace, and of the unattainability of beatitude in this life marks the final break between classical and Christian understandings of virtue, the will, and the happy life. The startling optimism of classical philosophy, with its unerring conviction of man's autonomous will, his capacity for rational self-determination and for perfectibility through knowledge . . . , has been dealt a death blow by Augustine's uncompromising picture of man subject to original Sin following the fall of Adam. Without the help of grace, man can do nothing to achieve salvation, his flawed and vitiated will can no longer do anything but sin, his grasp of the truth is marred by ignorance and blindness." Carol Harrison, *Augustine: Christian Truth and Fractured Humanity* (Oxford: Oxford University Press, 2000), 100.

91. Walton, *Jonathan Edwards, "Religious Affections" and the Puritan Analysis of True Piety, Spiritual Sensation and Heart Religion,* 220, 181.

92. Fiering, *Moral Philosophy at Seventeenth-Century Harvard,* 117. In this psychology, the soul is thought to consist of two rather than three faculties or powers—the understanding, which includes the powers of perception and speculation, and the will, which embraces the affections and the power of volition. Moreover, advocates insist that these faculties are not distinct, but act as a single substance that is united and governed by the "heart." Cf. Walton, *Jonathan Edwards, "Religious Affections" and the Puritan Analysis of True Piety, Spiritual Sensation and Heart Religion,* 43, 149, 220; Richard J. Gaffin, "Some Epistemological Reflections on 1 Corinthians 2:6–16," *WTJ* 57 (Spring 1995): 120; J. Knox Chamblin, *Paul and the Self: Apostolic Teaching for Personal Wholeness* (Grand Rapids: Baker, 1993), 37–59; Peter T. O'Brien, *The Letter to the Ephesians* (Grand Rapids: Eerdmans, 1999), 320–22; T. Kermit Scott, *Augustine: His Thought in Context* (Mahwah, NJ: Paulist Press, 1995), Part Three, especially 193–216. On the rise and subsequent decline of Augustinian voluntarism in the Renaissance, see William J. Bouwsma, *The Waning of the Renaissance: 1550–1640* (New Haven, CT: Yale University Press, 2000), chapters 2, 3, 11. Please note that I am using the term "Augustinian" largely in the sense that it is used by Perry Miller in his analysis of the New England Puritan mind. The Puritans in seventeenth-century New England were Augustinians, Miller argues, not because they "depended directly" on the writings of Augustine, but because Augustine is the "arch-exemplar" of a kind of piety that "centered upon . . . God, sin, and regeneration." Miller, *The New England Mind,* 3–34. The various elements of "Augustinian voluntarism" are evident in the following works of Augustine, which can be found in *Nicene and Post-Nicene Fathers,* ed. Philip Schaff (Peabody, MA: Hendrickson, 1995; 1887): *Conf.* 7.10.17 (*NPNF* 1:109–10, 111–12); *Civ.* 12–14 (*NPNF* 2:226–83); *Trin.* 8–13 (*NPNF* 3:115–82); *Enchir.* 1–5 (*NPNF* 3:237–38); *Trac. En. Jo.* 1 (*NPNF* 7:7–13); *Solil.* 1.1–4 (*NPNF* 7:537–38).

the object of near-universal loathing in the sixteenth, seventeenth, and eighteenth centuries because of what its critics regarded as an "almost obsessive emphasis . . . upon the fact of human depravity"[93]—the soul is not "a mere aggregation of discrete faculties, but . . . an integrated totality of perception and volition, [that is] determined by the basic affective inclination, or fundamental amative orientation,"[94] of "the inner essence of the whole man."[95] That is to say, Augustinian voluntarists conceive of the soul "not as a system of objectively distinguishable faculties" that have the ability to operate in more or less isolation from each other, "but as a 'mysterious organic unity'" that has "both an intellectual-percipient and a volitional-affective dimension," a two-dimensional unity that follows or takes its cues from the disposition or character of the "heart."[96]

What, then, is the "heart"? In the Augustinian tradition as in Scripture, the "heart" is "'that mysterious organ which is the center of the personality'" and "the single spring of thinking, feeling and acting."[97] The concept denotes the "bent" or "bias," the "inclination" or "fundamental amative orientation" of the personality "either toward the world of sin and self, or toward God and divine reality," and thus it indicates the underlying, preconscious "principle of psychic unity . . . [that] determines the manner in which one (1) perceives reality, and (2) wills, feels, and chooses."[98] Since the "heart" in this tradition is the principle that integrates and determines the "psychic totality" of the "whole soul," it has to do not with the emotions alone, but with "the simultaneous and interdependent operations of the cognitive and volitional-affective aspects of the personality, [aspects that are] unified, even fused, by its [inclination, or] fundamental amative orientation."[99] According to Augustinian voluntarists such as Charles Hodge, it is this emphasis on the heart that

---

93. Hoopes, *Right Reason in the English Renaissance*, 98.

94. Walton, *Jonathan Edwards, "Religious Affections" and the Puritan Analysis of True Piety, Spiritual Sensation and Heart Religion*, 220.

95. Fiering, *Moral Philosophy at Seventeenth-Century Harvard*, 117.

96. Walton, *Jonathan Edwards, "Religious Affections" and the Puritan Analysis of True Piety, Spiritual Sensation and Heart Religion*, 174, 227.

97. Ibid., 174, 184.

98. Ibid., 160, 227.

99. Ibid., 177, 220, 160.

forbids any such marked distinction between . . . [the soul's] cognitive and emotional faculties . . . , as is assumed in our philosophy, and therefore is impressed on our language. In Hebrew the same word designates what we commonly distinguish as separate faculties. The Scriptures speak of an "understanding heart," and of "the desires of the understanding," as well as of "the thoughts of the heart." They recognize that there is an element of feeling in our cognitions and an element of intelligence in our feelings. The idea that the heart may be depraved and the intellect unaffected is, according to the anthropology of the Bible, as incongruous as that one part of the soul should be happy and another miserable, one faculty saved and another lost.[100]

For those who stand in the tradition of Augustinian voluntarism, what this emphasis on the heart suggests is that the rightness or wrongness of the manner in which an agent apprehends and interacts with reality is determined not by the natural competence of the agent's distinct faculties, but by the moral character or underlying disposition that unites the two dimensions of the agent's soul into an organic thinking-feeling-willing whole. What this means for Protestants who are like Augustine and take the fall and original sin seriously, then, is that moral agents who are dead in sin and inclined to the world of sin and self acquire the ability to reason "rightly" not by gritting their teeth and resolving to follow the appetites of the head rather than the passions of the heart, as in the intellectualist view of "right reason," but by being given "hearts of flesh" (Ezek. 11:19), i.e., by being inclined to God and divine reality, in regeneration.[101] In regeneration, the Holy Spirit, working with and through the Word, becomes the new principle of life in the regenerated soul, and it is this new principle of life that inclines the soul to God and enables the moral agent to perceive, feel, and act "differently than before."[102] Among other things, the regenerated agent

100. Charles Hodge, *A Commentary on the Epistle to the Ephesians* (New York: Robert Carter and Brothers, 1866), 249–50.

101. On classically Protestant conceptions of the life of the mind, see Mark A. Noll, *America's God: From Jonathan Edwards to Abraham Lincoln* (New York: Oxford University Press, 2002), 95–102; Theodore Dwight Bozeman, *To Live Ancient Lives: The Primitivist Dimension in Puritanism* (Chapel Hill, NC: University of North Carolina Press, 1988), 51–80.

102. Walton, *Jonathan Edwards, "Religious Affections" and the Puritan Analysis of True Piety, Spiritual Sensation and Heart Religion*, 187.

not only sees all things in relationship to the God of the Bible because he looks at reality through the "spectacles" of Scripture,[103] but as an essential component of this seeing he also delights in and savors the spiritual excellence and beauty that is objectively present in and really radiating from the objects of his understanding.[104] He now recognizes with the likes of Charles Hodge that "Truth is not merely speculative, the object of cognition. It has moral [and spiritual] beauty."[105] Jonathan Edwards, one of the most thoughtful defenders of the bipartite, heart-centered psychology in the history of the Augustinian tradition, describes the regenerated agent's ability to discern what Hodge calls "the moral and spiritual excellence of truth"[106] as follows:

> Hence we learn that the prime alteration that is made in conversion, that which is first and the foundation of all, is the alteration of the temper and disposition and spirit of the mind; for what is done in conversion is nothing but conferring the Spirit of God, which dwells in the soul and becomes there a principle of life and action. 'Tis this is the new nature and the divine nature; and the nature of the soul being thus changed, it admits divine light. Divine things now appear excellent, beautiful, glorious, which did not when the soul was of another spirit.
>
> Indeed the first act of the Spirit of God, or the first that this divine temper exerts itself in, is in spiritual understanding, or in the sense of the mind, its perception of glory and excellency . . . in the ideas it has of divine things; and this is before any proper acts of the will. Indeed, the inclination of the soul is as immediately exercised in that sense of the mind which is called spiritual understanding, as the intellect. For it is not only the mere presence of ideas in the mind, but it is the mind's sense of their excellency, glory and delightfulness. By this

103. John Calvin, *Institutes of the Christian Religion*, 2 vols., ed. J. T. McNeill, trans. F. L. Battles (Philadelphia: Westminster Press, 1960), 1:70.

104. Cf. Walton, *Jonathan Edwards, "Religious Affections" and the Puritan Analysis of True Piety, Spiritual Sensation and Heart Religion*, 154–58, 189, 209, 222. Please note that by saying "objectively present in" I am *not* suggesting that the objects of the regenerated agent's understanding are themselves the ultimate *source* of the "spiritual excellence and beauty" that is perceived; I want to affirm with Reformed scholars generally that the glory of created things is *reflected* glory.

105. Hodge, *A Commentary on the Epistle to the Ephesians*, 250.

106. Ibid.

sense or taste of the mind, especially if it be lively, the mind in many things distinguishes truth from falsehood.[107]

Protestants who stand in the tradition of Augustine therefore insist that the regenerate alone "may rise to an understanding of the truth," because the regenerate alone have the moral ability to see revealed truth more or less for what it objectively is, namely glorious.[108] That is to say, regenerated knowers alone can know more or less "rightly" not only because they have an intellectual or speculative understanding of that which is true, but also because they have—as an essential component of their understanding—a love for the truth precisely because they see it declaring the glory, the moral excellence and beauty, of the one who is the source of truth and the epistemological key to interpreting all reality correctly (cf. Col. 2:3). For regenerated knowers, then, the eyes of faith—eyes that look at reality through the "spectacles" of Scripture—make a material difference not only in how they know, but also in what they know; they "are in a superior epistemic position," i.e., they are better knowers, because the Spirit, again working with and through the Word, helps them use "[their] natural epistemic faculties rightly."[109]

107. "Miscellanies" no. 397, in Jonathan Edwards, *The Works of Jonathan Edwards*, vol. 13, *The "Miscellanies," a-500*, ed. Thomas A. Schafer (New Haven, CT: Yale University Press, 1994), 462–63.

108. Hoopes, *Right Reason in the English Renaissance*, 64. Please note that Augustinian voluntarists do *not* claim that the "right" knowledge of the regenerate is comprehensive knowledge; thus they are amenable to robust yet chastened understandings of "perspectivalism." For example, see Poythress, *Symphonic Theology*; John M. Frame, *The Doctrine of the Knowledge of God* (Phillipsburg, NJ: Presbyterian and Reformed, 1987).

109. William J. Wainwright, *Reason and the Heart: A Prolegomenon to a Critique of Passional Reason* (Ithaca, NY, and London: Cornell University Press, 1995), 42–43. Note that if this is an accurate representation of how Augustinian voluntarists conceive of "right reason," then the work of Protestants who stand in this tradition should not be handled in a wooden, unimaginative fashion, for doing so will lead to serious misunderstandings, including the conclusion that such Protestants are rationalists. According to Carl Trueman, this is how progressive evangelicals have handled the Protestant scholastics. "As the work of scholars such as Richard Muller has indicated," Trueman argues, "confessional Reformed Orthodoxy . . . has theological moorings in an intelligent interaction with, and appropriation of, the best theological and exegetical work of the patristic and medieval authors, as well as the correctives of the sixteenth and seventeenth centuries. Yet this careful scholarship is so often aced in the evangelical culture by popular potboilers which tell a very different story. Thus, post-conservative evangelicals may take the worst bits of Hodge, read them back into Turretin, mix in a faulty understanding of scholasticism as an adumbration of Enlightenment rationalism,

Conclusion: Old Princeton's Humanism of "the Broken Heart"

As I have tried to suggest in this chapter, and as I have tried to argue throughout this study, there are good reasons for concluding that the theologians at Old Princeton Seminary stood squarely in what Robert Hoopes calls the "antihumanistic" heritage of the Reformation. Although the Princetonians did affirm a kind of humanism, the humanism they affirmed was "antihumanistic" in both the scholastic and Enlightenment senses because it was founded, as J. Gresham Machen argues in *Christianity and Liberalism*, "not upon human pride but upon divine grace."[110] That is to say, Old Princeton's humanism of "the broken heart" was founded on "the consciousness of sin" rather than an essentially "pagan" confidence in the competence of "existing [or fallen] human faculties," and thus it championed the need for the regeneration of the whole soul as the necessary means to "right reason" and saving faith.[111] In short, the Princetonians—along with their most thoughtful descendants in the mainstream of the "received evangelical tradition"—recognized that since the "heart" is "that prevailing moral disposition that determines the volitions and actions" of the whole person,[112] regeneration is of necessity at the foundation of the ability to reason "rightly" because reasoning itself is an activity involving all the powers of the soul, not simply the rational faculty alone. As Archibald Alexander Hodge makes clear in his *Outlines of Theology*, the Princetonians refused to grant a measure of autonomy to the rational faculty because they repudiated the foundational premise of both scholastic and Enlightenment

---

repeat, Mantra-style, superficially learned and portentous phrases such as 'Cartesian dualism' and 'modernist mindset,' and extrapolate from there to dismiss the whole of confessional Reformed Orthodoxy; but that is just one more example of the cod-theology which passes for scholarship in some evangelical quarters." Carl Trueman, review of *Is the Reformation Over?* by Mark A. Noll, Carolyn Nystrom (Grand Rapids: Baker, 2005), available at http://www .reformation21.org/shelf-life/is-the-reformation-over.php.

110. J. Gresham Machen, *Christianity and Liberalism* (Grand Rapids: Eerdmans, 1990; 1923), 66.

111. Ibid., 65–66.

112. A. A. Hodge, *Outlines of Theology* (Edinburgh: The Banner of Truth Trust, 1991; 1860), 459.

humanism. Indeed, they were simply not "rather bald rationalists,"[113] for they recognized that since

> The soul of man is one single indivisible agent . . . it is not true . . . that the understanding reasons, and the heart feels, and the conscience approves or condemns, and the will decides, as different members of the body work together, or as the different persons constituting a council deliberate and decide in mutual parts; but it is true that the one indivisible, rational, feeling, moral, self-determining soul reasons, feels, approves, or condemns and decides.[114]

This is the rather subtle point that has been overlooked by those who endorse the reigning interpretation of the Princeton Theology, and this is the reason why the presumption of rationalism at the heart of postconservatism's critique of the "received evangelical tradition" cannot be sustained.

113. Cf. William Livingstone, "The Princeton Apologetic as Exemplified by the Work of Benjamin B. Warfield and J. Gresham Machen: A Study of American Theology, 1880–1930" (PhD diss., Yale University, 1948), 186.
114. Hodge, *Outlines of Theology*, 280–81.

7

Conclusion: The Role and Function of Doctrine

I n Part Two of this study I have challenged an assessment of the Princeton Theology that has played an important—even if decidedly negative—role in the recent development of North American evangelicalism. According to this assessment, the ostensible defenders of Reformed orthodoxy throughout the nineteenth and early twentieth centuries were naïve rationalists who compromised "the original spirit of the Reformation"[1] by accommodating philosophical assumptions that fostered indifference to the subjective and experiential components of a consistently Reformed religious epistemology, thus engendering an exceedingly rigid approach to the task of theology both at Old Princeton and in conservative evangelicalism more generally. In Part Two of this study and more generally throughout, I have responded to this critique by arguing that the Princeton theologians simply were

---

1. Carl Raschke, *The Next Reformation: Why Evangelicals Must Embrace Postmodernity* (Grand Rapids: Baker, 2004), 9.

not rationalists, but more or less consistently Reformed scholars who conceived of reason in a moral rather than a merely rational sense. Indeed, they recognized that the reception of revealed truth is an activity involving the "whole soul" rather than the rational faculty alone, and as a consequence they insisted that the regenerate alone could apprehend this truth in a "right" or saving sense.

In this chapter I explore the relevance of my proposal to the assumptions at the heart of the ongoing debate within the evangelical camp over the role and function of doctrine. What I suggest is that despite what a growing consensus would have us believe, conservative and postconservative evangelicals are at odds not because conservatives have accommodated habits of mind that were "spawned by the Enlightenment"[2] and wittingly or unwittingly embraced by those at the fountainhead of the conservative mainstream. Rather, we are at odds because conservatives are committed to the convictions of their theological forefathers and thus refuse to conceive of moral and religious truth in what some have called an "anti-intellectual" or "feminized" sense.[3] Indeed, they are committed to a view of moral and religious truth that stands in self-conscious opposition to those cultural forces that have reduced moral and religious truth claims to little more than expressions of the subjective preferences of those who hold them, and thus their views on moral and religious matters are nothing if not out of step with the spirit of the age. As such, the forthcoming discussion challenges the assumptions at the heart of postconservative evangelicalism's critique of the "received evangelical tradition"[4] by considering those assumptions in light of the Princetonians' insistence that the regenerate alone can reason "rightly." It concludes that postconservatism's critique of the conservative evangelical mind is dubious at best because a key premise of that critique—which presumes that the rationalistic bent of some conservatives represents a faithful appropriation of the Princeton Theology—cannot be sustained because the best thinkers in

2. Roger E. Olson, "Postconservative Evangelicalism: An Update after a Decade," http://www.thedivineconspiracy.org/Z5209W.pdf.

3. Cf. Richard Hofstadter, *Anti-Intellectualism in American Life* (New York: Vintage Books, 1962); Ann Douglas, *The Feminization of American Culture* (New York: Noonday Press, 1998; 1977).

4. Olson, "Postconservative Evangelicalism: An Update after a Decade."

the conservative mainstream—like the best thinkers at Old Princeton Seminary—acknowledge that subjective and experiential factors are of critical importance not only to religious epistemology, but also to the life of the mind more generally.

The Historical Evangelical Consensus

Scholars with whom I am largely in agreement generally insist that since the Enlightenment a number of ideas "conspired" in the modern mind to both domesticate God and elevate man by obscuring if not completely erasing the Creator-creature distinction.[5] In the centuries following the Enlightenment, these scholars argue, the transcendent holiness of God was more or less rejected, the spiritual interconnectedness of the natural and supernatural orders was more or less affirmed, and the inherent goodness and ability of man were more or less presumed. According to scholars such as Ann Douglas, it was the "disestablishment" of America's God-centered heritage that posed a serious threat to the enduring integrity of Christian belief and practice, for it was the accommodation of these ideas that fostered a number of developments that had disturbing implications for the received understanding of both religion and theology.[6]

Among these developments was the widespread endorsement of a kind of spiritual orientation that locates the enduring essence of Christianity not in doctrines that are thought to be both objectively true and subjectively compelling, but in religious experiences that are thought to cultivate "the healthy and harmonious and joyous development of existing human faculties," to use the words of J. Gresham Machen in *Christianity and Liberalism*.[7] Indeed, those who called themselves theological liberals endorsed the prevailing agnosticism of the age, and as a consequence they came to think of Christianity not as a religion based on the appropriation of what God has revealed with the head

5. Please see the notes in Chapter Three of this study.

6. On the "vitiation and near disappearance of the Calvinist tradition," see Douglas, *The Feminization of American Culture*, 7; on the role that "sentimentality" played in the "disestablishment" of this tradition, see ibid., 3–164.

7. J. Gresham Machen, *Christianity and Liberalism* (Grand Rapids: Eerdmans, 1990; 1923), 65.

as well as the heart of the believing agent. Rather, they came to think of Christianity as the practical outworking of an ineffable encounter with an altogether impersonal spiritual presence that pervades what Machen calls "the mighty world process itself,"[8] erasing the distinctions between God and the world, God and man, good and evil, and religious truth and error. Not only was this form of religious expression thoroughly anthropocentric in that it presumed that the starting point for both moral and religious reflection as well as for religious life was the ineffable experience of the self "instead of God and his revelation."[9] More importantly, its controlling assumptions fostered the kind of moral and religious relativism that continues to manifest itself in the ecumenical commitments of those who mistakenly presume that religious expression is principally a matter of the heart rather than of the heart and the head, a matter that as such is essentially unaffected by the distinct doctrinal affirmations of one religious tradition or another.[10]

Throughout the nineteenth and twentieth centuries, evangelicals were largely united in their antipathy to what Machen calls the "paganism" of modern theological liberalism. While evangelicals in the nineteenth and twentieth centuries certainly had their differences, they were clearly on the same page with respect to their desire to champion the objective truthfulness of God's revelation along with our ability to know it, and they were united—at least in principle—in their rejection of the prevailing tendency to begin theologizing with the self and the self's experiences rather than with God and his Word. Indeed, evangelicals were confident that they had reliable access not just to their own ineffable experiences of an altogether vague and impersonal spiritual presence, but to transcendent truth that is revealed in both

8. Ibid., 63.

9. Stephen J. Wellum, "Postconservatism, Biblical Authority, and Recent Proposals for Re-Doing Evangelical Theology: A Critical Analysis," in *Reclaiming the Center: Confronting Evangelical Accommodation in Postmodern Times*, ed. Millard J. Erickson, Paul Kjoss Helseth, Justin Taylor (Wheaton, IL: Crossway, 2004), 186.

10. Please note that I am using the word "heart" in this sentence differently from the way I use it throughout the rest of this study. In this case, I am using it to refer not to the underlying "principle of psychic unity" that determines the movements of the "whole soul" (see the discussion in Chapter Six), but to a subjectivist tendency that is grounded in the denial that objective knowledge of God is possible.

nature and Scripture, discerned by those with the spiritual capacity to both see and hear, formulated in doctrines that are thought to be both objectively true and subjectively compelling, and centered on the sovereign Lord who is, as David Wells argues, both the source of truth and the meaning-bestowing norm "for all of the human centers, centers of private interest, of ethnicity, of gender, of sexuality, and of perspective."[11] Since those who stood in the mainstream of North American evangelicalism were convinced that it is the knowledge of what God has revealed that grounds, shapes, and gives meaning to Christian existence, they insisted that both the nature and the quality of this existence are invariably compromised when either the substance or the significance of this truth is undermined or abandoned. Indeed, many argued that when we lose confidence in the capacity of one doctrinal formulation or another to communicate information that is believed to be both objectively true and subjectively compelling we inevitably retreat into some manifestation of the self as the primary channel through which we presume to encounter that which we take to be sacred. In the process, we turn away from God to a form of spiritual narcissism that is characterized more by human striving than it is by humble receiving, a form of spirituality that at bottom is difficult to distinguish from a host of spiritualities that are more than at home in an increasingly secular world.[12]

The Contemporary Evangelical Divide

Unfortunately, the unanimity that North American evangelicals once enjoyed in this regard has largely come to an end because of a paradigm shift among some evangelicals known as postconservative evangelicalism. According to Justin Taylor, postconservative evangelicals are neither theological "conservatives" nor theological "liberals," but they are "self-professed evangelicals" who are eager to steer "a faithful course between the Scylla of conservative-traditionalism and

11. David F. Wells, *Above All Earthly Pow'rs: Christ in a Postmodern World* (Grand Rapids: Eerdmans, 2005), 233.

12. Recall Machen's critique of the "paganism" of theological liberalism; in particular, recall his opposition to its "imperative mood." Cf. Machen, *Christianity and Liberalism*, 46–47, 64–68.

the Charybdis of liberal-progressivism."[13] While postconservatives are more or less "conservative" because they affirm the universal truthfulness of the story of Scripture, at the same time they are more or less "liberal" because they regard attempts to elucidate this story in terms of doctrines that are thought to be both objectively true and subjectively compelling as misguided at best and destructive at worst. Indeed, postconservatives are convinced that conservative evangelicals are unable to speak effectively to those living in a postmodern world because conservatism's understanding of doctrinal truth is shaped by habits of mind that postmodernists believe are tragically outmoded. Since those living in a postmodern context are keenly aware of the contextual nature of all human knowledge, they regard the very idea of an objectively true doctrine as passé, and perhaps as nothing more than the divisive remnant of an altogether doctrinaire and spiritually oppressive past.

In order to speak effectively to those who have taken what is often called the "postmodern turn," postconservatives therefore argue that Christians must articulate what God has revealed in a fashion that affirms the universal truthfulness of the Christian story while simultaneously repudiating the rigid dogmatism that is grounded in what postmodernists believe is an anachronistic commitment to the notion of objective doctrinal truth.[14] Christians accomplish both of these ends at the same time, postconservatives contend, by distancing themselves from the enduring influence of the Princeton Theology—which they believe is the immediate source of those habits of mind that threaten the integrity of evangelicalism's contemporary witness[15]—and by embracing some of the more moderate building blocks of the postmodern mind, including those building blocks that inform what has come to be known as the "hermeneutics of finitude."[16] According to postconservative

13. Justin Taylor, "An Introduction to Postconservative Evangelicalism and the Rest of This Book," in *Reclaiming the Center*, 18.

14. For example, see my analysis of Robert Webber's "ancient-future" faith in Chapter Five.

15. For example, see Olson, "Postconservative Evangelicalism: An Update after a Decade"; Stanley J. Grenz, "Concerns of a Pietist with a Ph.D." *WesTJ* 37, 2 (Fall 2002): 58–76.

16. For example, see John R. Franke, *The Character of Theology: An Introduction to Its Nature, Task, and Purpose* (Grand Rapids: Baker, 2005), 27.

evangelicals and notwithstanding the claims of the Princeton theologians, there is no such thing as objective doctrinal knowledge because there is no such thing as an objective, transcultural vantage point from which to assess and interpret the revelation of God. Indeed, postconservatives are convinced that objective doctrinal knowledge is beyond the reach of finite human beings because every attempt that human beings make to understand what God has revealed is tied to a particular social and historical context, a context that affords a unique perspective on the revelation of God, but not a perspective that is either comprehensive or free of bias. Postconservatives therefore maintain that conservatives who follow the Princetonians by claiming to possess objective doctrinal knowledge not only naïvely deny that the outlooks of human beings "are always limited and shaped by the particular circumstances in which they emerge,"[17] but more importantly they inevitably fall prey to a kind of theological "hubris," for they wind up presuming that when they are thinking God's thoughts after him, they are thinking God's thoughts precisely like him.[18]

What this emphasis on human finitude suggests for postconservative evangelicals, then, is that Christians who would speak effectively to postmodern seekers must affirm on the one hand that the story of Scripture informs and shapes the true perspective on reality while acknowledging on the other that the role played by doctrinal elucidations of this story is significantly less foundational than is generally imagined by conservative evangelicals. Since they are convinced that spiritual fulfillment is found in participation in a believing community rather than in submission to doctrines that are thought to be objectively true, postconservatives insist that doctrinal elucidations of the Christian story play a truthful role in the life of the believing community not primarily because of the cognitive substance of the information that they convey, but because of the formative or pragmatic function that they perform. Whereas conservatives are convinced that doctrines are true when they communicate the information that is believed to ground, shape, and give meaning to the life of faith, postconservatives

17. Ibid., 28.
18. On the "hubris" of many conservatives, see, for example, Olson, "Postconservative Evangelicalism: An Update after a Decade."

are convinced that doctrines are true when they enable believers who are located in one sociohistorical context or another to see reality in a fashion that is shaped by the story of Scripture, and thus to think and live in a manner that is true because it is authentically Christian. Exactly why authentic Christian living and not, say, authentic Muslim living is true living, we might note in passing, is apparently not a point that postconservatives believe is in need of rational justification.

It is in the rather subtle nature of this disagreement over the role and function of doctrine, then, that the heart of the tension within contemporary evangelicalism is found. For postconservative evangelicals, doctrines play an important role not because they communicate the information that is believed to be at the foundation of the faith that informs both the life and the practice of the believing community. Rather, doctrines play an important role because they encourage those who have stepped into the experience of the believing community to see reality in a fashion that is shaped by the story of Scripture, and thus to think and live in a manner that is true because it is authentically Christian, whatever that might mean in a world devoid of objective doctrinal standards. While conservative evangelicals are eager to acknowledge that true doctrines do in fact encourage believers to think and live in a manner that is true because it is authentically Christian—consider, for example, the painstaking efforts of conservative Presbyterians to catechize the children of believing parents—they disagree with their postconservative brethren by insisting that the authentically Christian nature of this function is tied necessarily to the objective substance of the information that is conveyed by the doctrinal formulations themselves. In short, conservative evangelicals—particularly those who are indebted to the dogmatic approach to theology advanced at Old Princeton Seminary—have yet to be convinced that the formative capacity of distinctively Christian doctrines either can or should be separated from the objective truth-value of the doctrinal formulations themselves, for they are convinced that the faith that informs authentic Christian living is itself an activity involving the appropriation of what God has revealed with the whole soul—the head as well as the heart—of the believing agent.

Postconservative Evangelicalism and Doctrinal Agnosticism

Despite the rather serious nature of their disagreement over the role and function of doctrine, conservative evangelicals applaud the eagerness of their postconservative brethren to reach those living in a postmodern world with the good news of the gospel of Jesus Christ. Nevertheless, they are convinced that postconservatism's attempt to contextualize the faith has been compromised by a form of agnosticism that continues to threaten the integrity of the Christian religion. Like their more progressive forerunners in the nineteenth and twentieth centuries, postconservatives insist that objective knowledge of God and of his revelation is beyond the reach of finite human beings because of the manifold limitations of the creaturely condition. Whereas the liberals of old were convinced that objective knowledge of God and of his revelation is unattainable because finite human beings cannot transcend the limitations of their individual experience, postconservative evangelicals are convinced that such knowledge is beyond the reach of finite human beings because of the worldview-shaping limitations of communities that are located in one sociohistorical context or another. Although postconservatives acknowledge that a community's social location does afford a particular perspective on what God has made known, they believe this perspective is biased by the cultural baggage that is peculiar to that community's social context. As a consequence, postconservatives not only reject the possibility of objective knowledge of God and of his revelation, but they also insist that doctrinal elucidations of this revelation must change from one social location to another because doctrines *qua* doctrines can neither communicate truth that is transculturally true, nor function in a fashion that is pragmatically relevant to every social context. Doctrines, they maintain, are merely "attempts within a particular cultural moment and geographical place to express the faith in a fresh way."[19]

While most conservatives are eager to acknowledge that postmodern thinkers are "entirely right to remind us that all human knowing is necessarily the knowledge of finite beings, and is therefore in some

19. Robert Webber, *Ancient-Future Faith: Rethinking Evangelicalism for a Postmodern World* (Grand Rapids: Baker, 1999), 16.

ways partial, non-final, conditional, [and] dependent on a specific culture (after all, language itself is a cultural artifact),"[20] nevertheless they are distressed by the doctrinal agnosticism of their postconservative brethren for two important reasons. In the first place, it is disturbing to conservative evangelicals because it reflects what they regard as indebtedness to the "most-modern" inclination to begin theologizing with that which is human rather than with that which is divine.[21] Whereas the liberals of old insisted that the starting point for both moral and religious reflection was the ineffable experience of the autonomous self instead of the knowledge of God and of his revelation, postconservatives insist that the starting point for such reflection is the experience of the self as a member of a community that is located in one sociohistorical context or another. Rather than insisting that what distinguishes contemporary evangelicalism from other postmodern spiritualities is its commitment to doctrinal truth that is believed to correspond to the way reality objectively is, postconservatives instead baptize a mind-set that "carries within it the seeds of destruction for evangelical faith," for it minimizes the significance of such truth "in order to become attractive to postmodern seekers."[22] Indeed, by abandoning the notion of truth that distinguishes evangelical faith from the plethora of spiritualities that are at home in the postmodern world, postconservatives are not only demonstrating remarkable affinity with progressives who drank the Kool-Aid of cultural accommodation more than a century ago, but more importantly they are embracing the justification for their own irrelevance, for as David Wells argues, they are reducing the Christian religion to a form of religious expression that is "just one of many spiritualities in the marketplace even as the liberal Protestants much earlier diminished Christianity by making it out to be just one among many religions, better than the others, perhaps, but not unique."[23]

20. D. A. Carson, "Domesticating the Gospel: A Review of Grenz's *Renewing the Center*," in *Reclaiming the Center*, 46.

21. For a discussion of the "most-modern" nature of popular postmodernism, see Michael Horton's contribution to *The Church in Emerging Culture: Five Perspectives*, ed. Leonard Sweet (Grand Rapids: Zondervan, 2003).

22. Wells, *Above All Earthly Pow'rs*, 158, 123.

23. Ibid., 123.

In the second place, postconservatism's doctrinal agnosticism is also distressing to conservative evangelicals because it is grounded in what they regard as a profound misunderstanding of the conservative evangelical mind, a misunderstanding that in their estimation exposes the rather tenuous justification for the postconservative project. As we have seen, postconservative evangelicals justify their postconservatism in part by insisting that conservatism's commitment to objective truth—which postconservatives imagine is grounded in rationalistic tendencies derived largely from the theologians at Old Princeton Seminary—is based on habits of mind that are passé. In fact, postconservatives are convinced that progressive inclinations are warranted because conservative evangelicals—like their theological forefathers at Old Princeton Seminary—are naïve rationalists whose essentially pagan confidence in the cognitive powers of the fallen human mind is evidence of their decidedly modern indifference to the subjective and experiential factors that play an important role in our apprehension of God and the truth of his revelation. But unlike committed modernists and despite what their postconservative brethren would have us believe, conservatives at their best have always acknowledged that objective as well as subjective factors play an important role in our ability to know God and the truth of his revelation. Indeed, they have argued that such knowledge is possible not because finite human beings have the capacity to lay hold of what God has revealed in an unbiased, comprehensive, and mathematically indubitable fashion, but because those who have been given eyes to see and ears to hear lay hold of this revelation in a fashion that is biased by the work of the Spirit and the formative assumptions of the biblical worldview. While committed postconservatives will find this assertion difficult if not impossible to swallow because of an entrenched prejudice against the approach to theology advanced at Old Princeton Seminary, nevertheless it is true that the best thinkers in the conservative mainstream have always insisted that the possibility of objective doctrinal knowledge is not undermined, but established by the subjective and experiential factors that play a decisive role in our ability to lay hold of God and the truth of what he has revealed.

Conclusion: Necessary Dogmatism

Unlike their postconservative brethren, conservative evangelicals are convinced that the church, in order to fulfill its mission, "must be dogmatic."[24] While postconservative evangelicals would have us believe that this dogmatism is grounded in some manifestation of either scholastic or Enlightenment rationalism—a leftover, they believe, of the warmed-over humanism that was embraced and then passed on by the theologians at Old Princeton Seminary—in fact the best thinkers in the mainstream of conservative evangelicalism are neither witting nor unwitting rationalists, for they approach the task of theology much like the best thinkers at Old Princeton did. As I have argued in Part Two and throughout this study more generally, the Princetonians were neither scholastic nor Enlightenment rationalists, but more or less consistently Reformed theologians who regarded the science of theology as an aesthetic enterprise involving the work of the Spirit on the whole soul—the head as well as the heart—of a moral agent. We may conclude, therefore, that if some conservatives ought to be chastised for rationalistic tendencies that threaten the integrity of evangelicalism's contemporary witness, they ought to be chastised for tendencies that were acquired from some place other than Old Princeton, for at their best the Princeton theologians approached the task of theology not as arrogant rationalists would have done, but as biblically faithful Christians have always done. Indeed, they sought to discern the difference between truth and error not by appealing to the magisterial conclusions of the rational faculty alone, but by hearing the message of the text with "right reason," which for them was a biblically informed kind of theological aesthetic that presupposes the work of the Spirit on the whole soul of the believing theologian.

24. Cf. David Mills, "Necessary Doctrine: Why Dogma Is Needed and Why Substitutes Fail," *Touchstone* 15, 2 (March 2002); http://www.touchstonemag.com/archives/article.php?id=15-02-023-f.

Bibliography

Ahlstrom, Sydney. "The Scottish Philosophy and American Theology." *CH* 24 (1955): 257–72.

Alexander, Archibald. *A Brief Compendium of Bible Truth*. Grand Rapids: Reformed Heritage Books, 2005; 1846.

———. "A Practical View of Regeneration." *BRTR* 8, 4 (1836): 477–500.

———. "An Inquiry into that Inability under Which the Sinner Labours, and Whether It Furnishes Any Excuse for His Neglect of Duty." *BRTR* 3, 3 (1831): 360–83.

———. "Christ Our Wisdom, Righteousness, Sanctification, and Redemption." In *Evangelical Truth: Practical Sermons for the Christian Home*, 195–207. Birmingham, AL: Solid Ground Christian Books, 2004; 1850.

———. "Christ the Believer's Life." In *Practical Truths*, 62–65. Harrisonburg, VA: Sprinkle Publications, 1998; 1857.

———. "Deceitfulness of Sin." In *Practical Truths*, 57–59. Harrisonburg, VA: Sprinkle Publications, 1998; 1857.

———. "Deceitfulness of the Heart." In *Evangelical Truth: Practical Sermons for the Christian Home*, 161–76. Birmingham, AL: Solid Ground Christian Books, 2004; 1850.

———. *Evidences of the Authenticity, Inspiration, and Canonical Authority of the Holy Scriptures*. Philadelphia: Presbyterian Board of Publication, 1836.

———. "Excellency of the Knowledge of Christ." In *Evangelical Truth: Practical Sermons for the Christian Home*, 437–46. Birmingham, AL: Solid Ground Christian Books, 2004; 1850.

———. "Faith's Victory Over the World." In *Evangelical Truth: Practical Sermons for the Christian Home*, 407–23. Birmingham, AL: Solid Ground Christian Books, 2004; 1850.

———. "Holding Forth the Word of Life." In *Evangelical Truth: Practical Sermons for the Christian Home*, 447–57. Birmingham, AL: Solid Ground Christian Books, 2004; 1850.

———. "Love of the Truth." In *Practical Truths*, 80–81. Harrisonburg, VA: Sprinkle Publications, 1998; 1857.

———. "Love to Christ." In *Evangelical Truth: Practical Sermons for the Christian Home*, 229–45. Birmingham, AL: Solid Ground Christian Books, 2004; 1850.

———. "Obedience to Christ Gives Assurance of the Truth of His Doctrines." In *Evangelical Truth: Practical Sermons for the Christian Home*, 7–24. Birmingham, AL: Solid Ground Christian Books, 2004; 1850.

———. "Privileges of the Sons of God." In *Evangelical Truth: Practical Sermons for the Christian Home*, 151–60. Birmingham, AL: Solid Ground Christian Books, 2004; 1850.

———. "The Bible, A Key to the Phenomena of the Natural World." *Biblical Repertory. A Journal of Biblical Literature and Theological Science*, Conducted by an Association of Gentlemen New Series 5, 1 (1829): 99–120.

———. "The New Creation." In *Evangelical Truth: Practical Sermons for the Christian Home*, 106–25. Birmingham, AL: Solid Ground Christian Books, 2004; 1850.

———. *Thoughts on Religious Experience*. Edinburgh: Banner of Truth, 1989; 1844.

———. "Why Halt Thou between Two Opinions?" In *Practical Truths*, 68–70. Harrisonburg, VA: Sprinkle Publications, 1998; 1857.

Aquinas, Thomas. *Summa Contra Gentiles*. Notre Dame, IN: University of Notre Dame Press, 1975.

Armstrong, Maurice, Lefferts Loetscher, and Charles Anderson. *The Presbyterian Experience: Sources of American Presbyterian History*. Philadelphia: Westminster, 1956.

Averill, Lloyd. *American Theology in the Liberal Tradition*. Philadelphia: Westminster Press, 1967.

Bahnsen, Greg. "Machen, Van Til, and the Apologetical Tradition of the OPC." In *Pressing Toward the Mark: Essays Commemorating Fifty Years of the Orthodox Presbyterian Church*, edited by Charles Dennison and Richard Gamble, 259–94. Philadelphia: The Committee for the Historian of the Orthodox Presbyterian Church, 1986.

Baird, Forrest, and Walter Kaufmann, eds. *Ancient Philosophy*. 3rd edition. Upper Saddle River, NJ: Prentice Hall, 2000.

Baker, Herschel. *The Wars of Truth: Studies in the Decay of Christian Humanism in the Earlier Seventeenth Century*. Cambridge, MA: Harvard University Press, 1952.

Balmer, Randall H. "The Princetonians and Scripture: Towards an Evaluation of the Rogers and McKim Proposal." *WTJ* 44 (1982): 352–65.

Barker, William. "System Subscription." *WTJ* 63 (2001): 1–14.

Bethell, S. L. *The Cultural Revolution of the Seventeenth Century*. London: Dennis Dobson, 1951.

Bourke, Vernon J. *History of Ethics*. Garden City, NY: Doubleday & Company, 1968.

Bouwsma, William J. *The Culture of Renaissance Humanism*. Washington, D.C.: American Historical Association, 1973.

———. *The Waning of the Renaissance: 1550–1640*. New Haven, CT: Yale University Press, 2000.

Bozeman, Theodore Dwight. *Protestants in an Age of Science: The Baconian Ideal and Antebellum American Religious Thought*. Chapel Hill, NC: University of North Carolina Press, 1977.

———. *To Live Ancient Lives: The Primitivist Dimension in Puritanism*. Chapel Hill, NC: University of North Carolina Press, 1988.

Breitenbach, William. "Piety *and* Moralism: Edwards and the New Divinity." In *Jonathan Edwards and the American Experience*, edited by Nathan O. Hatch and Harry S. Stout, 177–204. New York: Oxford University Press, 1988.

———. "The Consistent Calvinism of the New Divinity Movement." *WMQ* 41 (April 1984): 241–64.

Bush, Douglas. *Paradise Lost in Our Time*. Ithaca, NY: Cornell University Press, 1945.

Calhoun, David B. *The Majestic Testimony, 1869–1929*. Vol. 2 of *Princeton Seminary*. Edinburgh: Banner of Truth, 1996.

Calvin, John. *Institutes of the Christian Religion*. 2 vols., edited by J. T. McNeill. Translated by F. L. Battles. Philadelphia: Westminster Press, 1960.

Caneday, Ardel B. "Is Theological Language Functional or Propositional? Postconservatism's Use of Language Games and Speech-Act Theory." In *Reclaiming the Center: Confronting Evangelical Accommodation in Postmodern Times*, edited by Millard J. Erickson, Paul Kjoss Helseth, and Justin Taylor, 137–59. Wheaton, IL: Crossway, 2004.

Caneday, Ardel B., and Thomas R. Schreiner. *The Race Set Before Us: A Biblical Theology of Perseverance and Assurance*. Downers Grove, IL: InterVarsity Press, 2001.

Carson, D. A. "Domesticating the Gospel: A Review of Grenz's *Renewing the Center*." In *Reclaiming the Center: Confronting Evangelical Accommodation in Postmodern Times*, edited by Millard J. Erickson, Paul Kjoss Helseth, and Justin Taylor, 33–55. Wheaton, IL: Crossway, 2004.

Cauthen, Kenneth. *The Impact of American Religious Liberalism*. New York: Harper & Row, 1962.

Chamblin, J. Knox. *Paul and the Self: Apostolic Teaching for Personal Wholeness*. Grand Rapids: Baker, 1993.

Chrisope, Terry. "The Bible and Historical Scholarship in the Early Life and Thought of J. Gresham Machen, 1881–1915." PhD diss., Kansas State University, 1988.

Clapp, Rodney. "How Firm a Foundation: Can Evangelicals Be Nonfoundationalists?" In *The Nature of Confession: Evangelicals and Liberals in Conversation*, edited by Timothy Phillips and Dennis Okholm, 81–92. Downers Grove, IL: InterVarsity Press, 1996.

Conforti, Joseph. *Samuel Hopkins and the New Divinity Movement*. Grand Rapids: Christian University Press, 1981.

Cragg, Gerald R. "Introduction." In *The Cambridge Platonists*, edited by Gerald R. Cragg, 3–31. New York: Oxford University Press, 1968.

———. *From Puritanism to the Age of Reason: A Study of Changes in Religious Thought within the Church of England 1660 to 1700*. Cambridge: Cambridge University Press, 1950.

———. *The Church in the Age of Reason, 1648–1789*. London: Hodder and Stoughton, 1960.

Craig, Samuel G. Introduction to *Biblical and Theological Studies*, by B. B. Warfield, edited by Samuel G. Craig, xi-xlviii. Philadelphia: Presbyterian and Reformed, 1952.

Danhof, Ralph. *Charles Hodge as Dogmatician*. Goes, Netherlands: Oosterbaan and le Cointre, 1929.

Davis, William C. "Contra Hart: Christian Scholars Should Not Throw in the Towel." *CSR* 34, 2 (Winter 2005): 187–200.

Dorrien, Gary. *The Remaking of Evangelical Theology*. Louisville: Westminster John Knox, 1998.

Douglas, Ann. *The Feminization of American Culture*. New York: Noonday Press, 1998; 1977.

Dowey, Edward. *The Knowledge of God in Calvin's Theology*. New York: Columbia University Press, 1952.

Edwards, Jonathan. *The Works of Jonathan Edwards*, 2 vols. Edinburgh: Banner of Truth, 1992; 1834.

———. *The "Miscellanies," a-500*. Vol. 13 of *The Works of Jonathan Edwards, edited by* Thomas A. Schafer. New Haven, CT: Yale University Press, 1994.

———. *The Freedom of the Will*. New Haven, CT: Yale University Press, 1957.

Erickson, Millard J. *The Evangelical Left: Encountering Postconservative Evangelical Theology*. Grand Rapids: Baker, 1997.

Fesko, J. V. "The Legacy of Old School Confession Subscription in the OPC." *JETS* 46 (December 2003): 673–98.

Fiering, Norman. *Moral Philosophy at Seventeenth-Century Harvard: A Discipline in Transition*. Chapel Hill, NC: University of North Carolina Press, 1981.

———. "Will and Intellect in the New England Mind." *WMQ* 29 (1972): 515–58.

Fosdick, Harry Emerson. "Shall the Fundamentalists Win?" *CC* 39 (June 8, 1922): 713–14.

———. *The Modern Use of the Bible*. New York: Macmillan, 1924.

Frame, John M. *Cornelius Van Til: An Analysis of His Thought*. Phillipsburg, NJ: P&R Publishing, 1995.

———. *The Doctrine of the Knowledge of God*. Phillipsburg, NJ: P&R Publishing, 1987.

Franke, John. *The Character of Theology: An Introduction to Its Nature, Task, and Purpose*. Grand Rapids: Baker, 2005.

Fuller, Donald, and Richard Gardiner. "Reformed Theology at Princeton and Amsterdam in the Late Nineteenth Century: A Reappraisal." *Presbyterion* 12, 2 (1995): 89–117.

Gadamer, Hans-Georg. *Truth and Method*. London: Sheed & Ward, 1995.

Gaffin, Richard B. "Some Epistemological Reflections on 1 Corinthians 2:6–16." *WTJ* 57 (Spring 1995): 103–24.

Gerrish, B. A. "The New Evangelical Theology and the Old: An Opportunity for the Next Century?" http://www.union-psce.edu/news/Publications/archive/aisit-gerrish.html.

Gerstner, John. "The Contributions of Hodge, Warfield, and Machen to the Doctrine of Inspiration." In *Challenges to Inerrancy*, edited by Gordon Lewis and Bruce Demarest, 347–81. Chicago: Moody, 1984.

Gerstner, Jonathan A. "Reason as Starting Point: The Rationality of Classical Apologetics." *ModRef* 7, 1 (January/February 1998): 17–20.

Grave, S. A. *The Scottish Philosophy of Common Sense*. Oxford: Clarendon Press, 1960.

Grenz, Stanley J. "Concerns of a Pietist with a Ph.D.," *WesTJ* 37, 2 (Fall 2002): 58–76.

———. *Renewing the Center: Evangelical Theology in a Post-Theological Era*. Grand Rapids: Baker, 2000.

———. *Revisioning Evangelical Theology: A Fresh Agenda for the Twenty-First Century*. Downers Grove, IL: InterVarsity Press, 1993.

Guelzo, Allen. "Jonathan Edwards and the New Divinity, 1758–1858." In *Pressing Toward the Mark: Essays Commemorating Fifty Years of the Orthodox Presbyterian Church*, edited by Charles Dennison and Richard Gamble, 147–67. Philadelphia: The Committee for the Historian of the Orthodox Presbyterian Church, 1986.

Gundlach, Bradley John. "The Evolution Question at Princeton, 1845–1929." PhD diss., University of Rochester, 1995.

Hall, David W. "Angels Unaware: The Ascendancy of Science over Orthodoxy in Nineteenth Century Reformed Orthodoxy." Unpublished paper.

———. "Holding Fast the Concession of Faith: Science, Apologetics, and Orthodoxy." Paper presented to the 47th Annual Meeting of the Evangelical Theological Society, November 1995, Philadelphia.

Haroutunian, Joseph. *Piety versus Moralism: The Passing of the New England Theology*. New York: Holt, 1932.

Harrison, Carol. *Augustine: Christian Truth and Fractured Humanity*. Oxford: Oxford University Press, 2000.

Hart, D. G. *Defending the Faith: J. Gresham Machen and the Crisis of Conservative Protestantism in Modern America*. Grand Rapids: Baker, 1995; 1994.

———. "'Doctor Fundamentalis': An Intellectual Biography of J. Gresham Machen, 1881–1937." PhD diss., Johns Hopkins University, 1988.

———. "Christian Scholars, Secular Universities, and the Problem with the Antithesis." *CSR* 30, 1 (Summer 2001): 383–402.

———. "*Christianity and Liberalism* in a Postliberal Age." *WTJ* 56 (1994): 329–44.

———. "The Critical Period for Protestant Thought in America." In *Reckoning with the Past: Historical Essays on American Evangelicalism from the Institute for the Study of American Evangelicals*, edited by D. G. Hart, 181–99. Grand Rapids: Baker, 1995.

———. "The Forgotten Machen?" In *Selected Shorter Writings of J. Gresham Machen*, edited by D. G. Hart, 1–22. Phillipsburg, NJ: P&R Publishing, 2004.

———. "The Princeton Mind in the Modern World and the Common Sense of J. Gresham Machen." *WTJ* 46 (1984): 1–25.

Helm, Paul. "Thomas Reid, Common Sense and Calvinism." In *Rationality in the Calvinian Tradition*, edited by Hendrik Hart, Johan Van Der Hoven, Nicholas Wolterstorff, 71–89. Lanham, MD: University Press of America, 1983.

———. *John Calvin's Ideas*. Oxford: Oxford University Press, 2004.

Heppe, Heinrich. *Reformed Dogmatics*, edited by Ernst Bizer, translated by G. T. Thomson, foreword by Karl Barth. London: George Allen and Unwin, Ltd., 1950.

Heslam, Peter S. "Architects of Evangelical Intellectual Thought: Abraham Kuyper and Benjamin Warfield." *Themelios* 24, 2 (Fall 1999): 3–20.

———. *Creating a Christian Worldview: Abraham Kuyper's Lectures on Calvinism*. Grand Rapids: Eerdmans; Carlisle: Paternoster, 1998.

Hewitt, Glenn. *Regeneration and Morality: A Study of Charles Finney, Charles Hodge, John Nevin, and Horace Bushnell*. Vol. 7 of Chicago Studies in the History of American Religion, edited by Jerald Brauer and Martin Marty. New York: Carlson, 1991.

Hicks, Peter. *The Philosophy of Charles Hodge: A Nineteenth-Century Evangelical Approach to Reason, Knowledge and Truth*. Lewiston, NY: Edwin Mellen Press, 1997.

Hodge, Archibald Alexander. *Outlines of Theology*. Edinburgh: Banner of Truth, 1991; 1860.

Hodge, Charles. *A Commentary on the Epistle to the Ephesians*. New York: Robert Carter and Brothers, 1866.

———. *A Commentary on the Epistle to the Romans*. Grand Rapids: Eerdmans, 1993; 1835.

———. "Delighting in the Law of God." In *Conference Papers*, 249–50. New York: Charles Scribner's Sons, 1879.

———. "Evidences of Regeneration." In *Conference Papers*, 137–39. New York: Charles Scribner's Sons, 1879.

———. "Except Ye Be Converted and Become As Little Children, Ye Shall Not Enter into the Kingdom of Heaven." In *Conference Papers*, 124–25. New York: Charles Scribner's Sons, 1879.

———. "Free Agency." *BRPR* 29 (January 1857): 101–35.

———. "Memoir of Dr. Alexander." *BRPR* 27 (1855): 133–59.

———. "Mortify the Deeds of the Body." In *Conference Papers*, 150–52. New York: Charles Scribner's Sons, 1879.

———. "My Son, Give Me Thy Heart." In *Conference Papers*, 131–32. New York: Charles Scribner's Sons, 1879.

———. "Regeneration." In *Conference Papers*, 136–37. New York: Charles Scribner's Sons, 1879.

———. "Regeneration, and the Manner of its Occurrence." *BRPR* 2 (1830): 250–97.

———. "Reid's Collected Writings." *BRPR* 32 (1860): 472–510.

———. "Remarks on the Princeton Review." *BRPR* 23 (1851): 306–47.

———. "Review of an Article in the June Number of *The Christian Spectator*, entitled 'Inquiries Respecting the Doctrine of Imputation.'" *BRPR* 2 (1830): 425–72.

———. *Systematic Theology*, 3 vols. Grand Rapids: Eerdmans, 1989; 1871–73.

———. "The Constitutional History of the Presbyterian Church in the United States of America." In *Paradigms in Polity: Classic Readings in Reformed and Presbyterian Church Government*, edited by David W. Hall and Joseph H. Hall, 365–92. Grand Rapids: Eerdmans, 1994.

———. "The Elements of Psychology." *BRPR* 28, 2 (1856): 331–87.

———. "The Excellency of the Knowledge of Christ Jesus our Lord." In *Conference Papers*, 214–15. New York: Charles Scribner's Sons, 1879.

———. "The First and Second Adam." *BRPR* 32 (April 1860): 335–76.

———. "The Indwelling of the Spirit." In *Conference Papers*, 77–78. New York: Charles Scribner's Sons, 1879.

———. "The Nature of Man." *BRPR* 37 (January 1865): 111–35.

———. "The Necessity of the Spirit's Teaching in Order to the Right Understanding of the Scriptures." In *Conference Papers*, 75–77. New York: Charles Scribner's Sons, 1879.

———. "The Sin of Unbelief." In *Conference Papers*, 97–98. New York: Charles Scribner's Sons, 1879.

———. "The Theology of the Intellect and that of the Feelings." *BRPR* 22 (1850): 642–74.

———. *The Way of Life*. Edinburgh: Banner of Truth, 1978; 1841.

———. *The Way of Life*. Introduction by Mark A. Noll. Mahwah, NJ: Paulist, 1987; 1841.

———. "What Is Christianity?" *BRPR* 32 (1860): 118–61.

———. *What Is Darwinism? And Other Writings on Science and Religion*, edited by Mark A. Noll and David N. Livingstone. Grand Rapids: Baker, 1994.

———. "What Is Meant by Adopting the Westminster Confession?" In *The Confession of Faith*, by A. A. Hodge, 420–26. Edinburgh: Banner of Truth, 1992; 1869.

Hoffecker, W. Andrew. "Benjamin B. Warfield." In *The Princeton Theology*, edited by David F. Wells, 63–91. Grand Rapids: Baker, 1989.

———. *Piety and the Princeton Theologians: Archibald Alexander, Charles Hodge, and Benjamin Warfield*. Phillipsburg, NJ: Presbyterian and Reformed; and Grand Rapids: Baker, 1981.

Hofstadter, Richard. *Anti-Intellectualism in American Life*. New York: Vintage Books, 1962, 1963.

Holifield, E. Brooks. "Hodge, the Seminary, and the American Theological Context." In *Charles Hodge Revisited: A Critical Appraisal of His Life and Work*, edited by John W. Stewart and James H. Moorhead, 103–28. Grand Rapids: Eerdmans, 2002.

———. *The Gentlemen Theologians: American Theology in the Southern Culture, 1795–1860*. Durham, NC: Duke University Press, 1978.

———. *Theology in America: Christian Thought from the Age of the Puritans to the Civil War*. New Haven, CT: Yale University Press, 2005.

Hoopes, Robert. *Right Reason in the English Renaissance*. Cambridge, MA: Harvard University Press, 1962.

Horton, Michael S. "Better Homes and Gardens." In *The Church in Emerging Culture: Five Perspectives*, edited by Leonard Sweet, 105–42. Grand Rapids: Zondervan, 2003.

———. *Covenant and Eschatology: The Divine Drama*. Louisville: Westminster John Knox, 2002.

Horton, Michael S., and Roger E. Olson. "Reflection and Response." *CSR* 31, 2 (2001): 131–68.

———. "Response to Roger Olson's Reply." *CSR* 31, 2 (2001): 163–68.

Hutchinson, George. *The Problem of Original Sin in American Presbyterian Theology*. Nutley, NJ: Presbyterian and Reformed, 1972.

Hutchison, William. *The Modernist Impulse in American Protestantism*. Cambridge, MA: Harvard University Press, 1976.

Jackson, Gordon E. "Archibald Alexander's *Thoughts on Religious Experience*, a Critical Revisiting." *JPH* 51, 2 (1973): 141–54.

Johnson, Alan F., and Robert E. Webber. *What Christians Believe: A Biblical and Historical Summary*. Grand Rapids: Zondervan, 1989.

Johnson, Phillip E. *Reason in the Balance: The Case against Naturalism in Science, Law & Education*. Downers Grove, IL: InterVarsity Press, 1995.

Jones, Peter. *Spirit Wars: Pagan Revival in Christian America*. Mukilteo, WA: WinePress Publishing, and Escondido, CA: Main Entry Editions, 1997.

Kelsey, David. *The Uses of Scripture in Recent Theology*. Philadelphia: Fortress Press, 1975.

Kuklick, Bruce. *A History of Philosophy in America: 1720–2000*. New York: Oxford University Press, 2001.

———. "On Critical History." In *Religious Advocacy and American History*, edited by Bruce Kuklick and D. G. Hart, 54–64. Grand Rapids: Eerdmans, 1997.

———. "The Place of Charles Hodge in the History of Ideas in America." In *Charles Hodge Revisited: A Critical Appraisal of His Life and Work*, edited by John W. Stewart and James H. Moorhead, 63–76. Grand Rapids: Eerdmans, 2002.

Lindbeck, George A. *The Nature of Doctrine: Religion and Theology in a Postliberal Age*. Philadelphia: Westminster, 1984.

Lindsay, James. "Psychology of the Soul." *PTR* 6, 3 (1908): 437–54.

Livingstone, David N. "Science, Region, and Religion: The Reception of Darwinism in Princeton, Belfast, and Edinburgh." In *Disseminating Darwinism: The Role of Place, Race, Religion, and Gender*, edited by Ronald L. Numbers and John Stenhouse, 7–38. Cambridge: Cambridge University Press, 1999.

Livingstone, William. "The Princeton Apologetic as Exemplified by the Work of Benjamin B. Warfield and J. Gresham Machen: A Study of American Theology, 1880–1930." PhD diss., Yale University, 1948.

Loetscher, Lefferts. *Facing the Enlightenment and Pietism: Archibald Alexander and the Founding of Princeton Theological Seminary*. Westport, CT: Greenwood, 1983.

———. *The Broadening Church: A Study of Theological Issues in the Presbyterian Church Since 1869*. Philadelphia: University of Pennsylvania Press, 1957.

Machen, J. Gresham. "A Debate: Is the Teaching of Dr. Harry Emerson Fosdick Opposed to the Christian Religion? Yes." *The Christian Work* 117 (December 13, 1924): 686–88.

———. Address at the Second Annual Symposium on Religion at Columbia University, 2 April 1930, Machen Archives. Montgomery Memorial Library, Westminster Theological Seminary, Philadelphia.

———. "An Earnest Plea for Christian Freedom—and Honesty!" *The Lookout: Magazine of Christian Education* 36 (March 2, 1924): 6.

———. "Christianity and Culture." In *Selected Shorter Writings of J. Gresham Machen*, edited by D. G. Hart, 399–410. Phillipsburg, NJ: P&R Publishing, 2004.

———. *Christianity and Liberalism*. Grand Rapids: Eerdmans, 1990; 1923.

———. "Christianity and Liberty: A Challenge to the 'Modern Mind.'" *The Forum* (March 1931): 162–66.

———. "Christianity in Conflict." In *Contemporary American Theology*. Vol. 1, edited by Vergilius Ferm, 245–74. New York: Round Table Press, 1932.

———. "Christian Scholarship and Evangelism." In *What Is Christianity? And Other Addresses*, edited by Ned Stonehouse. Grand Rapids: Eerdmans, 1951.

———. "Christian Scholarship and the Building up of the Church." In *What Is Christianity? And Other Addresses*, edited by Ned Stonehouse. Grand Rapids: Eerdmans, 1951.

————. "Christian Scholarship and the Defence of the Faith." In *What Is Christianity? And Other Addresses*, edited by Ned Stonehouse. Grand Rapids: Eerdmans, 1951.

————. "Christianity vs. Modern Liberalism." *Moody Bible Institute Monthly* 13 (April 1923): 349–52.

————. "Creeds Old and New." *PJ* 9 (February 1966): 13, 24.

————. "Faith and Knowledge." *Fourth Biennial Meeting of the Conference of Theological Seminaries and Colleges in the United States and Canada: Bulletin* 4 (August 1924): 12–23.

————. "For Christ or Against Him." *The Presbyterian* 20 (January 1921): 8–9.

————. "Forty Years of New Testament Research." *USR* 40 (1928): 1–12.

————. "God, the Creator." In *The Christian Faith in the Modern World*, 103–16. Grand Rapids: Eerdmans, 1936.

————. "God's Image in Man." In *The Christian View of Man*, 137–48. Edinburgh: Banner of Truth, 1984; 1937.

————. "God's Works of Creation and Providence." In *The Christian View of Man*, 79–89. Edinburgh: Banner of Truth, 1984; 1937.

————. "History and Faith." In *What Is Christianity? And Other Addresses*, edited by Ned Stonehouse. Grand Rapids: Eerdmans, 1951.

————. "Isaiah's Scorn of Idolatry." In *God Transcendent*, edited by Ned Stonehouse, 22–27. Edinburgh: Banner of Truth, 1982; 1949.

————. "Karl Barth and 'The Theology of Crisis.'" *WTJ* 53 (1991): 197–207.

————. "Liberalism or Christianity?" *PTR* 20 (1923): 93–176.

————. "Miracles." In *The Christian View of Man*, 102–13. Edinburgh: Banner of Truth, 1984; 1937.

————. "My Idea of God." In *My Idea of God: A Symposium of Faith*, edited by Joseph Fort Newton, 37–50. Boston: Little, Brown, and Company, 1926.

————. "Objections to Predestination." In *The Christian View of Man*, 69–78. Edinburgh: Banner of Truth, 1984; 1937.

————. "Premillennialism." *Guardian* (October 24, 1936): 21.

————. "Prophets False and True." In *God Transcendent*, edited by Ned Stonehouse, 116–27. Edinburgh: Banner of Truth, 1982; 1949.

———. "Rejoice with Trembling." Unpublished sermon, Machen Archives. Montgomery Memorial Library, Westminster Theological Seminary, Philadelphia.

———. "Religion and Fact." *The Real Issue* 1 (April 15, 1924): 3–4.

———. Review of *Apology and Polemic in the New Testament*, by Andrew D. Heffern. *Presbyterian* 93 (September 13, 1923): 10–11.

———. "Shall We Defend the Bible?" In *The Christian Faith in the Modern World*, 59–72. Grand Rapids: Eerdmans, 1936.

———. "Sinners Saved by Grace." In *The Christian View of Man*, 233–46. Edinburgh: Banner of Truth, 1984; 1937.

———. "The Active Obedience of Christ." In *God Transcendent*, edited by Ned Stonehouse, 187–96. Edinburgh: Banner of Truth, 1982; 1949.

———. "The Bible Versus Human Authority." In *The Christian Faith in the Modern World*, 73–86. Grand Rapids: Eerdmans, 1936.

———. "The Covenant of Life." In *The Christian View of Man*, 149–60. Edinburgh: Banner of Truth, 1984; 1937.

———. "The Creeds and Doctrinal Advance." In *God Transcendent*, edited by Ned Stonehouse, 157–67. Edinburgh: Banner of Truth, 1982; 1949.

———. "The Decrees of God." In *The Christian View of Man*, 24–34. Edinburgh: Banner of Truth, 1984; 1937.

———. "The Gospel and Modern Substitutes." In *God Transcendent*, edited by Ned Stonehouse, 93–103. Edinburgh: Banner of Truth, 1982; 1949.

———. *The Literature and History of New Testament Times, Teachers Manual*. The Westminster Departmental Graded Series, edited by John T. Faris. Philadelphia: The Presbyterian Board of Publication and Sabbath School Work, 1916.

———. "The Majesty of the Law of God." In *The Christian View of Man*, 184–95. Edinburgh: Banner of Truth, 1984; 1937.

———. "The Modern Use of the Bible." In *What Is Christianity? And Other Addresses*, edited by Ned Stonehouse. Grand Rapids: Eerdmans, 1951.

———. *The New Testament: An Introduction to Its Literature and History*, edited by W. John Cook. Edinburgh: Banner of Truth, 1990.

———. "The Progress of Christian Doctrine." *Guardian* 7 (January 10, 1940): 1–2, 8–9.

———. "The Real Issue Stated: What Evangelical Christians Stand For." *The Bible for China* 22 (October 1925): 11–17.

———. "The Relation of Religion to Science and Philosophy." *PTR* 24 (1926): 38–66.

———. "The Second General Assembly of the Presbyterian Church of America." *Guardian* (November 14, 1936): 41–45, 69–71.

———. *The Virgin Birth of Christ.* Grand Rapids: Baker, 1967; 1930.

———. J. Gresham Machen to Edward Holder, 28 January 1925, Machen Archives. Montgomery Memorial Library, Westminster Theological Seminary, Philadelphia.

———. J. Gresham Machen to Minnie Gresham Machen, 3 March 1912, Machen Archives. Montgomery Memorial Library, Westminster Theological Seminary, Philadelphia.

———. J. Gresham Machen to Rev. Charles H. Parkhurst, 28 February 1924, Machen Archives. Montgomery Memorial Library, Westminster Theological Seminary, Philadelphia.

———. J. Gresham Machen to Rev. Ralph W. Nelson, 2 April 1924, Machen Archives. Montgomery Memorial Library, Westminster Theological Seminary, Philadelphia.

———. "What Fundamentalism Stands for Now." In *What Is Christianity? And Other Addresses*, edited by Ned Stonehouse. Grand Rapids: Eerdmans, 1951.

———. *What Is Faith?* Edinburgh: Banner of Truth, 1991; 1925.

———. "What Is Original Sin?" In *The Christian View of Man*, 220–32. Edinburgh: Banner of Truth, 1984; 1937.

———. "What Is the Gospel?" *USR* 38 (1927): 158–70.

Maier, Bryan M. *The Separation of Psychology and Theology at Princeton, 1868–1903: The Intellectual Achievement of James McCosh and James Mark Baldwin.* Lewiston, NY: Edwin Mellen Press, 2005.

Marsden, George. *Fundamentalism and American Culture: The Shaping of Twentieth Century Evangelicalism, 1870–1925.* New York: Oxford University Press, 1980.

———. "J. Gresham Machen, History, and Truth." *WTJ* 42 (1979): 157–75.

———. "Reformed and American." In *The Princeton Theology*, edited by David F. Wells, 1–12. Grand Rapids: Baker, 1989.

———. "Scotland and Philadelphia: Common Sense Philosophy from Jefferson to Westminster." *RTJ* 29 (1979): 8–12.

———. "The Collapse of American Evangelical Academia." In *Faith and Rationality: Reason and Belief in God*, edited by Alvin Plantinga and Nicholas Wolterstorff, 219–64. Notre Dame, IN: Notre Dame University Press, 1983.

———. *The Evangelical Mind and the New School Presbyterian Experience.* New Haven, CT: Yale University Press, 1970.

———. "The Evangelical Love Affair with Enlightenment Science." In *Understanding Fundamentalism and Evangelicalism*, 122–52. Grand Rapids: Eerdmans, 1991.

———. *The Outrageous Idea of Christian Scholarship.* New York: Oxford University Press, 1997.

———. *The Soul of the American University: From Protestant Establishment to Established Nonbelief.* New York: Oxford University Press, 1994.

———. "Understanding J. Gresham Machen." *PSB: New Series* 11, 1 (1990): 46–60.

Marty, Martin. *The Irony of It All, 1893–1919.* Vol. 1 of Modern American Religion. Chicago: University of Chicago Press, 1986.

Masselink, William. "Professor J. Gresham Machen: His Life and Defense of the Bible." ThD diss., Free University of Amsterdam, 1938.

Mathews, Shailer. *New Faith for Old.* New York: Macmillan, 1936.

———. *The Faith of Modernism.* New York: Macmillan, 1924.

May, Henry. *The Enlightenment in America.* New York: Oxford University Press, 1976.

McGiffert, A. C. *Protestant Thought before Kant.* New York: Duckworth, 1912. Quoted in Conrad Wright, *The Liberal Christians* (Boston: Beacon Press, 1970), 5.

McKim, Donald. "Archibald Alexander and the Doctrine of Scripture." *JPH* 54, 3 (1976): 356.

McLoughlin, William, ed. *The American Evangelicals, 1800–1900.* New York: Harper Torchbooks, 1968.

Miller, Perry. *The Life of the Mind in America from the Revolution to the Civil War.* New York: Harcourt, Brace and World, 1965.

———. *The New England Mind: The Seventeenth Century.* Boston: Beacon Press, 1961; 1939.

Mills, David. "Necessary Doctrine: Why Dogma Is Needed and Why Substitutes Fail." *Touchstone* 15, 2 (March 2002). http://www.touchstonemag.com/archives/article.php?id=15-02-023-f.

Moreland, J. P., and William Lane Craig. *Philosophical Foundations for a Christian Worldview*. Downers Grove, IL: InterVarsity Press, 2003.

Mouw, Richard J. "Comments on Grenz Paper and 'The Word Made Fresh.'" Paper presented at the Annual Meeting of the American Academy of Religion, Toronto, November 2002.

———. "How Should Evangelicals Do Theology? Delete the 'Post' from 'Postconservative.'" *Books and Culture* (May/June 2001): 21–22.

Muller, Richard A. *Dictionary of Latin and Greek Theological Terms*. Grand Rapids: Baker, 1985.

———. *Prolegomena to Theology*. Vol. 1 of Post-Reformation Reformed Dogmatics. 2nd ed. Grand Rapids: Baker, 2003.

———. *The Unaccommodated Calvin: Studies in the Formation of a Theological Tradition*. New York: Oxford University Press, 2000.

Murphy, Nancey. "Phillip Johnson on Trial: A Critique of His Critique of Darwin." In *Perspectives on Science & Christian Faith* 45, 1 (March 1993): 26–36.

Murray, Iain H. *Evangelicalism Divided: A Record of Crucial Change in the Years 1950 to 2000*. Edinburgh: Banner of Truth, 2000.

———. *Revival and Revivalism: The Making and Marring of American Evangelicalism, 1750–1858*. Edinburgh: Banner of Truth, 1994.

Nelson, John O. "The Rise of Princeton Theology: A Generic History of American Presbyterianism Until 1850." PhD diss., Yale University, 1935.

Newby, James R., and Elizabeth Newby. *Between Peril and Promise*. Nashville: Thomas Nelson, 1984.

Nichols, Stephen J. "Contemporary Apologetics and the Nature of Truth." Paper presented at the Annual Meeting of the Evangelical Theological Society, Orlando, November 1998.

Noll, Mark A. *America's God: From Jonathan Edwards to Abraham Lincoln*. New York: Oxford University Press, 2002.

———. "Charles Hodge and B. B. Warfield on Science, the Bible, Evolution, and Darwinism." *ModRef* 7, 3 (May/June 1998): 18–22.

———. "Charles Hodge as an Expositor of the Spiritual Life." In *Charles Hodge Revisited: A Critical Appraisal of His Life and Work*, edited by John W. Stewart and James H. Moorhead, 181–216. Grand Rapids: Eerdmans, 2002.

———. "Jonathan Edwards and Nineteenth-Century Theology." In *Jonathan Edwards and the American Experience*, edited by Nathan O. Hatch and Harry S. Stout, 260–87. New York: Oxford University Press, 1988.

———. "New Haven Theology." In *Evangelical Dictionary of Theology*, edited by Walter Elwell, 762–63. Grand Rapids: Baker, 1984.

———. "The Contested Legacy of Jonathan Edwards in Antebellum Calvinism." In *Reckoning with the Past: Historical Essays on American Evangelicalism from the Institute for the Study of American Evangelicals*, edited by D. G. Hart, 200–217. Grand Rapids: Baker, 1995.

———. "The Founding of Princeton Seminary." *WTJ* 42 (1979): 72–110.

———. "The Irony of the Enlightenment for Presbyterians in the Early Republic." In *Reckoning with the Past: Historical Essays on American Evangelicalism from the Institute for the Study of American Evangelicals*, edited by D. G. Hart, 131–53. Grand Rapids: Baker, 1995.

———, ed. *The Princeton Theologians, 1812–1921*. Grand Rapids: Baker, 1983.

———. "The Princeton Theology." In *The Princeton Theology*, edited by David F. Wells, 13–35. Grand Rapids: Baker, 1989.

———. *The Scandal of the Evangelical Mind*. Grand Rapids: Eerdmans, 1994.

O'Brien, Peter T. *The Letter to the Ephesians*. Grand Rapids: Eerdmans, 1999.

Oliphint, K. Scott. "Jonathan Edwards, Reformed Apologist." *WTJ* 57, 1 (Spring 1995): 165–86.

———. *Reasons for Faith: Philosophy in the Service of Theology*. Phillipsburg, NJ: P&R Publishing, 2006.

Olson, Roger E. "Does Evangelical Theology Have a Future?" *Christianity Today* 42 (February 9, 1998): 40–48.

———. *How to Be Evangelical without Being Conservative*. Grand Rapids: Zondervan, 2008.

———. "Postconservative Evangelicals Greet the Postmodern Age." *CC* 112 (May 3, 1995): 480–83.

———. "Postconservative Evangelicalism: An Update after a Decade." http://www.thedivineconspiracy.org/Z5209W.pdf.

———. *Reformed and Always Reforming: The Postconservative Approach to Evangelical Theology*. Grand Rapids: Baker, 2007.

———. *The Story of Christian Theology: Twenty Centuries of Tradition and Reform*. Downers Grove, IL: InterVarsity Press, 1999.

Parkhurst, Charles. "Theology Is the Product of Intellect's Futile Effort to Reduce Religion to Forms of Thought." Machen Archives. Montgomery Memorial Library, Westminster Theological Seminary, Philadelphia.

Pearcey, Nancy. *Total Truth: Liberating Christianity from Its Cultural Captivity* (Study Guide Edition). Wheaton, IL: Crossway, 2005.

Piper, John. *God's Passion for His Glory: Living the Vision of Jonathan Edwards*. Wheaton, IL: Crossway, 1998.

Placher, William. *Unapologetic Theology: A Christian Voice in a Pluralistic Conversation*. Louisville: Westminster John Knox, 1989.

Pope, Earl. *New England Calvinism and the Disruption of the Presbyterian Church*. New York: Garland, 1987.

Porter, Jean. *The Recovery of Virtue: The Relevance of Aquinas for Christian Ethics*. Louisville: Westminster John Knox, 1990.

Poythress, Vern S. *Symphonic Theology: The Validity of Multiple Perspectives in Theology*. Phillipsburg, NJ: P&R Publishing, 2001; 1987.

Raschke, Carl. *The Next Reformation: Why Evangelicals Must Embrace Postmodernity*. Grand Rapids: Baker, 2004.

Reynolds, John Mark, and Paul Nelson. "Young Earth Creationism." In *Three Views on Creation and Evolution*, edited by J. P. Moreland and John Mark Reynolds, 39–75. Grand Rapids: Zondervan, 1999.

Riddlebarger, Kim. "The Lion of Princeton: Benjamin Breckinridge Warfield on Apologetics, Theological Method and Polemics." PhD diss., Fuller Theological Seminary, 1997.

Rogers, Jack. *Scripture in the Westminster Confession: A Problem of Historical Interpretation for American Presbyterianism*. Grand Rapids: Eerdmans, 1967.

———. "Van Til and Warfield on Scripture in the Westminster Confession." In *Jerusalem and Athens: Critical Discussions on the Philosophy and Apologetics of Cornelius Van Til*, edited by E. R. Geehan, 154–64. Phillipsburg, NJ: Presbyterian and Reformed, 1980.

Rogers, Jack, and Donald McKim. *The Authority and Interpretation of the Bible*. San Francisco: Harper & Row, 1979.

Sandeen, Ernest. "The Princeton Theology: One Source of Biblical Literalism in American Protestantism." *CH* 31 (1962): 307–21.

———. *The Roots of Fundamentalism: British and American Millenarianism, 1800–1930*. Chicago: University of Chicago Press, 1970.

Schaff, Philip, ed. *Nicene and Post-Nicene Fathers*. Peabody, MA: Hendrickson, 1995; 1887.

Schultz, Roger. "Evangelical Meltdown: The Trouble with Evangel*histoire*." *Contra Mundum* 2 (Winter 1992): 45–46.

Scott, T. Kermit. *Augustine: His Thought in Context*. Mahwah, NJ: Paulist Press, 1995.

Sherman, Steven B. *Revitalizing Theological Epistemology: Holistic Evangelical Approaches to the Knowledge of God*. Princeton Theological Monograph Series 83. Eugene, OR: Pickwick Publications, 2008.

Shults, F. LeRon. "Truth Happens? The Pragmatic Conception of Truth and the Postliberal Research Program." *PTR* 4 (February 1997): 26–36.

Smith, Gary Scott. *The Seeds of Secularization: Calvinism, Culture, and Pluralism in America 1870–1915*. Grand Rapids: Christian University Press, 1985.

Smith, H. Shelton. *Changing Conceptions of Original Sin: A Study in American Theology Since 1750*. New York: Charles Scribner's Sons, 1955.

Smith, James K. A. *Introducing Radical Orthodoxy: Mapping a Post-Secular Theology*. Grand Rapids: Baker, 2004.

Smith, R. Scott. "Language, Theological Knowledge, and the Postmodern Paradigm." In *Reclaiming the Center: Confronting Evangelical Accommodation in Postmodern Times*, edited by Millard J. Erickson, Paul Kjoss Helseth, and Justin Taylor, 109–33. Wheaton, IL: Crossway, 2004.

———. *Truth and the New Kind of Christian: The Emerging Effects of Postmodernism in the Church*. Wheaton, IL: Crossway, 2005.

Sproul, R. C., John Gerstner, and Arthur Lindsley. *Classical Apologetics: A Rational Defense of the Christian Faith and a Critique of Presuppositional Apologetics*. Grand Rapids: Zondervan, 1984.

Spurr, John. " 'Rational Religion' in Restoration England." *JHI* 49 (October–December 1988): 563–85.

Stewart, John W. "Introducing Charles Hodge to Postmoderns." In *Charles Hodge Revisited: A Critical Appraisal of His Life and Work*, edited by John W. Stewart and James H. Moorhead, 1–40. Grand Rapids: Eerdmans, 2002.

———. *Mediating the Center: Charles Hodge on American Science, Language, Literature, and Politics*. Princeton: Princeton Theological Seminary, 1995.

———. Review of *The Philosophy of Charles Hodge*, by Peter Hicks. *JPH* 77 (Spring 1999): 64–65.

———. "The Tethered Theology: Biblical Criticism, Common Sense Philosophy, and the Princeton Theologians, 1812–1860." PhD diss., University of Michigan, 1990.

Stewart, Kenneth J. "That Bombshell of a Book: Gaussen's *Theopneustia* and Its Influence on Subsequent Evangelical Theology." Paper presented at the Wheaton Theology Conference, Spring 2001.

Swanton, Robert. "Warfield and Progressive Orthodoxy." *RTR* 23 (October 1964): 74–87.

Sweeney, Douglas A. "Historiographical Dialectics: On Marsden, Dayton, and the Inner Logic of Evangelical History." *CSR* 23, 1 (1993): 48–52.

Sweeney, Douglas A., and Allen C. Guelzo. "Theology in New Haven." In *The New England Theology: From Jonathan Edwards to Edwards Amasa Park*, edited by Douglas A. Sweeney and Allen C. Guelzo, 187–218. Grand Rapids: Baker, 2006.

Szasz, Ferenc Morton. *The Divided Mind of Protestant America, 1880–1930*. Tuscaloosa, AL: University of Alabama Press, 1982.

Taylor, Justin. "An Introduction to Postconservative Evangelicalism and the Rest of This Book." In *Reclaiming the Center: Confronting Evangelical Accommodation in Postmodern Times*, edited by Millard J. Erickson, Paul Kjoss Helseth, and Justin Taylor. Wheaton, IL: Crossway, 2004, 17–32.

Trueman, Carl R. "Admiring the Sistine Chapel: Reflections on Carl F. H. Henry's *God, Revelation and Authority*." *Themelios* 25, 2 (2000): 48–58.

———. Review of *Is the Reformation Over?* by Mark A. Noll, Carolyn Nystrom. http://www.reformation21.org/shelf-life/is-the-reformation-over.php.

Turner, James. *Without God Without Creed: The Origins of Unbelief in America*. Baltimore: Johns Hopkins University Press, 1985.

Turretin, Francis. *Institutes of Elenctic Theology*. 3 vols. Translated by George Musgrave Giger, edited by James T. Dennison, Jr. Phillipsburg, NJ: P&R Publishing, 1992.

Van Til, Cornelius. "My Credo." In *Jerusalem and Athens: Critical Discussions on the Philosophy and Apologetics of Cornelius Van Til*, edited by E. R. Geehan, 1–22. Phillipsburg, NJ: Presbyterian and Reformed, 1980.

———. *Christian Apologetics*, 2nd ed., edited by William Edgar. Phillipsburg, NJ: P&R Publishing, 2003.

———. *The Defense of the Faith*, 3rd ed. Philadelphia: Presbyterian and Reformed, 1972.

Vander Stelt, John. *Philosophy and Scripture: A Study of Old Princeton and Westminster Theology*. Marlburg, NJ: Mack Publishing, 1978.

Wacker, Grant. *Augustus H. Strong and the Dilemma of Historical Consciousness*. Macon, GA: Mercer University Press, 1985.

Wainwright, William J. *Reason and the Heart: A Prolegomenon to a Critique of Passional Reason.* Ithaca, NY, and London: Cornell University Press, 1995.

Walton, Brad. *Jonathan Edwards, "Religious Affections" and the Puritan Analysis of True Piety, Spiritual Sensation and Heart Religion.* Vol. 74 of Studies in American Religion. Lewiston, NY: Edwin Mellen Press, 2002.

Warfield, Benjamin B. "A Calm View of the Freedman's Case." In *Selected Shorter Writings of Benjamin B. Warfield*, 2 vols., edited by John E. Meeter, 2:735–42. Phillipsburg, NJ: P&R Publishing, 2001.

———. "A Review of Herman Bavinck's *De Zekerheid des Geloofs.*" In *Selected Shorter Writings of Benjamin B. Warfield*, 2 vols., edited by John E. Meeter, 2:106–23. Phillipsburg, NJ: P&R Publishing, 2001.

———. "Apologetics." In *Studies in Theology.* Vol. 9 of *The Works of Benjamin Breckinridge Warfield*, 3–21. Grand Rapids: Baker, 1932.

———. "Augustine and the Pelagian Controversy." In *Tertullian and Augustine.* Vol. 4 of *The Works of Benjamin Breckinridge Warfield*, 289–412. Grand Rapids: Baker, 1991; 1930.

———. "Augustine's Doctrine of Knowledge and Authority." In *Tertullian and Augustine.* Vol. 4 of *The Works of Benjamin Breckinridge Warfield*, 135–225. Grand Rapids: Baker, 1991; 1930.

———. "Authority, Intellect, Heart." In *Selected Shorter Writings of Benjamin B. Warfield*, 2 vols., edited by John E. Meeter, 2:668–71. Phillipsburg, NJ: P&R Publishing, 2001.

———. "Autosoterism." In *The Plan of Salvation*, 37–63. Philadelphia: Presbyterian Board of Publication, 1918; 1915.

———. "Calvin's Doctrine of the Knowledge of God." In *Calvin and Calvinism.* Vol. 5 of *The Works of Benjamin Breckinridge Warfield*, 29–130. Grand Rapids: Baker, 1991; 1931.

———. "Christian Supernaturalism." In *Studies in Theology.* Vol. 9 of *The Works of Benjamin Breckinridge Warfield*, 25–48. Grand Rapids: Baker, 1991; 1932.

———. "Christianity and Revelation." In *Selected Shorter Writings of Benjamin B. Warfield*, 2 vols., edited by John E. Meeter, 1:23–30. Phillipsburg, NJ: P&R Publishing, 2001.

———. "Christianity the Truth." In *Selected Shorter Writings of Benjamin B. Warfield*, 2 vols, edited by John E. Meeter, 2:213–18. Phillipsburg, NJ: P&R Publishing, 2001.

———. "Drawing the Color Line." In *Selected Shorter Writings of Benjamin B. Warfield*, 2 vols., edited by John E. Meeter. 2:743–50. Phillipsburg, NJ: P&R Publishing, 2001.

———. "Evading the Supernatural." In *Selected Shorter Writings of Benjamin B. Warfield*, 2 vols., edited by John E. Meeter, 2:680–84. Phillipsburg, NJ: P&R Publishing, 2001.

———. *Evolution, Science and Scripture, Selected Writings*, edited by Mark A. Noll and David N. Livingstone. Grand Rapids: Baker, 2000.

———. "Faith and Life." In *Selected Shorter Writings of Benjamin B. Warfield*, 2 vols., edited by John E. Meeter, 1:365–68. Phillipsburg, NJ: P&R Publishing, 2001.

———. "God and Human Religion and Morals." In *Selected Shorter Writings of Benjamin B. Warfield*, 2 vols., edited by John E. Meeter, 1:41–45. Phillipsburg, NJ: P&R Publishing, 2001.

———. "God's Providence Over All." In *Selected Shorter Writings of Benjamin B. Warfield*, 2 vols., edited by John E. Meeter, 1:111–15. Phillipsburg, NJ: P&R Publishing, 2001.

———. "Heresy and Concession." In *Selected Shorter Writings of Benjamin B. Warfield*, 2 vols., edited by John E. Meeter, 2:672–79. Phillipsburg, NJ: P&R Publishing, 2001.

———. "How to Get Rid of Christianity." In *Selected Shorter Writings of Benjamin B. Warfield*. 2 vols., edited by John E. Meeter, 2:51–60. Phillipsburg, NJ: P&R Publishing, 2001.

———. "Imputation." In *Studies in Theology*. Vol. 9 of *The Works of Benjamin Breckinridge Warfield*, 301–12. Grand Rapids: Baker, 1991; 1932.

———. "Introduction to Francis R. Beattie's *Apologetics*." In *Selected Shorter Writings of Benjamin B. Warfield*, 2 vols., edited by John E. Meeter, 2:93–105. Phillipsburg, NJ: P&R Publishing, 2001.

———. "Light and Shining." In *Faith and Life*, 53–64. Edinburgh: Banner of Truth, 1974; 1916.

———. "Looking to Men." In *Faith and Life*, 93–102. Edinburgh: Banner of Truth, 1974; 1916.

———. "Mysticism and Christianity." In *Studies in Theology*. Vol. 9 of *The Works of Benjamin Breckinridge Warfield*, 649–66. Grand Rapids: Baker, 1932.

———. "*Mysticism in Christianity*, by W. K. Fleming, and *Mysticism and Modern Life*, by John W. Buckham." In *CR*. Vol. 10 of *The Works of Benjamin Breckinridge Warfield*, 366–72. Grand Rapids: Baker, 1991; 1932.

———. "New Testament Terms Descriptive of the Great Change." In *Selected Shorter Writings of Benjamin B. Warfield*, 2 vols., edited by John E. Meeter, 1:267–77. Phillipsburg, NJ: P&R Publishing, 2001.

———. "On Faith in its Psychological Aspects." In *Studies in Theology*. Vol. 9 of *The Works of Benjamin Breckinridge Warfield*, 313–44. Grand Rapids: Baker, 1991; 1932.

———. "On the Doctrine of the Holy Spirit." In *Selected Shorter Writings of Benjamin B. Warfield*, 2 vols., edited by John E. Meeter, 1:203–22. Phillipsburg, NJ: P&R Publishing, 2001.

———. "Presbyterian Churches and the Westminster Confession." *PR* 10, 4 (1889): 646–57.

———. "Recent Reconstructions of Theology." In *Selected Shorter Writings of Benjamin B. Warfield*, 2 vols., edited by John E. Meeter, 2:289–99. Phillipsburg, NJ: P&R Publishing, 2001.

———. " 'Redeemer' and 'Redemption.' " In *Biblical Doctrines*. Vol. 2 of *The Works of Benjamin Breckinridge Warfield*, 375–400. Grand Rapids: Baker, 1991; 1929.

———. "Repentance and Original Sin." In *Selected Shorter Writings of Benjamin B. Warfield*, 2 vols., edited by John E. Meeter, 1:278–82. Phillipsburg, NJ: P&R Publishing, 2001.

———. "Review of *Foundations: A Statement of Christian Belief in Terms of Modern Thought*, by Seven Oxford Men." In *CR*. Vol. 10 of *The Works of Benjamin Breckinridge Warfield*, 320–33. Grand Rapids: Baker, 1991; 1932.

———. "Review of *God's Image in Man, and Its Defacement, in the Light of Modern Denials*, by James Orr." In *CR*. Vol. 10 of *The Works of Benjamin Breckinridge Warfield*, 136–40. Grand Rapids: Baker, 1991; 1932.

———. "Review of *Mystik und Geschichtliche Religion*, by Wilhelm Frensenius." In *CR*. Vol. 10 of *The Works of Benjamin Breckinridge Warfield*, 357–65. Grand Rapids: Baker, 1991; 1932.

———. "Review of *The Christian Faith: A System of Dogmatics*, by Theodore Haering." In *CR*. Vol. 10 of *The Works of Benjamin Breckinridge Warfield*, 405–27. Grand Rapids: Baker, 1991; 1932.

———. "Review of *Van Den Eeuwigen Vrede Tusshen Wetenshap en Religie*, by H. Visscher, and *Professor Visscher's Rectorale Rede*, by H. W. van der Vaart Smit." In CR. Vol. 10 of *The Works of Benjamin Breckinridge Warfield*, 475–83. Grand Rapids: Baker, 1991; 1932.

———. "The Confession of Faith as Revised in 1903." In *Selected Shorter Writings of Benjamin B. Warfield*, 2 vols., edited by John E. Meeter, 2:370–410. Phillipsburg, NJ: P&R Publishing, 2001.

———. "The Dogmatic Spirit." In *Selected Shorter Writings of Benjamin B. Warfield*, 2 vols., edited by John E. Meeter, 2:663–68. Phillipsburg, NJ: P&R Publishing, 2001.

———. "The Fullness of God." In *Faith and Life*, 279–88. Edinburgh: Banner of Truth, 1974; 1916.

———. "The Idea of Systematic Theology." In *Studies in Theology*. Vol. 9 of *The Works of Benjamin Breckinridge Warfield*, 49–90. Grand Rapids: Baker, 1991; 1932.

———. "The Latest Phase of Historical Rationalism." In *Studies in Theology*. Vol. 9 of *The Works of Benjamin Breckinridge Warfield*, 585–648. Grand Rapids: Baker, 1932.

———. *The Plan of Salvation*. Philadelphia: Presbyterian Board of Publications, 1915.

———. *The Power of God Unto Salvation*. Philadelphia: The Presbyterian Board of Publishing and Sabbath-School Work, 1903.

———. "The Proposed Union with the Cumberland Presbyterians." *PTR* 2 (1904): 295–316.

———. "The Significance of the Westminster Standards as a Creed." In *Selected Shorter Writings of Benjamin B. Warfield*, 2 vols., edited by John E. Meeter, 2:660–62. Phillipsburg, NJ: P&R Publishing, 2001.

———. "The Task and Method of Systematic Theology." In *Studies in Theology*. Vol. 9 of *The Works of Benjamin Breckinridge Warfield*, 91–108. Grand Rapids: Baker, 1991; 1932.

———. "Theology a Science." In *Selected Shorter Writings of Benjamin B. Warfield*, 2 vols., edited by John E. Meeter, 2:207–212. Phillipsburg, NJ: P&R Publishing, 2001.

———. "This- and Other-Worldliness." In *Faith and Life*, 43–52. Edinburgh: Banner of Truth, 1974; 1916.

———. "What Is Calvinism?" In *Selected Shorter Writings of Benjamin B. Warfield*, 2 vols., edited by John E. Meeter, 1:389–92. Phillipsburg, NJ: P&R Publishing, 2001.

Webber, Robert E. "An Evangelical and Catholic Methodology." In *The Use of the Bible in Theology: Evangelical Options*, edited by Robert K. Johnston, 137–58. Atlanta: John Knox, 1985.

———. *Ancient-Future Faith: Rethinking Evangelicalism for a Postmodern World*. Grand Rapids: Baker, 1999.

———. "Out With the Old." *Christianity Today* (February 19, 1990): 16–17.

———. *The Younger Evangelicals: Facing the Challenges of the New World*. Grand Rapids: Baker, 2002.

———. *Who Gets to Narrate the World? Contending for the Christian Story in an Age of Rivals*. Downers Grove, IL: InterVarsity Press, 2008.

Wells, David F. *Above All Earthly Pow'rs: Christ in a Postmodern World*. Grand Rapids: Eerdmans, 2005.

———. *Losing Our Virtue: Why the Church Must Recover Its Moral Vision*. Grand Rapids: Eerdmans, 1998.

———. "Charles Hodge." In *The Princeton Theology*, edited by David Wells, 37–62. Grand Rapids: Baker, 1989.

Wellum, Stephen J. "Postconservatism, Biblical Authority, and Recent Proposals for Re-Doing Evangelical Theology: A Critical Proposal." In *Reclaiming the Center: Confronting Evangelical Accommodation in Postmodern Times*, edited by Millard J. Erickson, Paul Kjoss Helseth, and Justin Taylor, 161–97. Wheaton, IL: Crossway, 2004.

Willey, Basil. *The Seventeenth Century Background: Studies in the Thought of the Age in Relation to Poetry and Religion*. New York: Doubleday Anchor, 1955.

Wolterstorff, Nicholas. "Thomas Reid on Rationality." In *Rationality in the Calvinian Tradition*, edited by Hendrik Hart, Johan Van Der Hoven, and Nicholas Wolterstorff, 43–69. Lanham, MD: University Press of America, 1983.

Woodbridge, John D. "Biblical Authority: Towards an Evaluation of the Rogers and McKim Proposal." *TrinJ* n.s. 1 (1980): 165–236.

———. *Biblical Authority: A Critique of the Rogers/McKim Proposal*. Grand Rapids: Zondervan, 1982.

Woodbridge, John D., and Randall H. Balmer. "The Princetonians and Biblical Authority: An Assessment of the Ernest Sandeen Proposal." In *Scripture and Truth*, edited by John D. Woodbridge and D. A. Carson, 245–79. Grand Rapids: Zondervan, 1983.

Index of Subjects and Names